SECOND EDITION

INTRODUCTORY READINGS IN PHILOSOPHY

SECOND EDITION

INTRODUCTORY READINGS IN PHILOSOPHY

EDITED BY

Marcus G. Singer
University of Wisconsin

AND

Robert R. Ammerman
University of Wisconsin

CHARLES SCRIBNER'S SONS
New York

COPYRIGHT © 1974, 1962 CHARLES SCRIBNER'S SONS
COPYRIGHT © 1960 ROBERT R. AMMERMAN AND MARCUS G. SINGER

Library of Congress Cataloging in Publication Data

Singer, Marcus George, 1926–   ed.
  Introductory readings in philosophy, 2nd ed.

  Bibliography: p.
  1. Philosophy—Collected works. I. Ammerman,
Robert R., joint ed. II. Title.
B21.S53   1974   108   73-5194
ISBN 0-684-13680-5 (pbk)

This book published simultaneously in the
United States of America and in Canada—
Copyright under the Berne Convention

All rights reserved. No part of this book
may be reproduced in any form without the
permission of Charles Scribner's Sons.

1 3 5 7 9 11 13 15 17 19 H/P 20 18 16 14 12 10 8 6 4 2

Printed in the United States of America

FOR
CARL BÖGHOLT
WHO INSPIRED IT

CONTENTS

PREFACE TO THE SECOND EDITION		xi
HOW TO USE THIS BOOK		xv
HOW TO READ PHILOSOPHY		xix

PART I THE NATURE AND USES OF PHILOSOPHY

1	WISDOM • Alfred North Whitehead	3
2	PHILOSOPHY • Arthur Kenyon Rogers	5
3	THE PHILOSOPHIC MIND AND THE CONTEMPORARY WORLD • Arthur E. Murphy	10

PART II LOGIC AND PHILOSOPHY OF SCIENCE

4	ELEVEN BLUE MEN • Berton Roueché	23
5	LOGIC AND SCIENCE • Morris R. Cohen and Ernest Nagel	31
6	SCIENCE AND HUMAN NATURE • John Stuart Mill	39
7	UMBRELLAOLOGY AND PROBLEMATICS • John Somerville	43
8	WHAT THE TORTOISE SAID TO ACHILLES • Lewis Carroll	47
9	TRUTH AND VALIDITY • Irving M. Copi	50
10	SCIENCE AND HYPOTHESIS • Irving M. Copi	53
11	ON EXPLANATION • John Hospers	70

PART III THEORY OF KNOWLEDGE

12 OF DOUBT AND CERTITUDE • René Descartes — 91

13 TWO KINDS OF KNOWLEDGE • David Hume — 102

14 THE FIXATION OF BELIEF • Charles Sanders Peirce — 106

15 THE ETHICS OF BELIEF • W. K. Clifford — 115

16 HUMAN FALLIBILITY • Herbert Spencer — 121

17 IS TRUTH RELATIVE? • William Pepperell Montague — 123

18 EPISTEMOLOGICAL SKEPTICISM • C. E. M. Joad — 126

19 THE WORLD WE PERCEIVE • Arthur E. Murphy — 127

PART IV METAPHYSICS

20 WHAT IS METAPHYSICS? • A. E. Taylor — 135

21 MIND AND MATTER • George Berkeley — 145

22 IS A CAUSE ALWAYS NECESSARY? • David Hume — 150

23 CRIME AND FREE WILL • Clarence Darrow — 153

24 FREE WILL • John Stuart Mill — 154

25 A DEFENCE OF FREE WILL • C. Arthur Campbell — 160

26 HISTORY AND DETERMINISM • John Stuart Mill — 168

27 ECONOMIC DETERMINISM AND HISTORICAL DEVELOPMENT • Friedrich Engels — 177

28 EXISTENTIALISM • Jean-Paul Sartre — 179

29 THE ELIMINATION OF METAPHYSICS • Alfred Jules Ayer — 194

PART V PHILOSOPHY OF RELIGION

30 RELIGION • George Santayana — 209

31 THE NECESSARY EXISTENCE OF GOD • St. Anselm — 211

32 REASON, FAITH, AND GOD'S EXISTENCE • St. Thomas Aquinas — 213

33 ON EVIL AND THE ARGUMENT FROM DESIGN • David Hume — 219

34 THE POSSIBILITY OF RELIGIOUS KNOWLEDGE • A. J. Ayer — 225

35 THE WILL TO BELIEVE • William James — 230

36 FAITH, BELIEF, AND ACTION • William James — 238

37 RELIGION AND THE WILL TO BELIEVE • Morris R. Cohen — 242

38 HONEST TO GOD • John A. T. Robinson — 245

PART VI ETHICS AND VALUES

39 THE RING OF GYGES • Plato — 263

40 ON THE GOOD • Aristotle — 264

41 REASON, PASSION, AND MORALS • David Hume — 267

42 HEDONISTIC UTILITARIANISM • Jeremy Bentham — 274

43 THE CATEGORICAL IMPERATIVE • Immanuel Kant — 281

44 ETHICAL ABSOLUTISM AND ETHICAL RELATIVISM • Walter T. Stace — 286

45 THE EMOTIVE MEANING OF ETHICAL TERMS • C. L. Stevenson — 296

46 THE CONTINUUM OF ENDS-MEANS • John Dewey — 313

47 THE CONTEXT OF MORAL JUDGMENT • Arthur E. Murphy — 317

CONTENTS

48 THE CRITERION OF TASTE • George Santayana — 336

49 CAN WE DISPUTE ABOUT TASTES? • Monroe C. Beardsley — 343

50 HOW DO YOU KNOW IT'S GOOD? • Marya Mannes — 350

PART VII SOCIAL AND POLITICAL PHILOSOPHY

51 THE STATE OF NATURE • Thomas Hobbes — 359

52 LIBERTY, EQUALITY, AND THE STATE OF NATURE • John C. Calhoun — 363

53 AUTHORITY AND SOCIETY • Alexis de Tocqueville — 367

54 LIBERTY AND EQUALITY • R. H. Tawney — 370

55 LIBERTY AND LEGISLATION • Bernard Bosanquet — 379

56 DEMOCRACY, POLITICS, AND EDUCATION • John Dewey — 387

57 REMARKS AT THE PEACE BANQUET • William James — 393

58 FALLACIES IN POLITICAL THINKING • C. D. Broad — 396

BIOGRAPHICAL NOTES — 407

SELECTED BIBLIOGRAPHY — 419

CHRONOLOGICAL TABLE OF CONTENTS — 427

PREFACE TO THE SECOND EDITION

The first edition of this book, which was published in 1962, consisted in large part of the reading materials actually used by nearly all of the instructors of the Introduction to Philosophy course at the University of Wisconsin (Madison). This is not true of the present edition. In the intervening years vast changes have occurred, with the department from which we operate increasing greatly in size and diversity, and the book has now taken on an independent life of its own. We are gratified to have the opportunity, in this second edition, to make the book better than it was, and we hope that those who have been using it in this period agree with our judgment that it is a better book in this revised version.

Sixteen new selections are included in this second edition. In order to make room for them, twelve pieces were dropped altogether and two were substantially reduced in bulk. Consequently, the book is about the same size as it was before: not too heavy to be carried to class, and not heavy enough to be used for breaking windows. We have also brought the Bibliography up to date, and, where necessary, the Biographical Notes. This process of adding and deleting has resulted in the inclusion of twelve new authors in this edition, and an increase from thirty-eight to forty-five in the number of authors represented. We have also, it should be noted, improved the editing of selection 47 (Murphy) by adding a couple of paragraphs which had been previously omitted which, in our present judgment, make the selection somewhat easier to follow.

The reader should not suppose, however, that the selections in this volume offer a reliable guide to the philosophies of the authors included. The selections have been chosen as vehicles for the presentation and discussion of certain philosophical ideas and problems, and not as keys to the philosophies of the authors. Those readers who are interested in ascertaining the views of a particular author will find reference to many of his important works in the Biographical Notes and perhaps some clues in the Bibliography.

Thus, as before, some of the selections are relatively complete (and most of the new ones have been included absolutely complete), but most have been internally edited, and some are no more than excerpts. This editing and excerpting is by design, and is neither an accident nor an error. The main criterion for including a selection has been its actual usability in and value for introducing students to philosophy, and philosophy to students, students who are not likely to go on to make the study of philosophy their life's work, or even to take another course in the subject. If one can reach students, beginning students, at this level, one can reach others; whereas if one aims mainly at those who plan to major in it in college, or, strangely enough, those who plan to go on to teach the subject, one is not likely to reach any. This same criterion also has been used to determine whether and to what extent a selection should be edited.

What strikes us as important in a collection of this kind is that a selection should be likely to be both interesting and intelligible to undergraduates with no special preparation in the subject. Ideally, also, a selection should be likely to stimulate thought and discussion (and some selections, especially the briefer ones, have been included solely for their stimulus value), or else of such importance for thinking on these matters that it would be absurd for it not to be included (and hardly anything fits this category). Thus it is essential that a selection be intelligible as it stands, that knowledge of some special vocabulary, some previous controversy, or some esoteric tradition not be necessary to appreciate it—or, if it is intelligible only by reference to some other piece of writing to which it refers, that the other selection be included.

These criteria were followed to a certain extent in the previous edition, and rigorously in this revision. But, even though an attempt has been made to keep the selections intelligible and interesting to beginners, there are, to be sure, gradations of difficulty and variations in interest and intelligibility, and some selections, no doubt, are relatively difficult. This, presumably, is why there are teachers. There is certainly more material included here than could possibly be used in any single semester. There is enough for several courses. And this is as it should be.

Furthermore, it was deemed important that the selections be genuinely philosophical in character, though they need not have been written by persons who would be called philosophers by either themselves or others. This then is not a collection of controversies on the personal, social, national, or international issues of the day. It is a collection of philosophical writings, many of which are relevant to, though they were not directly written about, such issues.

The selections have been divided into a number of groups, according to the branches of philosophy they seem best to fit, though admittedly some selections could easily have gone in more than one place. It was thought best to keep the number of section headings to a minimum. There is no one principle governing the arrangement within each grouping. In some places chronology has operated, in others obvious connections of ideas, in others no special principle. The philosophical connections amongst various selections scattered throughout the book, which might not otherwise be apparent, are indicated by a number of cross references to be found in the source notes on the opening page of each selection.

One criticism of the previous edition that was made with some frequency was that the section on metaphysics was defective, since, apart from a few miscellaneous selections, it gave the appearance of concentrating almost solely on the free will-determinism issue, and thus the impression that this is the only issue in metaphysics. We have attempted to meet this criticism by eliminating most of the isolated and miscellaneous selections in that section and adding a couple of pieces that meet the general problems of metaphysics head on—selections 20 (Taylor) and 29 (Ayer). It should also be pointed out that philosophy of religion can properly and reasonably be regarded as a branch of metaphysics. Consequently if the sections entitled "Metaphysics" and "Philosophy of Religion" be taken together, it becomes apparent that there is plenty of material dealing with problems of metaphysics (one of which is simply "What is metaphysics?", and another of which is "Is metaphysics possible?"). This also should dispel the impression that the free will issue is the only issue in metaphysics. In this edition the section on philosophy of religion has been revised so as to eliminate a couple of pieces that just as easily could have been in the part "Ethics and Values," replacing them with two that bring out clearly and well the relation between problems in the philosophy of religion and the problems of metaphysics—selections 38 (Robinson) and 34 (Ayer).

Editorial omissions are in all cases indicated by the usual ellipses, and editorial additions by the usual brackets. Editorial footnotes are denoted by asterisks; numbered footnotes are those of the author of the selection in question. The sources of the selections have been indicated in the source note to each selection, as have acknowledgments, where required.

We wish to thank Professors Claudia Card, William H. Hay, Douglas Hosler, Ellen Kappy, Gerald Paske, and Aaron Snyder for their useful advice in connection with this revision; in two instances this advice took the form of very extensive critiques, based on extensive classroom experience. We also wish to acknowledge our debt to Professors Hay, Eugene Kaelin, and Julius Weinberg (now deceased) for their advice and assistance in preparing the first edition. One of the translations used was prepared by the late Professor Weinberg expressly for this work (Part II of selection 32, by Aquinas).

A preliminary edition of this book, for local use, was published in 1960 by the William C. Brown Book Company of Dubuque, Iowa. The experience gained in using this preliminary edition proved invaluable. We would also like

PREFACE TO THE SECOND EDITION

to express our gratitude to Professors William Baumer, Monroe Beardsley, C. J. Ducasse (now deceased), Vergil Dykstra, A. Campbell Garnett (now deceased), Ernest Nagel, Glenn Riddle, Calvin Rollins, and Herbert Spiegelberg, who examined the preliminary edition of this book and offered various comments and suggestions. Some of these suggestions we were glad to adopt, and only limitations of space prevented us from adopting more.

Perhaps it is due to something in the nature of the subject, or perhaps merely to the way it is often taught, but it is a fact that beginning students of philosophy, and even some who get well beyond the beginning stage, often retain the conviction that in philosophy it is all a matter of opinion or taste, and that philosophical discussion is really just a vehement debate about matters that, despite the appearances, are really far from momentous, and in which the cards are stacked in advance in favor of the teacher, since he has learned in graduate school *all the arguments there are* one way or the other on any philosophical issue. This often leads to the discouraged view that it doesn't matter what one believes, since no matter what it is the teacher can come up with arguments to refute it, and consequently the whole subject consists in fruitless debate on arid technicalities.

It does no good merely to say that this is not so. One has to show that this is not so. We hope that this book will be useful in this enterprise. Alfred North Whitehead, in the first selection in this volume, has some wise remarks to make about Wisdom. In the following passage, he has some wise remarks to make about the point just mentioned, remarks which deserve to be taken very seriously indeed:

> Philosophy is not a mere collection of noble sentiments. A deluge of such sentiments does more harm than good. Philosophy is at once general and concrete, critical and appreciative of direct intuition. It is not—or, at least, should not be—a ferocious debate between irritable professors.*

Madison, Wisconsin   M.G.S.
February 28, 1973   R.R.A.

---

*Alfred North Whitehead, *Adventures of Ideas* (Cambridge: The University Press, 1933), p. 125.

HOW TO USE
THIS BOOK

No body of introductory and teaching apparatus is included in this collection. Such matter is often extraneous and misleads students into raising issues irrelevant to the selections they are reading, or reading into them things that are just not there. Also, such matter takes up space, which is always limited, and which we judged could be used more effectively by including more and a greater variety of selections. Other collections are available that contain such apparatus, for those who find it useful or valuable to have; some are listed in the Bibliography.

There are, however, a number of important interconnections among the selections included, which are not brought out by their arrangement in the book (though most of them are indicated in special footnotes), and it seems desirable to say a few words about them.

One obviously related set of materials consists of selections 15 (Clifford) and 35 and 36 (James). These were intended to be taken together, even though all three have not been located in the same part of the book. The Clifford selection, on "the Ethics of Belief," fits best in the part entitled "Theory of Knowledge." The connection with religion and faith, especially religious faith, is obviously more prominent in the pieces by James, on the Will to Believe. Hence, these pieces are in the "Philosophy of Religion" section. But this connection can, if one chooses, be ignored altogether.

Some selections might seem to overlap, but such duplication is really only apparent. For example, selections 23 (Darrow) and 24 (Mill) cover much the same material, but the Darrow piece is an extreme and provocative statement of a position which the selection by Mill modifies almost to the point of reversal. By the same token, although selections 5 (Cohen and Nagel) and 14 (Peirce) deal with the same subject, the Peirce selection is loaded with irony, and partly for this reason is often obscure on crucial issues. Cohen and Nagel are clearer and more precise. The two pieces supplement rather than duplicate each other: the Peirce, in addition to its almost overriding importance, is useful as a stimulus for discussion, while the piece by Cohen and Nagel helps to clarify thought on the subject.

Some selections were included mainly because they are useful as stimuli

XV

for discussion: for example, Part I of selection 7 (Somerville), and selections 8 (Carroll), 16 (Spencer), 18 (Joad), 23 (Darrow), 39 (Plato), and 53 (de Tocqueville) seldom fail to excite interest and discussion among beginners and even more advanced students.

Some reference should be made to the paucity of materials on aesthetics (an area of philosophy often shortchanged in both introductory books and introductory courses in philosophy). Space limitations have prevented the inclusion of more than selections 48 (Santayana), 49 (Beardsley), and 50 (Mannes). These pieces, however, in their emphasis on matters of taste and judgment, go nicely together, as well as with other selections on ethics and values, and should serve to introduce the reader to one of the more important problems in that area. We have indicated in the Bibliography other works, including anthologies in aesthetics or the philosophy of art, for the benefit of those who are interested in pursuing the subject more extensively. We have followed the same practice with regard to the Bibliography for each of the subject categories we have used.

It may be useful to sketch two possible ways of using the materials of this book in a course of semester length.

One such arrangement, used by one of the editors, is the following. After a brief introduction to the nature of the subject, for which selection 3 (Murphy) serves very well, begin with problems of logic and the theory of knowledge, using at the outset selections 18 (Joad) and 12 (Descartes). Then take up as one related group selections 14 (Peirce), 5 (Cohen and Nagel), and 53 (de Tocqueville). Then proceed to selections 13 (Hume) and 19 (Murphy), along with 9 (Copi). The nature of science could be dealt with by reading 4 (Roueché), 7 (Somerville), 10 (Copi), and 11 (Hospers). The questions about causality and the establishment of empirical laws that arise here can be sharpened by reading selection 22 (Hume). In any case, they provide an obvious bridge to the second part of the course dealing with the problem of free will and necessity, the reading consisting of selections 23 (Darrow), 27 (Engels), and 24, 26, and 6 (Mill).

Questions about belief and evidence arising in the first part of the course provide a useful transition to Part III of the course, dealing with the ethics of belief, using selections 15 (Clifford), 35 and 36 (James), and 37 (Cohen). This then leads to questions of ethics, where selections 41 (Hume) and 47 (Murphy) are excellent foils for each other. The consideration of ethical questions leads in a very natural way to questions of social and political philosophy. A useful start here is provided by selections 51 (Hobbes) and 52 (Calhoun). This provides a stimulus to considering selections 55 (Bosanquet), 58 (Broad), 56 (Dewey), and 54 (Tawney), which go well together and which, collectively, deal with some of the most profound and interesting problems of political philosophy. One could end, if not with wisdom, at least with a selection on it, 1 (Whitehead).

It should be noticed that in the course just outlined each part begins with some selection that presents a skeptical position on the matter under discussion. This is a good way for beginners to be introduced to philosophical problems, because it challenges customary ideas. There are, naturally, other ways.

An alternate way of arranging the course would be to begin with a general description of the nature of philosophy. Selection 2 (Rogers) should be useful for this purpose. Selection 9 (Copi) provides useful background for considering substantive problems of philosophy. One might then introduce the students to some of the questions of ethics, a subject in which most beginning students are already interested. Selections 39 (Plato), 42 (Bentham), 43 (Kant), 44 (Stace), and 45 (Stevenson) might be read, for example. The second part of the course would deal with issues concerning religion. Here, various proofs for the existence of God can be considered, using selections 31 (Anselm), 32 (Aquinas), and 33 (Hume), as well as the problem of justifying belief in God on the basis of faith. Selections 15 (Clifford), 35 and 36 (James), and 37 (Cohen) provide a well-rounded discussion of this issue. Selections 34 (Ayer) and 38 (Robinson) would be valuable in introducing the student to some of the contemporary debates concerning these matters. Part II of selection 33 (Hume), dealing as it does with the problem of evil, raises the problem of free will. Selections 23 (Darrow), 24 (Mill), 25 (Campbell) and 28 (Sartre) provide excellent discussions of many facets of that problem. Finally, selection 12 (Descartes) is very useful for introducing the basic problem of skepticism, which can be discussed in connection with 14 (Peirce), 17 (Montague), and possibly selections 10 (Copi) and 11 (Hospers) on scientific knowledge. The final assignments would be selections 1 (Whitehead) and 3 (Murphy), which deal with the nature of wisdom and the relation of philosophy to life.

Neither of these two possible courses, naturally, finds a use for all of the materials included in the book, and they have, admittedly, considerable overlap. Yet they should serve to bring out the flexibility inherent in the book. Many more arrangements are possible, perhaps some of them better.

HOW TO READ PHILOSOPHY

All philosophical reading should be directed by a plan. This is especially true of the material contained in this book. The student should not attempt to read it without guidance. "Books are tools, which wise men use to suit their own ends," it has been said, and this book is pre-eminently a tool for teaching. Nevertheless, some general advice on how to read philosophical writings can be given in this place.

One of the difficulties beginners have is that they do not know how to approach the reading of a philosophical essay. Philosophical writings should always be read with certain questions in mind, and they almost always should be read more than once, for a single reading will seldom bring them into focus. "In all . . . philosophical studies," according to Professor G. E. Moore (perhaps with some exaggeration), "the difficulties and disagreements, of which its history is full, are mainly due to a very simple cause: namely to the attempt to answer questions, without first discovering precisely what question it is which you desire to answer." Of course, to discover just what problem a philosopher is trying to solve is not always easy.

In studying philosophy, the student is not usually expected to absorb and memorize large amounts of material. This deadens the capacity for reflection, and leaves no zest for it. And reflection here is of the essence. The student should read a selection carefully and thoroughly, several times, asking himself the following questions:

(1) What question is this philosopher trying to answer?
(2) How did the question arise? i.e., Why is he trying to answer this question?
(3) What answer does he give?
(4) Why does he give this answer instead of some other one? i.e., What reasons does he have for the answer at which he arrives?
(5) Is the answer he gives a good one—does it really answer the question?

In other words, one should always try first to determine the *point* of a selection, to decide *what* the author is trying to prove. Then one should consider *why* he is trying to prove that point. Thirdly, one should ask: How

xix

does he go about proving it?, i.e., What reasons or arguments does he give? What evidence does he present? Finally one may raise the critical questions: Are his reasons good ones? Does he really prove his point? Has he met all the objections that might bear the other way? Has he overlooked any facts he should have considered?

One should therefore first read through an assignment fairly rapidly in an attempt to get a general picture of what it is about, not worrying on first reading about details. Then one should read it again, more slowly, attempting to fit the details into the general picture. Reading a philosophical essay intelligently is analogous to the procedure involved in solving a jigsaw puzzle: it is much easier to put the separate pieces together if you have an idea of what the picture is about. The student ought not to feel discouraged if at first it seems difficult. It often is difficult. But nothing really worthwhile comes easy. Lewis Carroll once said:

> When you come to any passage you don't understand, *read it again;* if you still don't understand it, *read it again;* if you fail, even after *three* readings, very likely your brain is getting a little tired. In that case, put the book away, and take to other occupations, and next day, when you come to it fresh, you will very likely find that it is quite easy.

It is remarkable how often a procedure like this works. However, the student will be well advised not to allow himself to be stopped by *just one* passage. If you come to a passage you don't understand, read on a bit; maybe the context will make it clear.

The above remarks provide merely some general hints to help the student with his reading. They will not take the place of the student's own reflection. Nor will they take the place of discussion, which is often invaluable in clearing up a point and helping one settle one's own ideas.

PART I
THE NATURE AND USES OF PHILOSOPHY

1 WISDOM

ALFRED NORTH WHITEHEAD
(1861-1947)

The fading of ideals is sad evidence of the defeat of human endeavor. In the schools of antiquity philosophers aspired to impart wisdom, in modern colleges our humbler aim is to teach subjects. The drop from the divine wisdom, which was the goal of the ancients, to text-book knowledge of subjects, which is achieved by the moderns, marks an educational failure, sustained through the ages. I am not maintaining that in the practice of education the ancients were more successful than ourselves. You have only to read Lucian, and to note his satiric dramatizations of the pretentious claims of philosophers, to see that in this respect the ancients can boast over us no superiority. My point is that, at the dawn of our European civilisation, men started with the full ideals which should inspire education, and that gradually our ideals have sunk to square with our practice.

But when ideals have sunk to the level of practice, the result is stagnation. In particular, so long as we conceive intellectual education as merely consisting in the acquirement of mechanical mental aptitudes, and of formulated statements of useful truths, there can be no progress; though there will be much activity, amid aimless re-arrangement of syllabuses, in the fruitless endeavour to dodge the inevitable lack of time. We must take it as an unavoidable fact, that God has so made the world that there are more topics desirable for knowledge than any one person can possibly acquire. It is hopeless to approach the problem by the way of the enumeration of subjects which every one ought to have mastered. There are too many of them, all with excellent title-deeds. Perhaps, after all, this plethora of material is fortunate; for the world is made interesting by a delightful ignorance of important truths. . . . Though knowledge is one chief aim of intellectual education, there is another ingredient, vaguer but greater, and more dominating in its importance. The ancients called it "wisdom." You cannot be wise without some basis of knowledge; but you may easily acquire knowledge and remain bare of wisdom.

SOURCE: Excerpted from chapter 3 of *The Aims of Education;* copyright 1929 by The Macmillan Company, renewed 1957. Used by permission of The Macmillan Company, New York, and Ernest Benn Limited, London. The title of this selection has been supplied by the editors. Compare with selection 3.

Now wisdom is the way in which knowledge is held. It concerns the handling of knowledge, its selection for the determination of relevant issues, its employment to add value to our immediate experience. This mastery of knowledge, which is wisdom, is the most intimate freedom obtainable. The ancients saw clearly—more clearly than we do—the necessity for dominating knowledge by wisdom. But, in the pursuit of wisdom in the region of practical education, they erred sadly. To put the matter simply, their popular practice assumed that wisdom could be imparted to the young by procuring philosophers to spout at them. Hence the crop of shady philosophers in the schools of the ancient world. The only avenue towards wisdom is by freedom in the presence of knowledge. But the only avenue towards knowledge is by discipline in the acquirement of ordered fact. . . .

The importance of knowledge lies in its use, in our active mastery of it—that is to say, it lies in wisdom. It is a convention to speak of mere knowledge, apart from wisdom, as of itself imparting a peculiar dignity to its possessor. I do not share in this reverence for knowledge as such. It all depends on who has the knowledge and what he does with it. That knowledge which adds greatness to character is knowledge so handled as to transform every phase of immediate experience. It is in respect to the activity of knowledge that an over-vigorous discipline in education is so harmful. The habit of active thought, with freshness, can only be generated by adequate freedom. Undiscriminating discipline defeats its own objects by dulling the mind. If you have much to do with the young as they emerge from school and from the university, you soon note the dulled minds of those whose education has consisted in the acquirement of inert knowledge. . . . Furthermore, this overhaste to impart mere knowledge defeats itself. The human mind rejects knowledge imparted in this way. The craving for expansion, for activity, inherent in youth is disgusted by a dry imposition of disciplined knowledge. The discipline, when it comes, should satisfy a natural craving for the wisdom which adds value to bare experience. . . .

In my own work at universities I have been much struck by the paralysis of thought induced in pupils by the aimless accumulation of precise knowledge, inert and unutilised. It should be the chief aim of a university professor to exhibit himself in his own true character—that is, as an ignorant man thinking, actively utilising this small share of knowledge. In a sense, knowledge shrinks as wisdom grows: for details are swallowed up in principles. The details of knowledge which are important will be picked up *ad hoc* in each avocation of life, but the habit of the active utilisation of well-understood principles is the final possession of wisdom. . . .

2 PHILOSOPHY

ARTHUR KENYON ROGERS
(1868-1936)

No man who is able to learn from experience at all, can live very long in the world without finding himself continually passing judgment, in one way or another, on the meaning and the value of life. At the very least there will be some things which it will seem to him to be worth the while to do, and other things, again, which will fail to interest him, and which by implication therefore he will condemn; but besides such fragmentary and instinctive judgments, he also, if he reflects at all, can hardly help but ask himself at times whether life has not some meaning as a whole, which would serve to throw light on the scattered and chaotic fragments of his everyday experience, and bring them into some degree of unity. Now philosophy, apart from technicalities of definition, is nothing but an attempt, in a reasoned and comprehensive way, to answer this question, What is the meaning of life? Every one, therefore, in so far as he adopts a certain general attitude towards the problems that meet him, looks at them from a certain point of view, and does not simply let himself drift from one experience to another without any purpose or unity to connect them, is taking the standpoint of philosophy. Such an attitude we call his philosophy of life, and if he is more or less clearly conscious of what this attitude is, and is able to express it in a unified and consistent way, we say in a popular sense that he is a philosopher. Technical philosophy differs from this only in the fact that it tries to do thoroughly, and in full consciousness of itself, what in popular thinking we do in a loose and unsystematic fashion. Instead of picking out those factors in life which appeal to us more personally and directly, it tries to set individual prejudices and limitations aside, and to include, as impartially as it can, all the elements which experience presents. It is true that in doing this it frequently gets far enough from what seem to be living interests; but back of all technical discussions, there is still the underlying conviction that by this path, and this alone, can we get at the vital and essential meaning of the world, or else we have no longer philosophy, but mere pedantry and hair-splitting. It is natural, then, that we

SOURCE: From the Introduction to *A Brief Introduction to Modern Philosophy* (New York: The Macmillan Company, 1899). The title of this selection has been supplied by the editors.

should find the definitions which men have given of philosophy at different times are not by any means the same. They are not the same because, under different circumstances, men's interests are directed to different points, now to the importance of conduct, now to the nature of the external world, now to the existence of supersensible realities. But to say that their interest lies at one point or another, is only to say in other words that here they find the value of life; this is the test that can always be applied, the real motive, if not the apparent one. So we can speak of the philosophy of any pursuit whatever in which men can engage, or of any subject which can occupy them, of science, of history, of the technical arts. Between science and the philosophy of science, history and the philosophy of history, there is indeed no hard and fast separation; but what in the one case we are specially concerned with is the positive nature and the laws of a certain group of facts, which have been selected out from the rest of the world to be studied by themselves, while in the other we restore that connection with the whole which for the time being we had set aside, and try to look at our facts in the light of the meaning which they have for life in its entirety.

Even when it is stated in this preliminary way, the definition which has been given of philosophy will be seen to have a bearing on the disputes which have been common about the value of the study, and the very unequal estimation in which it has been held. There are many people to whom the pursuit of philosophy has seemed to be, at best, of very doubtful utility. Sometimes it is one who, like Matthew Arnold, is so impressed with the concrete values of art and conduct that the world of the philosopher seems to him abstract and barren in comparison. More often it is the man of science, who feels that he has got hold of reality so immediately and palpably in the world of matter, and of reality which is so far-reaching in its significance, that he has no interest left to give the supersensuous and very doubtful world which he understands that philosophy is trying to construct by merely thinking about it. Now the answer to be made the scientist is this, that he is not getting along without philosophy, as he supposes, but only is adopting one particular kind of philosophy, whose implications, however, he does not try to understand. And he can hardly hold that this refusal to examine into the presuppositions of his thinking is, in opposition to the metaphysician's course, a highly meritorious thing, without stultifying his whole scientific procedure. He may, indeed, as a scientist, merely devote himself to the discovery of facts; but unless he is prepared to say that the bare objective fact is everything, and its meaning, its value for us, is nothing (which is very like a contradiction in terms), he cannot avoid encroaching on the philosopher's field. In reality he always does bring with him his own interpretation of the facts of science, and they differentiate the way in which he looks at the world from the way in which other men look at it; the only question is as to whether this should be conscious and thoroughgoing, or whether it should be unconscious, and unaware of the possible difficulties that may be involved. In any case the mere facts of the objective world, as objective, cannot exhaust the problems which arise, and arise necessarily, for this external world would not exist, for us, if it did not have a value as coming within our conscious life, and so it forms but a part of experience, not the whole. Whatever it may be in itself, for human interest at least the objective fact or law as such cannot possibly be a final and sufficient goal. Even the man who thinks that it is so, must have some reason why the search for objective truth appeals to him; its simple existence in itself does not explain why he should want to know it. It may of course be that, in the end, one might be driven to admit that no vital relation to human life could be discovered; in that case science at once would cease to be pursued. But answerable or not, at least it cannot be said that when the problems go beyond mere scientific matter of fact they cease to have any *interest* for us; knowing the chemical composition of water will not satisfy us in face of the larger question, What is this world of which our lives form a part? what is its meaning and destiny? And it is through philosophy, not through science, that this latter question must receive an answer, if it is answered at all.

Nevertheless there is some justification for this contemptuous attitude which science is apt to adopt towards philosophy, and which grows out of the true feeling that any value which is really worth our consideration must attach to the actual world in which we live, not to some far-away abstract world, which only can be got at by the occasional philosopher, and through the colorless medium of thought. What we are after is the meaning of life as we live it, and if we come out at the end with something that finds no place for the concrete values with which we are familiar, then certainly a large factor in the problem has without any justification been juggled out of sight. So that we have to insist, in the second place, that the data which the philosopher uses are not something which, by a pure act of intellectual creation, he spins out of his own head, but the same facts with which science, and history, and everyday living, deal. In this sense, therefore, the philosopher is dependent on the scientist; he cannot go his own way and construct his world *a priori,* but he must continually be falling back upon the concrete knowledge which science represents. So, also, philosophy does not "give us God, freedom, immortality," if by this we mean that it somehow puts us in possession of values which we had not before suspected. Religion, morality, the social life, all come before philosophy, and are presupposed by it; and philosophy, in turn, in so far as it is only a bare recognition of truths, and not a vital appreciation of them, in so far as it stops with itself as mere knowing, and does not hand back the material which it has been elaborating intellectually, to the immediate experience in which this originated, is forgetting its place as the handmaid of life, and so is rendering itself barren and formal. All that philosophy can do is to take the actual values which come to us in experience, work out their implications and their mutual relationships, and, it may be, get at some unitary point of view, from which each element can be looked at, and have full justice done it. But by this very process it will be making a positive addition to the value of experience itself, not by creating truths which are entirely new, but by clearing up and throwing new light upon the meaning which already has been present in our lives, and so making it more real to us.

And this will also serve to indicate the answer to a very common complaint against philosophy, in which it is set over against feeling, as something quite opposed. It is common to hear people say, After all, it is feeling truth, not reasoning about it, which is the important thing; and philosophy, by translating everything over into the cold and impersonal medium of thought, and by introducing all sorts of doubts and limitations, is a foe to that immediate enjoyment of truth which alone is worth the having. Whether this is true or not depends entirely on what we mean by it. If we mean by feeling unintelligent, blind feeling, just the mere confused sense of satisfaction, it is not true at all. But this is not what we mean when we speak of feeling as it is aroused by poetry or art: that is equivalent rather to insight, intelligent appreciation. It is, therefore, not something which is opposed to reason, but its highest, most immediate exercise. But here again we shall be doing an injustice if we oppose immediacy too sharply to the more laborious and reflective work of thought. It is not philosophy which comes in to spoil the fineness of the enjoyment we get in immediate feeling, but it is the fact that feeling breaks down, and will no longer satisfy us, that compels us to betake ourselves to thought. Feelings are sure to clash, and then they possess no criterion within themselves which shall say whether this feeling or that one is the truer; merely as feeling they cannot tell us whether they are valid objectively, or whether we are only deluding ourselves with subjective emotions. To compare their values, and to bring them to the test of their consonancy with the whole of life, thought is needed; but that does not mean that we pass from immediate experience to something higher, thought; it means that, through thought, we get from an immediacy which is limited and partial, to one which is truer, richer, and more inclusive.

Now systems of philosophy are simply attempts to get at a unified way of looking at things.... In a general way we may say that they all of them have to do with a few very simple-looking assumptions, which every one is accustomed to make, and which are so natural that when our attention is first called to them we hardly see how anybody can be so foolish as to bring them into question. We all feel very sure, that is, that out there in space a lot of things exist,—trees, stones, houses,—which we know are there because we see them when we open our eyes, and touch them when we stretch out our hands. To be sure, we are not looking at them all the time, but that makes no difference to the things themselves; they still are there, whether we see them or not. Then again we are sure that we ourselves exist. If we were asked to define this "self," we might indeed have difficulty in determining just in what it consisted, but in general it is that which thinks and feels, has sensations and desires, and acts according to conscious purposes, none of which attributes are we ready to suppose belong to things in the external world. Finally, it is not only my own self that I believe in, but I am just as firmly convinced of the existence of other selves, with whom I am continually in communication. These three assumptions it never enters into the head of the ordinary man to doubt.

Now in these beliefs, on which every one, including the philosopher himself, continually is acting, there are involved the various problems of philosophy, even the most abstract. This world of men and things which we assume seems clear and unambiguous in its nature only so long as we refrain from thinking about it; a very little consideration shows the necessity of defining more exactly in what the reality of these things consists, how they are to be thought. In so far as philosophy has this problem, of determining the true nature of the real, it is called Ontology. If we start by assuming the separation between mind and matter, we must ask precisely what it is we mean by these two terms, and then the more they seem to differ from and exclude each other, the more insistent becomes the problem as to how that still more basal form of reality is to be conceived, which shall restore the unity of which philosophy is in search. But things not only exist, they have a history; and this brings us into still more evident contact with the practical values of experience. For any inquiry into the laws which govern the history of the material world, into the nature and connection of the world processes, raises at once and inevitably the question, what relation these have to our own conscious lives and purposes, whether they are mechanical merely, and indifferent to human interests, or whether something in the nature of meaning and aim can be detected in them. This in general is the field of Cosmology. But now the fact that we started with individuals more or less distinct from the world, gives rise to a third set of problems. It is soon apparent that we cannot talk about the nature of reality, without also giving some account of the source from which we get our knowledge, a problem which again becomes more difficult, the more we insist upon the separation between the knower and the object which is known. An answer to this question, What is the nature of knowledge? or How is knowledge possible? constitutes Epistemology.

Of course it would be a mistake to suppose that these three provinces of philosophy deal with problems that are in any strict sense distinct; in reality it is all the while a single problem which we are approaching from different sides. That problem is, to get some way of looking at things as a whole, some unitary conception which shall find a place for the actual facts of life, and by reference to which we may have some reasonable ground for believing that these facts possess real validity and worth. Philosophical systems are simply the most general points of view from which this unity has been sought. . . .

3 THE PHILOSOPHIC MIND AND THE CONTEMPORARY WORLD

ARTHUR E. MURPHY (1901-1962)

When the Humanities are afforded as handsome an opportunity as this Conference presents to explain themselves and their reason for being in an American University, the question that is at the back of nearly everybody's mind is a direct, if not a simple one. What is to be got out of humanistic studies —how many students who devote their time and effort to them expect to come away richer, or more skillful, or in some other assignable way better off than when they started? This question arises with particular urgency in the case of philosophy—a queer sort of subject in common repute, which seems to fit in nowhere and to lead to nothing in particular, and which yet, for some reason, men keep coming back to when they are deeply troubled and perplexed. What, within the general pattern of the humanistic studies, is to be got out of philosophy and for whom and under what conditions is it worth having? These are the questions which, without further preface, I propose to try to answer.

The first thing one might normally expect to get out of the study of philosophy is information about what various men called "philosophers" have taught in the past and about the circumstances under which their doctrines were developed and the kind of influence they had in their own time, and beyond.

SOURCE: An address delivered at the University of Rochester Conference on the Humanities, March 27, 1947. First published in *Reason and the Common Good: Selected Essays of Arthur E. Murphy*, edited by W. H. Hay and M. G. Singer (Prentice Hall, 1963), from which it is here reprinted with the kind consent of Dr. Frederick H. Ginascol, the executor of the Murphy estate.

Some of these men—Plato, Aristotle, Augustine, Descartes, Kant, Hegel, Nietzsche—have profoundly influenced the course of subsequent thought in all manner of interesting ways, and it is hardly possible to be well informed about the roots and meaning of contemporary culture without some knowledge of who they were and what they said. In the field of "general education," which tends in practice to be largely that of general information, they bulk large. A student at the University of Illinois who had elected a somewhat varied program told me a year or two ago that he was hearing about Plato's *Republic* in every course he was taking except plant pathology. Now Plato's *Republic* is indubitably philosophy, if anything is, and that some information about it should be considered important in so many different connections is to be accounted, I suppose, a tribute to the importance of our subject.

In philosophy, however, information is not enough. This is, for some students, a disquieting discovery. They come, notebook in hand, from classes in which they have faithfully recorded the material that the lecturer has got together on whatever subject, from geology to labor management, they have elected to study, and which they will be expected to remember and rewrite on examination papers. If the lecturer speaks slowly and clearly, and the student's pen, paper and memory are adequate to the demands made upon them, there is no reason why he should not, thus equipped, come well and bravely through the ordeal of very much of what is called a general education. But in philosophy the ordinary rules no longer hold. Here the student must not only acquire some information about thinking, he must actually participate in the activity of thinking for himself. And since it is notoriously hard to think and take notes at the same time, the novel exercise is likely to get in the way of what he takes to be the main business of the hour—the writing down of the information which, together with the grade which records his faithful memory of it at the right time, will quite literally be what he has "got out of" the course. To lose his notebook would be, for all practical educational purposes, to lose his mind. But this, as a little reflection will show, is not the philosophic mind that we are seeking.

Nor is this, as the troubled student sometimes suspects, just one more proof of the oddity of philosophers. It follows rather from the special nature of their subject, which is *ideas* considered not as events but as ideas. To understand an idea of Aristotle's it is not enough to know that Aristotle had it and where he wrote it down and what somebody else said about it afterward. To grasp it as an idea one must think it for oneself, and that means actually to participate in the activity of problem solving in which it is offered as an answer and to see what the conditions of the problem are and to what extent it really *is* an answer. In this field at least Santayana's aphorism applies: "We cannot cease to think and still continue to know." Or, to put the same point another way: in philosophy ideas must be known at first hand or by acquaintance and not merely by description if they are to be understood. The student who is not prepared to engage in this activity of thinking ought not to undertake the study of philosophy. If at any future time he needs to locate items of information about the great philosophers, he or his secretary or research assistant will find in easily accessible encyclopedias everything that is relevant to his purpose.

But if something more than information is to be got out of philosophy, what is it? The answer currently popular among professional educators and moralists as well as with many students is that it is sound doctrine and right attitudes of belief on issues of ultimate importance. Philosophers discuss such issues —the reality of God and of the human soul—the moral order and its ground and sanctions—the nature of political obligation and the justifying reasons, if any, behind the claims of constituted authorities. A person's convictions on such matters may properly, in ordinary usage, be referred to as his "philosophy" and it is important to any well-constituted society that its members should have the right beliefs on these subjects rather than the wrong ones. To inculcate such beliefs, or to fortify and confirm them in those who, through their cultural heritage and political allegiance, already possess them is a part of the service which education is expected to render to the state, and where, if not in philosophy, is this work properly to be done? "Render unto Caesar the things that are Caesar's" is an admonition we are not likely in these times to forget. For it has been discovered that ideas are weapons, and in the struggle for power which now divides the world their importance will hardly be neglected.

Is this what is to be "got out" of philosophy and philosophers today? I hope and believe that it is not. Yet the request seems reasonable enough. If the philosophers *have* the right beliefs on these high matters, why should they be reluctant to teach their conclusions with authority? And if they should turn out to be the wrong kind of philosophers—if their conclusions are not unequivocally on our side in the ideological battle—why should they be allowed to teach at all? To see the answer to these questions is to have advanced a long way in the understanding of what philosophy is and what it is worth to those who are prepared to meet its standards.

The essential point is this. In philosophy it is not only a question of what is believed but of the way in which and the grounds on which it is accepted. Kierkegaard put the matter drastically when he said that one may be "in the truth" on ultimate issues even when what he believes is by any external or objective standard false, while an objectively true belief, accepted in the wrong way, is a lie in the soul of the believer. Men may indeed be "given" an accredited philosophy by state or church, or by educational philosophers duly responsive to the demands of both, but they will not become the wiser, better or more enlightened in the process of thus receiving it. They will become instead the readily manipulatable partisans of doctrines whose merits they are neither intellectually nor morally in a position to judge, but to which by indoctrination they are committed at all cost. Such a doctrine may be identical in content with what some of the greatest philosophers and sages have taught. But, for those who thus receive it, it is not philosophy for all that, in the sense in which philosophy is the love of wisdom or the effective possession and use of it.

Philosophy does have profoundly to do with our beliefs or commitments on ultimate issues of life, value and human destiny—and when we are asked to say *where we stand* on such issues we are being asked, in substance, for our philosophy. Philosophy in this sense, like the poor, we have always with us. For we all have such commitments, whether we are aware of them or not, and when they are challenged we become conscious of them and remain uneasy until in one way or another they have been reinforced or substantiated. To invoke them, thus supported, against those who disagree, is an inspiring and exhilarating experience and a stimulus to resolute action with an undivided mind. It is a natural confusion to suppose that the philosophers who are lovers of and seekers for wisdom, and whose works are often posthumously honored as literary and cultural monuments, are the men to whom we ought to look for this sort of ideological comfort and support.

It is a confusion, nonetheless. For in philosophy as a rational discipline such commitments are the beginning, not the end, of inquiry. We do indeed want to know where we stand with regard to them, and the philosopher's search is for just such a standpoint—for a way of judging and correcting them that can carry us beyond our starting point and out into the larger world of truth and meaning that lies beyond their partisan and parochial limitations. What develops in this process of inquiry and must be achieved if we are to pursue it successfully is a distinctive way of understanding such commitments—a philosophic habit or attitude of mind. It is this way of looking at the world and our own commitments within it which, borrowing from Wordsworth, I have called "the philosophic mind." This, I think, is what the student who is prepared to devote himself to its study can reasonably expect to get out of philosophy. It is time now to go on to say more explicitly what it is and why it is worth having.

The philosophic mind is, in the first place, an inquiring mind. It is right and illuminating to say, with Aristotle, that philosophy begins in wonder. But not just any kind of wonder. The marvelous, the occult, the merely freakish and "colossal," are objects of wonder for the popular mind and arouse an interest that illustrated weeklies, motion pictures, sideshows and various forms of commercialized superstition exist to satisfy. The wonder that generates a philosophical inquiry is of a different sort—it is elicited not by the marvelous but by the familiar, by the things that everybody "knows" and takes for granted. Socrates liked to describe himself as an ignorant man, and there are ill-furnished minds today that pride themselves on being, in this at least, his disciples. The point was, however, that Socrates knew that he did not know the things that his fellow citizens were sure about, not because he lacked some information that they possessed, but because he saw, as they did not, the dubiety of the obvious, the oddity of the commonplace, the insecurity of the preconceptions to which "right thinking men" unthinkingly subscribe. Whitehead made the same essential point when he said with penetrating brevity that philosophy is "an attitude of mind toward doctrines ignorantly entertained"—that attitude, specifically, in which an awareness of initial ignorance as to the ground and meaning of one's preconceptions is the beginning of the quest for the wisdom that will clarify and correct them. To have doubted one's preconceptions, said Justice Holmes, is the mark of a civilized mind. It is, at least, the mark of the philosophic mind and those who are not prepared to undergo its discipline, for whom philosophy is a cushion of ultimate ideological self-satisfaction on which to rest a tired mind, or a brickbat to hurl at those of a different faith, are ignorant men indeed, but they are not in the Socratic sense philosophers.

Such questioning, however, if it is philosophical, is never merely captious. The lover of wisdom is by no means unaware of the substantial store of that too rare commodity that is embedded in our preconceptions and in the traditions and loyalties that they represent. If he is dissatisfied with them as *ultimate* criteria of truth and value, it is because, as Plato's description of the true philosopher makes clear, he is a lover not of a part of wisdom only, but of the whole. He therefore takes the responsibility for relating the ultimate assurances of any special segment of experience, and of any limited perspective within it, to what lies outside that area or point of view. He can discount nothing that is humanly significant, for nothing human can be alien to his purpose, his sympathy and his understanding. This demand for inclusiveness, and consequent discontent with anything partial or partisan which claims an absoluteness and finality which, in a wider view, it cannot rationally maintain, is the second distinguishing mark of the philosophic mind.

There is something genial and easygoing in the picture which such a description naturally calls to mind. To see all sides of every question, and good in everything, is, it would seem, to be very good natured indeed. One thinks of William James, with his kindly hospitality to the ideas of cranks and his appreciation of all varieties of human aspiration and experience. Such generosity is indeed a mark of philosophic insight, but it would be a mistake to think of it as easily come by. The method of attaining it is more accurately, if allegorically, outlined in the Myth of the Cave in Plato's *Republic*. The truth at which philosophy is aiming in its quest for wisdom is as plain and public as the sunlight of that common world in which men live and work together when they understand each other and themselves. But to be a free man in that world one must first have turned his back on the illusions of perspective which are, as Spinoza memorably said, the instruments of human bondage. "When half gods go, the gods arrive," but we know today that the manner of their going is sometimes more like the casting out of demons than Emerson seems ever to have realized.

The intellectual process in which the partiality of every limited interest and idea is exposed in the interest of a more inclusive wisdom is called dialectic, and a philosophy that must cut its way through prejudice and special pleading toward wholeness of understanding will in this sense be dialectical in its method. The philosophic mind is one that tries to see such absolutistic pretensions for what they are and, without denying or disparaging the genuineness of the values they represent, to see through them to the further truth they have distorted or denied.

No human insight can assess the truth from other than a partial standpoint, and the lover of wisdom would sin against the very light he seeks if he were to forget or deny his own humanity. He sees the world from where he is, and he cannot see everywhere—the divine omniscience and ubiquity are not for him. Hence he must make his own selection among the facts and values that present themselves for his interpretation, fixing on some as for his purposes fundamental, basic and real, and relegating others to the status of the apparent and peripheral. Everything that he can understand must have some sort of meaning and reality, but not everything will be real in the same way or on the same level. The ultimate or final things will be those which maintain themselves as genuine and reliable in the light of the most penetrating and comprehensive scrutiny he can bring to bear on them, and on these he will build his philosophy. Hence a third essential mark of the philosophic mind. The philosopher is the man who takes the responsibility for making the distinction between appearance and reality, which is inherent in all our thinking, wisely, from the standpoint of such wisdom as he has and for the sake of the further wisdom that in this way he can secure. A good philosophy is one that contributes to such understanding, that enables us to see more than we could have seen without it and to bring otherwise isolated or discrepant aspects of experiences into fruitful relation to the rest of what we know. A bad philosophy is one that blocks the path of understanding in just these ways.

It is notorious that philosophers, like other men, differ in their identifications of the realities by reference to which experience can most wisely be organized and understood. The way in which they agree among themselves and differ from others is that they are prepared to see this identification as a problem rather than a preconception and to justify their theories by reference to their contribution to the larger undertaking which is the quest for comprehensive wisdom. It is often taken as a matter of reproach that philosophers go on and on arguing with each other about the ultimate realities and seem to reach no final conclusions. It should rather be made an occasion for thankfulness and congratulation. For to achieve finality in a process in which all claims to finality are and must be partial and in which all partiality is subject to correction as we live and learn would be to reach a state of mind in which both living and learning had ceased to function as sources of wisdom. And to refuse to argue on such matters would be not to free ourselves from ultimate commitments, which are inescapable in all human thinking, but to withdraw them from the sphere of rational discussion and correction. It is by arguing and by changing our minds, not arbitrarily or blindly but with reasons, that we become as wise in these matters as at any time it is humanly possible to be. For the philosopher who has not confused himself, or his ecclesiastical superior, or the state, with God, and who knows his human limitations, a finality exempt from such criticism and correction would not be the fulfilment of his purpose but its negation. For he is a lover not only of that part of wisdom which his own particular doctrine or school of thought has selected for preferential attention, but of the whole, and he knows that it is only in the process of rational inquiry that the limitations inherent in every partial standpoint are corrected in the quest for the wider good he seeks.

A further characteristic of the philosophic mind—its "detachment"—appears directly as a consequence of the traits that we have so far been considering. The philosopher, just because he is concerned wih the truth that is not exhausted in any human insight, will refuse to put all his eggs in one basket, even if that basket be his own. He will see each particular good against the background of a world in which there are other goods as well and possibilities of good not realized, and will strive to estimate the significance of all local enthusiasms and causes from a standpoint in which neither partisanship nor special pleading has the final word. This does not mean that he is without preferences and enthusiasms of his own; it does mean that he is prepared to see them in a perspective in which their limits and relativity are made plain and their immediate urgency thereby qualified and corrected.

Samuel Alexander, whose philosophizing happily exemplified this coolness of judgment, offers a pleasing illustration of its working."On a certain occasion Boswell had invited Johnson with some others to supper at his lodging. But, the landlord having proved disagreeable, Boswell was obliged to change the place of meeting from his house to the Mitre, and waited on Johnson to explain his 'serious distress.' 'Consider, sir,' said Johnson, 'how insignificant this will appear a twelvemonth hence.' That was a philosophic answer, and Johnson had in practical conduct, though certainly not in speculation, the philosophic mind."[1]

It is not through levity or indifference that the philosopher has the temerity to view with some degree of detachment the claims and counterclaims in which the circumstances of his life involve him. He refuses to be wholly serious about some of the major preoccupations of his contemporaries and in this may sometimes affront the common sense of his time and country. Common sense has had its revenge, from the story about the first Greek philosopher who fell into a well "in a fit of abstraction" while looking at the stars, to more recent and ill-natured gibes at those who seek refuge in an "ivory tower" of speculation from the "realities" of practical life. The genuine philosopher is not much bothered by that, nor should he be. He means to keep out of wells, where possible, and also to take his bearings by the stars where larger issues are at stake. As for "realities," he is pretty sure that his "practical" critic does not know one when he sees it and is constantly being cheated with second-rate and shoddy stuff in consequence. Like Thoreau, he does not propose to impoverish his life by paying the market price for goods which the values of the market place do not justly measure, and "practical" has therefore a somewhat different meaning for him than for his critics. Hence, without wishing to be at all unsociable, he sometimes finds himself going in one direction while the crowd is hurrying in another. He thinks, however, that he knows where he is going while the crowd does not and would not be greatly surprised to find that in the long run they have shifted their direction and were coming his way so that, in the larger perspective of history, he might even appear to have been leading a parade. Stranger things have happened. Meanwhile he must be about his business, which is not that of leading parades or of following them, and is glad to welcome to that enterprise all who have a mind to share it with him.

It would be a misconception of his work, however, to suppose that such detachment was the philosopher's final response to the problems of the world in which he finds himself. Rather is his detachment the consequence and expression of a different loyalty. He is committed to an undertaking in whose worth he believes, and it is this commitment which makes sense of all the rest. Since it is an attitude and an affirmation, a claim to the reality of things not seen as yet, it may properly be called a faith. The fifth and, for our purposes, final mark of the philosophic mind is the quality and object of its faith.

It is a faith in the capacity of the human mind to achieve in some rewarding

---

[1] Samuel Alexander, *Space, Time, and Deity* (London: Macmillan and Co., Limited, 1920), I, 3–4.

measure the wisdom that it seeks, and to live, in the light of it, a juster and more generous life than would otherwise be attainable. This is not always the faith the professed philosopher professes, when called on to edify, instruct or entertain, but it is the faith he works by and justifies to the extent that his work attains its goal. No man who remembers his human limitations will claim to have reached the end of his search for wisdom or to possess the wholeness of truth that he is seeking. But if, within the present situation in which, like the rest of us, he lives, he has achieved a standpoint from which a man may see something of the scope and greatness of the world beyond the end of his nose and the urgency of his appetites and suspicions and if, reporting what he sees, he can bring into the heat and clutter of contemporary life a range of insight, steadiness of purpose and magnanimity of spirit which can lift it somewhat above the routine, exclusiveness, and mediocrity into which, without such insight, it regularly tends to fall, then he has done his job as a philosopher. He thinks it is a job worth doing.

Such is the philosophic mind which those who undertake the study and discipline of philosophical inquiry may expect in some measure to achieve. What, now, does it offer that is pertinent to the needs and interests of the contemporary world and of those who wish to participate in it as fully and intelligently as possible? There is time for no more than a brief answer; I shall try to make it to the point. One thing that the contemporary world is deeply concerned about is "peace of mind." The sense of both personal and national insecurity is widespread. We are confronted by alien and apparently hostile forces in a world that is larger and less congenial than we had been led to suppose. We seek a form of faith or ideological security that will give us something to hold on to, that will put a sure foundation under our shaken and half-undermined conviction. And it is natural that we should do so.

The situation, however, has its dangers. An examination paper I read recently told me that what most people were looking for now-a-days was "piece" of mind. Even an unintended pun may have a moral for the philosophic mind, and this is a case in point. For it seems dangerously near the truth to say that that is exactly what many people today are after. They want to purchase peace of mind by retreating into some fragment or aspect of experience to which they can cling no matter what, and to shut out all those wider and disturbing meanings which might upset their meager absolutes. Thus Mr. Aldous Huxley tells us that we shall be philosophers indeed—"perennial philosophers"—if we become "poor in spirit" and thus find in the mystical immediacy of an unutterable experience the solution, which is also the negation, of our deepest problems.

Another instance of a somewhat similar poverty of spirit is that frightened nationalism which, finding its preconceptions challenged by "alien ideologies," seeks the protection of its own ideals in the exclusion of such dangerous doctrines from public hearing and those suspected of any sort of sympathy with them from the public pay roll. The alarm thus manifested is understandable. But those of us who wish not only to sympathize with but to put into practice the ideals of democracy will be blind indeed if we do not see that it is an unwholesome thing for free men to be afraid of ideas, even if they are radical and mistaken ideas. It sets up the defensive reaction appropriate to a closed and frightened mind. We dare not seek a basis of common understanding with nations with whose economic, political and religious ideals we differ for fear of giving aid and comfort to an ideological enemy. And yet it is only on the basis of such an understanding that any genuine international community can be established. Those who profess to honor the ideal of such a community and at the same time cut off that free competition of ideas in terms of which alone, as a great American jurist affirmed in a period of similar panic, the truth is reliably established, may mean well, but they do not think well or act wisely. And their country may pay a heavy price in the future for their meagerness of mind.

Finally, to make a long story short enough for present purposes, we should consider the practical men who think that they can find security in concentration on small aims and tangible goods, and who resent as "metaphysical" the introduction into their calculations of any question of the meaning in human terms of the instruments and accessories toward whose production and sale their effort is untiringly addressed. Mr. Santayana's saying that "fanaticism is redoubling your effort when you have forgotten your aim" is well known. I doubt its applicability to many sorts of fanatics now abroad in the world. But it might well be modified to read "specialization is redoubling your effort when you have forgotten your aim." In that form the dictum would apply with justice to a good deal of contemporary American life, and not least to American universities. We all know this well enough, and have by now so far acquiesced in it that it seems both trite and impolite to refer to it. My point is that this "practicality" too is a kind of deliberate fragmentariness or poverty of spirit, a way of living with a piece of one's mind and securing, in this simplification, a partial respite from the claims of the larger world with which the specialist in his professional capacity is not prepared to deal. It is to be understood and judged as such.

As against such dubious and desperate expedients as these, it is surely the part of sanity and courage to insist once more that peace of mind is to be reliably secured only in wholeness and integrity of mind and that the business of a sound philosophy is not to protect our conceptions against the hazards of an uncertain world and a growing experience but rather to give us the means of growing up to the demands of that world and laying hold of and using its resources for all that they are worth. Clearly this is a risky business. The peace it promises is the steady assurance of a mind adequate to its business and not afraid in consequence to put its powers and ideals to the test of the widest experience that can be brought to bear on them. We shall need that sort of mind if America is to play its part cooperatively in the world community which our present situation makes both possible and necessary, but also tragically improbable, and if we are to do our part in America. Simple-mindedness may have been a virtue in simpler times than ours; it is a tragic misfit today, for it can only be the artificial and willful simple-mindedness that is also self-deception. Between such narrowness of mind and poverty of spirit on the one side and the full acceptance of our intellectual and moral responsibilities on the other we have now to choose. If we should choose the first alternative there will not in the near future be much place in America for the kind of philosophy of which I have been speaking. But if, as I believe, the spiritual resources of our country are great enough for choosing the second then we shall be called upon to make use of just the qualities of mind that have so far been described, not as an academic exercise but as a steady attitude of preference and sound judgment in the conduct of affairs. For we shall have to question and enlarge our traditional preconceptions from the standpoint of a more inclusive good, and to prefer the integrity of the process in which public understanding is won to the victory of our side in recurrent controversies and conflicts of interest. We shall have, in short, to be lovers not only of those parts of wisdom and goodness which we have come to regard as our peculiar possession but of the whole toward which, as partners in a common enterprise, all men may work together. And we shall have to learn to make that devotion decisive at crucial moments in our political behavior.

This is a large undertaking. I do not know that we shall succeed in it, or even that we shall be given any real chance to try. But of this I am sure. Nothing less than this is demanded of us by our situation in the contemporary world, and if we do not succeed at this level we shall fail no less surely and more ignominiously on the lower level to which the faint of heart and small of mind now ask us to retreat. This is the plain meaning of the task before us. It is not the business of education, if it is honest, to make hard things look easy, or to sell cheap the goods on which our civilization depends. It is its business to show them forth as the good they are and to invite those who see and honor them to share in the continuing work by which they are fostered and advanced. With such an invitation addressed, in customary fashion, "to whom it may concern," this discussion reaches its appropriate conclusion.

PART II
LOGIC AND PHILOSOPHY OF SCIENCE

4 ELEVEN BLUE MEN

BERTON ROUECHÉ (1911-   )

At about eight o'clock on Monday morning, September 25, 1944, a ragged, aimless old man of eighty-two collapsed on the sidewalk on Dey Street, near the Hudson Terminal. Innumerable people must have noticed him, but he lay there alone for several minutes, dazed, doubled up with abdominal cramps, and in an agony of retching. Then a policeman came along. Until the policeman bent over the old man, he may have supposed that he had just a sick drunk on his hands; wanderers dropped by drink are common in that part of town in the early morning. It was not an opinion that he could have held for long. The old man's nose, lips, ears, and fingers were sky-blue. The policeman went to the telephone and put in an ambulance call to Beekman-Downtown Hospital, half a dozen blocks away. The old man was carried into the emergency room there at eight-thirty. By that time, he was unconscious and the blueness had spread over a large part of his body. The examining physician attributed the old man's morbid color to cyanosis, a condition that usually results from an insufficient supply of oxygen in the blood, and also noted that he was diarrheic and in a severe state of shock. The course of treatment prescribed by the doctor was conventional. It included an instant gastric lavage, heart stimulants, bed rest, and oxygen therapy. Presently, the old man recovered an encouraging, if painful, consciousness and demanded, irascibly and in the name of God, to know what had happened to him. It was a question that, at the moment, nobody could answer with much confidence.

For the immediate record, the doctor made a free-hand diagnosis of carbon-monoxide poisoning—from what source, whether an automobile or a gas pipe, it was, of course, pointless even to guess. Then, because an isolated instance of gas poisoning is something of a rarity in a section of the city as crammed with human beings as downtown Manhattan, he and his colleagues in the emergency room braced themselves for at least a couple more victims. Their foresight was promptly and generously rewarded. A second man was rolled in at ten-twenty-five. Forty minutes later, an ambulance drove up with

SOURCE: From *Eleven Blue Men* (1954) by Berton Rouché, pp. 87–99, by permission of Little, Brown and Co. Copyright, 1948, by Berton Roueché. This story originally appeared in *The New Yorker.* Compare with selections 6, 10, and 11.

23

three more men. At eleven-twenty, two others were brought in. An additional two arrived during the next fifteen minutes. Around noon, still another was admitted. All of these nine men were also elderly and dilapidated, all had been in misery for at least an hour, and all were rigid, cyanotic, and in a state of shock. The entire body of one, a bony, seventy-three-year-old consumptive named John Mitchell, was blue. Five of the nine, including Mitchell, had been stricken in the Globe Hotel, a sunless, upstairs flophouse at 190 Park Row, and two in a similar place, called the Star Hotel, at 3 James Street. Another had been found slumped in the doorway of a condemned building on Park Row, not far from City Hall Park, by a policeman. The ninth had keeled over in front of the Eclipse Cafeteria, at 6 Chatham Square. At a quarter to seven that evening, one more aged blue man was brought in. He had been lying, too sick to ask for help, on his cot in a cubicle in the Lion Hotel, another flophouse, at 26 Bowery, since ten o'clock that morning. A clerk had finally looked in and seen him.

By the time this last blue man arrived at the hospital, an investigation of the case by the Department of Health, to which all outbreaks of an epidemiological nature must be reported, had been under way for five hours. Its findings thus far had not been illuminating. The investigation was conducted by two men. One was the Health Department's chief epidemiologist, Dr. Morris Greenberg, a small, fragile, reflective man of fifty-seven, who is now acting director of the Bureau of Preventable Diseases; the other was Dr. Ottavio Pellitteri, a field epidemiologist, who, since 1946, has been administrative medical inspector for the Bureau. He is thirty-six years old, pale, and stocky, and has a bristling black mustache. One day, when I was in Dr. Greenberg's office, he and Dr. Pellitteri told me about the case. Their recollection of it is, understandably, vivid. The derelicts were the victims of a type of poisoning so rare that only ten previous outbreaks of it had been recorded in medical literature. Of these, two were in the United States and two in Germany; the others had been reported in France, England, Switzerland, Algeria, Australia, and India. Up to September 25, 1944, the largest number of people stricken in a single outbreak was four. That was in Algeria, in 1926.

The Beekman-Downtown Hospital telephoned a report of the occurrence to the Health Department just before noon. As is customary, copies of the report were sent to all the Department's administrative officers. "Mine was on my desk when I got back from lunch," Dr. Greenberg said to me. "It didn't sound like much. Nine persons believed to be suffering from carbon-monoxide poisoning had been admitted during the morning, and all of them said that they had eaten breakfast at the Eclipse Cafeteria, at 6 Chatham Square. Still, it was a job for us. I checked with the clerk who handles assignments and found that Pellitteri had gone out on it. That was all I wanted to know. If it amounted to anything, I knew he'd phone me before making a written report. That's an arrangement we have here. Well, a couple of hours later I got a call from him. My interest perked right up."

"I was at the hospital," Dr. Pellitteri told me, "and I'd talked to the staff and most of the men. There were ten of them by then, of course. They were sick as dogs, but only one was in really bad shape."

"That was John Mitchell," Dr. Greenberg put in. "He died the next night. I understand his condition was hopeless from the start. The others, including the old boy who came in last, pulled through all right. Excuse me, Ottavio, but I just thought I'd get that out of the way. Go on."

Dr. Pellitteri nodded. "I wasn't at all convinced that it was gas poisoning," he continued. "The staff was beginning to doubt it, too. The symptoms weren't quite right. There didn't seem to be any of the headache and general dopiness that you get with gas. What really made me suspicious was this: Only two or three of the men had eaten breakfast in the cafeteria at the same time. They had straggled in all the way from seven o'clock to ten. That meant that the place would have had to be full of gas for at least three hours, which is preposterous. It also indicated that we ought to have had a lot more sick people than we did. Those Chatham Square eating places have a big turnover. Well, to make sure, I checked with Bellevue, Gouverneur, St. Vincent's, and the other downtown hospitals. None of them had seen a trace of cyanosis. Then I talked to the sick men some more. I learned two interesting things. One was that they had all got sick right after eating. Within thirty minutes. The other was that all but one had eaten oatmeal, rolls, and coffee. He ate just oatmeal. When ten men eat the same thing in the same place on the same day and then all come down with the same illness . . . I told Greenberg that my hunch was food poisoning."

"I was willing to rule out gas," Dr. Greenberg said. A folder containing data on the case lay on the desk before him. He lifted the cover thoughtfully, then let it drop. "And I agreed that the oatmeal sounded pretty suspicious. That was as far as I was willing to go. Common, ordinary, everyday food poisoning —I gathered that was what Pellitteri had in mind—wasn't a very satisfying answer. For one thing, cyanosis is hardly symptomatic of that. On the other hand, diarrhea and severe vomiting are, almost invariably. But they weren't in the clinical picture, I found, except in two or three of the cases. Moreover, the incubation periods—the time lapse between eating and illness—were extremely short. As you probably know, most food poisoning is caused by eating something that has been contaminated by bacteria. The usual offenders are the staphylococci—they're mostly responsible for boils and skin infections and so on—and the salmonella. The latter are related to the typhoid organism. In a staphylococcus case, the first symptoms rarely develop in under two hours. Often, it's closer to five. The incubation period in the other ranges from twelve to thirty-six hours. But here we were with something that hit in thirty minutes or less. Why, one of the men had got only as far as the sidewalk in front of the cafeteria before he was knocked out. Another fact that Pellitteri had dug up struck me as very significant. All of them told him that the illness had come on with extraordinary suddenness. One minute they were feeling fine, and the next minute they were practically helpless. That was another point against the ordinary food-poisoning theory. Its onset is never that fast. Well, that suddenness began to look like a lead. It led me to suspect that some drug might be to blame. A quick and sudden reaction is characteristic of a great many drugs. So is the combination of cyanosis and shock."

"None of the men were on dope," Dr. Pellitteri said. "I told Greenberg I was sure of that. Their pleasure was booze."

"That was O.K.," Dr. Greenberg said. "They could have got a toxic dose of some drug by accident. In the oatmeal, most likely. I couldn't help thinking that the oatmeal was relevant to our problem. At any rate, the drug idea was very persuasive."

"So was Greenberg," Dr. Pellitteri remarked with a smile. "Actually, it was the only explanation in sight that seemed to account for everything we knew about the clinical and environmental picture."

"All we had to do now was prove it," Dr. Greenberg went on mildly. "I asked Pellitteri to get a blood sample from each of the men before leaving the hospital for a look at the cafeteria. We agreed he would send the specimens to the city toxicologist, Dr. Alexander O. Gettler, for an overnight analysis. I wanted to know if the blood contained methemoglobin. Methemoglobin is a compound that's formed only when any one of several drugs enters the blood. Gettler's report would tell us if we were at least on the right track. That is, it would give us a yes-or-no answer on drugs. If the answer was yes, then we could go on from there to identify the particular drug. How we would go about that would depend on what Pellitteri was able to turn up at the cafeteria. In the meantime, there was nothing for me to do but wait for their reports. I'd theorized myself hoarse."

Dr. Pellitteri, having attended to his bloodletting with reasonable dispatch, reached the Eclipse Cafeteria at around five o'clock. "It was about what I'd expected," he told me. "Strictly a horse market, and dirtier than most. The sort of place where you can get a full meal for fifteen cents. There was a grind house on one side, a cigar store on the other, and the 'L' overhead. Incidentally, the Eclipse went out of business a year or so after I was there, but that had nothing to do with us. It was just a coincidence. Well, the place looked deserted and the door was locked. I knocked, and a man came out of the back and let me in. He was one of our people, a health inspector for the

Bureau of Food and Drugs, named Weinberg. His bureau had stepped into the case as a matter of routine, because of the reference to a restaurant in the notification report. I was glad to see him and to have his help. For one thing, he had put a temporary embargo on everything in the cafeteria. That's why it was closed up. His main job, though, was to check the place for violations of the sanitation code. He was finding plenty."

"Let me read you a few of Weinberg's findings," Dr. Greenberg said, extracting a paper from the folder on his desk. "None of them had any direct bearing on our problem, but I think they'll give you a good idea of what the Eclipse was like—what too many restaurants are like. This copy of his report lists fifteen specific violations. Here they are: 'Premises heavily infested with roaches. Fly infestation throughout premises. Floor defective in rear part of dining room. Kitchen walls and ceiling encrusted with grease and soot. Kitchen floor encrusted with dirt. Refuse under kitchen fixtures. Sterilizing facilities inadequate. Sink defective. Floor and walls at serving tables and coffee urns encrusted with dirt. Kitchen utensils encrusted with dirt and grease. Storage-cellar walls, ceiling, and floor encrusted with dirt. Floor and shelves in cellar covered with refuse and useless material. Cellar ceiling defective. Sewer pipe leaking. Open sewer line in cellar.' Well . . ." He gave me a squeamish smile and stuck the paper back in the folder.

"I can see it now," Dr. Pellitteri said. "And smell it. Especially the kitchen, where I spent most of my time. Weinberg had the proprietor and the cook out there, and I talked to them while he prowled around. They were very coöperative. Naturally. They were scared to death. They knew nothing about gas in the place and there was no sign of any, so I went to work on the food. None of what had been prepared for breakfast that morning was left. That, of course, would have been too much to hope for. But I was able to get together some of the kind of stuff that had gone into the men's breakfast, so that we could make a chemical determination at the Department. What I took was ground coffee, sugar, a mixture of evaporated milk and water that passed for cream, some bakery rolls, a five-pound carton of dry oatmeal, and some salt. The salt had been used in preparing the oatmeal. That morning, like every morning, the cook told me, he had prepared six gallons of oatmeal, enough to serve around a hundred and twenty-five people. To make it, he used five pounds of dry cereal, four gallons of water—regular city water—and a handful of salt. That was his term—a handful. There was an open gallon can of salt standing on the stove. He said the handful he'd put in that morning's oatmeal had come from that. He refilled the can on the stove every morning from a big supply can. He pointed out the big can—it was up on a shelf— and as I was getting it down to take with me, I saw another can, just like it, nearby. I took that one down, too. It was also full of salt, or, rather, something that looked like salt. The proprietor said it wasn't salt. He said it was saltpetre —sodium nitrate—that he used in corning beef and in making pastrami. Well, there isn't any harm in saltpetre; it doesn't even act as an antiaphrodisiac, as a lot of people seem to think. But I wrapped it up with the other loot and took it along, just for fun. The fact is, I guess, everything in that damn place looked like poison."

After Dr. Pellitteri had deposited his loot with a Health Department chemist, Andrew J. Pensa, who promised to have a report ready by the following afternoon, he dined hurriedly at a restaurant in which he had confidence and returned to Chatham Square. There he spent the evening making the rounds of the lodging houses in the neighborhood. He had heard at Mr. Pensa's office that an eleventh blue man had been admitted to the hospital, and before going home he wanted to make sure that no other victims had been overlooked. By midnight, having covered all the likely places and having rechecked the downtown hospitals, he was satisfied. He repaired to his office and composed a formal progress report for Dr. Greenberg. Then he went home and to bed.

The next morning, Tuesday, Dr. Pellitteri dropped by the Eclipse, which was still closed but whose proprietor and staff he had told to return for questioning. Dr. Pellitteri had another talk with the proprietor and the cook. He also had a few inconclusive words with the rest of the cafeteria's employees—two dishwashers, a busboy, and a counterman. As he was leaving, the cook, who had apparently passed an uneasy night with his conscience, remarked that it was possible that he had absent-mindedly refilled the salt can on the stove from the one that contained saltpetre. "That was interesting," Dr. Pellitteri told me, "even though such a possibility had already occurred to me, and even though I didn't know whether it was important or not. I assured him that he had nothing to worry about. We had been certain all along that nobody had deliberately poisoned the old men." From the Eclipse, Dr. Pellitteri went on to Dr. Greenberg's office, where Dr. Gettler's report was waiting.

"Gettler's test for methemoglobin was positive," Dr. Greenberg said. "It had to be a drug now. Well, so far so good. Then we heard from Pensa."

"Greenberg almost fell out of his chair when he read Pensa's report," Dr. Pellitteri observed cheerfully.

"That's an exaggeration," Dr. Greenberg said. "I'm not easily dumfounded. We're inured to the incredible around here. Why, a few years ago we had a case involving some numskull who stuck a fistful of potassium-thiocyanate crystals, a very nasty poison, in the coils of an office water cooler, just for a practical joke. However, I can't deny that Pensa rather taxed our credulity. What he had found was that the small salt can and the one that was supposed to be full of sodium nitrate both contained sodium *nitrite*. The other food samples, incidentally, were O.K."

"That also taxed my credulity," Dr. Pellitteri said.

Dr. Greenberg smiled. "There's a great deal of difference between nitrate and nitrite," he continued. "Their only similarity, which is an unfortunate one, is that they both look and taste more or less like ordinary table salt. Sodium nitrite isn't the most powerful poison in the world, but a little of it will do a lot of harm. If you remember, I said before that this case was almost without precedent—only ten outbreaks like it on record. Ten is practically none. In fact, sodium-nitrite poisoning is so unusual that some of the standard texts on toxicology don't even mention it. So Pensa's report was pretty startling. But we accepted it, of course, without question or hesitation. Facts are facts. And we were glad to. It seemed to explain everything very nicely. What I've been saying about sodium-nitrite poisoning doesn't mean that sodium nitrite itself is rare. Actually, it's fairly common. It's used in the manufacture of dyes and as a medical drug. We use it in treating certain heart conditions and for high blood pressure. But it also has another important use, one that made its presence at the Eclipse sound plausible. In recent years, and particularly during the war, sodium nitrite has been used as a substitute for sodium nitrate in preserving meat. The government permits it but stipulates that the finished meat must not contain more than one part of sodium nitrite per five thousand parts of meat. Cooking will safely destroy enough of that small quantity of the drug." Dr. Greenberg shrugged. "Well, Pellitteri had had the cook pick up a handful of salt—the same amount, as nearly as possible, as went into the oatmeal—and then had taken this to his office and found that it weighed approximately a hundred grams. So we didn't have to think twice to realize that the portion of nitrite in that batch of cereal was considerably higher than one to five thousand. Roughly, it must have been around one to about eighty before cooking destroyed part of the nitrite. It certainly looked as though Gettler, Pensa, and the cafeteria cook between them had given us our answer. I called up Gettler and told him what Pensa had discovered and asked him to run a specific test for nitrites on his blood samples. He had, as a matter of course, held some blood back for later examination. His confirmation came through in a couple of hours. I went home that night feeling pretty good."

Dr. Greenberg's serenity was a fugitive one. He awoke on Wednesday morning troubled in mind. A question had occurred to him that he was unable to ignore. "Something like a hundred and twenty-five people ate oatmeal at the Eclipse that morning," he said to me, "but only eleven of them got sick. Why? The undeniable fact that those eleven old men were made sick by the ingestion of a toxic dose of sodium nitrite wasn't enough to rest on. I wanted to know exactly how much sodium nitrite each portion of that cooked oatmeal had contained. With Pensa's help again, I found out. We prepared a batch just like the one the cook had made on Monday. Then Pensa measured out six ounces, the size of the average portion served at the Eclipse, and analyzed it. It contained two and a half grains of sodium nitrite. That explained why the hundred and fourteen other people did not become ill. The toxic dose of sodium nitrite is three grains. But it didn't explain how each of our eleven old men had received an additional half grain. It seemed extremely unlikely that the extra touch of nitrite had been in the oatmeal when it was served. It had to come in later. Then I began to get a glimmer. Some people sprinkle a little salt, instead of sugar, on hot cereal. Suppose, I thought, that the busboy, or whoever had the job of keeping the table salt shakers filled, had made the same mistake that the cook had. It seemed plausible. Pellitteri was out of the office—I've forgotten where—so I got Food and Drugs to step over to the Eclipse, which was still under embargo, and bring back the shakers for Pensa to work on. There were seventeen of them, all good-sized, one for each table. Sixteen contained either pure sodium chloride or just a few inconsequential traces of sodium nitrite mixed in with the real salt, but the other was point thirty-seven per cent nitrite. That one was enough. A spoonful of that salt contained a bit more than half a grain."

"I went over to the hospital Thursday morning," Dr. Pellitteri said. "Greenberg wanted me to check the table-salt angle with the men. They could tie the case up neatly for us. I drew a blank. They'd been discharged the night before, and God only knew where they were."

"Naturally," Dr. Greenberg said, "it would have been nice to know for a fact that the old boys all sat at a certain table and that all of them put about a spoonful of salt from that particular shaker on their oatmeal, but it wasn't essential. I was morally certain that they had. There just wasn't any other explanation. There was one other question, however. Why did they use so *much* salt? For my own peace of mind, I wanted to know. All of a sudden, I remembered Pellitteri had said they were all heavy drinkers. Well, several recent clinical studies have demonstrated that there is usually a subnormal concentration of sodium chloride in the blood of alcoholics. Either they don't eat enough to get sufficient salt or they lose it more rapidly than other people do, or both. Whatever the reasons are, the conclusion was all I needed. Any animal, you know, whether a mouse or a man, tends to try to obtain a necessary susbstance that his body lacks. The final question had been answered."

5 LOGIC AND SCIENCE
MORRIS R. COHEN (1880-1947)
AND ERNEST NAGEL (1901-   )

I. Logic and the Method of Science
Formal logic . . . deals with the possible relations (in regard to truth and falsity) between propositions, no matter what their subject matter. This gives us the *necessary* conditions for valid inference and enables us to eliminate false reasoning, but that is not *sufficient* to establish any material or factual truth in any particular field. Formal logic shows us that any such proposition must be true *if* certain others are so. The categorical assertion that our premises are actually true cannot be a matter of logic alone without making the latter identical with all knowledge. Logic, then, is involved in all reasoned knowledge (which is the original meaning of "science") but is not the whole of it. This enables us to regard all science as applied logic, which was expressed by the Greeks in calling the science of any subject, for example, man, or the earth, the logic of it—*anthropology,* or *geology.*

The great prestige of the natural sciences, acquired largely by their aid to modern technology and by their successful fight against the ancient mythology that was sanctified by various authorities, has led us to apply the term "science" only to these or to similarly highly developed branches of knowledge and to deny it to ordinary knowledge of affairs, no matter how well founded. Thus no one thinks of a railroad time-table or of a telephone book as science even though the knowledge in it is accurate, verifiable, and organized in a definite order. We reserve the term "science" for knowledge which is general and systematic, that is, in which specific propositions are all deduced from a few general principles. Now we need not enter here into the quarrel which arises because archeologists, historians, descriptive sociologists, and others wish to call their more empirical knowledge science. . . . All the logical methods involved in proving the existence of laws are involved in establishing the truth of any historical event. In determining the weight of

SOURCE: Part I is from chapter 10 and part II is section 2 of chapter 20 of *An Introduction to Logic and Scientific Method,* by Morris R. Cohen and Ernest Nagel, copyright 1934, by Harcourt Brace Jovanovich, Inc., and used with their permission. The title of this selection has been supplied by the editors. This selection should be compared with selection 13. See also selection 53.

evidence for any human event we must reason from general propositions in regard to human affairs, though such propositions are generally implicitly rather than explicitly assumed.

If we look at all the sciences not only as they differ among each other but also as each changes and grows in the course of time, we find that the constant and universal feature of science is its general method, which consists in the persistent search for truth, constantly asking: Is it so? To what extent is it so? Why is it so?—that is, What general conditions or considerations determine it to be so? And this can be seen on reflection to be the demand for the best available evidence, the determination of which we call logic. Scientific method is thus the persistent application of logic as the common feature of all reasoned knowledge. From this point of view scientific method is simply the way in which we test impressions, opinions, or surmises by examining the best available evidence for and against them. And thus a critical historian like Thucydides can be more scientific than the more credulous Livy, and a sound philologist like Whitney can be more scientific than the more hastily speculative Max Müller. The various features of scientific method can naturally be seen more clearly in the more developed sciences; but in essence scientific method is simply the pursuit of truth as determined by logical considerations. Before determining this in detail, it is well to distinguish between scientific method and other ways of banishing doubt and arriving at stable beliefs.

Most of our beliefs . . . rest on the tacit acceptance of current attitudes or on our own unreflective assumptions. Thus we come to believe that the sun revolves around the earth daily because we see it rise in the east and sink in the west; or we send a testimonial to the makers of a certain toothpaste to the effect that it is an excellent preserver of teeth because we have had no dental trouble since we have used that preparation; or we offer alms to some beggar because we perceive his poverty by his rags and emaciated appearance. But too often and sometimes, alas! too late, we learn that not all "seeing" is "believing." Beliefs so formed do not stand up against a more varied experience. There is too little agreement in opinions so formed and too little security in acting upon them. Most of us then find ourselves challenged to support or change our opinions. And we do so by diverse methods.

The Method of Tenacity. Habit or inertia makes it easier for us to continue to believe a proposition simply because we have always believed it. Hence, we may avoid doubting it by closing our mind to all contradictory evidence. That frequent verbal reiteration may strengthen beliefs which have been challenged is a truth acted upon by all organized sects or parties. If anyone questions the superior virtues of ourselves, our dear ones, our country, race, language, or religion, our first impulse and the one generally followed is to repeat our belief as an act of loyalty and to regard the questioning attitude as ignorant, disloyal, and unworthy of attention. We thus insulate ourselves from opinions or beliefs contrary to those which we have always held. As a defense of this attitude the believer often alleges that he would be unhappy if he were to believe otherwise than he in fact does. But while a change in opinion may require painful effort, the new beliefs may become habitual, and perhaps more satisfying than the old ones.

This method of tenacity cannot always secure the stability of one's beliefs. Not all men believe alike, in part because the climate of opinion varies with historical antecedents, and in part because the personal and social interests which men wish to guard are unlike. The pressure of opinions other than one's own cannot always be so disregarded. The man who tenaciously holds on to his own way occasionally admits that not all those who differ from him are fools. When once the incidence of other views is felt, the method of tenacity is incapable of deciding between conflicting opinions. And since a lack of uniformity in beliefs is itself a powerful souce of doubt concerning them, some method other than the method of tenacity is required for achieving stable views.

The Method of Authority. Such a method is sometimes found in the appeal to authority. Instead of simply holding on doggedly to one's beliefs, appeal is made to some highly respected source to substantiate the views held. Most propositions of religion and conduct claim support from some sacred text, tradition, or tribunal whose decision on such questions is vested with finality. Political, economic, and social questions are frequently determined in similar fashion. What one should wear at a funeral, what rule of syntax one should follow in writing, what rights one has in the product of his labor, how one should behave in some social crisis like war—these are problems repeatedly resolved by the authoritative method.

We may distinguish two forms of the appeal to authority. One form is inevitable and reasonable. It is employed whenever we are unable for lack of time or training to settle some problem, such as, What diet or exercise will relieve certain distressing symptoms? or, What was the system of weights which the Egyptians used? We then leave the resolution of the problem to experts, whose authority is acknowledged. But their authority is only relatively final, and we reserve the right to others (also competent to judge), or to ourselves (finding the time to acquire competence), to modify the findings of our expert. The second form of the appeal to authority invests some sources with infallibility and finality and invokes some external force to give sanction to their decisions. On questions of politics, economics, and social conduct, as well as on religious opinions, the method of authority has been used to root out, as heretical or disloyal, divergent opinions. Men have been frightened and punished into conformity in order to prevent alternative views from unsettling our habitual beliefs.

The aim of this method, unanimity and stability of belief, cannot be achieved so long as authorities differ. Buddhists do not accept the authorities of the Christians, just as the latter reject the authority of Mahomet and the Koran. In temporal matters experts frequently disagree and are often found in error. Moreover, authoritative regulation of all beliefs is not feasible practically, and much must be left to be decided in some other way. The method of authority has thus to be supplemented, if not replaced, by some other method for resolving doubt and uncertainty.

The Method of Intuition. A method repeatedly tried in order to guarantee stable beliefs is the appeal to "self-evident" propositions—propositions so "obviously true" that the understanding of their *meaning* will carry with it an indubitable conviction of their *truth*. Very few men in the history of philosophy and that of the sciences have been able to resist at all times the lure of intuitively revealed truths. Thus all the great astronomers, including Copernicus, believed it to be self-evident that the orbits of the planets must be circular, and no mathematician or physicist before Gauss seriously doubted the proposition that two straight lines cannot enclose an area. Other examples of propositions which have been, or still are, believed by some to be self-evident are: that the whole is greater than any one of its parts; that the right to private property is inalienable; that bigamy is a sin; that nothing can happen without an adequate cause.

Unfortunately, it is difficult to find a proposition for which at some time or other "self-evidence" has not been claimed. Propositions regarded as indubitable for many, for example, that the earth is flat, have been shown to to be false. It is well known that "self-evidence" is often a function of current fashions and of early training. The fact, therefore, that we feel absolutely certain, or that a given proposition has not before been questioned, is no guarantee against its being proved false. Our intuitions must, then, be tested.

The Method of Science or Reflective Inquiry. None of the methods for settling doubts we have examined so far is free from human caprice and willfulness. As a consequence, the propositions which are held on the basis of those methods are uncertain in the range of their application and in their accuracy. If we wish clarity and accuracy, order and consistency, security and cogency, in our actions and intellectual allegiances we shall have to resort to some method of fixing beliefs whose efficacy in resolving problems is independent of our desires and wills. Such a method, which takes advantage of the objective connections in the world around us, should be found reasonable not because of its appeal to the idiosyncrasies of a selected few individuals, but because it can be tested repeatedly and by all men.

The other methods discussed are all inflexible, that is, none of them can admit that it will lead us into error. Hence none of them can make provision for correcting its own results. What is called *scientific method* differs radically from these by encouraging and developing the utmost possible doubt, so that what is left after such doubt is always supported by the best available evidence. As new evidence or new doubts arise it is the essence of scientific method to incorporate them—to make them an integral part of the body of knowledge so far attained. Its method, then, makes science progressive because it is never too certain about its results.

It is well to distinguish between scientific method and general skepticism. The mere resolution to doubt all things is not necessarily effective. For the propositions most in need of questioning may seem to us unquestionable. We need a technique that will enable us to discover possible alternatives to propositions which we may regard as truisms or necessarily true. In this process formal logic aids us in devising ways of formulating our propositions explicitly and accurately, so that their possible alternatives become clear. When thus faced with alternative hypotheses, logic develops their consequences, so that when these consequences are compared with observable phenomena we have a means of testing which hypothesis is to be eliminated and which is most in harmony with the facts of observation. . . .

II. The Value of Scientific Method

The desire for knowledge for its own sake is more widespread than is generally recognized by anti-intellectualists. It has its roots in the animal curiosity which shows itself in the cosmological questions of children and in the gossip of adults. No ulterior utilitarian motive makes people want to know about the private lives of their neighbors, the great, or the notorious. There is also a certain zest which makes people engage in various intellectual games or exercises in which one is required to find out something. But while the desire to know is wide, it is seldom strong enough to overcome the more powerful organic desires, and few indeed have both the inclination and the ability to face the arduous difficulties of scientific method in more than one special field. The desire to know is not often strong enough to sustain critical inquiry. Men generally are interested in the results, in the story or romance of science, not in the technical methods whereby these results are obtained and their truth continually is tested and qualified. Our first impulse is to accept the plausible as true and to reject the uncongenial as false. We have not the time, inclination, or energy to investigate everything. Indeed, the call to do so is often felt as irksome and joy-killing. And when we are asked to treat our cherished beliefs as mere hypotheses, we rebel as violently as when those dear to us are insulted. This provides the ground for various movements that are hostile to rational scientific procedure (though their promoters do not often admit that it is science to which they are hostile).

Mystics, intuitionists, authoritarians, voluntarists, and fictionalists are all trying to undermine respect for the rational methods of science. These attacks have always met with wide acclaim and are bound to continue to do so, for they strike a responsive note in human nature. Unfortunately they do not offer any reliable alternative method for obtaining verifiable knowledge. The great French writer Pascal opposed to logic the spirit of subtlety or finesse *(esprit geometrique* and *esprit de finesse)* and urged that the heart has its reasons as well as the mind, reasons that cannot be accurately formulated but which subtle spirits apprehend none the less. Men as diverse as James Russell Lowell and George Santayana are agreed that:

"The soul is oracular still,"

and

"It is wisdom to trust the heart . . .
To trust the soul's invincible surmise."

Now it is true that in the absence of omniscience we must trust our soul's surmise; and great men are those whose surmises or intuitions are deep or penetrating. It is only by acting on our surmise that we can procure the evidence in its favor. But only havoc can result from confusing a surmise with a proposition for which there is already evidence. Are all the reasons of the heart sound? Do all oracles tell the truth? The sad history of human experience is distinctly discouraging to any such claim. Mystic intuition may give men absolute subjective certainty, but can give no proof that contrary intuitions are erroneous. It is obvious that when authorities conflict we must weigh the evidence in their favor logically if we are to make a rational choice. Certainly, when a truth is questioned it is no answer to say, "I am convinced," or, "I prefer to rely on this rather than on another authority." The view that physical science is no guide to proof, but is a mere fiction, fails to explain why it has enabled us to anticipate phenomena of nature and to control them. These attacks on scientific method receive a certain color of plausibility because of some indefensible claims made by uncritical enthusiasts. But it is of the essence of scientific method to limit its own pretension. Recognizing that we do not know everything, it does not claim the ability to solve all of our practical problems. It is an error to suppose, as is often done, that science denies the truth of all unverified propositions. For that which is unverified today may be verified tomorrow. We may get at truth by guessing or in other ways. Scientific method, however, is concerned with verification. Admittedly the wisdom of those engaged in this process has not been popularly ranked as high as that of the sage, the prophet, or the poet. Admittedly, also, we know of no way of supplying creative intelligence to those who lack it. Scientists, like all other human beings, may get into ruts and apply their techniques regardless of varying circumstances. There will always be formal procedures which are fruitless. Definitions and formal distinctions may be a sharpening of tools without the wit to use them properly, and statistical information may conform to the highest technical standards and yet be irrelevant and inconclusive. Nevertheless, scientific method is the only way to increase the general body of tested and verified truth and to eliminate arbitrary opinion. It is well to clarify our ideas by asking for the precise meaning of our words, and to try to check our favorite ideas by applying them to accurately formulated propositions.

In raising the question as to the social need for scientific method, it is well to recognize that the suspension of judgment which is essential to that method is difficult or impossible when we are pressed by the demands of immediate action. When my house is on fire, I must act quickly and promptly—I cannot stop to consider the possible causes, not even to estimate the exact probabilities involved in the various alternative ways of reacting. For this reason, those who are bent upon some specific couse of action often despise those devoted to reflection; and certain ultramodernists seem to argue as if the need for action guaranteed the truth of our decision. But the fact that I must either vote for candidate X or refrain from doing so does not of itself give me adequate knowledge. The frequency of our regrets makes this obvious. Wisely ordered society is therefore provided with means for deliberation and reflection *before* the pressure of action becomes irresistible. In order to assure the most thorough investigation, all possible views must be canvassed, and this means toleration of views that are *prima facie* most repugnant to us.

In general the chief social condition of scientific method is a widespread desire for truth that is strong enough to withstand the powerful forces which make us cling tenaciously to old views or else embrace every novelty because it is a change. Those who are engaged in scientific work need not only leisure for reflection and material for their experiments, but also a community that respects the pursuit of truth and allows freedom for the expression of intellectual doubt as to its most sacred or established institutions. Fear of offending established dogmas has been an obstacle to the growth of astronomy and geology and other physical sciences; and the fear of offending patriotic or respected sentiment is perhaps one of the strongest hindrances to scholarly history and social science. On the other hand, when a community indiscriminately acclaims every new doctrine the love of truth becomes subordinated to the desire for novel formulations.

On the whole it may be said that the safety of science depends on there being men who care more for the justice of their methods than for any results obtained by their use. For this reason it is unfortunate when scientific research in the social field is largely in the hands of those not in a favorable position to oppose established or popular opinion.

We may put it the other way by saying that the physical sciences can be more liberal because we are sure that foolish opinions will be readily eliminated by the shock of facts. In the social field, however, no one can tell what harm may come of foolish ideas before the foolishness is finally, if ever, demonstrated. None of the precautions of scientific method can prevent human life from being an adventure, and no scientific investigator knows whether he will reach his goal. But scientific method does enable large numbers to walk with surer step. By analyzing the possibilities of any step or plan, it becomes possible to anticipate the future and adjust ourselves to it in advance. Scientific method thus minimizes the shock of novelty and the uncertainty of life. It enables us to frame policies of action and of moral judgment fit for a wider outlook than those of immediate physical stimulus or organic response.

Scientific method is the only effective way of strengthening the love of truth. It develops the intellectual courage to face difficulties and to overcome illusions that are pleasant temporarily but destructive ultimately. It settles differences without any external force by appealing to our common rational nature. The way of science, even if it is up a steep mountain, is open to all. Hence, while sectarian and partisan faiths are based on personal choice or temperament and divide men, scientific procedure unites men in something nobly devoid of all pettiness. Because it requires detachment, disinterestedness, it is the finest flower and test of a liberal civilization.

6 SCIENCE AND HUMAN NATURE

JOHN STUART MILL (1806-1873)

1. It is a common notion, or at least it is implied in many common modes of speech, that the thoughts, feelings, and actions of sentient beings are not a subject of science, in the same strict sense in which this is true of the objects of outward nature. This notion seems to involve some confusion of ideas, which it is necessary to begin by clearing up.

Any facts are fitted, in themselves, to be a subject of science, which follow one another according to constant laws; although those laws may not have been discovered, nor even be discoverable by our existing resources. Take, for instance, the most familiar class of meteorological phenomena, those of rain and sunshine. Scientific inquiry has not yet succeeded in ascertaining the order of antecedence and consequence among these phenomena, so as to be able, at least in our regions of the earth, to predict them with certainty or even with any high degree of probability. Yet no one doubts that the phenomena depend on laws, and that these must be derivative laws resulting from known ultimate laws, those of heat, electricity, vaporisation, and elastic fluids. Nor can it be doubted that if we were acquainted with all the antecedent circumstances, we could, even from those more general laws, predict (saving difficulties of calculation) the state of the weather at any future time. Meteorology, therefore, not only has in itself every natural requisite for being, but actually is, a science; though, from the difficulty of observing the facts on which the phenomena depend (a difficulty inherent in the peculiar nature of those phenomena), the science is extremely imperfect; and were it perfect, might probably be of little avail in practice, since the data requisite for applying its principles to particular instances would rarely be procurable.

A case may be conceived of an intermediate character between the perfection of science and this its extreme imperfection. It may happen that the greater causes, those on which the principal part of the phenomena depends, are within the reach of observation and measurement; so that if no other causes intervened, a complete explanation could be given not only of the

SOURCE: Bk. VI, ch. 3 of *A System of Logic* (1843). The title of this selection has been supplied by the editors. Compare with selections 24 and 26.

phenomenon in general, but of all the variations and modifications which it admits of. But inasmuch as other, perhaps many other causes, separately insignificant in their effects, co-operate or conflict in many or in all cases with those greater causes, the effect, accordingly, presents more or less of aberration from what would be produced by the greater causes alone. Now if these minor causes are not so constantly accessible, or not accessible at all to accurate observation, the principal mass of the effect may still, as before, be accounted for, and even predicted; but there will be variations and modifications which we shall not be competent to explain thoroughly, and our predictions will not be fulfilled accurately, but only approximately.

It is thus, for example, with the theory of the tides. No one doubts that Tidology is really a science. As much of the phenomena as depends on the attraction of the sun and moon is completely understood, and may in any, even unknown, part of the earth's surface be foretold with certainty; and the far greater part of the phenomena depends on those causes. But circumstances of a local or casual nature, such as the configuration of the bottom of the ocean, the degree of confinement from shores, the direction of the wind, etc., influence in many or in all places the height and time of the tide; and a portion of these circumstances being either not accurately knowable, not precisely measurable, or not capable of being certainly foreseen, the tide in known places commonly varies from the calculated result of general principles by some difference that we cannot explain, and in unknown ones may vary from it by a difference that we are not able to foresee or conjecture. Nevertheless, not only is it certain that these variations depend on causes, and follow their causes by laws of unerring uniformity; not only, therefore, is tidology a science, like meteorology, but it is what, hitherto at least, meteorology is not, a science largely available in practice. General laws may be laid down respecting the tides; predictions may be founded on those laws, and the result will in the main, though often not with complete accuracy, correspond to the predictions.

And this is what is or ought to be meant by those who speak of sciences which are not *exact* sciences. Astronomy was once a science, without being an exact science. It could not become exact until not only the general course of the planetary motions, but the perturbations also, were accounted for, and referred to their causes. It has become an exact science, because its phenomena have been brought under laws comprehending the whole of the causes by which the phenomena are influenced, whether in a great or only in a trifling degree, whether in all or only in some cases, and assigning to each of those causes the share of effect which really belongs to it. But in the theory of the tides, the only laws as yet accurately ascertained are those of the causes which affect the phenomenon in all cases, and in a considerable degree;

while others which affect it in some cases only, or, if in all, only in a slight degree, have not been sufficiently ascertained and studied to enable us to lay down their laws, still less to deduce the completed law of the phenomenon, by compounding the effects of the greater with those of the minor causes. Tidology, therefore, is not yet an exact science; not from any inherent incapacity of being so, but from the difficulty of ascertaining with complete precision the real derivative uniformities. By combining, however, the exact laws of the greater causes, and of such of the minor ones as are sufficiently known, with such empirical laws of such approximate generalisations respecting the miscellaneous variations as can be obtained by specific observation, we can lay down general propositions which will be true in the main, and on which, with allowance for the degree of their probable inaccuracy, we may safely ground our expectations and our conduct.

2. The science of human nature is of this description. It falls far short of the standard of exactness now realised in Astronomy; but there is no reason that it should not be as much a science as Tidology is, or as Astronomy was when its calculations had only mastered the main phenomena, but not the perturbations.

The phenomena with which this science is conversant being the thoughts, feelings, and actions of human beings, it would have attained the ideal perfection of a science if it enabled us to foretell how an individual would think, feel, or act throughout life, with the same certainty with which astronomy enables us to predict the places and occultations of the heavenly bodies. It needs scarcely be stated that nothing approaching to this can be done. The actions of individuals could not be predicted with scientific accuracy, were it only because we cannot foresee the whole of the circumstances in which those individuals will be placed. But further, even in any given combination of (present)) circumstances, no assertion, which is both precise and universally true, can be made respecting the manner in which human beings will think, feel, or act. This is not, however, because every person's modes of thinking, feeling, and acting do not depend on causes; nor can we doubt that if, in the case of any individual, our data could be complete, we even now know enough of the ultimate laws by which mental phenomena are determined to enable us in many cases to predict, with tolerable certainty, what, in the greater number of supposable combinations of circumstances, his conduct or sentiments would be. But the impressions and actions of human beings are not solely the result of their present circumstances, but the joint result of those circumstances and of the characters of the individuals; and the agencies which determine human character are so numerous and diversified (nothing which has happened to the person throughout life being without its portion of influence), that in the aggregate they are never in any two cases exactly similar. Hence, even if our science of human nature were theoretically perfect, that is, if we could calculate any character as we can calculate the orbit of any planet, *from given data;* still, as the data are never all given, nor ever precisely alike in different cases, we could neither make positive predictions, nor lay down universal propositions.

Inasmuch, however, as many of those effects which it is of most importance to render amenable to human foresight and control are determined, like the tides, in an incomparably greater degree by general causes, than by all partial causes taken together; depending in the main on those circumstances and qualities which are common to all mankind, or at least to large bodies of them, and only on a small degree on the idiosyncrasies of organisation or the peculiar history of individuals; it is evidently possible, with regard to all such effects, to make predictions which will *almost* always be verified, and general propositions which are almost always true. And whenever it is sufficient to know how the great majority of the human race, or of some nation or class of persons, will think, feel, and act, these propositions are equivalent to universal ones. For the purposes of political and social science this *is* sufficient. . . . An approximate generalisation is, in social inquiries, for most practical purposes equivalent to an exact one; that which is only probable when asserted of individual human beings indiscriminately selected, being certain when affirmed of the character and collective conduct of masses.

It is no disparagement, therefore, to the science of Human Nature that those of its general propositions which descend sufficiently into detail to serve as a foundation for predicting phenomena in the concrete are for the most part only approximately true. But in order to give a genuinely scientific character to the study, it is indispensable that these approximate generalisations, which in themselves would amount only to the lowest kind of empirical laws, should be connected deductively with the laws of nature from which they result—should be resolved into the properties of the causes on which the phenomena depend. In other words, the science of Human Nature may be said to exist in proportion as the approximate truths which compose a practical knowledge of mankind can be exhibited as corollaries from the universal laws of human nature on which they rest, whereby the proper limits of those approximate truths would be shown, and we should be enabled to deduce others for any new state of circumstances, in anticipation of specific experience. . . .

7 UMBRELLAOLOGY AND PROBLEMATICS

JOHN SOMERVILLE (1905-   )

I. Umbrellaology

... Dear Sir:

I am taking the liberty of calling upon you to be the judge in a dispute between me and an acquaintance who is no longer a friend. The question at issue is this: Is my creation, umbrellaology, a science? Allow me to explain this situation. For the past eighteen years, assisted by a few faithful disciples, I have been collecting materials on a subject hitherto almost wholly neglected by scientists, the umbrella. The results of my investigations to date are embodied in the nine volumes which I am sending to you under a separate cover. Pending their receipt, let me describe to you briefly the nature of their contents and the method I pursued in compiling them. I began on the Island of Manhattan. Proceeding block by block, house by house, family by family and individual by individual I ascertained (1) the number of umbrellas possessed, (2) their size, (3) their weight, (4) their color. Having covered Manhattan after many years, I eventually extended the survey to the other boroughs of the City of New York, and at length completed the entire city. Thus I was ready to carry forward the work to the rest of the state and indeed the rest of the United States and the whole known world.

It was at this point I approached my erstwhile friend. I am a modest man, but I felt I had the right to be recognized as the creator of a new science. He, on the other hand, claimed that umbrellaology was not a science at all. First, he said, it was silly to investigate umbrellas. Now this argument is false because science scorns not to deal with any object, however humble and lowly, even to the "hind leg of a flea." Then why not umbrellas? Next he said that umbrellaology could not be recognized as a science because it was of

SOURCE: Part I is part of an essay entitled "Umbrellaology" that originally appeared in *Philosophy of Science*, Vol. VIII, no. 1 (January, 1941). Reprinted with the kind permission of the author and publisher, The Williams and Wilkins Co., Baltimore. Part II is from "Problematics: A Methodological Aspect of Philosophy of Science," which originally appeared in Vol. VI of the *Proceedings of the XIth International Congress of Philosophy*, 1953. Reprinted with the kind permission of the author and publisher, North-Holland Publishing Company, Amsterdam. The title of this selection has been supplied by the editors. Compare with selections 10 and 11.

no use or benefit to mankind. But is not the truth the most precious thing in life? And are not my nine volumes filled with the truth about my subject? Every word is true. Every sentence contains a hard, cold fact. When he asked me what was the object of umbrellaology I was proud to say, "To seek and discover the truth is object enough for me." I am a pure scientist; I have no ulterior motives. Hence it follows that I am satisfied with truth alone. Next, he said my truths were dated and that any one of my findings might cease to be true tomorrow. But this, I pointed out, is not an argument against umbrellaology, but rather an argument for keeping it up to date, which is exactly what I propose. Let us have surveys monthly, weekly or even daily to keep our knowledge abreast of the changing facts. His next contention was that umbrellaology had entertained no hypotheses and had developed no theories or laws. This is a great error. In the course of my investigations, I employed innumerable hypotheses. Before entering each new block and each new section of the city, I entertained an hypothesis as regards the number and characteristics of the umbrellas that would be found there, which hypotheses were either verified or nullified by my subsequent observations, in accordance with proper scientific procedure, as explained in authoritative texts. (In fact, it is interesting to note that I can substantiate and document every one of my replies to these objections by numerous quotations from standard works, leading journals, public speeches of eminent scientists and the like.) As for theories and laws, my work presents an abundance of them. I will here mention only a few, by way of illustration. There is the Law of Color Variation Relative to Ownership by Sex. (Umbrellas owned by women tend to great variety of color, whereas those owned by men are almost all black.) To this law I have given exact statistical formulation. (See vol. 6, Appendix 1, Table 3, p. 582.) There are the curiously interrelated Laws of Individual Ownership of Plurality of Umbrellas, and Plurality of Owners of Individual Umbrellas. The interrelationship assumes the form, in the first law, of almost direct ratio to annual income, and in the second, of almost inverse ratio to annual income. (For an exact statement of the modifying circumstances, see vol. 8, p. 350.) There is also the Law of Tendency towards Acquisition of Umbrellas in Rainy Weather. To this law I have given experimental verification in chapter 3 of volume 3. In the same way I have performed numerous other experiments in connection with my generalizations.

Thus I feel that my creation is in all respects a genuine science, and I appeal to you for substantiation of my opinion. . . .

II. Problematics

By the word problematics I mean to indicate a phase of scientific methodology which, for some strange reason, has never been systematically worked out. Indeed, it seems to have been scarcely noticed and never named, although it is of cardinal importance. I refer to that aspect of scientific method which has to do with the selection of problems. The study of it I propose to call problematics. . . .

The history of science shows that in many cases there was a long groping for the fruitful problems to work upon, and that once these were precisely formulated, fruitful solutions were not long in coming forth. Indeed, it is self-evident that the original selection of problems must in a sense determine the whole quality of what is subsequently done. If people are not working on significant problems, they will never arrive at significant solutions, even though they find what they are looking for. On the other hand, once the right problem has been formulated, that in itself represents an enormous step forward. For this reason the wrong solution or even no solution of the right problem is infinitely preferable to the right solution of the wrong problem.

But what is the criterion of significance as regards problems? How can we tell what are the right problems to work upon? Is there a subjective determinant operative in the situation? On what basis is the selection of problems actually made in science? . . .

Let us look at the matter from the viewpoint of what actually takes place in the procedures of the scientists. What makes one problem more significant, more worth working upon, than another? For example, it is quite likely scientists would unanimously agree that to find the cause of cancer is, scientifically speaking, a more significant problem than to find the average number of letters in the names of all living people. That is, it would probably be agreed that the solution of the first mentioned problem would mean much more to science than the solution of the second. But on what basis? Can we discover any common criterion which is being employed, consciously or unconsciously? . . .

Our thesis is that this criterion is prognosis. Scientists generally regard one problem as more significant than another if the solving of it would yield more new predictions than the solving of the other. To take the example mentioned, we know (before any work is done) that if we discover the cause of cancer we shall be able to make a multitude of predictions which we cannot make now. Under present conditions, multitudes of people get cancer, and we do not know what specific causal agent is common to these cases, in the sense that we know bacillus tuberculosis is a common causal agent in consumption. If we discovered the full cause of cancer, we could then predict not only what would be found common to a multitude of cancer cases; we could also predict that wherever that specific factor or complex of factors appeared, cancer would follow; wherever it was eliminated, cancer would be eliminated; wherever it was decreased, cancer would be decreased, and so on. If we could not make correct predictions of that kind, it would show we had not really found the cause. Conversely, the only way to prove we have found the cause is to make correct predictions of that kind, among other things.

Now, what would follow if we solved the problem of the average number of letters in the names of all living persons? We need not do it first in order to realize that we would have a great deal of truth, but that truth would add little to our present ability either to explain or to predict. Perhaps we should say it would add little to our present ability to explain *because* it would add little to our ability to predict. For it would seem that *scientific* explanation always involves prognosis, although this may not be true of other forms of explanation, which are more subjective. . . .

There are certainly other factors besides prognosis entering into scientific explanation, but prognosis is an important one. However, the decisive point is seen in the converse sense: whenever newly discovered relationships, connections or other facts add greatly to predictability, it is always considered that they add greatly to explanation. There are other things that make a science grow, but one of the main ones is the continued discovery of the kind of facts which significantly increase predictability. This is true of every field of knowledge universally recognized as a science in the modern sense of that term (such fields as astronomy, physics, chemistry, biology). . . .

. . . *Insofar as the natural sciences are concerned* . . . the selection of problems has become almost automatic, although the criterion employed is rarely formulated, or perhaps even consciously apprehended. If we believed in scientific instincts, we might say that natural scientists manifest an instinct to work on problems which, if solved, would significantly promote predictability.

However, the situation is very different in the social sciences, where the most urgent need of a clearly worked out problematics is evident. In these fields there seems to be no common criterion used, either consciously or unconsciously, for the selection of problems. There seems to be no agreement, either explicit or implicit, in regard to what constitutes explanation. At least, there seems to be no general tendency to use the criterion of predictability. And this, I think, is one of the reasons why the social sciences have made little progress as compared to the natural sciences. . . .

8 WHAT THE TORTOISE SAID TO ACHILLES

LEWIS CARROLL (1832-1898)

Achilles had overtaken the Tortoise, and had seated himself comfortably on its back.

"So you've got to the end of our race-course?" said the Tortoise. "Even though it *does* consist of an infinite series of distances? I thought some wiseacre or other had proved that the thing couldn't be done?"

"It *can* be done," said Achilles. "It *has* been done! *Solvitur ambulando.* You see the distances were constantly *diminishing;* and so—"

"But if they had been constantly *increasing?*" the Tortoise interrupted. "How then?"

"Then I shouldn't be *here,*" Achilles modestly replied; "and *you* would have got several times round the world, by this time!"

"You flatter me—*flatten,* I mean," said the Tortoise; "for you *are* a heavy weight, and *no* mistake! Well now, would you like to hear of a race-course, that most people fancy they can get to the end of in two or three steps, while it *really* consists of an infinite number of distances, each one longer than the previous one?"

"Very much indeed!" said the Grecian warrior, as he drew from his helmet (few Grecian warriors possessed *pockets* in those days) an enormous note-book and a pencil. "Proceed! And speak *slowly,* please! *Shorthand* isn't invented yet!"

"That beautiful First Proposition of Euclid!" the Tortoise murmured dreamily. "You admire Euclid?"

"Passionately! So far, at least, as one *can* admire a treatise that wo'n't be published for some centuries to come!"

"Well, now, let's take a little bit of the argument in that First Proposition —just *two* steps, and the conclusion drawn from them. Kindly enter them in your note-book. And in order to refer to them conveniently, let's call them A, B, and Z:—

(A) Things that are equal to the same are equal to each other.

(B) The two sides of this Triangle are things that are equal to the same.

SOURCE: Reprinted from *Mind,* N. S. vol. IV (1895), pp. 278–80. Compare with selection 9.

(Z) The two sides of this Triangle are equal to each other.

Readers of Euclid will grant, I suppose, that *Z* follows logically from *A* and *B*, so that any one who accepts *A* and *B* as true, *must* accept *Z* as true?"

"Undoubtedly! The youngest child in a High School—as soon as High Schools are invented, which will not be till some two thousand years later—will grant *that.*"

"And if some reader had *not* yet accepted *A* and *B* as true, he might still accept the *sequence* as a *valid* one, I suppose?"

"No doubt such a reader might exist. He might say 'I accept as true the Hypothetical Proposition that, *if A* and *B* be true, *Z* must be true; but, I *don't* accept A and B as true.' Such a reader would do wisely in abandoning Euclid, and taking to football."

"And might there not *also* be some reader who would say 'I accept *A* and *B* as true, but I *don't* accept the Hypothetical'?"

"Certainly there might. *He,* also, had better take to football."

"And *neither* of these readers," the Tortoise continued, "is *as yet* under any logical necessity to accept *Z* as true?"

"Quite so," Achilles assented.

"Well, now, I want you to consider *me* as a reader of the *second* kind, and to force me, logically, to accept *Z* as true."

"A tortoise playing football would be—" Achilles was beginning

"—an anomaly, of course," the Tortoise hastily interrupted. "Don't wander from the point. Let's have *Z* first, and football afterwards!"

"I'm to force you to accept *Z,* am I?" Achilles said musingly. "And your present position is that you accept *A* and *B,* but you *don't* accept the Hypothetical—"

"Let's call it *C,*" said the Tortoise.

"—but you *don't* accept

(C) If *A* and *B* are true, *Z* must be true."

"That is my present position," said the Tortoise.

"Then I must ask you to accept *C.*"

"I'll do so," said the Tortoise, "as soon as you've entered it in that notebook of yours. What else have you got in it?"

"Only a few memoranda," said Achilles, nervously fluttering the leaves: "a few memoranda of—of the battles in which I have distinguished myself!"

"Plenty of blank leaves, I see!" the Tortoise cheerily remarked. "We shall need them *all!*" (Achilles shuddered.) "Now write as I dictate:—

(A) Things that are equal to the same are equal to each other.

(B) The two sides of this Triangle are things that are equal to the same.

(C) If *A* and *B* are true, *Z* must be true.

(Z) The two sides of this Triangle are equal to each other."

"You should call it *D*, not *Z,*" said Achilles. "It comes *next* to the other three. If you accept *A* and *B* and *C,* you *must* accept *Z.*"

"And why *must* I?"

"Because it follows *logically* from them. If *A* and *B* and *C* are true, *Z must* be true. You don't dispute *that,* I imagine?"

"If *A* and *B* and *C* are true, *Z must* be true," the Tortoise thoughtfully repeated. "That's *another* Hypothetical, isn't it? And, if I failed to see its truth, I might accept *A* and *B* and *C,* and *still* not accept *Z*, mightn't I?"

"You might," the candid hero admitted; "though such obtuseness would certainly be phenomenal. Still, the event is *possible*. So I must ask you to grant *one* more Hypothetical."

"Very good. I'm quite willing to grant it, as soon as you've written it down. We will call it

(D) If *A* and *B* and *C* are true, *Z* must be true.

Have you entered that in your note-book?"

"I *have!*" Achilles joyfully exclaimed, as he ran the pencil into its sheath. "And at last we've got to the end of this ideal race-course: Now that you accept *A* and *B* and *C* and *D, of course* you accept *Z.*"

"Do I?" said the Tortoise innocently. "Let's make that quite clear. I accept *A* and *B* and *C* and *D*. Suppose I *still* refused to accept *Z!*"

"Then Logic would take you by the throat, and *force* you to do it!" Achilles triumphantly replied. "Logic would tell you 'You ca'n't help yourself. Now that you've accepted *A* and *B* and *C* and *D,* you *must* accept *Z!*' So you've no choice, you see."

"Whatever *Logic* is good enough to tell me is worth *writing down,*" said the Tortoise. "So enter it in your book, please. We will call it

(E) If *A* and *B* and *C* and *D* are true, *Z* must be true. Until I've granted *that,* of course I needn't grant *Z*. So it's quite a *necessary* step, you see?"

"I see," said Achilles; and there was a touch of sadness in his tone.

Here the narrator, having pressing business at the Bank, was obliged to leave the happy pair, and did not again pass the spot until some months afterwards. When he did so, Achilles was still seated on the back of the much-enduring Tortoise, and was writing in his note-book, which appeared to be nearly full. The Tortoise was saying "Have you got that last step written down? Unless I've lost count, that makes a thousand and one. There are several millions more to come. And *would* you mind, as a personal favour, considering what a lot of instruction this colloquy of ours will provide for the Logicians of the Nineteenth Century—*would* you mind adopting a pun that my cousin the Mock-Turtle will then make, and allowing yourself to be re-named *Taught-Us?*"

"As you please!" replied the weary warrior, in the hollow tones of despair, as he buried his face in his hands. "Provided that *you*, for *your* part, will adopt a pun the Mock-Turtle never made, and allow yourself to be re-named *A Kill-Ease!*"

9 TRUTH AND VALIDITY
IRVING M. COPI (1917-   )

An argument . . . is any group of propositions of which one is claimed to follow from the others, which are regarded as providing evidence for the truth of that one. . . . An argument is not a mere collection of propositions, but has a structure. In describing this structure, the terms "premiss" and "conclusion" are usually employed. The *conclusion* of an argument is that proposition which is affirmed on the basis of the other propositions of the argument, and these other propositions which are affirmed as providing evidence or reasons for accepting the conclusion are the *premisses* of that argument.

It should be noted that "premiss" and "conclusion" are relative terms: one and the same proposition can be a premiss of one argument and a conclusion in another. Consider, for example, the following argument:

> No act performed involuntarily should be punished.
> Some criminal acts are performed involuntarily.
> Therefore some criminal acts should not be punished.

Here the proposition *some criminal acts should not be punished* is the conclusion, and the other two propositions are the premisses. But the first premiss in this argument, *no acts performed involuntarily should be punished,* is the conclusion in the following (different) argument:

> No act beyond the control of the agent should be punished.
> All involuntary acts are beyond the control of the agent.
> Therefore no act performed involuntarily should be punished.

No proposition, taken all by itself, in isolation, is either a premiss or a conclusion. It is a premiss only when it occurs in an argument which assumes it for the sake of showing that some other proposition is thereby justified. And it is a conclusion only when it occurs in an argument which attempts to establish or prove it on the basis of other propositions which are assumed. This

SOURCE: From chapter 1, pp. 8–12, of *Introduction to Logic;* copyright 1953 by The Macmillan Company and used with their permission. The title of this selection has been supplied by the editors. Compare with selection 8.

notion is common enough: it is like the fact that a man, taken by himself, is neither an employer nor an employee, but may be either in different contexts, employer to his gardener, employee of the firm for which he works.

Arguments are traditionally divided into two different types, *deductive* and *inductive*. While every argument involves the claim that its premises provide evidence for the truth of its conclusion, only a *deductive* argument claims that its premises provide *conclusive* evidence. In the case of deductive arguments the technical terms "valid" and "invalid" are used in place of "correct" and "incorrect." A deductive argument is *valid* when its premises do provide conclusive evidence for its conclusion, that is, when premises and conclusion are so related that it is absolutely impossible for the premises to be true unless the conclusion is true also. Every deductive argument is either valid or invalid, and the task of deductive logic is to clarify the nature of the relationship which holds between premises and conclusion in a valid argument, and thus to allow us to discriminate between valid and invalid arguments. . . .

An inductive argument, on the other hand, does not claim that its premises give conclusive evidence for the truth of its conclusion, but only that they provide *some* evidence for it. Inductive arguments are neither *valid* nor *invalid* in the sense in which those terms are applied to deductive arguments. Inductive arguments may, of course, be evaluated as better or worse, according to the degree of likelihood or probability which their premises confer upon their conclusions. . . .

Truth and falsehood may be predicated of propositions, but never of arguments. And the properties of validity and invalidity can belong only to deductive arguments, never to propositions. There is a connection between the validity or invalidity of an argument and the truth or falsehood of its premises and conclusion, but this connection is by no means a simple one. Some valid arguments contain only true propositions, as, for example:

All whales are mammals.
All mammals have lungs.
Therefore all whales have lungs.

But an argument may contain false propositions exclusively, and be valid nevertheless, as, for example:

All spiders have six legs.
All six legged creatures have wings.
Therefore all spiders have wings.

This argument is valid because *if* its premises were true its conclusion would have to be true also, even though in fact they are all false. On the other hand, if we reflect upon the argument:

> If I owned all the gold in Fort Knox, then I would be very wealthy.
> I do not own all the gold in Fort Knox.
> Therefore I am not very wealthy.

we see that although its premisses and conclusion are true, the argument is invalid. That the premisses *could* be true and the conclusion false, if not immediately apparent, may be made clear by considering that if I were to inherit a million dollars, the premisses would remain true while the conclusion would become false. This point is further illustrated by the following argument, which is of the same form as the preceding one:

> If Rockefeller owned all the gold in Fort Knox, then Rockefeller would be very wealthy.
> Rockefeller does not own all the gold in Fort Knox.
> Therefore Rockefeller is not very wealthy.

The premisses of this argument are true, and its conclusion is false. Such an argument cannot be valid, because it is impossible for the premisses of a valid argument to be true while its conclusion is false.

The preceding examples show that there are valid arguments with false conclusions, as well as invalid arguments with true conclusions. Hence the truth or falsehood of its conclusion does not determine the validity or invalidity of an argument. Nor does the validity of an argument guarantee the truth of its conclusion. There are perfectly valid arguments which have false conclusions—but any such argument must have at least one false premiss. The term "sound" is introduced to characterize a valid argument all of whose premisses are true. Clearly the conclusion of a *sound* argument is true. A deductive argument fails to establish the truth of its conclusion if it is *unsound*, which means either that it is not *valid*, or that not all of its premisses are *true*. To test the truth or falsehood of premisses is the task of science in general, since premisses may deal with any subject matter at all. The logician is not so much interested in the truth or falsehood of propositions as in the logical relations between them, where by the "logical" relations between propositions we mean those which determine the correctness or incorrectness of arguments in which they may occur. Determining the correctness or incorrectness of arguments falls squarely within the province of logic. The logician is interested in the correctness even of arguments whose premisses might be false. . . .

10 SCIENCE AND HYPOTHESIS
IRVING M. COPI (1917-   )

I. Explanations: Scientific and Unscientific

In everyday life it is the unusual or startling for which we demand explanations. An office boy may arrive at work on time every morning for ever so long, and no curiosity will be aroused. But let him come an hour late one day, and his employer will demand an *explanation*. What is it that is wanted when an explanation for something is requested? An example will help to answer this question. The office boy might reply that he had taken the seven-thirty bus to work as usual, but the bus had been involved in a traffic accident which had entailed considerable delay. In the absence of any other transportation, the boy had had to wait for the bus to be repaired, and that had taken a full hour. This account would probably be accepted as a satisfactory explanation. It can be so regarded because from the statements which constitute the explanation the fact to be explained follows logically and no longer appears puzzling. An explanation is a group of statements . . . from which the thing to be explained can logically be inferred and whose assumption removes or diminishes its problematic or puzzling character. . . . Explanation and inference are very closely related. They are, in fact, the same process regarded from opposite points of view. Given certain premises, any conclusion which can logically be inferred from them is regarded as being explained by them. And given a fact to be explained, we say that we have found an explanation for it when we have found a set of premises from which it can logically be inferred.

Of course some proposed explanations are better than others. The chief criterion for evaluating explanations is *relevance*. If the tardy office boy had offered as explanation for his late arrival the fact that there is a war in China or a famine in India, that would properly be regarded as a very poor explanation, or rather as "no explanation at all." Such a story would have "nothing to do with the case"; it would be *irrelevant*, because from it the fact to be explained can *not* be inferred. The relevance of a proposed explanation, then, corresponds exactly to the cogency of the argument by which the fact

SOURCE: From chapter 13, sections 2–4, of *Introduction to Logic*. Copyright 1953 by The Macmillan Company and used with their permission. See selections 7 and 11.

to be explained is inferred from the proposed explanation. Any acceptable explanation must be relevant, but not all . . . which are relevant in this sense are acceptable explanations. There are other criteria for deciding the worth or acceptability of proposed explanations.

The most obvious requirement to propose is that the explanation be *true*. In the example of the office boy's lateness, the crucial part of his explanation was a particular fact, the traffic accident, of which he was (presumably) an eye witness. But the explanations of science are for the most part *general* rather than particular. The keystone of Newtonian Mechanics is the Law of Universal Gravitation, whose statement is:

> Every particle of matter in the universe attracts every other particle with a force which is directly proportional to the product of the masses of the particles and inversely proportional to the square of the distance between them.

Newton's law is not directly verifiable in the same way that a bus accident is at the time it occurs. There is simply no way in which we can inspect *all* particles of matter in the universe and see that they do attract each other in precisely the way that Newton's law asserts. Few propositions of science are *directly* verifiable as true. In fact, none of the important ones are. For the most part they concern *unobservable* entities, such as molecules and atoms, electrons and protons, and the like. Hence the proposed requirement of truth is not *directly* applicable to most scientific explanations. Before considering more useful criteria for evaluating scientific theories, it will be helpful to compare scientific with unscientific explanations.

Science is supposed to be concerned with facts, and yet in its further reaches we find it apparently committed to highly speculative notions which are far removed from the possibility of direct experience. How then are scientific explanations to be distinguished from those which are frankly mythological or superstitious? An unscientific "explanation" of the regular motions of the planets was the doctrine that each heavenly body was the abode of an "Intelligence" or "Spirit" which controlled its movement. A certain humorous currency was achieved during World War II by the unscientific explanation of certain aircraft failures as being due to "gremlins," which were said to be invisible but mischievous little men who played pranks on aviators. The point to note here is that from the point of view of observability and direct verifiability, there is no great difference between modern scientific theories and the unscientific doctrines of mythology or theology. One can no more see or touch a Newtonian "particle," an atom, or electron, than an "Intelligence" or a "gremlin." What then are the differences beween scientific and unscientific explanations?

There are two important and closely related differences between the kind of explanation sought by science and the kind provided by superstitions of various sorts. The first significant difference lies in the attitudes taken towards the explanations in question. The typical attitude of one who really *accepts* an unscientific explanation is *dogmatic*. What he accepts is regarded as being absolutely true and beyond all possibility of improvement or correction. During the Middle Ages and the early modern period the word of Aristotle was the ultimate authority to which scholars appealed for deciding questions of fact. However empirically and openmindedly Aristotle himself may have arrived at his views, they were accepted by the non-scientific schoolmen in a completely different and unscientific spirit. One of the schoolmen to whom Galileo offered his telescope to view the newly discovered moons of Jupiter declined to look, being convinced that none could possibly be seen because no mention of them could be found in Aristotle's treatise on astronomy! Because unscientific beliefs are absolute, ultimate, and final, within the framework of any such doctrine or dogma there can be no rational method of ever considering the question of its truth. The scientist's attitude toward his explanations is altogether different. Every explanation in science is put forward tentatively and provisionally. Any proposed explanation is regarded as a mere hypothesis, more or less probable on the basis of the available facts or relevant evidence. It must be admitted that the scientist's vocabulary is a little misleading on this point. When what was first suggested as a "hypothesis" becomes well confirmed, it is frequently elevated to the position of a "theory." And when, on the basis of a great mass of evidence, it achieves well nigh universal acceptance, it is promoted to the lofty status of a "law." This terminology is not always strictly adhered to: Newton's discovery is still called the "Law of Gravitation," while Einstein's contribution, which supersedes or at least improves on Newton's, is referred to as the "Theory of Relativity." The vocabulary of "hypothesis," "theory," and "law" is unfortunate, since it obscures the important fact that *all* of the general propositions of science are regarded as hypotheses, never as dogmas.

Closely allied with the difference in the way they are regarded is the second and more fundamental difference between scientific and unscientific explanations or theories. This second difference lies in the basis for accepting or rejecting the view in question. Many unscientific views are mere prejudices, which their adherents could scarcely give any reason for holding. Since they are regarded as "certain," however, any challenge or question is likely to be regarded as an affront and met with abuse. If one who accepts an unscientific explanation *can* be persuaded to discuss the basis for its acceptance, there are only a few grounds on which he will attempt to "defend" it. It is true because "we've always believed it," or because "everyone knows it." These all too familiar phrases express appeals to tradition or popularity rather than evidence. Or a questioned dogma may be defended on the grounds of revelation or authority. The absolute truth of their religious creeds and the absolute falsehood of all others have been revealed from on high, at various times, to Moses, to Paul, to Mohammed, to Joseph Smith, and to many others. That there are rival traditions, conflicting authorities, and revelations which contradict one another does not seem disturbing to those who have embraced an absolute creed. In general, unscientific beliefs are held independently of anything we should regard as *evidence* in their favor. Because they are *absolute,* questions of evidence are regarded as having little or no importance.

The case is quite different in the realm of science. Since every scientific explanation is regarded as a hypothesis, it is regarded as worthy of acceptance only to the extent that there is *evidence* for it. As a hypothesis, the question of its truth or falsehood is *open,* and there is continual search for more and more evidence to decide that question. The term "evidence" as used here refers ultimately to experience; *sensible* evidence is the ultimate court of appeal in verifying scientific propositions. Science is *empirical* in holding that sense experience is the *test of truth* for all its pronouncements. Consequently, it is of the essence of a *scientific* proposition that it be capable of being tested by observation.

Some propositions can be tested *directly*. To decide the truth or falsehood of the proposition which asserts that it is now raining outside, we need only look out the window. To tell whether a traffic light shows green or red, all we have to do is to look at it. But the propositions which scientists usually offer as explanatory hypotheses are not of this type. Such general propositions as Newton's Laws or Einstein's Theory are not *directly testable* in this fashion. They can, however, be tested *indirectly*. The *indirect method* of testing the truth of a proposition is familiar to all of us, though we may not be familiar with this name for it. For example, if his employer had been suspicious of the office boy's explanation of his tardiness, he might have checked up on it by telephoning the bus company to find out whether an accident had really happened to the seven-thirty bus. If the bus company's report checked with the boy's story, this would serve to dispel the employer's suspicions; whereas if the bus company denied that an accident had occurred, it would probably convince the employer that his office boy's story was false. This inquiry would constitute an *indirect test* of the office boy's explanation.

The pattern of *indirect testing* or *indirect verification* consists of two parts. First one deduces from the proposition to be tested one or more other propositions which *are* capable of being tested *directly*. Then these consequences are tested and found to be either true or false. If the consequences are false, any proposition which implies them must be false also. On the other hand, if the consequences are true, they are evidence for the truth of the proposition being tested, which is thus confirmed *indirectly*.

It should be noted that indirect testing is never demonstrative or certain. To deduce directly testable conclusions from a proposition usually requires additional premises. The conclusions that the bus company will *reply* that the seven-thirty bus had an accident this morning does not follow validly from the proposition that the seven-thirty bus *did* have an accident. Additional premises are needed, for example, that all accidents are reported to the company's office, that the reports are not mislaid or forgotten, and the company does not make a policy of denying its accidents. So the bus company's denying that an accident occurred would not demonstrate the office boy's story to be false, for the discrepancy might be due to the falsehood of one of the other premises mentioned. Those others, however, ordinarily have such a high degree of probability that a negative reply on the part of the bus company would render the office boy's story very doubtful indeed.

Similarly, establishing the truth of a conclusion does not demonstrate the truth of the premises from which it was deduced. We know very well that a valid argument may have a true conclusion even though its premises are not all true. In the present example, the bus company might affirm that an accident occurred to the seven-thirty bus because of some mistake in their records, even though no accident had occurred. So the inferred consequent *might* be true even though the *premises* from which it was deduced were not. . . .

It must be admitted that every proposition, scientific or unscientific, which is a relevant explanation for any observable fact, has *some* evidence in its favor, namely the fact to which it is relevant. Thus the regular motions of the planets must be conceded to constitute evidence for the (unscientific) theory that the planets are inhabited by "Intelligences" which cause them to move in just the orbits which are observed. The motions themselves are as much evidence for that myth as they are for Newton's or Einstein's theories. The difference lies in the fact that that is the only evidence for the unscientific hypothesis. Absolutely no other *directly* testable propositions can be deduced from the myth. On the other hand, a very large number of directly testable propositions can be deduced from the scientific explanations mentioned. Here, then, *is the* difference between scientific and unscientific explanations. A scientific explanation for a given fact will have directly testable propositions deducible from it other than the one asserting the fact to be explained. But an unscientific explanation will have no other directly testable propositions deducible from it. . . .

It is clear that we have been using the term "scientific explanation" in a quite general sense. As here defined, an explanation may be scientific even though it is not a part of one of the various special sciences like physics or psychology. Thus the office boy's explanation of his tardiness would be classified as a *scientific* one, for it is testable, even if only indirectly. But had he offered as explanation the proposition that God *willed him to be late that morning, and God is omnipotent,* that explanation would have been unscientific. For although his being late that morning is deducible from the proffered explanation, no other directly testable proposition is, and so the explanation is not even indirectly testable, and hence is unscientific.

II. Evaluating Scientific Explanations

The question naturally arises as to how scientific explanations are to be evaluated, that is, judged as good or bad, or at least as better or worse. This question is especially important because there is usually more than a single scientific explanation for one and the same fact. A man's abrupt behavior may be explained either by the hypothesis that he is shy or by the hypothesis that he is unfriendly. In a criminal investigation two different and incompatible hypotheses about the identity of the criminal may equally well account for the known facts. In the realm of science proper, that an object expands when heated is explained by both the caloric theory of heat and the kinetic theory. The caloric theory regarded heat as an invisible weightless fluid called "caloric," with the power of penetrating, expanding, and dissoving bodies, or dissipating them in vapor. The kinetic theory, on the other hand, regards the heat of a body as consisting of random motions of the molecules of which the body is composed. These are *alternative* scientific explanations which serve equally well to explain some of the phenomena of thermal expansion. They cannot both be true, however, and the problem is to evaluate or choose between them.

What is wanted here is a list of conditions which a good hypothesis can be expected to fulfill. It must not be thought that such a list of conditions can constitute a *recipe* by whose means anyone at all can construct good hypotheses. No one has ever pretended to lay down a set of rules for the invention or discovery of hypotheses. It is likely that none could ever be laid down, for that is the *creative* side of the scientific enterprise. Ability to create is a function of a person's imagination and talent and cannot be reduced to a mechanical process. A great scientific hypothesis, with wide explanatory powers like those of Newton's or Einstein's, is as much the product of genius as a great work of art. There is no formula for discovering new hypotheses, but there are certain rules to which acceptable hypotheses can be expected to conform. These can be regarded as the criteria for evaluating hypotheses.

There are five criteria which are used in judging the worth or acceptability of hypotheses. They may be listed as (1) relevance, (2) testability, (3) compatibility with previously well established hypotheses, (4) predictive or explanatory power, and (5) simplicity. The first two have already been discussed, but we shall review them briefly here.

1. Relevance. No hypothesis is ever proposed for its own sake but is always intended as an explanation of some fact or other. Therefore it must be *relevant* to the fact which it is intended to explain, that is, the fact in question must be *deducible* from the proposed hypotheses—either from the hypothesis alone or from it together with certain causal laws which may be presumed to have already been established as highly probable, or from these together with certain assumptions about particular initial conditions. A hypothesis which is not relevant to the fact it is intended to explain simply fails to explain it and can only be regarded as having failed to fulfill its intended function. . . .

2. Testability. The chief distinguishing characteristic of scientific hypotheses (as contrasted with unscientific ones) is that they are testable. That is, there must be the possibility of making observations which tend to confirm or disprove any scientific hypothesis. It need not be *directly* testable, of course. As has already been observed, most of the really important scientific hypotheses are formulated in terms of such unobservable entities as electrons or electromagnetic waves. . . . But there must be some way of getting from statements about such unobservables to statements about directly observable entities such as tables and chairs, or pointer readings, or lines on a photographic plate. In other words, there must be some connection between any scientific hypothesis and empirical data or facts of experience.

3. Compatibility with Previously Well Established Hypotheses. The requirement that an acceptable hypothesis must be compatible or consistent with other hypotheses which have already been well confirmed is an eminently reasonable one. Science, in seeking to encompass more and more facts, aims at achieving a *system* of explanatory hypotheses. Of course such a system must be self-consistent, for no self-contradictory set of propositions could possibly be true—or even intelligible. Ideally, the way in which scientists hope to make progress is by gradually expanding their hypotheses to comprehend more and more facts. For such progress to be made each new hypothesis must be consistent with those already confirmed. Thus Leverrier's hypothesis that there was an additional but not yet charted planet beyond the orbit of Uranus was perfectly consistent with the main body of accepted astronomical theory. A new theory must *fit in* with older theories if there is to be orderly progress in scientific inquiry.

It is possible, of course, to overestimate the importance of the third criterion. Although the ideal of science may be the gradual growth of theoretical knowledge by the addition of one new hypothesis after another, the actual history of scientific progress has not always followed that pattern. Many of the most important of new hypotheses have been inconsistent with older theories and have in fact replaced them rather than fitted in with them. Einstein's Relativity Theory was of that sort, shattering many of the preconceptions of the older Newtonian theory. . . .

The foregoing is not intended to give the impression that scientific progress is a helter-skelter process in which theories are abandoned right and left in favor of newer and shinier ones. Older theories are not so much abandoned as corrected. Einstein himself has always insisted that his own work is a modification rather than a rejection of Newton's. . . . Every established theory has been established through having proved adequate to explain a considerable mass of data, of observed facts. And it cannot be dethroned or discredited by any new hypothesis unless that new hypothesis can account for the same facts as well or even better. There is nothing capricious about the development of science. Every change represents an improvement, a more comprehensive and thus more adequate explanation of the way in which the world manifests itself in experience. Where inconsistencies occur between hypotheses, the greater age of one does not automatically prove it to be correct and the newer one wrong. The *presumption* is in favor of the older one if it has already been extensively confirmed. But if the new one in conflict with it *also* receives extensive confirmation, considerations of age or priority are definitely irrelevant. Where there is a conflict between two hypotheses, we must turn to the observable facts to decide between them. Ultimately, our last court of appeal in deciding between rival hypotheses is experience. What our third criterion, compatibility with previously well established hypotheses, comes to is this: the totality of hypotheses accepted at any time should be consistent with each other, and—other things being equal—of two new hypotheses, the one which fits in better with the accepted body of scientific theory is to be preferred. The question of what is involved in "other things being equal" takes us directly to our fourth criterion.

4. *Predictive or Explanatory Power.* By the predictive or explanatory power of hypothesis is meant the range of observable facts that can be deduced from it. This criterion is related to, but different from, that of testability. A hypothesis is testable if *some* observable fact is deducible from it. If one of two testable hypotheses has a greater number of observable facts deducible from it than from the other, then it is said to have greater predictive or explanatory power. For example, Newton's hypothesis of universal gravitation together with his three laws of motion had greater predictive power than either Kepler's or Galileo's hypotheses, because all observable consequences of the latter two were also consequences of the former, and the former had many more besides. An observable fact which can be deduced

SCIENCE AND HYPOTHESIS

from a given hypothesis is said to be explained by it and also can be said to be predicted by it. The greater the predictive power of a hypothesis, the more it explains, and the better it contributes to our understanding of the phenomena with which it is concerned.

Our fourth criterion has a negative side which is of crucial importance. If a hypothesis is inconsistent with any well attested fact of observation, the hypothesis is false and must be rejected. Where two different hypotheses are both relevant to explaining some set of facts and both are testable, and both are compatible with the whole body of already established scientific theory, it may be possible to choose between them by deducing incompatible propositions from them which are directly testable. . . .

5. *Simplicity.* It sometimes happens that two rival hypotheses satisfy the first four criteria equally well. Historically the most important pair of such hypotheses were those of Ptolemy (fl. 127–151) and Copernicus (1473–1543). Both were intended to explain all of the then known data of astronomy. According to the Ptolemaic theory, the earth is the center of the universe, and the heavenly bodies move about it in orbits which require a very complicated geometry of epicycles to describe. Ptolemy's theory was relevant, testable, and compatible with previously well established hypotheses, satisfying the first three criteria perfectly. According to the Copernican theory, the sun rather than the earth is at the center, and the earth itself moves around the sun along with the other planets. Copernicus' theory too satisfied the first three criteria perfectly. And with respect to the fourth criterion, the two theories were almost exactly on a par. . . . To all intents and purposes, the Ptolemaic and Copernican theories were of equal predictive or explanatory power. There was only one significant difference between the two rival hypotheses. Although both required the clumsy method of epicycles to account for the observed positions of the various heavenly bodies, *fewer* such epicycles were required within the Copernican theory. The Copernican system was therefore *simpler,* and on this basis it was accepted by all later astronomers, despite the greater age and equal predictive power of the Ptolemaic system, and in the teeth of persecution by the Medieval Church!

The criterion of simplicity is a perfectly natural one to invoke. In ordinary life as well as in science, the simplest theory which fits all the available facts is the one we tend to accept. In court trials of criminal cases the prosecution attempts to develop a hypothesis which includes the guilt of the accused and fits in with all the available evidence. Opposing him, the defense attorney seeks to set up a hypothesis which includes the innocence of the accused and also fits all the available evidence. Often both sides succeed, and then the case is usually decided—or *ought* to be decided—in favor of that hypothesis which is simpler or more "natural." Simplicity, however, is a very difficult term to define. Not all controversies are as straight-forward as the Ptolemaic-Copernican one, in which the latter's greater simplicity consisted merely in requiring a smaller number of epicycles. And of course "naturalness" is an almost hopelessly deceptive term—for it seems much more "natural" to believe that the earth is still while the apparently moving sun really does move. The fifth and last criterion, simplicity, is an important and frequently decisive one, but it is vague and not always easy to apply.

III. The Detective As Scientist

Now that we have formulated and explained the criteria by which hypotheses are evaluated, we are in a position to describe the general pattern of scientific research. . . . It will be instructive to examine an illustration of that method. A perennial favorite in this connection is the detective, whose problem is not quite the same as that of the pure scientist, but whose approach and technique illustrate the method of science very clearly. The classical example of the astute detective who can solve even the most baffling mystery is A. Conan Doyle's immortal creation, Sherlock Holmes. Holmes, his stature undiminished by the passage of time, will be our hero in the following account.

1. The Problem. Some of our most vivid pictures of Holmes are those in which he is busy with magnifying glass and tape measure, searching out and finding essential clues which had escaped the attention of those stupid bunglers, the "experts" of Scotland Yard. Or those of us who are by temperament less vigorous may think back more fondly on Holmes the thinker, ". . . who, when he had an unsolved problem upon his mind, would go for days, and even for a week, without rest, turning it over, rearranging his facts, looking at it from every point of view until he had either fathomed it or convinced himself that his data were insufficient."[1] At one such time, according to Dr. Watson:

> He took off his coat and waistcoat, put on a large blue dressing-gown, and then wandered about the room collecting pillows from his bed and cushions from the sofa and armchairs. With these he constructed a sort of Eastern divan, upon which he perched himself cross-legged, with an ounce of shag tobacco and a box of matches laid out in front of him. In the dim light of the lamp I saw him sitting there, an old briar pipe between his lips, his eyes fixed vacantly upon the corner of the ceiling, the blue smoke curling up from him, silent, motionless, with the light shining upon his strong-set aquiline features. So he sat as I dropped off to sleep, and so he sat when a sudden ejaculation caused me to wake up, and I found the summer sun shining into the apartment. The pipe was still between

[1] "The Man with the Twisted Lip."

his lips, the smoke still curled upward, and the room was full of a dense tobacco haze, but nothing remained of the heap of shag which I had seen upon the previous night.[2]

But such memories are incomplete. Holmes was not always searching for clues or pondering over solutions. . . . When there is no mystery to be unraveled, no man in his right mind would go out to look for clues. Clues, after all, must be *clues* for something. Nor could Holmes, or anyone else, for that matter, engage in profound thought unless he had something to think *about*. Sherlock Holmes was a genius at solving problems, but even a genius must *have* a problem before he can solve it. All reflective thinking, and this term includes criminal investigation as well as scientific research, is a problem-solving activity. . . . There must be a problem felt before either the detective or the scientist can go to work.

Of course the active mind sees problems where the dullard sees only familiar objects. One Christmas season Dr. Watson visited Holmes to find that the latter had been using a lens and forceps to examine ". . . a very seedy and disreputable hard-felt hat, much the worse for wear, and cracked in several places."[3] After they had greeted each other, Holmes said of it to Watson, "I beg that you will look upon it not as a battered billycock but as an intellectual problem." It so happened that the hat led them into one of their most interesting adventures, but it could not have done so had Holmes not seen a problem in it from the start. A problem may be characterized as a fact or group of facts for which we have no acceptable explanation, which seem unusual, or which fail to fit in with our expectations or preconceptions. It should be obvious that *some* prior beliefs are required if anything is to appear problematic. If there are no expectations, there can be no surprises.

Sometimes, of course, problems came to Holmes already labeled. The very first adventure recounted by Dr. Watson began with the following message from Gregson of Scotland Yard:

> My Dear Mr. Sherlock Holmes:
> There has been a bad business during the night at 3, Lauriston Gardens, off the Brixton Road. Our man on the beat saw a light there about two in the morning, and as the house was an empty one, suspected that something was amiss. He found the door open, and in the front room, which is bare of furniture, discovered the body of a gentleman, well dressed, and having cards in his pocket bearing the name of 'Enoch J. Drebber, Cleveland, Ohio, U.S.A.' There had been no robbery, nor is there any evidence as to how the man met his death. There are marks of blood in the room, but there is no wound upon his person. We are

---

[2]"The Man with the Twisted Lip."
[3]"The Adventure of the Blue Carbuncle."

at a loss as to how he came into the empty house; indeed, the whole affair is a puzzler. If you can come round to the house any time before twelve, you will find me there. I have left everything in statu quo until I hear from you. If you are unable to come, I shall give you fuller details, and would esteem it a great kindness if you would favour me with your opinion.

Yours faithfully,
T.G.[4]

Here was a problem indeed. A few minutes after receiving the message, Sherlock Holmes and Dr. Watson "were both in a hansom, driving furiously for the Brixton Road."

2. *Preliminary Hypotheses.* On their ride out Brixton way, Holmes "prattled away about Cremona fiddles and the difference between a Stradivarius and an Amati." Dr. Watson chided Holmes for not giving much thought to the matter at hand, and Holmes replied: "No data yet. . . . It is a capital mistake to theorize before you have all the evidence. It biases the judgment." This point of view was expressed by Holmes again and again. On one occasion he admonished a younger detective that "The temptation to form premature theories upon insufficient data is the bane of our profession."[5] Yet for all of his confidence about the matter, on this one issue Holmes was completely mistaken. Of course one should not reach a *final judgment* until a great deal of evidence has been considered, but this procedure is quite different from *not theorizing*. As a matter of fact, it is strictly impossible to make any serious attempt to collect evidence unless one *has* theorized beforehand. . . . There are too many particular facts, too many data in the world, for anyone to try to become acquainted with them all. Everyone, even the most patient and thorough investigator, must pick and choose, deciding which facts to study and which to pass over. He must have some working hypothesis for or against which to collect relevant data. It need not be a *complete* theory, but at least the rough outline must be there. Otherwise how could one decide what facts to select for consideration out of the totality of all facts, which is too vast even to begin to sift?

Holmes' actions were wiser than his words in this connection. After all, the words were spoken in a hansom speeding towards the scene of the crime. If Holmes really had no theory about the matter, why go to Brixton Road? If facts and data were all that he wanted, any old facts and any old data, with no hypotheses to guide him in their selection, why should he have left Baker Street at all? There were plenty of facts in the rooms at 221-B, Baker Street. Holmes might just as well have spent his time counting all the words on all

---

[4] *A Study in Scarlet.*
[5] "The Valley of Fear."

the pages of all the books there, or perhaps making very accurate measurements of the distances between each separate pair of articles of furniture in the house. He coud have gathered data to his heart's content and saved himself cab fare into the bargain!

It may be objected that the facts to be gathered at Baker Street have nothing to do with the case, whereas those which awaited Holmes at the scene of the crime were valuable clues for solving the problem. It was, of course, just this consideration which led Holmes to ignore the "data" at Baker Street and hurry away to collect those off Brixton Road. It must be insisted, however, that the greater relevance of the latter could not be *known* beforehand but only conjectured on the basis of previous experience with crimes and clues. It was in fact a *hypothesis* which led Holmes to look in one place rather than another for his facts, the hypothesis that there was a murder, that the crime was committed at the place where the body was found, and that the murderer had left some trace or clue which could lead to his discovery. Some such hypothesis is always required to guide the investigator in his search for relevant data, for in the absence of any preliminary hypothesis there are simply too many facts in this world to examine. The preliminary hypothesis ought to be highly tentative, and it must be based on previous knowledge. But a preliminary hypothesis is as necessary as the existence of a problem for any serious inquiry to be begun.

It must be emphasized that a preliminary hypothesis, as here conceived, need not be a *complete* solution to the problem. The hypothesis that the man was murdered by someone who had left some clues to his identity on or near the body of his victim was what led Holmes to Brixton Road. This hypothesis is clearly incomplete: it does not say *who* committed the crime, or *how* it was done, or *why*. Such a preliminary hypothesis may be *very* different from the final solution to the problem. It will never be complete: it may be a tentative explanation of only *part* of the problem. But however partial and however tentative, a preliminary hypothesis is required for any investigation to proceed.

3. *Collecting Additional Facts.* Every serious investigation begins with some fact or group of facts which strike the detective or the scientist as problematic and which initiate the whole process of inquiry. The initial facts which constitute the problem are usually too meager to suggest a wholly satisfactory explanation for themselves, but they will suggest—to the competent investigator—some preliminary hypotheses which lead him to search out additional facts. These additional facts, it is hoped, will serve as clues to the final solution. The inexperienced or bungling investigator will overlook or ignore all but the most obvious of them; but the careful worker will aim at completeness in his examination of the additional facts to which his prelimi-

nary hypotheses lead him. Holmes, of course, was the most careful and painstaking of investigators.

Holmes insisted on dismounting from the hansom a hundred yards or so from their destination and approached the house on foot, looking carefully at its surroundings and especially at the pathway leading up to it. When Holmes and Watson entered the house, they were shown the body by the two Scotland Yard operatives, Gregson and Lestrade. ("There is no clue," said Gregson. "None at all," chimed in Lestrade.) But Holmes had already started his own search for additional facts, looking first at the body:

> ... his nimble fingers were flying here, there, and everywhere, feeling, pressing, unbuttoning, examining ... So swiftly was the examination made, that one would hardly have guessed the minuteness with which it was conducted. Finally, he sniffed the dead man's lips, and then glanced at the soles of his patent leather boots.

Then turning his attention to the room itself,

> ... he whipped a tape measure and a large round magnifying glass from his pocket. With these two implements he trotted noiselessly about the room, sometimes stopping, occasionally kneeling, and once lying flat upon his face. So engrossed was he with his occupation that he appeared to have forgotten our presence, for he chattered away to himself under his breath the whole time, keeping up a running fire of exclamations, groans, whistles, and little cries suggestive of encouragement and of hope. As I watched him I was irresistibly reminded of a pure-blooded, well-trained foxhound as it dashes backward and forward through the covert, whining in its eagerness, until it comes across the lost scent. For twenty minutes or more he continued his researches, measuring with the most exact care the distance between marks which were entirely invisible to me, and occasionally applying his tape to the walls in an equally incomprehensible manner. In one place he gathered up very carefully a little pile of gray dust from the floor and packed it away in an envelope. Finally he examined with his glass the word upon the wall, going over every letter of it with the most minute exactness. This done, he appeared to be satisfied, for he replaced his tape and his glass in his pocket.

"They say that genius is an infinite capacity for taking pains," he remarked with a smile. "It's a very bad definition, but it does apply to detective work."

One matter deserves to be emphasized very strongly. Steps (2) and (3) are not completely separable but are usually very intimately connected and interdependent. True enough, we require a preliminary hypothesis to begin any intelligent examination of facts, but the additional facts may themselves suggest new hypotheses, which may lead to new facts, which suggest still other hypotheses, which lead to still other additional facts, and so on. Thus having made his careful examination of the facts available in the house off Brixton Road, Holmes was led to formulate a further hypothesis which required the taking of testimony from the constable who found the body. The man was off duty at the moment, and Lestrade gave Holmes the constable's name and address.

Holmes took a note of the address.

> "Come along, Doctor," he said: "we shall go and look him up. I'll tell you one thing which may help you in the case," he continued, turning to the two detectives. "There has been murder done, and the murderer was a man. He was more than six feet high, was in the prime of life, had small feet for his height, wore coarse, square-toed boots and smoked a Trichinopoly cigar. He came here with his victim in a four-wheeled cab, which was drawn by a horse with three old shoes and one new one on his off fore-leg. In all probability the murderer had a florid face, and the fingernails of his right hand were remarkably long. These are only a few indications, but they may assist you."

Lestrade and Gregson glanced at each other with an incredulous smile.

"If this man was murdered, how was it done?" asked the former.

"Poison," said Sherlock Holmes curtly, and strode off.

4. Formulating the Hypothesis. At some stage or other of his investigation, any man—whether detective, scientist, or ordinary mortal—will get the feeling that he has all the facts needed for his solution. He has his "2 and 2," so to speak, but the task still remains of "putting them together." At such a time Sherlock Holmes might sit up all night, consuming pipe after pipe of tobacco, trying to think things through. The result or end product of such thinking, if it is successful, is a hypothesis which accounts for all the data, both the original set of facts which constituted the problem, and the additional facts to which the preliminary hypotheses pointed. The actual discovery of such an explanatory hypothesis is a process of creation, in which imagination as well as knowledge is involved. Logic has nothing to say about the *discovery* of hypotheses; this process is more properly to be investigated by psychologists. Holmes, who was a genius at inventing hypotheses, described the process as reasoning "backwards." As he put it,

> Most people, if you describe a train of events to them, will tell you what the result would be. They can put those events together in their minds, and argue from them that something will come to pass. There are few people, however, who, if you told them a result, would be able to evolve from their own inner consciousness what the steps were which led up to that result.

Here is Holmes' description of the process of formulating an explanatory hypothesis. When a hypothesis has been proposed, however, its evaluation must be along the lines that were sketched in Section II. Granted its relevance and testability, and its compatibility with other well attested beliefs, the ultimate criterion for evaluating a hypothesis is its predictive power.

5. Deducing Further Consequences. A really fruitful hypothesis will not only explain the facts which originally inspired it but will explain many others in addition. A good hypothesis will point beyond the initial facts in the direction of others whose existence might otherwise not have been suspected. And of course the verification of those further consequences will tend to confirm the hypothesis which led to them. Holmes' hypothesis that the murdered man had been poisoned was soon put to such a test. A few days later the murdered man's secretary and traveling companion was also found murdered. Holmes asked Lestrade, who had discovered the second body, whether he had found anything in the room which could furnish a clue to the murderer. Lestrade answered "Nothing," and went on to mention a few quite ordinary effects. Holmes was not satisfied and pressed him, asking "And was there nothing else?" Lestrade answered, "Nothing of any importance," and named a few more details, the last of which was "a small chip ointment box containing a couple of pills." At this information,

> Sherlock Holmes sprang from his chair with an exclamation of delight.
> "The last link," he cried, exultantly. "My case is complete."
> The two detectives stared at him in amazement.
> "I have now in my hands," my companion said, confidently, "all the threads which have formed such a tangle. . . . I will give you a proof of my knowledge. Could you lay your hands upon those pills?"
> "I have them," said Lestrade, producing a small white box . . .

On the basis of his hypothesis about the original crime, Holmes was able to predict that the pills found at the scene of the second crime must contain poison. Here deduction has an essential role in the process of any scientific or inductive inquiry. The ultimate value of any hypothesis lies in its predictive or explanatory power, which means that additional facts must be deducible from an adequate hypothesis. From his theory that the first man was poisoned and that the second victim met his death at the hands of the same murderer, Holmes inferred that the pills found by Lestrade must be poison. His theory, however sure he may have felt about it, was only a theory and needed further confirmation. He obtained that confirmation by testing the consequences deduced from the hypothesis and finding them to be true. Having used deduction to make a prediction, his next step was to test it.

6. *Testing the Consequences.* The consequences of a hypothesis, that is, the predictions made on the basis of that hypothesis, may require different means for their testing. Some require only observation. In some cases, Holmes needed only to watch and wait—for the bank robbers to break into the vault, in the "Adventure of the Red-headed League," or for Dr. Roylott to slip a venomous snake through a dummy ventilator, in the "Adventure of the Speckled Band." In the present case, however, an *experiment* had to be performed.

Holmes asked Dr. Watson to fetch the landlady's old and ailing terrier, which she had asked to have put out of its misery the day before. Holmes then cut one of the pills in two, dissolved it in a wineglass of water, added some milk, and

> ... turned the contents of the wineglass into a saucer and placed it in front of the terrier, who speedily licked it dry. Sherlock Holmes's earnest demeanour had so far convinced us that we all sat in silence, watching the animal intently, and expecting some startling effect. None such appeared, however. The dog continued to lie stretched upon the cushion, breathing in a laboured way, but apparently neither the better nor the worse for its draught.
>
> Holmes had taken out his watch, and as minute followed minute without result, an expression of the utmost chagrin and disappointment appeared upon his features. He gnawed his lip, drummed his fingers upon the table, and showed every other symptom of acute impatience. So great was his emotion that I felt sincerely sorry for him, while the two detectives smiled derisively, by no means displeased at this check which he had met.
>
> "It can't be a coincidence," he cried, at last springing from his chair and pacing wildly up and down the room: "it is impossible that it should be a mere coincidence. The very pills which I suspected in the case of Drebber are actually found after the death of Stangerson. And yet they are inert. What can it mean? Surely my whole chain of reasoning cannot have been false. It is impossible! And yet this wretched dog is none the worse. Ah, I have it! I have it!" With a perfect shriek of delight he rushed to the box, cut the other pill in two, dissolved it, added milk, and presented it to the terrier. The unfortunate creature's tongue seemed hardly to have been moistened in it before it gave a convulsive shiver in every limb, and lay as rigid and lifeless as if it had been struck by lightning.
>
> Sherlock Holmes drew a long breath, and wiped the perspiration from his forehead.

By the favorable outcome of his experiment, Holmes' hypothesis had received dramatic and convincing confirmation.

7. Application. The detective's concern, after all, is a practical one. Given a crime to solve, he has not merely to explain the facts but to apprehend and arrest the criminal. The latter involves making *application* of his theory, using it to predict where the criminal can be found and how he may be caught. He must deduce still further consequences from the hypothesis, not for the sake of additional confirmation but for practical purposes. From his general hypothesis Holmes was able to infer that the murderer was acting the role of a cabman. We have already seen that Holmes had formed a pretty clear description of the man's appearance, and he sent out his army of "Baker Street Irregulars," street urchins of the neighborhood, to search out and summon the cab driven by just that man. The successful "application" of this hypothesis can be described again in Dr. Watson's words. A few minutes after the terrier's death,

... there was a tap at the door, and the spokesman of the street Arabs, young Wiggins, introduced his insignificant and unsavoury person.

"Please, sir," he said, touching his forelock, "I have the cab downstairs."

"Good boy," said Holmes, blandly. "Why don't you introduce this pattern at Scotland Yard?" he continued, taking a pair of steel handcuffs from a drawer. "See how beautifully the spring works. They fasten in an instant."

"The old pattern is good enough," remarked Lestrade, "if we can only find the man to put them on."

"Very good, very good," said Holmes, smiling. "The cabman may as well help me with my boxes. Just ask him to step up, Wiggins."

I was surprised to find my companion speaking as though he were about to set out on a journey, since he had not said anything to me about it. There was a small portmanteau in the room, and this he pulled out and began to strap. He was busily engaged at it when the cabman entered the room.

"Just give me a help with this buckle, cabman," he said, kneeling over his task, and never turning his head.

The fellow came forward with a somewhat sullen, defiant air, and put down his hands to assist. At that instant there was a sharp click, the jangling of metal, and Sherlock Holmes sprang to his feet again.

"Gentlemen," he cried, with flashing eyes, "let me introduce you to Mr. Jefferson Hope, the murderer of Enoch Drebber and of Joseph Stangerson."

Here we have a picture of the detective as scientist, reasoning from observed facts to a testable hypothesis which not only explains the facts but permits of practical application. . . .

11 ON EXPLANATION

JOHN HOSPERS (1918-   )

We are sometimes presented with a statement describing some observed fact, and when we ask "Why?" we are presented with another statement which is said to constitute an "explanation" of the first. What is the relation between these two statements? What is it that constitutes the second statement an "explanation" of the first? By virtue of what does it "explain"? Though

SOURCE: Originally published in the *Journal of Philosophy*, vol. XLIII, no. 13 (June 20, 1946), pp. 337–56. Reprinted with permission of the author and the editors of the *Journal of Philosophy*. A much modified version of the present essay appears in the anthology *Essays in Conceptual Analysis*, edited by Antony Flew (London: Macmillan & Co. Ltd., 1956), pp. 94–119. Compare with selections 10 and 58.

everyone is constantly uttering statements which are supposed in one way or another to explain, few persons are at all clear about what it is that makes such statements explanations.

It is sometimes assumed that when we set out to explain anything we are always trying to answer the question "Why?" But it should be evident at once that this is not the case. We offer many statements as explanations although they do not answer the question "Why?"; they sometimes explain how, or when, or who, or whither; and often when we are asked to explain some statement we merely make it clearer to the listener by stating it in other words. As the word is commonly used, any kind of clarification is likely to be called an explanation; and a statement can be clarified in many different ways.

Thus explanation covers a good deal more ground than merely answering the question "Why?"; and it might be worth while to disentangle various senses of the word "explain," showing what different kinds of questions are answered by statements which are commonly called explanations. In this paper, however, I shall be concerned only with the sense of "explain" which tries to answer the question "Why?" It may develop that to answer "Why?" also involves, or is involved in, answering the question "How?" but my present object is simply to inquire into the "Why?" I shall, moreover, restrict the field of inquiry to empirical concepts, neglecting explanations in mathematics and logic, where we would generally be said to ask for reasons rather than for explanations (although both these words are very loosely used, and overlap a good deal). My remarks will be designed not so much to add any new contribution to this issue as to analyze and correlate statements which have already been made about it. And considering the uncritical meekness with which people have accepted claims that "science has explained the universe," or, on the other hand, that "science doesn't really explain anything," the analysis of explanation has received little enough attention.

There have been a number of statements, some overlapping and others contradictory, of what the "true nature" of explanation is. (1) Perhaps the most obvious, and certainly the oldest, is that of "explanation in terms of purpose." We have explained why an event occurred when we have stated its purpose. "Why did you walk through the snow for ten miles when you could have taken the bus?" "I wanted to win a bet." "Why does that dog scratch at the door?" "He's cold and he wants to get in." In these cases, when such answers are given, we feel quite satisfied that our question has been answered and that the phenomenon in question has been explained; and it has been explained with reference to a purpose which some sentient being(s) had in attaining a certain end. This is the most primitive conception of explanation. People like to feel that there is a purposive explanation for everything: if not in terms of human purposes, then of divine ones, or mysterious forces and powers. The impulse to explain everything in terms of purpose doubtless springs in part from an attempt to extend what holds true of some events in the human realm to all events whatever: we know what conscious motivation is like from our own experience of it, hence we "feel at home" with this kind of explanation.

But if all explanation must be in terms of purpose, then physical science can never be said to give explanations. Surely, however animistically the nature of explanation was once conceived, this is not its meaning now. To have recourse to the whims of malignant demons to explain why the watch misbehaves is surely to desert explanation altogether. Many reasons could be adduced for this, but it is enough here to state that what we want is something that will tell us why this event happened rather than that one; and, outside contexts in which human (and perhaps also animal) agencies are operative, this can not be done by appealing simply to "purpose." (An account of the nature of purposive explanations, what renders them explanations, and their place among other explanations, will appear later in this paper.)

Another account of the nature of explanation is that (2) an event is explained when it has been shown to be an instance of some kind or class of events which is already familiar to us. For example, when a person's behavior seems strange to us, we are satisfied when it is "explained" to us as being really impelled by the same sort of motives and desires—love, greed, etc.—as occur in us, and are therefore familiar to us. "Why is he introducing the man he hates to the woman he loves?" "Because he wants them to fall in love with each other" would not generally be accepted as an explanation, for this very reason. When we observe that a balloon ascends rather than descends, unlike most objects, and it is made clear to us that air has weight and that the gas inside the balloon weighs less than an equal volume of air would weigh, we are satisfied; the phenomenon has been "explained" to us by "reducing" it to something already familiar to us in everyday experience, such as a dense object sinking in water while a hollow one floats. The event is no longer unusual, strange, or unique; it has been shown to illustrate a principle we were already acquainted with and accepted. When we want to know why gases diffuse when released into a chamber from which the air has been pumped out, the explanation offered by the kinetic theory of gases is satisfactory to us because it asserts that molecules behave *like* particles with which we are already acquainted in our everyday experience.

> Only those who have practised experimental physics, know anything by actual experience about the laws of gases; they are not things which force themselves on our attention in common life, and even those who are most familiar with them

never think of them out of working hours. On the other hand, the behavior of moving solid bodies is familiar to every one; every one knows roughly what will happen when such bodies collide with each other or with a solid wall, though they may not know the exact dynamical laws involved in such reactions. In all our common life we are continually encountering moving bodies, and noticing their reactions; indeed, if the reader thinks about it, he will realize that whenever we do anything which affects the external world, or whenever we are passively affected by it, a moving body is somehow involved in the transaction. Movement is just the most familiar thing in the world; it is through motion that everything and anything happens. And so by tracing a relation between the unfamiliar changes which gases undergo when their temperature or volume is altered, and the extremely familiar changes which accompany the motions and mutual reactions of solid bodies, we are rendering the former more intelligible; we are explaining them.[1]

Professor Bridgman holds that all explanation is of this kind: "I believe that examination will show that the essence of an explanation consists in reducing a situation to elements with which we are so familiar that we accept them as a matter of course, so that our curiosity rests."[2]

One might object to this that the term "familiar" is a rather subjective one. What is familiar and every-day to us may be strange and unfamiliar to the savage; what may be familiar to you may even be unfamiliar to me. Hence some statements will be explanations for some persons and not for others. Explanation will then be a relative matter—relative to the person to whom the explaining is done. Professor Bridgman is quite willing to accept this consequence: "An explanation is not an absolute sort of thing, but what is satisfactory for one man will not be for another."[3] But there is a more serious objection: we ask for explanations not merely of phenomena that are strange and unusual. We ask for explanations of the simplest and most familiar phenomena in the world. We can ask not only why balloons rise, but why heavier-than-air objects fall. We can ask why trees grow, why our memories fail as we get old, why January is colder than July. And the principles in terms of which the scientist claims to explain these things are principles which most of us have never heard of before. Surely the fact that light blinds you as you emerge from the darkness but not after you have been in the light for a few minutes, and the fact that you can see better in darkness when you have been in it for a while, is more familiar than its explanation in terms of the contraction and expansion of the pupil of the eye. And surely the formation of rust

---

[1] Norman Campbell, *What Is Science?*, p. 84.
[2] P. W. Bridgman, *The Logic of Modern Physics*, p. 37.
[3] *Ibid.*, p. 38.

on iron is more familiar than the chemical combination of iron with oxygen, of which most observers of iron rust have never heard.[4]

It is sometimes asserted that (3) an event is explained when it has been classed as an instance of some general law (the degree of familiarity of this law being irrelevant). A seemingly isolated phenomenon is shown to be an instance of a general law, and thus is explained. "Why are there more suicides (in proportion to the population) in New York City than in Mudville Flats?" "There are always more suicides in large cities." But surely this is no explanation. It is true that we have learned something—in this case, that the size of the city is relevant to the frequency of suicide, rather than, say, its longitude. Moreover, by showing that the phenomenon in question is not unique, that it is only one of many occurrences in a class, or subsumed under some law, we have taken away from most questioners the curiosity which prompted them to ask for an explanation in the first place; people most frequently (though not always, as we have seen) ask for explanations of what is bizarre or strange, and when an event has been shown not to be so ("It's just like a lot of other things") they are no longer so curious. But to have removed the impulse to ask the question is surely not to have answered it. And if people were asked whether a statement such as the one above really explained the phenomenon in question, they would very probably answer "No"; they would still know nothing about the phenomenon except that it belongs to a class of similar phenomena.

> I do not believe that laws can ever be explained by inclusion in more general laws; and I hold that, even if it were possible so to explain them, the explanation would not be that which science, developing the tendencies of common sense, demands. . . . To say that all gases expand when heated is not to explain why hydrogen expands when heated; it merely leads us to ask immediately why all gases expand. An explanation which leads immediately to another question of the same kind is no explanation at all.[5]

---

[4]We must beware, however, of a misuse of this argument. The freezing of the water-pipes in my basement in winter may be more familiar to me than the principle that water expands when it freezes, but once we have learned that water does expand when it freezes (unfamiliar though that fact may have been), the principle employed as explanation is indeed more familiar than the phenomenon we wanted explained: namely, that when things expand they "have to go some place" and in doing so can be expected to break whatever they are enclosed in. This is surely one of the most familiar facts of experience. Thus in one sense, at least, the explanation is really more familiar than the thing explained—the general phenomenon (things bursting other things when pressure is exerted) is more familiar, but not the fact that this class of phenomena (the expansion of water on freezing) is an instance of it. It is probable that many explanations are actually in terms of something more familiar although at first they may not seem to be so. On the other hand, many do not seem to be so in any sense. And, I am tempted to ask, what does it matter? Does the familiarity of a principle to some person or group really affect its value as an explanation? Many phenomena which are more familiar than others are not explanations of them; and many which are less familiar, are.

[5]Norman Campbell, *What Is Science?*, pp. 79–80.

Let us compare the two answers given to each of the following questions:

(1) Why do the water-pipes in my basement burst in winter?

(a) It always happens under certain specific conditions (cold weather, a certain pressure on the pipes, etc.).

(b) The pipes are filled with water, which expands when it freezes, bursting the pipes.

(2) Why are there more suicides in New York City than in Mudville Flats?

(a) Suicides are always more prevalent in large cities.

(b) In large cities, conditions leading to discouragement and despair are more prevalent: loneliness, mass unemployment, poverty. . . . When people are in such situations, they more often commit suicide.

(3) Why do animals in the arctic so often have white fur?

(a) Many animals exhibit protective coloration.

(b) Those that don't have protective coloration are more easily seen against their snowy background by animals which prey on them, with the result that they are more likely to be killed by them; the white ones live to perpetuate the species and their young, in turn, have a better chance for survival; thus, the white ones multiply in increasing numbers, while the others are gradually obliterated.

We have, in the first of the two cases in each example, a simple general statement ("explanation by generalization," which I have just described); in the second, a principle or set of principles in terms of which the phenomenon can be understood. In each case we have shown the phenomenon to be an instance of a general law which is accepted as true. (These laws are not necessarily more familiar—so long as they are accepted as true, that is sufficient. In more cases than not, they are both more familiar and more general than the phenomena to be explained. But their familiarity has nothing to do with the validity of the explanation. "If they aren't familiar they should be.") How, then, does the second kind differ from the first? In that it does not simply repeat the statement in general form. Instead of saying with regard to the broken water-pipes, "This regularly happens when it is cold, etc.," we give another general law, "Water expands when it freezes," which, when we combine it with other statements, of whose truth in this case we are already aware (e.g., that when things expand they may break whatever stands in the way of their expansion), yields us a satisfying explanation of why the pipes burst. We have not simply made a statement which generalizes on the instance adduced: we have, at last, shown *why* the phenomenon occurred. Or again: it is true (as well as familiar) that animals beget other animals like them, that animals that prey on others often kill them and keep them from propagating their species, that animals are most likely to catch the animals they can most easily see, etc. These things being true, it is understandable that so many animals in a white environment are white. In this example, many such general principles are involved; but be they many or few, every explanation involves them and is made on the basis of them.

Before discussing this view of explanation further I want to mention a closely related one: namely, the notion that (4) we are said to explain the concurrence of two phenomena (the reason for whose concurrence we do not understand) when we indicate intermediate factors which provide a connection between them. For example, we may explain the high correlation between the presence of cats in a certain region and the abundance of clover there, by showing that the cats catch the mice which would otherwise eat the bees (and other insects) that are required to pollinate the clover.

It will be seen that this—"explanation by intermediary agencies"—is really a special case of explanation in terms of general principles, just discussed. The links are fitted into the chain by general principles: in this case, that cats eat mice, that bees pollinate clover, etc. Illustrations of the other type could equally well be made to fall under this one: we could say, for example, that we are trying to explain the correlation between sub-freezing temperature and the bursting of the water-pipes, and the principle of the expansion of water on freezing supplies us with the required connection; it is the intermediate link in the chain, so to speak, just as the predatory habits of cats and mice and the fact that bees pollinate clover are general principles constituting the intermediate links in the other chain. A large proportion of explanations are of this type: they break down gross phenomena into components which are, or are instances of, general principles which serve to explain the concurrence of these phenomena.

It is sometimes said that (5) an event is explained by reference to its *cause*. Now I do not propose here to attempt an analysis of just what the causal relation is—the volumes devoted to this subject constitute a large fraction of the entire literature of philosophy—except to say that the word "cause" is used so vaguely, and often ambiguously as well, that to say that an event is explained in terms of its cause is to substitute for a term that requires analysis one that requires analysis still more. So loosely is this weasel-word used that I feel safe in saying that every explanation is in *some* sense or other a causal explanation.

For example: When someone asks, "Why did that book fall to the floor?" he may receive such diverse answers as "Somebody accidentally dropped it" and "On account of the law of gravitation." Both of these answers may be claimed to state the *cause* of the book's falling—and yet they are manifestly answers of quite a different order. The first answer would be more likely to satisfy the average inquirer than the second. What he wants to know is the particular circumstance in this case—did someone drop it in anger, did the cat playing on the table dislodge it, etc. But he may, on the other hand, know the circumstances of the book's falling—may have seen it fall—and then when he asks why it fell he is not asking for the same sort of thing at all. He is asking for some general principle, a law, not a particular event in time. (Perhaps the timeless principle enunciated in the law of gravitation will not satisfy him, on grounds that it merely classifies the event, just as "All gases expand when heated" did not satisfy the person who asked "Why does hydrogen expand when heated?" In this case he is asking for a general principle, but not one that merely generalizes on the present instance. Sometimes no other answer is possible, however—"explanation by generalization," if this can be called explanation at all, is all that can be offered; but this will be discussed below under the heading of "brute fact.") Without doing too much violence to Aristotle, we might call the first answer adduced the efficient cause of the event and the second, the general principle, the formal cause. In contemporary philosophical terminology the second would be unlikely to be called a cause at all.

Generally when we ask for the cause of an event we mean the efficient cause—though I shall not here try to describe an efficient cause (whether it is a necessary condition of the event, or a set of them, or a sufficient condition, or both, etc.) other than to say that it is a particular prior event or set of events. When we ask, "Why is the water in the lake frozen?" the answer we want is not "Because water freezes at 32° F." (a general law) but rather "Because the temperature dropped to below 32° F. during the night" (a particular prior event). In a case such as this we *presuppose* acquaintance with the general law that water freezes at 32° F. but want to know the efficient cause in this instance, just as in the case of the book we presuppose that objects do fall under certain circumstances and want to know the particular circumstances of the fall on this occasion.

To connect this now with the discussion of explanation: When the phenomenon requiring explanation is not a particular event but a general statement (law in its widest sense) referring to a class of events (Why do waterpipes burst in winter? etc.), then no particular event is needed by way of explanation—only general principles are involved. But when the phenomenon requiring explanation is a particular event, then the complete explanation consists not only of the general principle(s) but also of the particular antecedent(s) in this case. Thus, again: "Why did the water in the lake freeze?" "Water freezes at 32° F. (under standard conditions)" (general principle) *plus* "The temperature dropped to zero last night" (antecedent event), which together constitute an explanation of the phenomenon to be explained. But if we ask in general, "Why do lakes freeze in winter?" we are answered with the non-temporal principle that water freezes whenever the temperature reaches a certain low, which it generally does in winter in northern climates.

It should be evident here that explanation in terms of purpose is just one species of explanation in terms of general principles—or, in the case of a particular event, general principles plus particular antecendent events. If there is a satisfactory explanation, there is some general principle involved: "Why did you go to New York last night?" "There was an opera I wanted to see." Seeing the opera was the person's *purpose* in going; but there are general principles presupposed here, such as "People, in general, do what they want to do, unless prevented by some other force"—and it is only by virtue of such accepted general principles that wanting to do a thing is considered in any way an explanation of doing it. For example, in this instance it is presupposed that the act in question is something we *can* do if we want to; with many others this is not the case. "Why did the Allies win the war?" "Because they wanted to" would not be a sufficient explanation; after all both sides wanted to; wanting to and having the physical power to are *both* requisite, and all the wanting to in the world will not alone explain its happening, any more than the desire of a paralytic to walk is sufficient to enable him to do so.

In connection with explanations of particular events, it should be pointed out here that the analysis just given applies to all "genetic" explanations. On the tidal hypothesis, for example, the fact that the largest planets in the solar system are in the middle is explained by the fact that when the passing star approached the sun, the tides raised on the sun were the largest at the star's point of closest approach; this tidal material, ejected from the sun by the star's gravitational attraction, condensed into the planets, leaving the largest in the middle where the amount of ejected material was the greatest. Many principles are involved here: the law of gravitation, Newton's laws of motion, etc. Some, indeed, such as the principle of moment of momentum, can not be rendered consistent with certain consequences of the hypothesis and thus serve to cast doubt upon the whole hypothesis. But *if* this is what happened several billion years ago and if our formulation of the laws involved is correct, then surely the present state of affairs (the position of the larger planets, and many other things) is explained, exactly as in the case of the lake freezing.

I shall now touch on a number of points which I hope will clarify certain points in the above account, and which I consider more important than the analysis of explanation itself.

(1) The laws alleged must be true ones, else there is no true explanation. If, in the cats-clover sequence, we had been told that cats eat *books* and that the books in turn eat the bees, we would never have accepted the explanation, inasmuch as these statements are false. *If* true, they would provide a connecting link, but since we are quite sure that cats do not eat books and that books do not eat bees, we would reject any alleged explanation depend-

ing on such proffered laws. As it is, we may not believe that mice eat bees; and if they do not, the whole explanation breaks down and we must cast about for another one. A chain is no stronger than its weakest link.

Sometimes explanations are offered in terms of intra-molecular states and other unobservable entities, where we can not observe directly even a single instance of the truth of the general statement. But again the principle is the same: *if* the statements about intra-molecular states are true, they do indeed provide the explanations we are after; and if the truth of the statement is something that can not be determined for certain, then whether this explanation is true or not can not be determined either. (I do not want to become involved here in the question of whether the only *meaning* of saying that a statement, e.g., about atoms, is true is that certain phenomena—"pointer-readings"—are observable. This would be too lengthy a digression.)

The "simplicity" of explanations has been much emphasized, often at the expense of their truth. All other things being equal, I suppose, the simplest explanation is most likely to be accepted (not psychologically the simplest, i.e., the easiest to understand, but the one involving the fewest principles). But many accepted explanations are far less simple than rejected ones. The simplest explanation of the cats-clover correlation, I suppose, would be that certain effluvia released into the atmosphere in the exhalation of the cats' breath served to pollinate automatically all the clover in the region. A true explanation is often very complicated, and many alleged explanations turn out to be gross oversimplifications which overlook the actual complexity of events. Simple explanations could, I daresay, be devised for any occurrence whatever, in terms of principles which are dubious or false, like the one just mentioned. The explanation of many things remains unknown simply because of the complexities involved. This is true in submicroscopic phenomena as well: the atom can not be constructed on any such simple model as was accepted a century ago; if it is to explain the observed phenomena, it must be made bewilderingly complex, and there is much question of whether any model will suffice at all.

(2) Sometimes the explanatory principles are theories, and sometimes laws. (I have used the term "general principle" to cover both.) The relation between these two must be indicated.[6] It is usual in discussions of this kind to

---

[6] I am using the word "theory" as Campbell uses it, to denote statements involving unobservables, such as atoms and electrons. Generalizations involving only observables, such as that all crows are black and that bees pollinate clover and that ice melts at 32° F., are laws and not theories, even if some generalizations of this kind may be doubtful or even false—in this case they are false laws or dubious or alleged laws. It would be confusing to apply to these not-definitely-accepted laws the name "theories," and so confuse them with statements incapable of direct observation. Thus the statement that the hydrogen atom has one electron is a theory, but the statement that hydrogen burns is a law.

state that individual events are explained by laws, and that laws are explained by theories. But this is a misleading statement, to say the least. I may ask for the explanation of some individual event, such as the appearance of the aurora borealis on a certain night, and be answered with statements about electrical storms on the sun (sunspots) and streams of electrons flowing from the sun toward the earth's magnetic poles—most of which certainly comes under the head of theory, since it is not directly observable. Of course it might be objected that this is actually an explanation of why the aurora borealis occurs at any given time, and not why it appears tonight, and that thus we would still be explaining the individual event (its appearance tonight) in terms of laws (aurora occurs under certain observable conditions, e.g., involving sunspots), and the laws (specifying the conditions under which the aurora occurs) in terms of theories (about streams of electrons, etc.). But might it not be the case that there was no discoverable regularity in such an occurrence (if not in the aurora example, then in others), and hence no law under which the instance could be subsumed, and we would have to invoke theory to explain the individual event, no law being discoverable? Moreover, we have seen in the first part of this paper that when individual events are explained by laws they are not explained by laws alone but by laws *plus* antecedent events (to explain the state of the solar system at some future moment we must know not only the laws describing the behavior of bodies but also the state of the solar system at the present, or some past time). Nor is it always true that laws are explained in terms of theories. Both the explanation and the phenomenon to be explained may be laws, of which instances are directly observable. The explanation of the cats-clover correlation can be entirely in terms of other laws (not mere "explanation by generalization" such as "Cats are generally more plentiful when there's clover about" but rather statements about the predatory habits of cats and mice, etc.) and never once invoke theory; that is to say, the general principles in terms of which a law can be explained may very well be other laws, into which theory does not enter at all.

Nevertheless there is a substantial difference between laws and theories as explanations. To use an example I have used often before in this paper, we may perfectly well explain the bursting of the water-pipes on the principle of the expansion of water on freezing—a law of nature. Lest the phenomenon to be explained be taken for an individual event, we may put it in a general way: not "Why did they burst just now?" but "Why do they always do so under certain specifiable conditions (when it's cold, etc.)?" The explanation would be in terms of the expansion of water on freezing, a physical law referring again to something perfectly observable, with no theories involved. But suppose one goes on to ask, "Why does water expand when it freezes?"

Here the explanation is not in terms of any general law of which we can directly observe instances ("Most liquids do" would not be an explanation, but simply a generalization, as we have seen, even if it were true, which it isn't). The explanation generally offered, and the only *kind* of explanation I can think of, is in terms of the crystalline structure of the water molecule. This is theory; the structure of the water molecule has not been observed; but *if* we suppose it to have such a structure, we can see how water *would* expand on freezing.

(3) Perhaps the most important matter yet discussed in this paper is the extent to which explanation can be carried, and when it must stop.

To take again the case of the pipes bursting: we can explain this in terms of the expansion of water on freezing; and when we are asked in turn why this happens, then on the ordinary macroscopic level we can say nothing— "it just is that way"—although, as I have just indicated, attempts have been made to explain this in terms of the structure of the water molecule. (Whether this is actually a true explanation, and what precisely is meant by saying that it is true, I am not concerned with here. Assuming that the explanation is satisfactory, we can go on.) This only suggests the next question: "Why is the molecule constructed in this way?" Perhaps some explanation might be suggested in terms of intramolecular or intra-atomic forces; but when an explanation of these is demanded, it seems that we can only say, "That's just the way it is, that's all." Here, it appears, explanation comes to an end; we have reached the level of "brute fact." "This is the way things are, this is how the world is constituted, and that's all we can say about it." Most persons would probably say this before such a level of analysis had been reached; they would say it is just a brute fact that water starts to expand again below 39° F.[7]

There are many phenomena which were formerly considered "brute fact" which are no longer considered so. Why does this element have this color, this melting-point, these spectral lines? Why does it combine with this substance and not with that? etc. For many of these phenomena, of which formerly it was said "These are just (brute-fact) properties of this substance," explanations are now offered in terms chiefly of atomic structure and activity.

[7] There is a rather elementary but widely pervasive confusion on this point. It is said that unless an explanation has been given all the way down to the level of brute fact, no explanation has really been given for the phenomenon at all; e.g., unless we know why water expands on freezing, why the water-molecule has a crystalline structure, etc., we do not really know why our pipes burst. But surely this is not the case. Whether we know why water expands on freezing or not, we do know that it does so, and that it is because of its doing so that the pipes burst in cold weather. When we have asked why the pipes burst, the principle of expansion of water does give an explanation. When we ask why water expands on freezing, we are asking *another* question. The first *has* been answered, whether we can answer the second or not.

But are not these explanations (assuming that they are satisfactory) brute fact? or if not, then the explanations of these? Must we not sooner or later come to a standstill in our process of explaining?[8]

At any given stage of scientific investigation, surely, there is a level of brute fact, in which the phenomena can not be explained in terms of anything more ultimate though they themselves may afford an explanation of other phenomena on a "higher" level. As has just been said, a level that was once thought to be ultimate may turn out not to be so—like layers of varnish that keep peeling off, revealing others below. But how can we be sure, at any given point, that we have come to the end, reached *the* ultimate brute fact and not just what is thought at any particular time to be so? The answer is, of course, that we never can be sure. If ever we *have* arrived, no further explanation is possible; but that we have arrived, is never certain.

It is sometimes said that people who keep asking Why? Why? even with regard to what we now consider brute fact, are asking meaningless questions. It might be observed, however, that if such questions had not been asked in the past, we would not have reached such "deep" levels of explanation as we now have; and the progress of science depends in large measure on the fruitfulness of explanatory hypotheses. Moreover, I suggest that the question has meaning when we have some definite conception of a more ultimate structure in terms of which the structure now considered brute fact can be explained, even if such a conception be highly tenuous and hypothetical, e.g., if we know what kind of structure *would* explain the behavior of the electrons, etc., just as the present electron-proton hypothesis explains the failure of certain elements to combine with others. Explanation is always in terms of something else, and there can be no explanation (to request one is to make a demand logically impossible of fulfillment) if there is nothing even hypothecated in terms of which to make it. But once such a hypothesis has been conceived, our answers in terms of it will make sense even though they may not be true and even though it may seem unlikely that we shall ever know whether they are.[9]

---

[8] I am tempted to remark here that there has been much unjust criticism of the Humian doctrine of causation because the process of analysis is not carried far enough. Thus, in cases of death by arsenic poisoning, he would be no more content than would a physician to say that there was simply a constant conjunction and no connection (between arsenic and death); he would analyze it down further, to the action of this substance on the stomach, etc. To deny this is to reduce Hume's view of causation to an absurdity. But ultimately, having performed such a detailed analysis, do we not come to a series of brute-fact "constant conjunctions"? (One might say: Yes, if you like, there are connections, but those connections consist of a lot of constant conjunctions.) This, however, is too large a topic for me to explore any further here.

[9] Cf. Bridgman, *op. cit.,* p. 39: "Formally, there is no limit to the process of explanation, because we can always ask what is the explanation of the elements in terms of which we have given the last explanation. But the point of view of operations shows that this is a mere formalism which

ON EXPLANATION

There are many realms in which explanation, at the present stage of inquiry, comes to an end long before the molecular or sub-molecular level is reached. This is particularly true in cases dealing with biological behavior. And perhaps biological phenomena—some of them at any rate—are inherently incapable of explanation in this way; does not the controversy between vitalism and mechanism (in at least one of the many meanings of those much-abused terms) involve precisely this issue?

Nor do I want to leave the impression that all explanation must be in terms of the more minute. This is not even true in physics. As Bridgman says, speaking of the "elements" in terms of which an event or law is explained,

> There is no implication that the "element" is either a smaller or a larger scale thing than the phenomenon being explained; thus we may explain the properties of a gas in terms of its constituent molecules, or perhaps some day we shall become so familiar with the idea of a non-Euclidean space that we shall *explain* (instead of describe) the gravitational attraction of a stone by the earth in terms of a space-time curvature imposed by all the rest of the matter in the universe.[10]

The terms which we apply in trying to explain phenomena make it seem as if explanations are being given, while actually in many cases the terms are simply names for the phenomena themselves, or the class into which they fall, and nothing more. When someone asks, "Why do stones fall?" and the "explanation" is given, "All heavier-than-air objects tend to fall," it is clear at once that one is simply generalizing on an individual case—"explanation by generalization" which we have already seen to be unsatisfactory. But it is not so clear to most people that the answer "Because of the law of universal gravitation" is of exactly the same kind as the first one. The classification has been extended—the behavior of the stone is now of a kind in which all objects in the universe partake, not merely terrestrial ones—but neither statement does more than classify the present phenomenon. It has been classified but not explained. Appeals to gravitation are just ways of saying that all bodies behave in a certain manner, and this mode of behavior is entitled "gravitational attraction." We are not explaining the fall of bodies as we did the bursting of the pipes or the comparative abundance of white animals in arctic regions.

To make this quite clear let us compare it with another instance.

> All plants, so far as is known, I believe, *start* upwards as regard their stems, however these may begin soon afterwards in some cases to creep. And they all

ends only in meaningless jargon, for we soon arrive at the limit of our experimental knowledge, and beyond this the operations involved in the concepts of our explanations become impossible and the concepts become meaningless."

[10] *Ibid.,* p. 38.

> equally start downwards as regards their roots, whatever direction these may subsequently take. When we enquire as to the cause of this tendency, . . . the scientific man does not attempt here to interpose a technical term like "gravitation"; in fact, owing to the novelty of the enquiry he is not provided with such a term as yet. Had the particular question been raised a couple of centuries ago, the difficulty would probably have been smoothed away by the introduction of a well-selected expression, on the analogy of "plastic form" or "vital force." But this resource is not available, and consequently to the semi-scientific, who are greatly influenced by the appropriate introduction of a term, it often seems in such a case as if some admission were being made as to the inferior position which we occupy.[11]

To have given a name, however impressive it may be, is not to have given an explanation.

There seems to be one kind of case in which the brute-fact level is reached at once and bids fair to remain so: I mean the correlation of certain mental states with certain physical states. We can often explain physical phenomena in terms of other physical phenomena, as has been done constantly in this essay; but what can we do in the case of mental phenomena except note that certain of them seem to be uniquely correlated with certain physical states? *Why* do I have a certain color-sensation, which I call red, when light-waves of a certain frequency strike the retina of my eyes, and another and indescribably different sensation, which I call yellow, when rays of another frequency strike the retina? That this frequency is correlated with this unique experience, and that one with that experience, seems to be sheer brute fact, which no amount of information about physics and physiology alone could have enabled us to predict. Or, again, is it not just an ultimate brute fact that this peculiar and unique taste-sensation occurs when salt is in contact with my palate, and another when the substance is cinnamon?

But is not the salty taste of a certain food explained when we discover that one of its chief ingredients is salt? Yes, indirectly: I mean that *if* one grants the brute fact that this substance is correlated with this kind of sensation, then the occurrence of the salty taste in this dish is explained by the presence of salt in it; but that this taste is correlated with the presence of this substance, is still brute fact. (When we are ill the dish may not taste salty; but this shows only that the presence of salt is not the whole physical state; many other things enter into the picture as well; but the *whole* complex—or, some would say, the brain-event which is the end-product of a whole series of states in the brain, nerves, sense-organs, and external world—is what is, as a matter of brute fact, correlated with this particular sensation.) If we know that a

---

[11] John Venn, *Empirical Logic*, pp. 502–503.

physical state x is correlated with mental state x', the production or removal of that mental state can be explained indirectly in terms of the production or removal of the physical state x by means of agencies (in this case chemical) a, b, etc. Thus it is the physical state in each case that is explained, and the brute-fact character of the mind-matter correlation remains.

One further point should be made before leaving this subject. There are many cases in which the question "Why?" is asked and no answer is forthcoming. It may be that there is an explanation but we do not yet know what it is: for example, we do not as yet know why potassium thiocyanate relieves certain types of migraine, although we shall probably come to know this in the future. If, on the other hand, we are at the brute-fact level, then by definition we can no longer meaningfully ask for further explanations. Of course, as we have seen, we can not be sure at any given stage whether this level has been reached (with the possible exception, just noted, of the correlation of mental states with physical ones); it might be described as the theoretical limit of our investigations; and physical science can always keep on speculating and investigating the possibility of further explanations. But there are other cases in which the question "Why?" is asked, and the inquirer has no notion what he is really asking for. The child asks, "Why is Mummy sick?" and on being given a lengthy physical description of germs attacking certain blood-corpuscles which are necessary to the maintenance of health because they perform certain essential functions in the body, etc., the child, even if he understands the physical explanation, may still ask, "But *why* is she sick?" What is the child asking for? Perhaps he is asking for an explanation in terms of purpose (and might then be satisfied with "God willed it so" or even "Some evil spirit wanted to torture her") just as he receives an answer in terms of purpose to questions such as "Why did Daddy go to Chicago?" (I daresay that most of the first explanations a child receives are in terms of purpose, and he may assume that all others will be in those same terms.) It is notorious that uneducated persons as well as children demand explanations in such terms when none is in order. But on the other hand the child may have no idea what he is asking and may simply feel a general dissatisfaction which he voices by repeating the question "Why?" So too may the man in the street and the philosopher when they ask (respectively) "Why is life like that?" and "Why are there sense-data?"—little realizing that they have removed the very possibility of an answer by the very nature of the question —or group of words in the form of a question.

In such cases the word "why" simply becomes an "expectation-formula"; having received answers to questions beginning with "why" when these questions were meaningful and explanations could be given, they continue to use the word "why" even when they do not know what it means in this case, and really do not know what they are asking for. One need not be surprised that no answer is forthcoming to such questions. We are all too prone to terminate an exasperating series of questions beginning with "why" with a remark such as "That's just something we don't know," as if it were like the cases where something definite is being asked but we do not yet happen to know the principles which explain the phenomena we are asking about. If something in the case is not known, there must be something in the case which we could fail to know. If we are to ask a meaningful question, we must know what it is that we are asking for; only then can we recognize an answer as being one when we do find it. And if no statement, even if true, would satisfy as an answer, what does the question itself mean?

(4) Closely related to this is the contention that science actually explains nothing, but only describes. "Science doesn't tell us *why* things happen," the complaint runs, "it only tells us *how* things happen." Now I confess that the exact intention of the user of the question beginning with "why" is often not very clear—as we have just seen. In the way in which the term is commonly used, science *does* explain; once again, the bursting of the pipes, the formation of ice at the top of ponds rather than at the bottom, and many other phenomena, are explained by reference to the principle of the expansion of water on freezing. The phenomenon is now understandable to us, we see why it occurs as it does, and we say it has been explained. (If someone says we have *not* explained why the pipes burst, then what does he mean by "why"? What sort of thing is it that he is asking? What *would* answer his question? Let him state in other terms what it is that he wants to know.)

"But is not explanation after all merely description?" I have no objection to saying that when we explain something we actually describe, but this does not preclude the fact that we *are* explaining. When the question is asked why pressing the button turns on the light, we explain the phenomenon by describing just what (we believe) goes on—currents, closed and open circuits, conduction of electricity, dynamos in the power plant, etc. But have we not in so doing explained the phenomenon? We have explained *by* describing, if you will—by stating the principles which describe these states-of-affairs; but certainly we have explained. To deny this would be like saying that because an object is red it can not also be colored.

(5) In any given case the explanation that will satisfy us depends on our intent in asking the question. We may be interested in only one aspect of a phenomenon, and yet, roughly speaking, say that we have found "the explanation" whereas others, looking for something else, but asking the same question, may find "the explanation" to be quite different. Each of them is looking for some item in the total explanatory scheme, which in the case of human affairs is often bewilderingly complex. Why did the man steal the

money out of that safe? "He picked the lock," says the detective; "He knew that the Madame was out," says the maid; "We needed the money," states his wife; "Look at his background," says the sociologist, "and you'll discover why." These explanations do not exclude each other, but rather complete and supplement each other. In these cases we should speak not of *the* true explanation, but of *a* true explanation; or, more precisely still, a part or aspect of the complete explanation.

In this connection it is in point once again to allude to explanation in terms of purpose. What can be explained in terms of purpose can also be explained —in a different dimension, so to speak—on other levels. Whether the explanation satisfies depends on what the inquirer was asking for. "Why did he go downtown?" "Well, in response to impulses from certain centers in his brain, some muscles in his arms and legs started moving and. . . ." "No, that's not what I mean. I mean, why did he go? what purpose did he have in view?" "Oh—he wanted to buy a new suit." Contrast this with the following: "Why did he die?" "Well, a bullet entered his lung, puncturing some blood vessels, and the blood filled his lung so that he couldn't breathe any more, and. . . ." "No, that's not what I mean. I mean *why* did he die?" But here we can give no answer in terms of conscious purpose. (We could answer in terms of purpose in *another* sense, e.g., what purpose did it serve? How was the world benefited by his death?[12]) The inquirer here is assuming that just as the conscious purpose of some individual resulted in that individual's going downtown, so also the conscious will of some superhuman individual, presumably God, resulted in the death by shooting of the person in the second example. But unless we introduce *ad hoc* such an agency into the scene, the question in the second case is not in order (of the philosophical difficulties entailed by such an introduction I shall here say nothing), but merely derives its appearance of reasonableness from an analogy with cases like the former. Explanation in terms of purpose works only where there *is* a conscious agent purposing to do this or that; purposive explanations are out of order in cases where inanimate objects (and all others incapable of sensation and volition) alone enter into the picture, i.e., where there is nobody to have the purpose.

(6) Scientific explanation has been viewed with fear or abhorrence in some circles because it was believed that explaining meant "explaining away." The precise meaning of this latter term I have never been able to discover. Surely explanation deprives us of no facts we had before. To "explain color" in terms of light-waves is not, of course (as should have been obvious), to take away the fact of color-sensations. "Thinking is nothing but the occurrence of certain neural impulses" should be changed into "*When* thinking takes place

---

[12]Cf. the three senses of "purpose" given by Woodger in *Biological Principles*, pp. 432–434.

(and it is just as incontrovertible a fact as the neurons are), there are neural impulses." To "explain away" someone's politically reactionary tendencies by saying "He's old, and people get over-conservative when they get old" does not for a moment impugn whatever truth the person's opinions may have. The same reasoning could undermine his opponent's assertions: "You needn't pay any attention to that young upstart, they're all hot communists when they're young." Reference to biography may explain why a person held a certain belief at a certain time, but the truth or falsity of the belief is utterly unaffected by this and is tested on different grounds entirely. The idea that reference to a person's mental or physical condition could "explain away" the truth of any belief is one of the most flagrant blunders of the materialistically-inclined laity of our day.

In this paper I have tried (1) to analyze the nature of explanation, particularly in the natural sciences, and (2) to clarify several related questions, such as the ultimacy of explanations, laws and theories as explanations, and the relation of explanation to description. There are many other related topics, such as that of *ad hoc* explanations and the predictive value of explanations, which would require far too lengthy a treatment for a single essay, and which, moreover, are much more usual problems for discussion in current philosophy, having been amply discussed in a number of textbooks and articles in periodicals.

PART III
THEORY OF KNOWLEDGE

12 OF DOUBT AND CERTITUDE
RENÉ DESCARTES (1596-1650)

Meditation I
Of the Things of Which We May Doubt. Several years have now elapsed since I first became aware that I had accepted, even from my youth, many false opinions for true, and that consequently what I afterwards based on such principles was highly doubtful; and from that time I was convinced of the necessity of undertaking once in my life to rid myself of all the opinions I had adopted, and of commencing anew the work of building from the foundation, if I desired to establish a firm and abiding superstructure in the sciences. But as this enterprise appeared to me to be one of great magnitude, I waited until I had attained an age so mature as to leave me no hope that at any stage of life more advanced I should be better able to execute my design. On this account, I have delayed so long that I should henceforth consider I was doing wrong were I still to consume in deliberation any of the time that now remains for action. Today, then, since I have opportunely freed my mind from all cares, and am happily disturbed by no passions, and since I am in the secure possession of leisure in a peaceable retirement, I will at length apply myself earnestly and freely to the general overthrow of all my former opinions. But, to this end, it will not be necessary for me to show that the whole of these are false—a point, perhaps, which I shall never reach; but as even now my reason convinces me that I ought not the less carefully to withhold belief from what is not entirely certain and indubitable, than from what is manifestly false, it will be sufficient to justify the rejection of the whole if I shall find in each some ground for doubt. Nor for this purpose will it be necessary even to deal with each belief individually, which would be truly an endless labour; but, as the removal from below of the foundation necessarily involves the downfall of the whole edifice, I will at once approach the criticism of the principles on which all my former beliefs rested.

All that I have, up to this moment, accepted as possessed of the highest truth and certainty, I received either from or through the senses. I observed,

---

SOURCE: The first two of the six *Meditations on the First Philosophy* (1641); translated from the Latin by John Veitch (1853). The title of this selection has been supplied by the editors. See selections 14 and 19.

however, that these sometimes misled us; and it is the part of prudence not to place absolute confidence in that by which we have even once been deceived.

But it may be said, perhaps, that, although the senses occasionally mislead us respecting minute objects, and such as are so far removed from us as to be beyond the reach of close observation, there are yet many other of their informations (presentations), of the truth of which it is manifestly impossible to doubt; as for example, that I am in this place, seated by the fire, clothed in a winter dressing-gown, that I hold in my hands this piece of paper, with other intimations of the same nature. But how could I deny that I possess these hands and this body, and withal escape being classed with persons in a state of insanity, whose brains are so disordered and clouded by dark bilious vapours as to cause them pertinaciously to assert that they are monarchs when they are in the greatest poverty; or clothed in gold and purple when destitute of any covering; or that their head is made of clay, their body of glass, or that they are gourds? I should certainly be not less insane that they, were I to regulate my procedure according to examples so extravagant.

Though this be true, I must nevertheless here consider that I am a man, and that, consequently, I am in the habit of sleeping, and representing to myself in dreams those same things, or even sometimes others less probable, which the insane think are presented to them in their waking moments. How often have I dreamt that I was in these familiar circumstances,—that I was dressed, and occupied this place by the fire, when I was lying undressed in bed? At the present moment, however, I certainly look upon this paper with eyes wide awake; the head which I now move is not asleep; I extend this hand consciously and with express purpose, and I perceive it; the occurrences in sleep are not so distinct as all this. But I cannot forget that, at other times, I have been deceived in sleep by similar illusions; and, attentively considering those cases, I perceive so clearly that there exist no certain marks by which the state of waking can ever be distinguished from sleep, that I feel greatly astonished; and in amazement I almost persuade myself that I am now dreaming.

Let us suppose, then, that we are dreaming, and that all these particulars —namely, the opening of the eyes, the motion of the head, the forthputting of the hands—are merely illusions; and even that we really possess neither an entire body nor hands such as we see. Nevertheless, it must be admitted at least that the objects which appear to us in sleep are, as it were, painted representations which could not have been formed unless in the likeness of realities; and, therefore, that those general objects, at all events,—namely, eyes, a head, hands, and an entire body—are not simply imaginary, but really existent. For, in truth, painters themselves, even when they study to represent sirens and satyrs by forms the most fantastic and extraordinary, cannot bestow upon them natures absolutely new, but can only make a certain medley of the members of different animals; or if they chance to imagine something so novel that nothing at all similar has ever been seen before, and such as is, therefore, purely fictitious and absolutely false, it is at least certain that the colours of which this is composed are real.

And on the same principle, although these general objects, viz. a body, eyes, a head, hands, and the like, be imaginary, we are nevertheless absolutely necessitated to admit the reality at least of some other objects still more simple and universal than these, of which, just as of certain real colours, all those images of things, whether true and real, or false and fantastic, that are found in our consciousness, are formed.

To this class of objects seem to belong corporeal nature in general and its extension; the figure of extended things, their quantity or magnitude, and their number, as also the place in, and the time during, which they exist, and other things of the same sort. We will not, therefore, perhaps reason illegitimately if we conclude from this that Physics, Astronomy, Medicine, and all the other sciences that have for their end the consideration of composite objects, are indeed of a doubtful character; but that Arithmetic, Geometry, and the other sciences of the same class, which regard merely the simplest and most general objects, and scarcely inquire whether or not these are really existent, contain somewhat that is certain and indubitable; for whether I am awake or dreaming, it remains true that two and three makes five, and that a square has but four sides; nor does it seem possible that truths so apparent can ever fall under a suspicion of falsity or incertitude.

Nevertheless, the belief that there is a God who is all-powerful, and who created me, such as I am, has, for a long time, obtained steady possession of my mind. How, then, do I know that he has not arranged that there should be neither earth, nor sky, nor any extended thing, nor figure, nor magnitude, nor place, providing at the same time, however, for the rise in me of the perceptions of all these objects, and the persuasion that these do not exist otherwise than I perceive them? And further, as I sometimes think that others are in error respecting matters of which they believe themselves to possess a perfect knowledge, how do I know that I am not also deceived each time I add together two and three, or number the sides of a square, or form some judgment still more simple, if more simple indeed can be imagined? But perhaps Deity has not been willing that I should be thus deceived, for He is said to be supremely good. If, however, it were repugnant to the goodness of Deity to have created me subject to constant deception, it would seem likewise to be contrary to his goodness to allow me to be occasionally deceived; and yet it is clear that this is permitted. Some, indeed, might perhaps be found who would be disposed rather to deny the existence of a

Being so powerful than to believe that there is nothing certain. But let us for the present refrain from opposing this opinion, and grant that all which is here said of a Deity is fabulous; nevertheless in whatever way it be supposed that I reached the state in which I exist, whether by fate, or chance, or by an endless series of antecedents and consequents, or by any other means, it is clear (since to be deceived and to err is a certain defect) that the probability of my being so imperfect as to be the constant victim of deception, will be increased exactly in proportion as the power possessed by the cause, to which they assign my origin, is lessened. To these reasonings I have assuredly nothing to reply, but am constrained at last to avow that there is nothing of all that I formerly believed to be true of which it is impossible to doubt, and that not through thoughtlessness or levity, but from cogent and maturely considered reasons; so that henceforward, if I desire to discover anything certain, I ought not the less carefully to refrain from assenting to those same opinions than to what might be shown to be manifestly false.

But it is not sufficient to have made these observations; care must be taken likewise to keep them in remembrance. For those old and customary opinions perpetually recur—long and familiar usage giving them the right of occupying my mind, even almost against my will, and subduing my belief; nor will I lose the habit of deferring to them and confiding in them so long as I shall consider them to be what in truth they are, viz., opinions to some extent doubtful, as I have already shown, but still highly probable, and such as it is much more reasonable to believe than deny. It is for this reason I am persuaded that I shall not be doing wrong, if, taking an opposite judgment of deliberate design, I become my own deceiver, by supposing, for a time, that all those opinions are entirely false and imaginary, until at length, having thus balanced my old by my new prejudices, my judgment shall no longer be turned aside by perverted usage from the path that may conduct to the perception of truth. For I am assured that, meanwhile, there will arise neither peril nor error from this course, and that I cannot for the present yield too much to distrust, since the end I now seek is not action but knowledge.

I will suppose, then, not that Deity, who is sovereignly good and the fountain of truth, but that some malignant demon, who is at once exceedingly potent and deceitful, has employed all his artifice to deceive me; I will suppose that the sky, the air, the earth, colours, figures, sounds, and all external things, are nothing better than the illusions of dreams, by means of which this being has laid snares for my credulity; I will consider myself as without hands, eyes, flesh, blood, or any of the senses, and as falsely believing that I am possessed of these; I will continue resolutely fixed in this belief, and if indeed by this means it be not in my power to arrive at the knowledge of truth, I shall at least do what is in my power, viz., suspend my judgment, and guard with settled purpose against giving my assent to what is false, and being imposed upon by this deceiver, whatever be his power and artifice.

But this undertaking is arduous, and a certain indolence insensibly leads me back to my ordinary course of life; and just as the captive, who, perchance, was enjoying in his dreams an imaginary liberty, when he begins to suspect that it is but a vision, dreads awakening, and conspires with the agreeable illusions that the deception may be prolonged; so I, of my own accord, fall back into the train of my former beliefs, and fear to arouse myself from my slumber, lest the time of laborious wakefulness that would succeed this quiet rest, in place of bringing any light of day, should prove inadequate to dispel the darkness that will arise from the difficulties that have now been raised.

Meditation II
Of the Nature of the Human Mind; and That It Is More Easily Known Than the Body. The Meditation of yesterday has filled my mind with so many doubts, that it is no longer in my power to forget them. Nor do I see, meanwhile, any principle on which they can be resolved; and, just as if I had fallen all of a sudden into very deep water, I am so greatly disconcerted as to be unable either to plant my feet firmly on the bottom or sustain myself by swimming on the surface. I will, nevertheless, make an effort, and try anew the same path on which I had entered yesterday, that is, proceed by casting aside all that admits of the slightest doubt, not less than if I had discovered it to be absolutely false; and I will continue always in this track until I shall find something that is certain, or at least, if I can do nothing more, until I shall know with certainty that there is nothing certain. Archimedes, that he might transport the entire globe from the place it occupied to another, demanded only a point that was firm and immoveable; so also, I shall be entitled to entertain the highest expectations, if I am fortunate enough to discover only one thing that is certain and indubitable.

I suppose, accordingly, that all the things which I see are false (fictitious); I believe that none of those objects which my fallacious memory represents ever existed; I suppose that I possess no senses; I believe that body, figure, extension, motion, and place are merely fictions of my mind. What is there, then, that can be esteemed true? Perhaps this only, that there is absolutely nothing certain.

But how do I know that there is not something different altogether from the objects I have now enumerated, of which it is impossible to entertain the slightest doubt? Is there not a God, or some being, by whatever name I may designate him, who causes these thoughts to arise in my mind? But why suppose such a being, for it may be I myself am capable of producing them?

Am I, then, at least not something? But I before denied that I possessed senses or a body; I hesitate, however, for what follows from that? Am I so dependent on the body and the senses that without these I cannot exist? But I had the persuasion that there was absolutely nothing in the world, that there was no sky and no earth, neither minds nor bodies; was I not, therefore, at the same time, persuaded that I did not exist? Far from it; I assuredly existed, since I was persuaded. But there is I know not what being, who is possessed at once of the highest power and the deepest cunning, who is constantly employing all his ingenuity in deceiving me. Doubtless, then, I exist, since I am deceived; and, let him deceive me as he may, he can never bring it about that I am nothing, so long as I shall be conscious that I am something. So that it must, in fine, be maintained, all things being maturely and carefully considered, that this proposition, I am, I exist, is necessarily true each time it is expressed by me, or conceived in my mind.

But I do not yet know with sufficient clearness what I am, though assured that I am; and hence, in the next place, I must take care, lest perchance I inconsiderately substitute some other object in room of what is properly myself, and thus wander from truth, even in that knowledge which I hold to be of all others the most certain and evident. For this reason, I will now consider anew what I formerly believed myself to be, before I entered on the present train of thought; and of my previous opinion I will retrench all that can in the least be invalidated by the grounds of doubt I have adduced, in order that there may at length remain nothing but what is certain and indubitable. What then did I formerly think I was? Undoubtedly I judged that I was a man. But what is a man? Shall I say a rational animal? Assuredly not; for it would be necessary forthwith to inquire into what is meant by animal, and what by rational, and thus, from a single question, I should insensibly glide into others, and these more difficult than the first; nor do I now possess enough of leisure to warrant me in wasting my time amid subtleties of this sort. I prefer here to attend to the thoughts that sprung up of themselves in my mind, and were inspired by my own nature alone, when I applied myself to the consideration of what I was. In the first place, then, I thought that I possessed a countenance, hands, arms, and all the fabric of members that appears in a corpse, and which I called by the name of body. It further occurred to me that I was nourished, that I walked, perceived, and thought, and all those actions I referred to the soul; but what the soul itself was I either did not stay to consider, or, if I did, I imagined that it was something extremely rare and subtile, like wind, or flame, or ether, spread through my grosser parts. As regarded the body, I did not even doubt of its nature, but thought I distinctly knew it, and if I had wished to describe it according to the notions I then entertained, I should have explained myself in this manner: By body

I understand all that can be terminated by a certain figure; that can be comprised in a certain place, and so fill a certain space as therefrom to exclude every other body; that can be perceived either by touch, sight, hearing, taste, or smell; that can be moved in different ways, not indeed of itself, but by something foreign to it by which it is touched and from which it receives the impression; for the power of self-motion, as likewise that of perceiving and thinking, I held as by no means pertaining to the nature of body; on the contrary, I was somewhat astonished to find such faculties existing in some bodies.

But as to myself, what can I now say that I am, since I suppose there exists an extremely powerful, and, if I may so speak, malignant being, whose whole endeavours are directed towards deceiving me? Can I affirm that I possess any one of all those attributes of which I have lately spoken as belonging to the nature of body? After attentively considering them in my own mind, I find none of them that can properly be said to belong to myself. To recount them were idle and tedious. Let us pass, then, to the attributes of the soul. The first mentioned were the powers of nutrition and walking; but, if it be true that I have no body, it is true likewise that I am capable neither of walking nor of being nourished. Perception is another attribute of the soul; but perception too is impossible without the body: besides, I have frequently during sleep, believed that I perceived objects which I afterwards observed I did not in reality perceive. Thinking is another attribute of the soul; and here I discover what properly belongs to myself. This alone is inseparable from me. I am—I exist: this is certain; but how often? As often as I think; for perhaps it would even happen, if I should wholly cease to think, that I should at the same time altogether cease to be. I now admit nothing that is not necessarily true: I am therefore, precisely speaking, only a thinking thing, that is, a mind, understanding, or reason,—terms whose signification was before unknown to me. I am, however, a real thing, and really existent; but what thing? The answer was, a thinking thing. The question now arises, am I aught besides? I will stimulate my imagination with a view to discover whether I am not still something more than a thinking being. Now it is plain I am not the assemblage of members called the human body; I am not a thin and penetrating air diffused through all these members, or wind, or flame, or vapour, or breath, or any of all the things I can imagine; for I supposed that all these were not, and, without changing the supposition, I find that I still feel assured of my existence.

But it is true, perhaps, that those very things which I suppose to be nonexistent, because they are unknown to me, are not in truth different from myself whom I know. This is a point I cannot determine, and do not now enter into any dispute regarding it. I can only judge of things that are known to me: I am conscious that I exist, and I who know that I exist inquire into what I am. It is, however, perfectly certain that the knowledge of my existence, thus precisely taken, is not dependent on things, the existence of which is as yet unknown to me: and consequently it is not dependent on any of the things I can feign in imagination. Moreover, the phrase itself, I frame an image, reminds me of my error; for I should in truth frame one if I were to imagine myself to be anything, since to imagine is nothing more than to contemplate the figure or image of a corporeal thing; but I already know that I exist, and that it is possible at the same time that all those images, and in general all that relates to the nature of body, are merely dreams or chimeras. From this I discover that it is not more reasonable to say, I will excite my imagination that I may know more distinctly what I am, than to express myself as follows: I am now awake, and perceive something real; but because my perception is not sufficiently clear, I will of express purpose go to sleep that my dreams may represent to me the object of my perception with more truth and clearness. And, therefore, I know that nothing of all that I can embrace in imagination belongs to the knowledge which I have of myself, and that there is need to recall with the utmost care the mind from this mode of thinking, that it may be able to know its own nature with perfect distinctness.

But what, then, am I? A thinking thing, it has been said. But what is a thinking thing? It is a thing that doubts, understands, conceives, affirms, denies, wills, refuses, that imagines also, and perceives. Assuredly it is not little, if all these properties belong to my nature. But why should they not belong to it? Am I not that very being who now doubts of almost everything; who, for all that, understands and conceives certain things; who affirms one alone as true, and denies the others; who desires to know more of them, and does not wish to be deceived; who imagines many things, sometimes even despite his will; and is likewise percipient of many, as if through the medium of the senses. Is there nothing of all this as true as that I am, even although I should be always dreaming, and although he who gave me being employed all his ingenuity to deceive me? Is there also any one of these attributes that can be properly distinguished from my thought, or that can be said to be separate from myself? For it is of itself so evident that it is I who doubt, I who understand, and I who desire, that it is here unnecessary to add anything by way of rendering it more clear. And I am as certainly the same being who imagines; for, although it may be (as I before supposed) that nothing I imagine is true, still the power of imagination does not cease really to exist in me and to form part of my thought. In fine, I am the same being who perceives, that is, who apprehends certain objects as by the organs of sense, since, in truth, I see light, hear a noise, and feel heat. But it will be said that these presentations are false, and that I am dreaming. Let it be so. At all events it is certain that I seem to see light, hear a noise, and feel heat; this cannot be false, and this is what in me is properly called perceiving, which is nothing else than thinking. From this I begin to know what I am with somewhat greater clearness and distinctness than heretofore.

But, nevertheless, it still seems to me, and I cannot help believing, that corporeal things, whose images are formed by thought, which fall under the senses, and are examined by the same, are known with much greater distinctness than that I know not what part of myself which is not imaginable; although, in truth, it may seem strange to say that I know and comprehend with greater distinctness things whose existence appears to me doubtful, that are unknown, and do not belong to me, than others of whose reality I am persuaded, that are known to me, and appertain to my proper nature; in a word, than myself. But I see clearly what is the state of the case. My mind is apt to wander, and will not yet submit to be restrained within the limits of truth. Let us therefore leave the mind to itself once more, and, according to it every kind of liberty, permit it to consider the objects that appear to it from without, in order that, having afterwards withdrawn it from these gently and opportunely, and fixed it on the consideration of its being and the properties it finds in itself, it may then be the more easily controlled.

Let us now accordingly consider the objects that are commonly thought to be the most easily, and likewise the most distinctly known, viz., the bodies we touch and see; not, indeed, bodies in general, for these general notions are usually somewhat more confused, but one body in particular. Take, for example, this piece of wax; it is quite fresh, having been but recently taken from the bee-hive; it has not yet lost the sweetness of the honey it contained; it still retains somewhat of the odour of the flowers from which it was gathered; its colour, figure, size, are apparent to the sight, it is hard, cold, easily handled; and sounds when struck upon with the finger. In fine, all that contributes to make a body as distinctly known as possible, is found in the one before us. But, while I am speaking, let it be placed near the fire—what remained of the taste exhales, the smell evaporates, the colour changes, its figure is destroyed, its size increases, it becomes liquid, it grows hot, it can hardly be handled, and, although struck upon, it emits no sound. Does the same wax still remain after this change? It must be admitted that it does remain; no one doubts it, or judges otherwise. What, then, was it I knew with so much distinctness in the piece of wax? Assuredly, it could be nothing of all that I observed by means of the senses, since all the things that fell under taste, smell, sight, touch, and hearing are changed, and yet the same wax remains. It was perhaps what I now think, viz., that this wax was neither the sweetness of honey, the pleasant odour of flowers, the whiteness, the figure, nor the sound, but only a body that a little before appeared to me conspicuous under these forms, and which is now perceived under others. But, to speak precisely, what is it that I imagine when I think of it in this way? Let it be attentively considered, and, retrenching all that does not belong to the wax, let us see what remains. There certainly remains nothing, except something extended, flexible, and movable. But what is meant by flexible and movable? Is it not that I imagine that the piece of wax, being round, is capable of becoming square, or of passing from a square into a triangular figure? Assuredly such is not the case, because I conceive that it admits of an infinity of similar changes; and I am, moreover, unable to compass this infinity by imagination, and consequently this conception which I have of the wax is not the product of the faculty of imagination. But what now is this extension? Is it not also unknown? For it becomes greater when the wax is melted, greater when it is boiled, and greater still when the heat increases; and I should not conceive clearly and according to truth, the wax as it is, if I did not suppose that the piece we are considering admitted even of a wider variety of extension than I ever imagined. I must, therefore, admit that I cannot even comprehend by imagination what the piece of wax is, and that it is the mind alone which perceives it. I speak of one piece in particular; for, as to wax in general, this is still more evident. But what is the piece of wax that can be perceived only by the understanding or mind? It is certainly the same which I see, touch, imagine; and, in fine, it is the same which, from the beginning, I believed it to be. But (and this it is of moment to observe) the perception of it is neither an act of sight, of touch, nor of imagination, and never was either of these, though it might formerly seem so, but is simply an intuition of the mind, which may be imperfect and confused, as it formerly was, or very clear and distinct, as it is at present, according as the attention is more or less directed to the elements which it contains, and of which it is composed.

But, meanwhile, I feel greatly astonished when I observe the weakness of my mind, and its proneness to error. For although, without at all giving expression to what I think, I consider all this in my own mind, words yet occasionally impede my progress, and I am almost led into error by the terms of ordinary language. We say, for example, that we see the same wax when it is before us, and not that we judge it to be the same from its retaining the same colour and figure: whence I should forthwith be disposed to conclude that the wax is known by the act of sight, and not by the intuition of the mind alone, were it not for the analogous instance of human beings passing on in the street below, as observed from a window. In this case I do not fail to say that I see the men themselves, just as I say that I see the wax; and yet what do I see from the window beyond hats and cloaks that might cover artificial machines, whose motions might be determined by springs? But I judge that there are human beings from these appearances, and thus I comprehend, by the faculty of judgment alone which is in the mind, what I believed I saw with my eyes.

The man who makes it his aim to rise to knowledge superior to the common, ought to be ashamed to seek occasions of doubting from the vulgar forms of speech: instead, therefore, of doing this, I shall proceed with the matter in hand, and inquire whether I had a clearer and more perfect perception of the piece of wax when I first saw it, and when I thought I knew it by means of the external sense itself, or, at all events, by the comon sense, as it is called, that is, by the imaginative faculty; or whether I rather apprehend it more clearly at present, after having examined with greater care, both what it is, and in what way it can be known. It would certainly be ridiculous to entertain any doubt on this point. For what, in that first perception, was there distinct? What did I perceive which any animal might not have perceived? But when I distinguish the wax from its exterior form, and when, as if I had stripped it of its vestments, I consider it quite naked, it is certain, although some error may still be found in my judgment, that I cannot, nevertheless, thus apprehend it without possessing a human mind.

But, finally, what shall I say of the mind itself, that is, of myself? For as yet I do not admit that I am anything but mind. What, then! I who seem to possess so distinct an apprehension of the piece of wax,—do I not know myself, both with greater truth and certitude, and also much more distinctly and clearly? For if I judge that the wax exists because I see it, it assuredly follows, much more evidently, that I myself am or exist, for the same reason: for it is possible that what I see may not in truth be wax, and that I do not even possess eyes with which to see anything; but it cannot be that when I see, or, which comes to the same thing, when I think I see, I myself who think am nothing. So likewise, if I judge that the wax exists because I touch it, it will still also follow that I am; and if I determine that my imagination, or any other cause, whatever it be, persuades me of the existence of the wax, I will still draw the same conclusion. And what is here remarked of the piece of wax, is applicable to all the other things that are external to me. And further, if the notion or perception of wax appeared to me more precise and distinct, after that not only sight and touch, but many other causes besides, rendered it manifest to my apprehension, with how much greater distinctness must I now know myself, since all the reasons that contribute to the knowledge of the nature of wax, or of any body whatever, manifest still better the nature of my mind? And there are besides so many other things in the mind itself that contribute to the illustration of its nature, that those dependent on the body, to which I have here referred, scarcely merit to be taken into account.

But, in conclusion, I find I have insensibly reverted to the point I desired; for, since it is now manifest to me that bodies themselves are not properly perceived by the senses nor by the faculty of imagination, but by the intellect alone; and since they are not perceived because they are seen and touched, but only because they are understood or rightly comprehended by thought, I readily discover that there is nothing more easily or clearly apprehended than my own mind. But because it is difficult to rid one's self so promptly of an opinion to which one has been long accustomed, it will be desirable to tarry for some time at this stage, that, by long continued meditation, I may more deeply impress upon my memory this new knowledge.

13 TWO KINDS OF KNOWLEDGE
DAVID HUME (1711-1776)

All the objects of human reason or enquiry may naturally be divided into two kinds, to wit, *Relations of Ideas,* and *Matters of Fact.* Of the first kind are the sciences of Geometry, Algebra, and Arithmetic; and in short, every affirmation which is either intuitively or demonstratively certain. *That the square of the hypothenuse is equal to the square of the two sides,* is a proposition which expresses a relation between these figures. *That three times five is equal to the half of thirty,* expresses a relation between these numbers. Propositions of this kind are discoverable by the mere operation of thought, without dependence on what is anywhere existent in the universe. Though there never were a circle or triangle in nature, the truths demonstrated by Euclid would for ever retain their certainty and evidence.

Matters of fact, which are the second objects of human reason, are not ascertained in the same manner; nor is our evidence of their truth, however great, of a like nature with the foregoing. The contrary of every matter of fact is still possible; because it can never imply a contradiction, and is conceived by the mind with the same facility and distinctness, as if ever so conformable to reality. *That the sun will not rise tomorrow* is no less intelligible a proposition, and implies no more contradiction than the affirmation, *that it will rise.* We should in vain, therefore, attempt to demonstrate its falsehood. Were it demonstratively false, it would imply a contradiction, and could never be distinctly conceived by the mind.

It may, therefore, be a subject worthy of curiosity, to enquire what is the

SOURCE: From *An Enquiry Concerning Human Understanding,* 1748, sec. IV, pt. 1. The title of this selection has been supplied by the editors. Compare with selections 22 and 24.

nature of that evidence which assures us of any real existence and matter of fact, beyond the present testimony of our senses, or the records of our memory. This part of philosophy, it is observable, has been little cultivated, either by the ancients or moderns; and therefore our doubts and errors, in the prosecution of so important an enquiry, may be the more excusable; while we march through such difficult paths without any guide or direction. They may even prove useful, by exciting curiosity, and destroying that implicit faith and security, which is the bane of all reasoning and free enquiry. The discovery of defects in the common philosophy, if any such there be, will not, I presume, be a discouragement, but rather an incitement, as is usual, to attempt something more full and satisfactory than has yet been proposed to the public.

All reasonings concerning matter of fact seem to be founded on the relation of *Cause and Effect*. By means of that relation alone we can go beyond the evidence of our memory and senses. If you were to ask a man, why he believes any matter of fact, which is absent; for instance, that his friend is in the country, or in France; he would give you a reason; and this reason would be some other fact; as a letter received from him, or the knowledge of his former resolutions and promises. A man finding a watch or any other machine in a desert island, would conclude that there had once been men in that island. All our reasonings concerning fact are of the same nature. And here it is constantly supposed that there is a connexion between the present fact and that which is inferred from it. Were there nothing to bind them together, the inference would be entirely precarious. The hearing of an articulate voice and rational discourse in the dark assures us of the presence of some person: Why? Because these are the effects of the human make and fabric, and closely connected with it. If we anatomize all the other reasonings of this nature, we shall find that they are founded on the relation of cause and effect, and that this relation is either near or remote, direct or collateral. Heat and light are collateral effects of fire, and the one effect may justly be inferred from the other.

If we would satisfy ourselves, therefore, concerning the nature of that evidence, which assures us of matters of fact, we must enquire how we arrive at the knowledge of cause and effect.

I shall venture to affirm, as a general proposition, which admits of no exception, that the knowledge of this relation is not, in any instance, attained by reasonings *a priori;* but arises entirely from experience, when we find that any particular objects are constantly conjoined with each other. Let an object be presented to a man of ever so strong natural reason and abilities; if that object be entirely new to him, he will not be able, by the most accurate examination of its sensible qualities, to discover any of its causes or effects.

Adam, though his rational faculties be supposed, at the very first, entirely perfect, could not have inferred from the fluidity and transparency of water that it would suffocate him, or from the light and warmth of fire that it would consume him. No object ever discovers, by the qualities which appear to the senses, either the causes which produced it, or the effects which will arise from it; nor can our reason, unassisted by experience, ever draw any inference concerning real existence and matter of fact.

This proposition, *that causes and effects are discoverable, not by reason but by experience,* will readily be admitted with regard to such objects, as we remember to have once been altogether unknown to us; since we must be conscious of the utter inability, which we then lay under, of foretelling what would arise from them. Present two smooth pieces of marble to a man who has no tincture of natural philosophy; he will never discover that they will adhere together in such a manner as to require great force to separate them in a direct line, while they make so small a resistance to a lateral pressure. Such events, as bear little analogy to the common course of nature, are also readily confessed to be known only by experience; nor does any man imagine that the explosion of gunpowder, or the attraction of a loadstone, could ever be discovered by arguments *a priori.* In like manner, when an effect is supposed to depend upon an intricate machinery or secret structure of parts, we make no difficulty in attributing all our knowledge of it to experience. Who will assert that he can give the ultimate reason, why milk or bread is proper nourishment for a man, not for a lion or a tiger?

But the same truth may not appear, at first sight, to have the same evidence with regard to events, which have become familiar to us from our first appearance in the world, which bear a close analogy to the whole course of nature, and which are supposed to depend on the simple qualities of objects, without any secret structure of parts. We are apt to imagine that we could discover these effects by the mere operation of our reason, without experience. We fancy, that were we brought on a sudden into this world, we could at first have inferred that one Billiard-ball would communicate motion to another upon impulse; and that we needed not to have waited for the event, in order to pronounce with certainty concerning it. Such is the influence of custom, that, where it is strongest, it not only covers our natural ignorance, but even conceals itself, and seems not to take place, merely because it is found in the highest degree.

But to convince us that all the laws of nature, and all the operations of bodies without exception, are known only by experience, the following reflections may, perhaps, suffice. Were any object presented to us, and were we required to pronounce concerning the effect, which will result from it, without consulting past observation; after what manner, I beseech you, must the mind proceed in this operation? It must invent or imagine some event, which it ascribes to the object as its effect; and it is plain that this invention must be entirely arbitrary. The mind can never possibly find the effect in the supposed cause, by the most accurate scrutiny and examination. For the effect is totally different from the cause, and consequently can never be discovered in it. Motion in the second Billiard-ball is a quite distinct event from motion in the first; nor is there anything in the one to suggest the smallest hint of the other. A stone or piece of metal raised into the air, and left without any support, immediately falls: but to consider the matter *a priori,* is there anything we discover in this situation which can beget the idea of a downward, rather than an upward, or any other motion, in the stone or metal?

And as the first imagination or invention of a particular effect, in all natural operations, is arbitrary, where we consult not experience; so must we also esteem the supposed tie or connexion between the cause and effect, which binds them together, and renders it impossible that any other effect could result from the operation of that cause. When I see, for instance, a Billiard-ball moving in a straight line towards another; even suppose motion in the second ball should by accident be suggested to me, as the result of their contact or impulse; may I not conceive, that a hundred different events might as well follow from that cause? May not both these balls remain at absolute rest? May not the first ball return in a straight line, or leap off from the second in any line or direction? All these suppositions are consistent and conceivable. Why then should we give the preference to one, which is no more consistent or conceivable than the rest? All our reasonings *a priori* will never be able to show us any foundation for this preference.

In a word, then, every effect is a distinct event from its cause. It could not, therefore, be discovered in the cause, and the first invention or conception of it, *a priori,* must be entirely arbitrary. And even after it is suggested, the conjunction of it with the cause must appear equally arbitrary; since there are always many other effects, which, to reason, must seem fully as consistent and natural. In vain, therefore, should we pretend to determine any single event, or infer any cause or effect, without the assistance of observation and experience. . . .

14 THE FIXATION OF BELIEF
CHARLES SANDERS PEIRCE
(1839-1914)

... We generally know when we wish to ask a question and when we wish to pronounce a judgment, for there is a dissimilarity between the sensation of doubting and that of believing.

But this is not all which distinguishes doubt from belief. There is a practical difference. Our beliefs guide our desires and shape our actions. The Assassins, or followers of the Old Man of the Mountain, used to rush into death at his least command, because they believed that obedience to him would insure everlasting felicity. Had they doubted this, they would not have acted as they did. So it is with every belief, according to its degree. The feeling of believing is a more or less sure indication of there being established in our nature some habit which will determine our actions. Doubt never has such an effect.

Nor must we overlook a third point of difference. Doubt is an uneasy and dissatisfied state from which we struggle to free ourselves and pass into the state of belief; while the latter is a calm and satisfactory state which we do not wish to avoid, or to change to a belief in anything else. On the contrary, we cling tenaciously, not merely to believing, but to believing just what we do believe.

Thus, both doubt and belief have positive effects upon us, though very different ones. Belief does not make us act at once, but puts us into such a condition that we shall behave in a certain way, when the occasion arises. Doubt has not the least effect of this sort, but stimulates us to action until it is destroyed. This reminds us of the irritation of a nerve and the reflex action produced thereby; while for the analogue of belief, in the nervous system, we must look to what are called nervous associations—for example, to that habit of the nerves in consequence of which the smell of a peach will make the mouth water.

The irritation of doubt causes a struggle to attain a state of belief. I shall term this struggle *inquiry,* though it must be admitted that this is sometimes not a very apt designation.

SOURCE: From "The Fixation of Belief," *Popular Science Monthly,* November, 1877; the first of a series of six papers entitled "Illustrations of the Logic of Science." Compare with selections 5, 12, 15, and 53.

The irritation of doubt is the only immediate motive for the struggle to attain belief. It is certainly best for us that our beliefs should be such as may truly guide our actions so as to satisfy our desires; and this reflection will make us reject any belief which does not seem to have been so formed as to insure this result. But it will only do so by creating a doubt in the place of that belief. With the doubt, therefore, the struggle begins, and with the cessation of doubt it ends. Hence, the sole object of inquiry is the settlement of opinion. We may fancy that this is not enough for us, and that we seek not merely an opinion, but a true opinion. But put this fancy to the test, and it proves groundless; for as soon as a firm belief is reached we are entirely satisfied, whether the belief be false or true. And it is clear that nothing out of the sphere of our knowledge can be our object, for nothing which does not affect the mind can be a motive for a mental effort. The most that can be maintained is, that we seek for a belief that we shall *think* to be true. But we think each one of our beliefs to be true, and, indeed, it is mere tautology to say so.

That the settlement of opinion is the sole end of inquiry is a very important proposition. It sweeps away, at once, various vague and erroneous conceptions of proof. A few of these may be noticed here.

1. Some philosophers have imagined that to start an inquiry it was only necessary to utter a question or set it down on paper, and have even recommended us to begin our studies with questioning everything! But the mere putting of a proposition into the interrogative form does not stimulate the mind to any struggle after belief. There must be a real and living doubt, and without this all discussion is idle.

2. It is a very common idea that a demonstration must rest on some ultimate and absolutely indubitable propositions. These, according to one school, are first principles of a general nature; according to another, are first sensations. But, in point of fact, an inquiry, to have that completely satisfactory result called demonstration, has only to start with propositions perfectly free from all actual doubt. If the premises are not in fact doubted at all, they cannot be more satisfactory than they are.

3. Some people seem to love to argue a point after all the world is fully convinced of it. But no further advance can be made. When doubt ceases, mental action on the subject comes to an end; and, if it did go on, it would be without a purpose.

If the settlement of opinion is the sole object of inquiry, and if belief is of the nature of a habit, why should we not attain the desired end, by taking any answer to a question, which we may fancy, and constantly reiterating it to ourselves, dwelling on all which may conduce to that belief, and learning to turn with contempt and hatred from anything which might disturb it? This simple and direct method is really pursued by many men. I remember once being entreated not to read a certain newspaper lest it might change my opinion upon free-trade. "Lest I might be entrapped by its fallacies and misstatements," was the form of expression. "You are not," my friend said, "a special student of political economy. You might, therefore, easily be deceived by fallacious arguments upon the subject. You might, then, if you read this paper, be led to believe in protection. But you admit that free-trade is the true doctrine; and you do not wish to believe what is not true." I have often known this system to be deliberately adopted. Still oftener, the instinctive dislike of an undecided state of mind, exaggerated into a vague dread of doubt, makes men cling spasmodically to the views they already take. The man feels that, if he only holds to his belief without wavering, it will be entirely satisfactory. Nor can it be denied that a steady and immovable faith yields great peace of mind. It may, indeed, give rise to inconveniences, as if a man should resolutely continue to believe that fire would not burn him, or that he would be eternally damned if he received his *ingesta* otherwise than through a stomach pump. But then the man who adopts this method will not allow that its inconveniences are greater than its advantages. He will say, "I hold steadfastly to the truth and the truth is always wholesome." And in many cases it may very well be that the pleasure he derives from his calm faith overbalances any inconveniences resulting from its deceptive character. Thus, if it be true that death is annihilation, then the man who believes that he will certainly go straight to heaven when he dies, provided he have fulfilled certain simple observances in this life, has a cheap pleasure which will not be followed by the least disappointment. A similar consideration seems to have weight with many persons in religious topics, for we frequently hear it said, "Oh, I could not believe so-and-so, because I should be wretched if I did." When an ostrich buries its head in the sand as danger approaches, it very likely takes the happiest course. It hides the danger, and then calmly says there is no danger; and, if it feels perfectly sure there is none, why should it raise its head to see? A man may go through life, systematically keeping out of view all that might cause a change in his opinions, and if he only succeeds —basing his method, as he does, on two fundamental psychological laws— I do not see what can be said against his doing so. It would be an egotistical impertinence to object that his procedure is irrational, for that only amounts to saying that his method of settling belief is not ours. He does not propose to himself to be rational, and indeed, will often talk with scorn of man's weak and illusive reason. So let him think as he pleases.

But this method of fixing belief, which may be called the method of tenacity, will be unable to hold its ground in practice. The social impulse is against it. The man who adopts it will find that other men think differently from him, and it will be apt to occur to him in some saner moment that their opinions are quite as good as his own, and this will shake his confidence in his belief. This conception, that another man's thought or sentiment may be equivalent to one's own, is a distinctly new step, and a highly important one. It arises from an impulse too strong in man to be suppressed, without danger of destroying the human species. Unless we make ourselves hermits, we shall necessarily influence each other's opinions; so that the problem becomes how to fix belief, not in the individual merely, but in the community.

Let the will of the state act, then, instead of that of the individual. Let an institution be created which shall have for its object to keep correct doctrines before the attention of the people, to reiterate them perpetually, and to teach them to the young; having at the same time power to prevent contrary doctrines from being taught, advocated, or expressed. Let all possible causes of a change of mind be removed from men's apprehensions. Let them be kept ignorant, lest they should learn of some reason to think otherwise than they do. Let their passions be enlisted, so that they may regard private and unusual opinions with hatred and horror. Then, let all men who reject the established belief be terrified into silence. Let the people turn out and tar-and-feather such men, or let inquisitions be made into the manner of thinking of suspected persons, and, when they are found guilty of forbidden beliefs, let them be subjected to some signal punishment. When complete agreement could not otherwise be reached, a general massacre of all who have not thought in a certain way has proved a very effective means of settling opinion in a country. If the power to do this be wanting, let a list of opinions be drawn up, to which no man of the least independence of thought can assent, and let the faithful be required to accept all these propositions, in order to segregate them as radically as possible from the influence of the rest of the world.

This method has, from the earliest times, been one of the chief means of upholding correct theological and political doctrines, and of preserving their universal or catholic character. In Rome, especially, it has been practiced from the days of Numa Pompilius to those of Pius Nonus. This is the most perfect example in history; but wherever there is a priesthood—and no religion has been without one—this method has been more or less made use of. Wherever there is aristocracy, or a guild, or any association of a class of men whose interests depend or are supposed to depend on certain propositions, there will be inevitably found some traces of this natural product of social feeling. Cruelties always accompany this system; and when it is consistently carried out, they become atrocities of the most horrible kind in the eyes of any rational man. Nor should this occasion surprise, for the officer of a society does not feel justified in surrendering the interests of that society for the sake of mercy, as he might his own private interests. It is natural, therefore, that sympathy and fellowship should thus produce a most ruthless power.

In judging this method of fixing belief, which may be called the method of authority, we must in the first place, allow its immeasurable mental and moral superiority to the method of tenacity. Its success is proportionally greater; and in fact it has over and over again worked the most majestic results. The mere structures of stone which it has caused to be put together —in Siam, for example, in Egypt, and in Europe—have many of them a sublimity hardly more than rivaled by the greatest works of Nature. And, except the geological epochs, there are no periods of time so vast as those which are measured by some of these organized faiths. If we scrutinize the matter closely, we shall find that there has not been one of their creeds which has remained always the same; yet the change is so slow as to be imperceptible during one person's life, so that individual belief remains sensibly fixed. For the mass of mankind, then, there is perhaps no better method than this. If it is their highest impulse to be intellectual slaves, then slaves they ought to remain.

But no institution can undertake to regulate opinions upon every subject. Only the most important ones can be attended to, and on the rest men's minds must be left to the action of natural causes. This imperfection will be no source of weakness so long as men are in such a state of culture that one opinion does not influence another—that is, so long as they cannot put two and two together. But in the most priest-ridden states some individuals will be found who are raised above that condition. These men possess a wider sort of social feeling; they see that men in other countries and in other ages have held to very different doctrines from those which they themselves have been brought up to believe; and they cannot help seeing that it is the mere accident of their having been taught as they have, and of their having been surrounded with the manners and associations they have, that has caused them to believe as they do and not far differently. And their candor cannot resist the reflection that there is no reason to rate their own views at a higher value than those of other nations and other centuries; and this gives rise to doubts in their minds.

They will further perceive that such doubts as these must exist in their minds with reference to every belief which seems to be determined by the caprice either of themselves or of those who originated the popular opinions. The willful adherence to a belief, and the arbitrary forcing of it upon others, must, therefore, both be given up and a new method of settling opinions must be adopted, which shall not only produce an impulse to believe, but shall also decide what proposition it is which is to be believed. Let the action of natural preferences be unimpeded, then, and under their influence let men conversing together and regarding matters in different lights, gradually develop beliefs in harmony with natural causes. This method resembles that by which conceptions of art have been brought to maturity. The most perfect example of it is to be found in the history of metaphysical philosophy. Systems of this sort have not usually rested upon observed facts, at least not in any great degree. They have been chiefly adopted because their fundamental propositions seemed "agreeable to reason." This is an apt expression; it does not mean that which agrees with experience, but that which we find ourselves inclined to believe. Plato, for example, finds it agreeable to reason that the distances of the celestial spheres from one another should be proportional to the different lengths of strings which produce harmonious chords. Many philosophers have been led to their main conclusions by considerations like this; but this is the lowest and least developed form which the method takes, for it is clear that another man might find Kepler's (earlier) theory, that the celestial spheres are proportional to the inscribed and circumscribed spheres of the different regular solids, more agreeable to *his* reason. But the shock of opinions will soon lead men to rest on preferences of a far more universal nature. Take, for example, the doctrine that man only acts selfishly—that is, from the consideration that acting in one way will afford him more pleasure than acting in another. This rests on no fact in the world, but it has had a wide acceptance as being the only reasonable theory.

This method is far more intellectual and respectable from the point of view of reason than either of the others which we have noticed. But its failure has been the most manifest. It makes of inquiry something similar to the development of taste; but taste, unfortunately, is always more or less a matter of fashion, and accordingly, metaphysicians have never come to any fixed agreement, but the pendulum has swung backward and forward between a more material and a more spiritual philosophy, from the earliest times to the latest. And so from this, which has been called the *a priori* method, we are driven, in Lord Bacon's phrase, to a true induction. We have examined into this *a priori* method as something which promised to deliver our opinions from their accidental and capricious element. But development, while it is a process which eliminates the effect of some casual circumstances, only magnifies that of others. This method, therefore, does not differ in a very essential way from that of authority. The government may not have lifted its finger to influence my convictions; I may have been left outwardly quite free to choose, we will say, between monogamy and polygamy, and appealing to my conscience only, I may have concluded that the latter practice is in itself licentious. But when I come to see that the chief obstacle to the spread of Christianity among a people of as high culture as the Hindoos has been a conviction of the immorality of our way of treating women, I cannot help seeing that, though governments do not interfere, sentiments in their development will be very greatly determined by accidental causes. Now, there are some people, among whom I must suppose that my reader is to be found, who, when they see that any belief of theirs is determined by any circumstance extraneous to the facts, will from that moment not merely admit in words that that belief is doubtful, but will experience a real doubt of it, so that it ceases to be a belief.

To satisfy our doubts, therefore, it is necessary that a method should be found by which our beliefs may be caused by nothing human, but by some external permanency—by something upon which our thinking has no effect. Some mystics imagine that they have such a method in a private inspiration from on high. But that is only a form of the method of tenacity, in which the conception of truth as something public is not yet developed. Our external permanency would not be external, in our sense, if it was restricted in its influence to one individual. It must be something which affects, or might affect, every man. And, though these affections are necessarily as various as are individual conditions, yet the method must be such that the ultimate conclusion of every man shall be the same. Such is the method of science. Its fundamental hypothesis, restated in more familiar language, is this: There are real things, whose characters are entirely independent of our opinions about them; those realities affect our senses according to regular laws, and, though our sensations are as different as our relations to the objects, yet, by taking advantage of the laws of perception, we can ascertain by reasoning how things really are, and any man, if he have sufficient experience and reason enough about it, will be led to the one true conclusion. The new conception here involved is that of reality. It may be asked how I know that there are any realities. If this hypothesis is the sole support of my method of inquiry, my method of inquiry must not be used to support my hypothesis. The reply is this: (1) If investigation cannot be regarded as proving that there are real things, it at least does not lead to a contrary conclusion; but the method and the conception on which it is based remain ever in harmony. No doubts of the method, therefore, necessarily arise from its practice, as is the case with all the others. (2) The feeling which gives rise to any method of fixing belief is a dissatisfaction at two repugnant propositions. But here already is a vague concession that there is some *one* thing to which a proposition should conform. Nobody, therefore, can really doubt that there are realities, or if he did, doubt would not be a source of dissatisfaction. The hypothesis, therefore, is one which every mind admits. So that the social impulse does not cause me to doubt it. (3) Everybody uses the scientific method about a great many things, and only ceases to use it when he does not know how to apply it. (4) Experience of the method has not led me to doubt it, but, on the contrary, scientific investigation has had the most wonderful triumphs in the way of settling opinion. These afford the explanation of my not doubting the method or the hypothesis which it supposes; and not having any doubt, nor believing that anybody else whom I could influence has, it would be the merest babble for me to say more about it. If there be anybody with a living doubt upon the subject, let him consider it.

To describe the method of scientific investigation is the object of this series of papers. At present I have only room to notice some points of contrast between it and other methods of fixing belief.

This is the only one of the four methods which presents any distinction of a right and a wrong way. If I adopt the method of tenacity and shut myself out from all influences, whatever I think necessary to doing this is necessary according to that method. So with the method of authority: the state may try to put down heresy by means which, from a scientific point of view, seem very ill-calculated to accomplish its purposes; but the only test *on that method* is what the state thinks, so that it cannot pursue the method wrongly. So with the *a priori* method. The very essence of it is to think as one is inclined to think. . . . But with the scientific method the case is different. I may start with known and observed facts to proceed to the unknown; and yet the rules which I follow in doing so may not be such as investigation would approve. The test of whether I am truly following the method is not an immediate appeal to my feelings and purposes, but, on the contrary, itself involves the application of the method. Hence it is that bad reasoning as well as good reasoning is possible; and this fact is the foundation of the practical side of logic.

It is not to be supposed that the first three methods of settling opinion present no advantage whatever over the scientific method. On the contrary, each has some peculiar convenience of its own. The *a priori* method is distinguished for its comfortable conclusions. It is the nature of the process to adopt whatever belief we are inclined to, and there are certain flatteries to one's vanities which we all believe by nature, until we are awakened from our pleasing dream by rough facts. The method of authority will always govern the mass of mankind; and those who wield the various forms of organized force in the state will never be convinced that dangerous reasoning ought not to be suppressed in some way. If liberty of speech is to be untrammeled from the grosser forms of constraint, then uniformity of opinion will be secured by a moral terrorism to which the respectability of society will give its thorough approval. Following the method of authority is the path of peace. Certain non-conformities are permitted; certain others (considered unsafe) are forbidden. These are different in different countries and in different ages; but, wherever you are let it be known that you seriously hold a tabooed belief, and you may be perfectly sure of being treated with a cruelty no less brutal but more refined than hunting you like a wolf. Thus, the greatest intellectual benefactors of mankind have never dared, and dare not now, to utter the whole of their thought; and thus a shade of *prima facie* doubt is cast upon every proposition which is considered essential to the security of society. Singularly enough, the persecution does not all come from without; but a man torments himself and is oftentimes most distressed at finding himself believing propositions which he has been brought up to regard with aversion. The peaceful and sympathetic man will, therefore, find it hard to resist the temptation to submit his opinions to authority. But most of all I admire the method of tenacity for its strength, simplicity, and directness. Men who pursue it are distinguished for their decision of character, which becomes very easy with such a mental rule. They do not waste time in trying to make up their minds to what they want, but, fastening like lightning upon whatever alternative comes first, they hold to it to the end, whatever happens, without an instant's irresolution. This is one of the splendid qualities which generally accompany brilliant, unlasting success. It is impossible not to envy the man who can dismiss reason, although we know how it must turn out at last.

Such are the advantages which the other methods of settling opinions have over scientific investigation. A man should consider well of them; and then he should consider that, after all, he wishes his opinions to coincide with the fact, and that there is no reason why the results of these three methods should do so. To bring about this effect is the prerogative of the method of science. Upon such considerations he has to make his choice—a choice which is far more than the adoption of any intellectual opinion, which is one of the ruling decisions of his life, to which when once made he is bound to adhere. The force of habit will sometimes cause a man to hold on to old beliefs, after he is in a condition to see that they have no sound basis. But reflection upon the state of the case will overcome these habits, and he ought to allow reflection full weight. People sometimes shrink from doing this, having an idea that beliefs are wholesome which they cannot help feeling rest on nothing. But let such persons suppose an analogous though different case from their own. Let them ask themselves what they would say to a reformed Mussulman who should hesitate to give up his old notions in regard to the relations of the sexes; or to a reformed Catholic who should still shrink from the Bible. Would they not say that these persons ought to consider the matter fully, and clearly understand the new doctrine, and then ought to embrace it in its entirety? But, above all, let it be considered that what is more wholesome than any particular belief, is integrity of belief; and that to avoid looking into the support of any belief from a fear that it may turn out rotten is quite as immoral as it is disadvantageous. The person who confesses that there is such a thing as truth, which is distinguished from falsehood simply by this, that if acted on it will carry us to the point we aim at and not astray, and then though convinced of this, dares not know the truth and seeks to avoid it, is in a sorry state of mind, indeed.

Yes, the other methods do have their merits: a clear logical conscience does cost something—just as any virtue, just as all that we cherish, costs us dear. But, we should not desire it to be otherwise. The genius of a man's logical method should be loved and reverenced as his bride, whom he has chosen from all the world. He need not condemn the others; on the contrary, he may honor them deeply, and in doing so he only honors her the more. But she is the one that he has chosen, and he knows that he was right in making that choice. And having made it, he will work and fight for her, and will not complain that there are blows to take, hoping that there may be as many and as hard to give, and will strive to be the worthy knight and champion of her from the blaze of whose splendors he draws his inspiration and his courage.

15 THE ETHICS OF BELIEF
W. K. CLIFFORD (1845-1879)

A shipowner was about to send to sea an emigrant-ship. He knew that she was old, and not over-well built at the first; that she had seen many seas and climes, and often had needed repairs. Doubts had been suggested to him that possibly she was not seaworthy. These doubts preyed upon his mind and made him unhappy; he thought that perhaps he ought to have her thoroughly overhauled and refitted, even though this should put him to great expense. Before the ship sailed, however, he succeeded in overcoming these melancholy reflections. He said to himself that she had gone safely through so many voyages and weathered so many storms that it was idle to suppose she would not come safely home from this trip also. He would put his trust in Providence, which could hardly fail to protect all these unhappy families that were leaving their father-land to seek for better times elsewhere. He would dismiss from his mind all ungenerous suspicions about the honesty of builders and contractors. In such ways he acquired a sincere and comfortable conviction that his vessel was thoroughly safe and seaworthy; he watched her departure with a light heart, and benevolent wishes for the success of the

SOURCE: The first part of a three part essay which appeared originally in the *Contemporary Review,* January 1877, and was reprinted in Clifford's posthumous *Lectures and Essays,* 1879. Compare with selections 35 and 36.

exiles in their strange new home that was to be; and he got his insurance-money when she went down in mid-ocean and told no tales.

What shall we say of him? Surely this, that he was verily guilty of the death of those men. It is admitted that he did sincerely believe in the soundness of his ship; but the sincerity of his conviction can in no wise help him, because *he had no right to believe on such evidence as was before him.* He had acquired his belief not by honestly earning it in patient investigation, but by stifling his doubts. And although in the end he may have felt so sure about it that he could not think otherwise, yet inasmuch as he had knowingly and willingly worked himself into that frame of mind, he must be held responsible for it.

Let us alter the case a little, and suppose that the ship was not unsound after all; that she made her voyage safely, and many others after it. Will that diminish the guilt of her owner? Not one jot. When an action is once done, it is right or wrong for ever; no accidental failure of its good or evil fruits can possibly alter that. The man would not have been innocent, he would only have been not found out. The question of right or wrong has to do with the origin of his belief, not the matter of it; not what it was, but how he got it; not whether it turned out to be true or false, but whether he had a right to believe on such evidence as was before him.

There was once an island in which some of the inhabitants professed a religion teaching neither the doctrine of original sin nor that of eternal punishment. A suspicion got abroad that the professors of this religion had made use of unfair means to get their doctrines taught to children. They were accused of wresting the laws of their country in such a way as to remove children from the care of their natural and legal guardians; and even of stealing them away and keeping them concealed from their friends and relations. A certain number of men formed themselves into a society for the purpose of agitating the public about this matter. They published grave accusations against individual citizens of the highest position and character, and did all in their power to injure those citizens in the exercise of their professions. So great was the noise they made, that a Commission was appointed to investigate the facts; but after the Commission had carefully inquired into all the evidence that could be got, it appeared that the accused were innocent. Not only had they been accused on insufficient evidence, but the evidence of their innocence was such as the agitators might easily have obtained, if they had attempted a fair inquiry. After these disclosures the inhabitants of that country looked upon the members of the agitating society, not only as persons whose judgment was to be distrusted, but also as no longer to be counted honourable men. For although they had sincerely and conscientiously believed in the charges they had made, *yet they had no right to believe on such evidence as was before them.* Their sincere convictions, instead of being honestly earned by patient inquiring, were stolen by listening to the voice of prejudice and passion.

Let us vary this case also, and suppose, other things remaining as before, that a still more accurate investigation proved the accused to have been really guilty. Would this make any difference in the guilt of the accusers? Clearly not; the question is not whether their belief was true or false, but whether they entertained it on wrong grounds. They would no doubt say, "Now you see that we were right after all; next time perhaps you will believe us." And they might be believed, but they would not thereby become honourable men. They would not be innocent, they would only be not found out. Every one of them, if he chose to examine himself *in foro conscientiae,* would know that he had acquired and nourished a belief, when he had no right to believe on such evidence as was before him; and therein he would know that he had done a wrong thing.

It may be said, however, that in both of these supposed cases it is not the belief which is judged to be wrong, but the action following upon it. The shipowner might say, "I am perfectly certain that my ship is sound, but still I feel it my duty to have her examined, before trusting the lives of so many people to her." And it might be said to the agitator, "However convinced you were of the justice of your cause and the truth of your convictions, you ought not to have made a public attack upon any man's character until you had examined the evidence on both sides with the utmost patience and care."

In the first place, let us admit that, so far as it goes, this view of the case is right and necessary; right, because even when a man's belief is so fixed that he cannot think otherwise, he still has a choice in regard to the action suggested by it, and so cannot escape the duty of investigating on the ground of the strength of his convictions; and necessary, because those who are not yet capable of controlling their feelings and thoughts must have a plain rule dealing with overt acts.

But this being premised as necessary, it becomes clear that it is not sufficient, and that our previous judgment is required to supplement it. For it is not possible so to sever the belief from the action it suggests as to condemn the one without condemning the other. No man holding a strong belief on one side of a question, or even wishing to hold a belief on one side, can investigate it with such fairness and completeness as if he were really in doubt and unbiassed; so that the existence of a belief not founded on fair inquiry unfits a man for the performance of this necessary duty.

Nor is that truly a belief at all which has not some influence upon the actions of him who holds it. He who truly believes that which prompts him to an action has looked upon the action to lust after it, he has committed it already in his heart. If a belief is not realised immediately in open deeds, it is stored up for the guidance of the future. It goes to make a part of that aggregate of beliefs which is the link between sensation and action at every moment of all our lives, and which is so organised and compacted together that no part of it can be isolated from the rest, but every new addition modifies the structure of the whole. No real belief, however trifling and fragmentary it may seem, is ever truly insignificant; it prepares us to receive more of its like, confirms those which resembled it before, and weakens others; and so gradually it lays a stealthy train in our inmost thoughts, which may some day explode into overt action, and leave its stamp upon our character for ever.

And no one man's belief is in any case a private matter which concerns himself alone. Our lives are guided by that general conception of the course of things which has been created by society for social purposes. Our words, our phrases, our forms and processes and modes of thought, are common property, fashioned and perfected from age to age; an heirloom which every succeeding generation inherits as a precious deposit and a sacred trust to be handed on to the next one, not unchanged but enlarged and purified, with some clear marks of its proper handiwork. Into this, for good or ill, is woven every belief of every man who has speech of his fellows. An awful privilege, and an awful responsibility, that we should help to create the world in which posterity will live.

In the two supposed cases which have been considered, it has been judged wrong to believe on insufficient evidence, or to nourish belief by suppressing doubts and avoiding investigation. The reason of this judgment is not far to seek: it is that in both these cases the belief held by one man was of great importance to other men. But forasmuch as no belief held by one man, however seemingly trivial the belief, and however obscure the believer, is ever actually insignificant or without its effect on the fate of mankind, we have no choice but to extend our judgment to all cases of belief whatever. Belief, that sacred faculty which prompts the decisions of our will, and knits into harmonious working all the compacted energies of our being, is ours not for ourselves, but for humanity. It is rightly used on truths which have been established by long experience and waiting toil, and which have stood in the fierce light of free and fearless questioning. Then it helps to bind men together, and to strengthen and direct their common action. It is desecrated when given to unproved and unquestioned statements, for the solace and private pleasure of the believer; to add a tinsel splendour to the plain straight road of our life and display a bright mirage beyond it; or even to drown the common sorrows of our kind by a self-deception which allows them not only to cast down, but also to degrade us. Whoso would deserve well of his fellows in this matter will guard the purity of his belief with a very fanaticism of jealous care, lest at any time it should rest on an unworthy object, and catch a stain which can never be wiped away.

It is not only the leader of men, statesman, philosopher, or poet, that owes this bounden duty to mankind. Every rustic who delivers in the village alehouse his slow, infrequent sentences, may help to kill or keep alive the fatal superstitions which clog his race. Every hard-worked wife of an artisan may transmit to her children beliefs which shall knit society together, or rend it in pieces. No simplicity of mind, no obscurity of station, can escape the universal duty of questioning all that we believe.

It is true that this duty is a hard one, and the doubt which comes out of it is often a very bitter thing. It leaves us bare and powerless where we thought that we were safe and strong. To know all about anything is to know how to deal with it under all circumstances. We feel much happier and more secure when we think we know precisely what to do, no matter what happens, than when we have lost our way and do not know where to turn. And if we have supposed ourselves to know all about anything, and to be capable of doing what is fit in regard to it, we naturally do not like to find that we are really ignorant and powerless, that we have to begin again at the beginning, and try to learn what the thing is and how it is to be dealt with—if indeed anything can be learnt about it. It is the sense of power attached to a sense of knowledge that makes men desirous of believing, and afraid of doubting.

This sense of power is the highest and best of pleasures when the belief on which it is founded is a true belief, and has been fairly earned by investigation. For then we may justly feel that it is common property, and holds good for others as well as for ourselves. Then we may be glad, not that *I* have learned secrets by which I am safer and stronger, but that *we men* have got mastery over more of the world; and we shall be strong, not for ourselves, but in the name of Man and in his strength. But if the belief has been accepted on insufficient evidence, the pleasure is a stolen one. Not only does it deceive ourselves by giving us a sense of power which we do not really possess, but it is sinful, because it is stolen in defiance of our duty to mankind. That duty is to guard ourselves from such beliefs as from a pestilence, which may shortly master our own body and then spread to the rest of the town. What would be thought of one who, for the sake of a sweet fruit, should deliberately run the risk of bringing a plague upon his family and his neighbours?

And, as in other such cases, it is not the risk only which has to be considered; for a bad action is always bad at the time when it is done, no matter what happens afterwards. Every time we let ourselves believe for unworthy reasons, we weaken our powers of self-control, of doubting, of judicially and fairly weighing evidence. We all suffer severely enough from the maintenance and support of false beliefs and the fatally wrong actions which they lead to, and the evil born when one such belief is entertained is great and wide. But a greater and wider evil arises when the credulous character is maintained and supported, when a habit of believing for unworthy reasons is fostered and made permanent. If I steal money from any person, there may be no harm done by the mere transfer of possession; he may not feel the loss, or it may prevent him from using the money badly. But I cannot help doing this great wrong towards Man, that I make myself dishonest. What hurts society is not that it should lose its property, but that it should become a den of thieves; for then it must cease to be society. This is why we ought not to do evil that good may come; for at any rate this great evil has come, that we have done evil and are made wicked thereby. In like manner, if I let myself believe anything on insufficient evidence, there may be no great harm done by the mere belief; it may be true after all, or I may never have occasion to exhibit it in outward acts. But I cannot help doing this great wrong towards Man, that I make myself credulous. The danger to society is not merely that it should believe wrong things, though that is great enough; but that it should become credulous and lose the habit of testing things and inquiring into them; for then it must sink back into savagery.

The harm which is done by credulity in a man is not confined to the fostering of a credulous character in others, and consequent support of false beliefs. Habitual want of care about what I believe leads to habitual want of care in others about the truth of what is told to me. Men speak the truth to one another when each reveres the truth in his own mind and in the other's mind; but how shall my friend revere the truth in my mind when I myself am careless about it, when I believe things because I want to believe them, and because they are comforting and pleasant? Will he not learn to cry, "Peace," to me, when there is no peace? By such a course I shall surround myself with a thick atmosphere of falsehood and fraud, and in that I must live. It may matter little to me, in my cloud-castle of sweet illusions and darling lies; but it matters much to Man that I have made my neighbours ready to deceive. The credulous man is father to the liar and the cheat; he lives in the bosom of this his family, and it is no marvel if he should become even as they are. So closely are our duties knit together, that whoso shall keep the whole law, and yet offend in one point, he is guilty of all.

To sum up: it is wrong always, everywhere, and for any one, to believe anything upon insufficient evidence.

If a man, holding a belief which he was taught in childhood or persuaded of afterwards, keeps down and pushes away any doubts which arise about it in his mind, purposely avoids the reading of books and the company of men that call in question or discuss it, and regards as impious those questions which cannot easily be asked without disturbing it—the life of that man is one long sin against mankind.

If this judgment seems harsh when applied to those simple souls who have never known better, who have been brought up from the cradle with a horror of doubt, and taught that their eternal welfare depends on what they believe, then it leads to the very serious question, Who hath made Israel to sin? . . .

Inquiry into the evidence of a doctrine is not to be made once for all, and then taken as finally settled. It is never lawful to stifle a doubt; for either it can be honestly answered by means of the inquiry already made, or else it proves that the inquiry was not complete.

"But," says one, "I am a busy man; I have no time for the long course of study which would be necessary to make me in any degree a competent judge of certain questions, or even able to understand the nature of the arguments." Then he should have no time to believe. . . .

16 HUMAN FALLIBILITY
HERBERT SPENCER (1820-1903)

From time to time there returns on the cautious thinker, the conclusion that, considered simply as a question of probabilities, it is unlikely that his views upon any debatable topic are correct. "Here," he reflects, "are thousands around me holding on this or that point opinions differing from mine—wholly in many cases; partially in most others. Each is as confident as I am of the truth of his convictions. Many of them are possessed of great intelligence; and, rank myself high as I may, I must admit that some are my equals—perhaps my superiors. Yet, while every one of us is sure he is right, unquestionably most of us are wrong. Why should not I be among the mistaken? True, I cannot realize the likelihood that I am so. But this proves nothing; for though the majority of us are necessarily in error, we all labour under the inability to think we are in error. Is it not then foolish thus to trust myself? When I look back into the past, I find nations, sects, theologians, philosophers, cherishing beliefs in science, morals, politics, and religion, which we decisively reject. Yet they held them with a faith quite as strong as ours: nay

SOURCE: From the essay "Over-Legislation," first published in *The Westminster Review* for July 1853, and reprinted in Spencer's *Essays: Scientific, Political, and Speculative* (New York: D. Appleton and Company, 1891), pp. 229–31. The title of this selection has been supplied by the editors. Compare with selections 5, 12, and 14.

—stronger, if their intolerance of dissent is any criterion. Of what little worth, therefore, seems this strength of my conviction that I am right! A like warrant has been felt by men all the world through; and, in nine cases out of ten, has proved a delusive warrant. Is it not then absurd in me to put so much faith in my judgments?"

Barren of practical results as this reflection at first sight appears, it may, and indeed should, influence some of our most important proceedings. Though in daily life we are constantly obliged to act out our inferences, trustless as they may be—though in the house, in the office, in the street, there hourly arise occasions on which we may not hesitate; seeing that if to act is dangerous, never to act at all is fatal—and though, consequently, on our private conduct, this abstract doubt as to the worth of our judgments, must remain inoperative; yet, in our public conduct, we may properly allow it to weigh. Here decision is no longer imperative; while the difficulty of deciding aright is incalculably greater. Clearly as we may think we see how a given measure will work, we may infer, drawing the above induction from human experience, that the chances are many against the truth of our anticipations. Whether in most cases it is not wiser to do nothing, becomes now a rational question. Continuing his self-criticism, the cautious thinker may reason:—"If in these personal affairs, where all the conditions of the case were known to me, I have so often miscalculated, how much oftener shall I miscalculate in political affairs, where the conditions are too numerous, too wide-spread, too complex, too obscure to be understood. Here, doubtless, is a social evil and there a desideratum; and were I sure of doing no mischief I would forthwith try to cure the one and achieve the other. But when I remember how many of my private schemes have miscarried—how speculations have failed, agents proved dishonest, marriage been a disappointment—how I did but pauperize the relative I sought to help—how my carefully-governed son has turned out worse than most children—how the thing I desperately strove against as a misfortune did me immense good—how while the objects I ardently pursued brought me little happiness when gained, most of my pleasures have come from unexpected sources; when I recall these and hosts of like facts, I am struck with the incompetence of my intellect to prescribe for society. And as the evil is one under which society has not only lived but grown, while the desideratum is one it may spontaneously obtain, as it has most others, in some unforeseen way, I question the propriety of meddling." . . .

17 IS TRUTH RELATIVE?
WILLIAM PEPPERELL MONTAGUE
(1873-1953)

... There are, I believe, three ... reasons for the growth of ... relativism: (1) its apparent connection with the doctrine of evolution; (2) its apparent connection with the attitude of scepticism; (3) an ambiguity of the term "truth." Let us consider these reasons in turn.

The theory of evolution has made us familiar with the extent to which the universe is pervaded by change; even the things that appear to be most permanent, such as the heavenly bodies, the seas and mountains, and the species of plants and animals, are in a process of change. Human institutions and human beliefs that at one time seemed eternal are now being revised. It is natural for us to suppose that this evolutionary process to which all existing things are subject should extend to the realm of logical meaning; and consequently we tend to regard the notion of an unchangeable system of truth as a relic of the pre-Darwinian age. Yet while the extension of the notion of change from the things of physics to the things of logic may be natural, it is absolutely unjustifiable and leads only to confusion. In the first place, change itself has no meaning unless the terms of the process remain fixed. I cannot speak of a man changing from youth to age, or of a species changing from simian to human, unless the terms "youth," "age," "simian," "human," are supposed to preserve their meanings unchanged. What holds true of logical terms holds true equally of propositions which are relations between terms. If the proposition that the earth has been spherical for the ten billion years prior to the year 1900 is true at this moment, then that proposition will always be true on pain of losing its meaning as a proposition. The earth might change to-morrow from a globe to a disc without changing the truth of the above proposition. In short, the maxims: *True for one, true for all* and *once true, always true,* apply not only to all abstract or non-existential propositions, but to all other propositions in so far as they are made thoroughly unambiguous with respect to the time and space of the facts asserted. Change resides only

SOURCE: From chapter 5, section 3 of *The Ways of Knowing* (1925). Reprinted with the permission of the publisher, George Allen & Unwin Ltd., London. The title of this selection has been supplied by the editors.

in physical processes and in the psychological processes by which we become aware of physical processes. But between those processes and the logical relations which they reveal there is fixed a gulf which no change can cross.

Let us turn now to the second of the three causes for the spread of the doctrine of relativism, *viz.* its connection with scepticism. And here the relativistic pragmatist can make out a somewhat better case. We may imagine him to speak to us as follows: "You talk about an absolute truth, independent of anyone's belief in it or knowledge of it. Well, supposing that there were such a thing, we could never attain it; or at least if we did attain it, we could never recognize it for what it was. All that we can know in the way of truth is something that is believed. Each man calls his own belief by the eulogistic name of *truth,* and with respect to this as an absolute standard, he describes his neighbour's opinions by such uncomplimentary names as 'apparent truths' or 'subjective beliefs.' Consequently, we pragmatists, recognizing this universal shortcoming of human nature, are frank enough to say that there is no truth with a capital T; no absolute impersonal objective reality, not even our own, and that whether we like it or not we have to put up with *the best in the way of belief.* We may still use the word truth in this semi-subjective sense, and it is in this sense that truth is relative to different persons and subject to change."

Now, the only trouble with this reply of the pragmatist is that it is a virtual confession that the relativistic feature of his doctrine, when freed from ambiguities, reduces to pure scepticism. For scepticism is the theory that truth in its objective sense is unattainable by any means within our power. The only difference between pragmatic relativism and scepticism is that the former doctrine uses the word "truth" in a purely subjective sense that is different from the sense in which it is used by the other methodological theories. The thoroughgoing sceptic believes with the relativist that we possess beliefs which we prefer to those of our neighbours, but he gives himself no false verbal comfort by calling these preferred beliefs "truth." He reserves that word for the objective reality which he thinks lies beyond the reach of our knowledge. . . .

The third of the reasons for the popularity of Epistemological relativism may be stated as follows: *All truth depends upon or is in part created by individuals. It is, therefore, inseparable from them and relative to them; and as such, it changes as they change.* Now there are two meanings involved in this statement of relativism which depend upon the two meanings that can be given to the word truth. By "truth" may be meant (1) whatever is believed, or (2) whatever is real or is a fact. If the word is taken in the first or subjective sense, then the relativistic principle that truth changes becomes a truism, for it means only that *people's beliefs change as people's minds change*. If truth is taken in the second or objective sense, the relativistic principle ceases to be a truism and becomes a paradox, for it then means that *the facts or realities of the world change as people's minds change*. We may illustrate the difference by the following example: " 'That the earth is flat' was for the ancients an obvious truth; 'that the earth is round' is for us an established truth. Their truth was not our truth. Truth, therefore, is relative and changing, and what is true for one may be false for another." These statements sound pretty well, and we should probably pass them over unchallenged, because we should take for granted that the word "truth" was being used in its subjective sense as a synonym of belief. It is a truism that people's beliefs can differ, that one can believe what another disbelieves; and it is a commonplace that a change in beliefs took place with regard to the shape of the earth. The ancients believed it to be flat, and we believe it to be round. But if we were told that the author of the statements cited meant "truth" to be taken in the objective sense, we should suppose that he had been indulging in either a geological or a logical paradox. If he meant that the flatness of the earth was a truth (fact) in ancient times and also that its roundness was a truth (fact) in modern times, we should assume that he believed that the earth's shape had undergone a marvellous geological change from a disc to a globe. If in still adhering to the objective meaning of the term "truth" he denied that he intended any such geological absurdity as the above, we should have to assume that he was committing the still greater logical absurdity of supposing that the shape of the earth could be both flat and spherical at once.

The . . . doctrine of the relativity of truth is thus seen to owe some of its plausibility to an ambiguity. Before the ambiguity is revealed, the truism and the paradox conceal one another and unite to produce the appearance of a novel and important discovery. In exactly the same way a black cardboard seen through white tissue paper appears to be a single surface of grey. When we look at the thing edgewise, however, the effect of grey disappears and we see only the black and the white. So, when once we recognize the ambiguity of the term "truth," and insist upon the relativist . . . using the word in one sense or the other, we find only an ill-looking juxtaposition of the paradox that facts depend upon people believing them, and the truism that our beliefs about facts change and vary. In case the illustration chosen fails to satisfy the reader, I would suggest that he make up for himself examples of statements which can loosely be regarded as cases of "truth changing" or of "true for one but false for another," and see for himself whether a little analysis of the meanings involved in all such statements will not disclose the above-mentioned ambiguity or duplicity of the "truth" in question. . . .

18 EPISTEMOLOGICAL SKEPTICISM
C. E. M. JOAD (1891-1953)

... Let us suppose that I am looking at a star, Sirius say, on a dark night. If physics is to be believed, light waves which started to travel from Sirius many years ago reach (after a specified time which astronomers calculate) the earth, impinge upon my retinae and cause me to say that I am seeing Sirius. Now the Sirius about which they convey information to me is the Sirius which existed at the time when they started. This Sirius, may, however, no longer exist; it may have disappeared in the interim. To say that one can see what no longer exists is absurd. It follows that, whatever it is that I am seeing, it is not Sirius. What, in fact, I do see is a yellow patch of a particular size, shape and intensity. I infer that this yellow patch had an origin (with which it is connected by a continuous chain of physical events) several years ago and many million miles away. But this inference may be mistaken; the origin of the yellow patch, which I call a star, may be a blow on the nose, or a lamp hanging on the mast of a ship.

Nor is this the only inference involved. It is true that I *think* I am seeing a yellow patch, but am I really justified in holding this belief? So far as physics and physiology are concerned, all that we are entitled to say is that the optic nerve is being stimulated in a certain way, as a result of which certain events are being caused in the brain. Are we really justified in saying any more than this? Possibly we are ... but it is important to realize that once again an inference is involved, and once again the inference may be mistaken. Directly we go beyond the bare statement "the optic nerve is being stimulated in such and such a way" and conclude from this fact "therefore I am seeing an object of such and such a character," we are drawing an inference and are liable to fall into error. What, then, if the physicist and physiologist are right, we in fact know are certain events taking place in our own brains. The outside world is not itself known; its existence is merely an inference due to the fact that we think these events must have a cause....

If we accept the teaching of physics and physiology, what we know in perception are not the movements of matter, but certain events in ourselves

SOURCE: Excerpted from *Guide to Modern Thought* (London: Faber and Faber, Ltd., 1933), pp. 88–93. Reprinted here with the kind permission of the Executors of the late C. E. M. Joad. The title of this selection has been supplied by the editors. Compare with selections 12, 19, and 21.

connected with those movements; not objects external to ourselves, but the effects of the impact of light-rays and other forms of energy proceeding from these objects upon our bodies. . . .

What, then, is left in the world outside us? We cannot tell. . . .

19 THE WORLD WE PERCEIVE
ARTHUR E. MURPHY (1901-1962)

The contrast between mere ideas and their relations on the one hand and substantial matter of fact on the other is central to the common sense notion of a world we find and do not make, a world to which our ideas must conform if they are to be factually true and informationally reliable. And while common sense has had some very hard things said about it by sophisticated critics, it has the advantage, when it is about its own business, of being both common (that is, publicly sharable and testable) and sensible, which is more than can be said of many of the theories that the critics seek to put in its place. We shall do well, therefore, to start our inquiry from its standpoint, and see how far we can go with it. What is the world we find ourselves living in, the world which, to adapt a famous saying of Bishop Berkeley's, we need only open our eyes to see? The full answer to this question would require all the knowledge that men, starting by opening their eyes and looking, and proceeding by using their minds to inquire, and their eyes and hands again to test their ideas, have been able to accumulate, and all they may still accumulate by the further use of their senses and their minds. Fortunately we need not here undertake so full an answer. For whatever else or more this world may prove to be, it is at least the familiar world that we see with our eyes and handle with our hands, the world in which we move about and greet our friends and live and work together. It is also the world in which we do our thinking, and what we can observe of it provides the clue and the test for beliefs about its more remote and perceptually inaccessible areas. We can construct in our minds a more intellectually coherent world, and wish for a more emotionally satisfying one, but in so far as our wishes and our intellectual constructions claim informational accuracy with respect to what is actually going on, or has occurred, or is likely to happen in this world in which, for better or worse,

SOURCE: From Part I, chapter 1 of *The Uses of Reason*. Copyright 1943 by The Macmillan Company and used with their permission. Compare with selections 12, 18, and 21.

we find ourselves, they must meet the test of truthfulness by agreement with what we find this world to be when and in so far as we are able perceptually to observe it.

It is for this reason that the appeal to *experience,* to what we find when we actually observe things at first hand, as distinct from what we might antecedently think or desire them to be, has so important and honorable a place in the history of critical thought. The empiricists have been preeminently the *fact* men, where "fact" is simply something that is found to be so in tested experience, and their function has been to insist on the informational primacy (for reasonable belief) of what is thus discovered, whether we like it or not, and on the primary importance, for such discovery, of accurate observation through the senses, of what is going on around us. So far they have been plainly right, and we shall be on their side in all that follows. Nor is their doctrine a trivial or merely obvious one. There are indeed truths that a man need only open his eyes to see. But to open one's eyes and see what is there to be seen, honestly, accurately and without the bias of preconception, prejudice or tradition, is an intellectual, and not merely a physiological, achievement. The ability to *learn* by experience, that is, to derive ideas from what we observe and to correct beliefs in terms of what is found to be the case, is the most basic factor in our intellectual progress, when such progress actually occurs. And it involves as its precondition the capacity to see and report what happens in just those cases in which what happens does not agree with antecedent ideas, but stands in contrast to them as mere stubborn matter of fact, *to be* taken account of but not, as it stands, either "rational" or pleasant. It is no wonder, then, that modern philosophers have so often stressed the value of experience and tried to make it the standard for all thinking that pretends to informational accuracy concerning the world and ourselves.

But what do we *really* experience? What is the final and ultimate "given" to which our ideas have added nothing and about which, therefore, we cannot possibly be mistaken? . . . "Experience" in epistemological controversy may mean anything or nothing, and there have been appeals to all sorts of experience—"inner" or "outer," scientific, aesthetic or religious, fallible or infallible—for all sorts of purposes. What we propose to ask instead is what we experience, or are aware of, when we are observing the world perceptually, by seeing, hearing, smelling or handling the things in our more immediate bodily environment. This is *one* of the ways, at least, in which we find out, by observation, what is going on around us, and guide and correct our ideas by what we find. If we can see how experience functions in this capacity as a source of reliable information, we shall have a solid basis on which to proceed. . . .

There are three things about the process of perceptual observation, critically considered as a source of reliable information about ourselves and our bodily environment, that deserve special attention. First, this process, considered as a source of information, not merely as a physiological event, is fallible. Second, it is corrigible, and it is in the process of correction that the difference between reliable and unreliable information is reasonably made out. Third, it is quite ultimate for us as a source of information about the world, since there is no other or better way of finding out what we learn by its means. And what we learn in this way maintains itself, under philosophical scrutiny, as trustworthy information to which belief in other fields, so far as it refers to the same matters of fact, ought reasonably to conform.

First, perceptual observation is fallible. I use my eyes and my hands in observing objects in my bodily environment, and what I observe in this process is what is going on in the world, not what is going on in my body or in my mind when I observe it. And I observe such objects as they look, or feel or smell, under the conditions in which I can observe them; that is, in the relations in which they stand to me at that time. I can see objects under a variety of conditions, with the aid of a microscope or through blue spectacles or when I am so drunk that I cannot make out what they are. But I shall never see objects when I am not seeing them, or think of them when they are not objects of my thought. It has sometimes—rather oddly—been argued that this is proof that I am not "really" seeing them, or at least not seeing them as they "really" are. On the contrary, however, to see things as they look is evidently and naturally the way to see them, no other or better having yet been devised, and if what they "really" are is at all relevant to what as observable objects they are found to be, then it is through just this process that what they really are must be disclosed. It is quite true, however, that things, as thus observed, are not always what they seem. What looks to be a man may prove on inspection to have been a shadow, and the pink rats of drunken experience and epistemological controversy have no local habitation in my bodily environment, though under some conditions they seem to some people to be there. Hence, I must learn to look carefully, and to look again, and to guide my looking by the lessons of past experience, both my own and that of others as reliably reported to me. There is, however, no mystery about this. What we observe are objects and events in our bodily environment as they appear under the conditions in which we *can* observe them, and what they really are, in this context, is what they reliably prove to be on further perceptual inspection. . . .

Hence, secondly, perceptual observation is corrigible, and it is in this process of correction through further and more careful observation that the distinction between what is reliable in it, as information about the world, and what is unreliable appearance is reasonably made out. Those who seek to find in a single instance of such observation the infallible certainty in terms of which alone they can distinguish *real* knowledge from mere opinion, will stare fixedly at the object until it becomes transparent, and all they are aware of in it is what they *can* thus be certain about: the shape or color or feel of it which would be there even if they were drunk or dreaming, and about which there is, as they keep on telling themselves, "no reasonably probable shadow of doubt, no possible doubt whatever." The trouble is that while they will then know *something* certainly—unless, as their critics allege, they have been in error even here—what they know will no longer be a material object but only an impression, or sense-datum, which is not itself an object of perceptual observation at all, or a part of the material world. How to get from such disembodied fragments of epistemologically infallible experience to the outdoor world of men and events is a further problem, but for us a quite gratuitous one. The kind of criticism and correction that perceptual observation requires presupposes no such unprofitable quest for certainty. There are other means of correcting the illusion of the drunkard than that of retreating to a world so tenuous that there is nothing left in it that even a drunkard could be mistaken about. There is the process by which the sober man, or the drunkard when he becomes sober, learns, by observation, what sort of world he lives in. No single observation here is infallible; about any one the question can meaningfully be raised as to whether what is observed is, in fact, what it appears to be. Fortunately, however, while the question can be asked, it can also, sometimes, be answered beyond all reasonable doubt. The process of answering it, reasonably, is the process by means of which ideas are used in the pursuit of truth about the nature and behavior of the world of bodies of which our own bodies are a part. The aim of the rational criticism of belief on this subject is not to halt inquiry at the point at which we claim to know so little about the world that no question of error can arise, but to carry it through to a point at which we know enough to distinguish what is permanently reliable in our observations from what is random, superficial and misleading.

And, thirdly, this process of criticism is sufficient to show that, in the rational ordering of our beliefs, perceptual observation, as a self-correcting process, has a quite ultimate and fundamental place. We know that there is a world of bodies, because we perceive it, because we open our eyes and our minds to find ourselves involved in it and capable of learning the lessons it has to teach. If we did not know it in this way, it would be quite futile to try to "construct" it from private sense data, or deduce it from the necessities of speculative reason, or postulate it as the area in which our duty is to be done. Such constructions, postulations and deductions are familiar enough, but all are shamelessly parasitic on the information which perceptual observation provides about the kind of world we actually live in, the world to which, after many wanderings, their speculations somehow bring them back. There may . . . be much more in the "reality" to which they aspire than perceptual observation can disclose, but there cannot be less. Unless this "more" can be understood along with what we find out perceptually, and interpreted in conformity with its veracious and reliable testimony on the subjects with which it is competent to deal, the doctrine that reports it must remain suspect. What can we reason, but from what we know? And *part* of what we know —or have reliable information about—is the observable nature and behavior of objects in our bodily environment. The use of reason in the acquisition of this information, and the use of this information as a criterion for the credibility and authenticity of further beliefs to which it is pertinent are not the end and sum of human wisdom by any means. But they are somewhere near the beginning of it, and no theory, however exalted its pretensions, which ignores or falsifies their findings, can stand the test of rational examination.

PART IV
METAPHYSICS

20 WHAT IS METAPHYSICS?
A. E. TAYLOR (1869-1945)

§ 1. It is always difficult, in treating of any branch of knowledge, to put before the beginner a correct preliminary notion of the nature and scope of the study to which he is to be introduced, but the difficulty is exceptionally great in the case of the body of investigations traditionally known as Metaphysics.[1] The questions which the science seeks to answer are, indeed, in principle of the simplest and most familiar kind, but it is their very simplicity and familiarity which constitute the chief difficulty of the subject. We are naturally slow to admit that there is anything we do not understand in terms and ideas which we are constantly using, not only in the special sciences, but in our nonsystematised everyday thought and language about the course of the world. Hence, when the metaphysician begins to ask troublesome questions about the meaning and validity of these common and familiar notions, ordinary practical men, and even intelligent students of the special sciences, are apt to complain that he is wasting his time by raising idle and uncalled-for difficulties about the self-evident. Consequently the writer on Metaphysics is almost inevitably compelled to begin by rebutting the natural and current prejudice which regards his science as non-existent and its problems as illusory. The full vindication of metaphysical inquiry from this charge of futility can only be furnished by such a systematic examination of the actual problems of the study as will be attempted, in outline, in the succeeding chapters of this work. All that can be done in an Introduction is to present such a general description of the kind of questions to be subsequently discussed, and their relation to the more special problems of the various sciences, as may incline the reader to give an impartial hearing to what is to follow.

§ 2. The course of our ordinary experience, as well as our education in the rudiments of the sciences, has made us all familiar with the distinction between what really *is* or *exists* and what merely *appears* to be. There is no

---

[1] The name simply means "what comes after Physics," and probably owes its origin to the fact that early editors of Aristotle placed his writings on ultimate philosophical questions immediately after his physical treatises.

SOURCE: Reprinted from *Elements of Metaphysics* (London: Methuen & Co. Ltd., 1903; 13th ed., 1952), pp. 1-13, with the permission of Associated Book Publishers (International) Ltd. The title of this selection has been supplied by the editors. Compare with selection 29.

opposition more thoroughly enshrined in the language and literature of civilised races than the contrast of *seeming* with *reality*, of *substance* with *show*. We come upon it alike in our study of the processes of nature and our experience of human character and purpose. Thus we contrast the seeming stability of the earth with its real motion, the seeming continuity and sameness of a lump of solid matter with the real discontinuity and variety of its chemical constituents, the seeming friendliness of the hypocritical self-seeker with his real indifference to our welfare. In all these cases the motive which leads us to make the distinction is the same, namely, the necessity to escape from the admission of a contradiction in experience. So long as our various direct perceptions are not felt to conflict with one another, we readily accept them all as equally real and valid, and no question arises as to their relative truth or falsehood. Were all our perceptions of this kind, there would be no need for the correction, by subsequent reflection, of our first immediate impressions about the nature of ourselves and the world; error would be a term of no meaning for us, and science would have no existence. But when two immediate perceptions, both apparently equally authenticated by our senses, stand in direct conflict with one another,[2] we cannot, without doing violence to the fundamental law of rational thinking, regard both as equally and in the same sense true. Unless we abandon once for all the attempt to reconcile the course of our experience with the demand of our intellect for consistency in thinking, we are driven to make a momentous distinction. We have to recognise that things are not always what they seem to be; what appears to us is, sometimes at any rate, not real, and what really is does not always appear. Of our two conflicting perceptions, only one at best can be a correct representation of the real course of things; one of them at least, and possibly both, must be mere seeming or appearance, and we are thus cast upon the problem which every science tries, in its own sphere and its own way, to solve: what part of our conceptions about the world gives us reality and what part only appearance?[3] It is because of the importance of these puzzles of immediate perception as stimulating to such scientific reflection that Plato and Aristotle called philosophy the child of Wonder, and it is because the processes of change present them in a peculiarly striking form that the problem of change has always been a central one in Metaphysics.

§ 3. The attempt to harmonise by reflection the contradictions which beset

---

[2] For an example of these puzzles, compare the passage (*Republic*, 524) where Plato refers to cases in which an apparent contradiction in our sensations is corrected by *counting*.
[3] Of course we must not assume that "*every* appearance is *only* appearance," or that "nothing is both reality and appearance." This is just the uncritical kind of preconception which it is the business of Metaphysics to test. Whether "every appearance is only appearance" is a point we shall have to discuss later.

WHAT IS METAPHYSICS?

immediate perception in all its forms is one which is not confined to a single science; the common task of all sciences is to say what, in some special department and for special purposes, must be taken as reality and what as mere appearance, and, by degrading the contradictory to the level of appearance, to satisfy the instinctive demand of our intellect for coherency and consistency of thought. But the development of scientific reflection itself in its turn, while it solves some of our difficulties, is constantly giving rise to fresh perplexities of a higher order. Our scientific principles themselves frequently seem to present us with contradictions of a peculiarly distressing kind. Thus we find ourselves forced in some of our geometrical reasonings to treat a curve as absolutely continuous, in others to regard it as made up of a number of points. Or, again, we are alternately compelled to regard the particles of matter as inert and only capable of being moved by impact from without, and yet again as endowed with indwelling "central forces." Both the opposing views, in such a case, clearly cannot be ultimately true, and we are therefore compelled either to give up the effort to think consistently, or to face the question, Is either view ultimately true, and if so, which? Again, the principles of one branch of study may appear to contradict those of another. For instance, the absolute determination of every movement by a series of antecedent movements which we assume as a principle in our mechanical science, appears, at least, to conflict with the freedom of human choice and reality of human purpose which are fundamental facts for the moralist and the historian; and we have thus once more to ask, which of the two, mechanical necessity or intelligent freedom, is the reality and which the mere appearance? Finally, the results of our scientific reflection sometimes seem to be in violent disagreement with our deepest and most characteristic aspirations and purposes, and we cannot avoid the question, which of the two have the better title to credit as witnesses to the inmost nature of reality?

In all these cases of perplexity there are, short of the refusal to think about our difficulties at all, only two courses open to us. We may answer the question at haphazard and as it suits our momentary caprice, or we may try to answer it on an intelligible principle. If we choose the second course, then clearly before we formulate our principle we must undertake a systematic and impartial inquiry as to what we really mean by the familiar distinction between "seems" and "is," that is to say, a scientific inquiry into the general characteristics by which reality or real being is distinguished from mere appearance, not in some one special sphere of study, but universally. Now, such an inquiry into the general character of reality, as opposed to more or less unreal appearance, is precisely what is meant by Metaphysics. Metaphysics sets itself, more systematically and universally than any other science, to ask what, after all, is meant by being *real*, and to what degree our various scientific and non-scientific theories about the world are in harmony with the universal characteristics of real existence. Hence Metaphysics has been called "an attempt to become aware of and to doubt all preconceptions"; and again, "an unusually resolute effort to think consistently." As we cannot, so long as we allow ourselves to think at all, avoid asking these questions as to what "is" and what only "seems," it is clear that the attempt to dispense with metaphysical speculation altogether would be futile. We have really no choice whether we shall form metaphysical hypotheses or not, only the choice whether we shall do so consciously and in accord with some intelligible principle, or unconsciously and at random.

§ 4. Our preliminary account of the general character of the metaphysician's problem will enable us to distinguish Metaphysics from some other closely related forms of human thought, and to give it at least a provisional place in the general scheme of knowledge. (a) Clearly, Metaphysics, as an inquiry into the meaning of reality, will have some affinity with religion as well as with imaginative literature, both of which aim at getting behind mere appearances and interpreting the reality which lies beneath them. In one important respect its relation to both is closer than that of any other department of knowledge—inasmuch as it, like them, is directly concerned with *ultimate* reality, whereas the special sciences deal each with some one particular aspect of things, and avowedly leave all ultimate questions on one side. Where it differs from both is in its spirit and method. Unlike religion and imaginative literature, Metaphysics deals with the ultimate problems of existence in a purely scientific spirit; its object is *intellectual* satisfaction, and its method is not one of appeal to immediate intuition or unanalysed feeling, but of the critical and systematic analysis of our conceptions. Thus it clearly belongs, in virtue of its spirit and method, to the realm of science. (b) Yet it differs widely in method from the other types of science with which most of us are more familiar. It differs from the mathematical sciences in being non-quantitative and non-numerical in its methods. For we cannot employ the numerical and quantitative methods of Mathematics except on things and processes which admit of measurement, or, at least, of enumeration, and it is for Metaphysics itself, in the course of its investigations, to decide whether what is ultimately real, or any part of it, is numerical or quantitative, and if so, in what sense. It differs, again, from the experimental sciences in that, like Logic and Ethics, it does nothing to increase the stock of our knowledge of particular facts or events, but merely discusses the way in which facts or events are to be interpreted if we wish to think consistently. Its question is not what in detail we must regard as the reality of any special set of processes, but what are the *general* conditions to which all reality, as such, conforms. (Just in the same way, it will be remembered, Logic does not discuss the worth of the evidence for particular scientific theories, but the general conditions to which evidence must conform if it is to prove its conclusion.) Hence Aristotle correctly called Metaphysics a science of being *quà* being, ὄντα ᾗ ὄντα (as opposed, for instance, to Mathematics, which only studies existence in so far as it is quantitative or numerical).

Again, as an attempt to discover and get rid of baseless preconceptions about reality, Metaphysics may, in a sense, be said to be "sceptical." But it differs profoundly from vulgar scepticism both in its method and in its moral purpose. The method of vulgar scepticism is *dogmatic,*—it takes it for granted without inquiry that two perceptions or two speculative principles which conflict with one another must be equally false. Because such contradictions can be detected in all fields of knowledge and speculation, the sceptic dogmatically assumes that there is no means of getting behind these contradictory appearances to a coherent reality. For the metaphysician, on the contrary, the assumption that the puzzles of experience are insoluble and the contradictions in our knowledge irreconcilable is itself just one of those preconceptions which it is the business of his study to investigate and test. Until after critical examination, he refuses to pronounce which of the conflicting views is true, or, supposing both false, whether one may not be nearer the truth than the other. If he does not assume that truth can be got and reality known by our human faculties, he does at any rate assume that it is worth our while to make the attempt, and that nothing but the issue can decide as to its chances of success. Again, the metaphysician differs from the sceptic in respect of moral purpose. Both in a sense preach the duty of a "suspense of judgment" in the face of ultimate problems. The difference is that the sceptic treats "suspense," and the accompanying mental indolence, as an end in itself; the metaphysician regards it as a mere preliminary to his final object, the attainment of determinate truth.

§ 5. We can now see some of the reasons which make the science of Metaphysics a peculiarly difficult branch of study. It is difficult, in the first place, from the very simplicity and generality of its problems. There is a general conviction that every science, if it is to be anything more than a body of disputes about mere words, must deal with some definite subject-matter, and it is not easy to say precisely *what* is the subject dealt with by the metaphysician. In a certain sense this difficulty can only be met by admitting it; it is true, as we have already seen, that Metaphysics deals in some way with everything; thus it is quite right to say that you cannot specify any particular class of objects as its exclusive subject-matter. This must not, however, be understood to mean that Metaphysics is another name for the whole body of the sciences. What it does mean is that precisely because the distinction between the real and the apparent affects every department of our knowledge and enters into every one of the special sciences, the general problem as to the meaning of this distinction and the principle on which it rests cannot be dealt with by any one special science, but must form the subject of an independent inquiry. The parallel with Logic may perhaps help to make this point clearer. It is just because the principles of reasoning and the rules of evidence are, in the last resort, the same for all the sciences, that they have to be made themselves the subject of a separate investigation. Logic, like Metaphysics, deals with everything, not in the sense of being another name for the whole of our knowledge, but in the sense that it, unlike the special sciences, attacks a problem which confronts us in every exercise of our thought. The question of the difference between the two sciences will be discussed in a later section of this chapter.

There are two other minor sources of difficulty, arising out of the universality of the metaphysical problem, which ought perhaps to be mentioned, as they present a serious obstacle to the study of Metaphysics by minds of a certain stamp. In Metaphysics we have no such helps to the imagination as the figures and diagrams which are so useful in many branches of Mathematics; and again, we are, by the nature of the problem, entirely cut off from the aid of physical experiment. All our results have to be reached by the unassisted efforts of thought in the strictest sense of the word, that is, by the rigid and systematic mental analysis of conceptions. Thus Metaphysics stands alone among the sciences, or alone with Logic, in the demand it makes on the student's capacity for sheer hard continuous thought. This may help to explain why men who are capable of excellent work in the domain of mathematical or experimental science sometimes prove incompetent in Metaphysics; and again, why eminent metaphysical ability does not always make its possessor a sound judge of the results and methods of the other sciences.

§ 6. It is now time to consider one or two objections which are very commonly urged against the prosecution of metaphysical studies. It is often asserted, either that (1) such a science is, in its very nature, an impossibility; or (2) that, if possible, it is useless and superfluous, since the other sciences together with the body of our practical experience give us all the truth we need; or, again, (3) that at any rate the science is essentially unprogressive, and that all that can be said about its problems has been said long ago. Now, if any of these popular objections are really sound, it must clearly be a waste of time to study Metaphysics, and we are therefore bound to discuss their force before we proceed any further.

(1) To the objection that a science of Metaphysics is, from the nature of the case, impossible, it would be in principle correct to reply that, as the proverb says, "You never can tell till you try," and that few, if any, of those who urge this objection most loudly have ever seriously made the trial. If any

WHAT IS METAPHYSICS?

one thinks the task not worth his while, he is not called on to attempt it; but his opinion gives him no special claim to sit in judgment on those who think differently of the matter. Still, the anti-metaphysical prejudice is so common, and appears in so many different forms, that it is necessary to exhibit its groundlessness rather more in detail.

(a) It is sometimes maintained that Metaphysics is an impossibility because the metaphysician's problems, in their own nature, admit of no solution. To a meaningless question, of course, there can be no intelligible answer, and it is occasionally asserted, and often insinuated, that the questions of Metaphysics are of this kind. But to call the metaphysician's question a senseless one is as much as to say that there is no meaning in the distinction, which we are all constantly making, between the real and the apparent. If there is any meaning at all in the distinction, it is clearly a necessary as well as a proper question precisely by what marks the one may be distinguished from the other. Our right to raise this question can in fairness only be challenged by an opponent who is prepared to maintain that the contradictions which lead us to make the distinction may themselves be the ultimate truth about things. Now, whether this view is defensible or not, it is clearly not one which we have the right to assume without examination as self-evident; it is itself a metaphysical theory of first principles, and would have to be defended, if at all, by an elaborate metaphysical analysis of the meaning of the concepts "truth" and "reality." Again, the objection, if valid, would tell as much against experimental and mathematical science as against Metaphysics. If the self-contradictory can be true, there is no rational ground for preferring a coherent scientific theory of the world to the wildest dreams of superstition or insanity. Thus we have no escape from the following dilemma. Either there is no rational foundation at all for the distinction between reality and appearance, and then all science is an illusion, or there is a rational foundation for it, and then we are logically bound to inquire into the principle of the distinction, and thus to face the problems of Metaphysics.[4]

(b) What is essentially the same objection is sometimes put in the following form. Metaphysics, it is said, can have no place in the scheme of human knowledge, because all intelligible questions which we can ask about reality must fall within the province of one or other of the "sciences." There are no facts with which some one or other of the sciences does not deal, and there is therefore no room for a series of "metaphysical" inquiries over and above those inquiries which constitute the various sciences. Where there are facts to investigate and intelligible questions to be put, we are, it is contended, in the domain of "science"; where there are none, there can be no knowledge.

---

[4] Cf. F. H. Bradley, *Appearance and Reality*, pp. 1–4.

Plausible as this argument can be made to appear, it is easy to see that it is fallacious. From the point of view of pure Logic it manifestly contains a flagrant fallacy of *petitio principii*. For it simply assumes that there is no "science," in the most universal acceptation of the term—*i.e.* no body of reasoned truth—besides those experimental sciences which have for their object the accumulation and systematisation of facts, and this is the very point at issue between the metaphysician and his critics. What the metaphysician asserts is not that there are facts with which the various special branches of experimental science cannot deal, but that there are questions which can be and ought to be raised about the facts with which they do deal other than those which experimental inquiry can solve. Leaving it entirely to the special sciences to tell us what in particular are the true facts about any given part of the world's course, he contends that we still have to ask the more general question, what we mean by "real" and "fact," and how in general the "real" is to be distinguished from the unreal. To denounce the raising of this question as an attempt to exclude certain events and processes from the "province of science," is simply to misrepresent the issue at stake. Incidentally it may be added, the objection reveals a serious misunderstanding of the true principle of distinction between different sciences. The various sciences differ primarily, not as dealing with different *parts* of the world of reality, but as dealing with the whole of it so far as it can be brought under different *aspects*. They are different, not because they deal with different sets of facts, but because they look at the facts from different points of view. Thus it would be quite wrong to suppose that the difference between e.g., Physics, Physiology, and Psychology, is primarily that each studies a different group of facts. The facts studied may in great part be the same; it is the point of view from which they are regarded by which each of the three sciences is distinguished from the others. Thus every voluntary movement may be looked at either as a link in a series of displacements of mass-particles (Physics), as a combination of muscular contractions initiated from a centre in the cortex of the brain (Physiology), or as a step to the satisfaction of a felt want (Psychology). So Metaphysics does not profess to deal with a certain group of facts lying outside the province of the "sciences," but to deal with the same facts which form that province from a point of view which is not that of the experimental sciences. Its claim to do so can only be overthrown by proving what the criticism we are considering assumes, that there is no intelligible way of looking at the facts besides that of experimental science.

(c) More commonly still the intrinsic intelligibility of the metaphysician's problem is admitted, but our power to solve it denied. There may be, it is said, realities which are more than mere appearance, but at any rate with our human faculties we can know nothing of them. All our knowledge is strictly

WHAT IS METAPHYSICS?

limited to appearances, or, as they are often called, *phenomena*.[5] What lies behind them is completely inaccessible to us, and it is loss of time to speculate about its nature. We must therefore content ourselves with the discovery of general laws or uniformities of the interconnection of phenomena, and dismiss the problem of their real ground as insoluble. This doctrine, technically known as Phenomenalism, enjoys at the present time a widespread popularity, which is historically very largely due to an imperfect assimilation of the negative element in the philosophy of Kant. Its merits as a philosophical theory we may leave for later consideration; at present we are only concerned with it as the alleged ground of objection against the possibility of a science of Metaphysics. As such it has really no cogency whatever. Not only do the supporters of the doctrine constantly contradict their own cardinal assumption (as, for instance, when they combine with the assertion that we can know nothing about ultimate reality, such assertions as that it is a certain and ultimate truth that all "phenomena" are connected by general laws, or that "the course of nature is, without exception, uniform"), but the assumption itself is self-contradictory. The very statement that "we know only phenomena" has no meaning unless we know at least enough about ultimate realities to be sure that they are unknowable. The phenomenalist is committed to the recognition of at least one proposition as an absolute and ultimate truth, namely, the proposition, "I know that whatever I know is mere appearance." And this proposition itself, whatever we may think of its value as a contribution to Philosophy, is a positive theory as to first principles the truth or falsity of which is a proper subject for metaphysical investigation. Thus the arguments by which it has been sought to demonstrate the impossibility of Metaphysics themselves afford unimpeachable evidence of the necessity for the scientific examination of the metaphysical problem.[6]

§ 7. With the other two anti-metaphysical contentions referred to at the beginning of the last section we may deal much more briefly. (2) To the objector who maintains that Metaphysics, if possible, still is useless, because the sciences and the practical experience of life between them already supply us with a coherent theory of the world, devoid of contradictions, we may reply: *(a)* The fact is doubtful. For, whatever may be said by the popularisers of science when they are engaged in composing metaphysical theories for the multitude, the best representatives of every special branch of mathematical

---

[5] I may be pardoned for reminding the reader who may be new to our subject, that "facts" and "processes" are only properly called *phenomena* when it is intended to imply that as they stand they are *not* genuine realities but only the partially misleading appearance of reality which is non-phenomenal or ultra-phenomenal. (We shall do well to avoid the pretentious error of calling the ultra-phenomenal, *as such,* "noumenal.")

[6] *Appearance and Reality,* chap. 12, p. 129 (ed. 1).

and experimental science seem absolutely agreed that ultimate questions as to first principles are outside the scope of their sciences. The scope of every science, they are careful to remind us, is defined by certain initial assumptions, and what does not fall under those assumptions must be treated by the science in question as non-existent. Thus Mathematics is in principle restricted to dealing with the problems of number and quantity; whether there are realities which are in their own nature non-numerical and non-quantitative[7] or not, the mathematician, as mathematician, is not called upon to pronounce; if there are such realities, his science is by its initial assumptions debarred from knowing anything of them. So again with Physics; even if reduced to pure Kinematics, it deals only with displacements involving the dimensions of length and time, and has no means of ascertaining whether or not these dimensions are exhibited by all realities. The notion that the various sciences of themselves supply us with a body of information about ultimate reality is thus, for good reasons, rejected by their soundest exponents, who indeed are usually so impressed with the opposite conviction as to be prejudiced in favour of the belief that the ultimately real is unknowable. *(b)* Again, as we have already seen, the results of physical science, and the beliefs and aspirations which arise in the course of practical experience and take shape in the teachings of poetry and religion, often appear to be in sharp antagonism. "Science" frequently seems to point in one direction, our deepest ethical and religious experience in another. We cannot avoid asking whether the contradiction is only apparent or, supposing it real, what degree of authority belongs to each of the conflicting influences. And, apart from a serious study of Metaphysics, this question cannot be answered. *(c)* Even on the most favourable supposition, that there is no such contradiction, but that science and practical experience together afford a single ultimately coherent theory of the world, it is only after we have ascertained the general characteristics of ultimate reality, and satisfied ourselves by careful analysis that reality, as conceived in our sciences, possesses those characteristics, that we have the right to pronounce our theory finally true. If Metaphysics should turn out in the end to present no fresh view as to the nature of the real, but only to confirm an old one, we should still, as metaphysicians, have the advantage of knowing where we were previously only entitled to conjecture.

(3) The charge of unprogressiveness often brought against our science is easily disproved by careful study of the History of Philosophy. The problems of the metaphysician are no doubt, in a sense, always the same; but this is equally true of the problems of any other science. The methods by which the problems are attacked and the adequacy of the solutions they receive vary,

---

[7]As, for instance, all mental states are, according to certain psychologists, non-quantitative.

from age to age, in close correspondence with the general development of science. Every great metaphysical conception has exercised its influence on the general history of science, and, in return, every important movement in science has affected the development of Metaphysics. Thus the revived interest in mechanical science, and the great progress made in that branch of knowledge which is so characteristic of the seventeenth century, more than anything else determined the philosophical method and results of Descartes; the Metaphysics of Leibnitz were profoundly affected by such scientific influences as the invention of the calculus, the recognition of the importance of *vis viva* in dynamics, the contemporary discoveries of Leuwenhoeck in embryology; while, to come to our own time, the metaphysical speculation of the last half-century has constantly been revolving round the two great scientific ideas of the conservation of energy and the origin of species by gradual differentiation. The metaphysician could not if he would, and would not if he could, escape the duty of estimating the bearing of the great scientific theories of his time upon our ultimate conceptions of the nature of the world as a whole. Every fundamental advance in science thus calls for a restatement and reconsideration of the old metaphysical problems in the light of the new discovery.[8] . . .

[8] The student will find Höffding's *History of Modern Philosophy* (English translation in 2 vols., Macmillan) particularly valuable for the way in which the author brings out the intimate historical connection between the development of Metaphysics and the general progress of science.

21 MIND AND MATTER
GEORGE BERKELEY (1685-1753)

It is evident to anyone who takes a survey of the *objects of human knowledge,* that they are either *ideas* actually imprinted on the senses; or else such as are perceived by attending to the passions and operations of the mind; or lastly, *ideas* formed by help of memory and imagination—either compounding, dividing, or barely representing those originally perceived in the aforesaid ways. By sight I have the ideas of light and colours, with their several degrees and variations. By touch I perceive hard and soft, heat and cold, motion and

SOURCE: From *A Treatise Concerning the Principles of Human Knowledge* (1710), Part I, sections 1–10, 17–21. The title of this selection has been supplied by the editors. Compare with selections 12, 16, 17, and 19.

resistance; and of all these more and less either as to quantity or degree. Smelling furnishes me with odours; the palate with tastes; and hearing conveys sounds to the mind in all their variety of tone and composition.

And as several of these are observed to accompany each other, they come to be marked by one name, and so to be reputed as one *thing*. Thus, for example, a certain colour, taste, smell, figure and consistence having been observed to go together, are accounted one distinct thing, signified by the name apple; other collections of ideas constitute a stone, a tree, a book, and the like sensible things; which as they are pleasing or disagreeable excite the passions of love, hatred, joy, grief, and so forth.

But besides all that endless variety of ideas or objects of knowledge, there is likewise Something which knows or perceives them; and exercises divers operations, as willing, imagining, remembering, about them. This perceiving, active being is what I call *mind, spirit, soul* or *myself*. By which words I do not denote any one of my ideas, but a thing entirely distinct from them, wherein they exist, or, which is the same thing, whereby they are perceived; for the existence of an idea consists in being perceived.

That neither our thoughts, nor passions, nor ideas formed by the imagination, exist without the mind is what everybody will allow. And to me it seems no less evident that the various sensations or ideas imprinted on the Sense, however blended or combined together (that is, whatever objects they compose), cannot exist otherwise than in a mind perceiving them. I think an intuitive knowledge may be obtained of this, by any one that shall attend to what is meant by the term *exist* when applied to sensible things. The table I write on I say exists; that is, I see and feel it: and if I were out of my study I should say it existed; meaning thereby that if I was in my study I might perceive it, or that some other spirit actually does perceive it. There was an odour, that is, it was smelt; there was a sound, that is, it was heard; a colour or figure, and it was perceived by sight or touch. This is all that I can understand by these and the like expressions. For as to what is said of the *absolute* existence of unthinking things, without any relation to their being perceived, that is to me perfectly unintelligible. Their *esse* is *percipi;* nor is it possible they should have any existence out of the minds or thinking things which perceive them.

It is indeed an opinion strangely prevailing amongst men, that houses, mountains, rivers and in a word all sensible objects, have an existence, natural or real, distinct from their being perceived by the understanding. But, with how great an assurance and acquiescence soever this Principle may be entertained in the world, yet whoever shall find in his heart to call it in question may, if I mistake not, perceive it to involve a manifest contradiction. For, what are the aforementioned objects but the things we perceive by sense? and what do we perceive besides our own ideas or sensations? and is it not plainly repugnant that any one of these, or any combination of them, should exist unperceived?

If we thoroughly examine this tenet it will, perhaps, be found at bottom to depend on the doctrine of *abstract ideas*. For can there be a nicer strain of abstraction than to distinguish the existence of sensible objects from their being perceived, so as to conceive them existing unperceived? Light and colours, heat and cold, extension and figures—in a word the things we see and feel—what are they but so many sensations, notions, ideas or impressions on the sense? and is it possible to separate, even in thought, any of these from perception? For my part, I might as easily divide a thing from itself. I may, indeed, divide in my thoughts, or conceive apart from each other, those things which perhaps I never perceived by sense so divided. Thus, I imagine the trunk of a human body without the limbs, or conceive the smell of a rose without thinking on the rose itself. So far, I will not deny, I can abstract; if that may properly be called *abstraction* which extends only to the conceiving separately such objects as it is possible may really exist or be actually perceived asunder. But my conceiving or imagining power does not extend beyond the possibility of real existence or perception. Hence, as it is impossible for me to see or feel anything without an actual sensation of that thing, so is it impossible for me to conceive in my thoughts any sensible thing or object distinct from the sensation or perception of it. . . .

Some truths there are so near and obvious to the mind that a man need only open his eyes to see them. Such I take this important one to be, *viz.* that all the choir of heaven and furniture of the earth, in a word all those bodies which compose the mighty frame of the world, have not any subsistence without a mind; that their *being* is to be perceived or known; that consequently so long as they are not actually perceived by me, or do not exist in my mind, or that of any other created spirit, they must either have no existence at all, or else subsist in the mind of some Eternal Spirit: it being perfectly unintelligible, and involving all the absurdity of abstraction, to attribute to any single part of them an existence independent of a spirit. . . .

From what has been said it is evident there is not any other Substance than *Spirit,* or that which perceives. But, for the fuller proof of this point, let it be considered the sensible qualities are colour, figure, motion, smell, taste and such like, that is, the ideas perceived by sense. Now, for an idea to exist in an unperceiving thing is a manifest contradiction; for to have an idea is all one as to perceive: that therefore wherein colour, figure, and the like qualities exist must perceive them. Hence it is clear there can be no unthinking substance or substratum of those ideas.

But, say you, though the ideas themselves do not exist without the mind, yet there may be things like them, whereof they are copies or resemblances; which things exist without the mind, in an unthinking substance. I answer, an idea can be like nothing but an idea; a colour or figure can be like nothing but another colour or figure. If we look but never so little into our thoughts, we shall find it impossible for us to conceive a likeness except only between our ideas. Again I ask whether those supposed *originals,* or external things, of which our ideas are the pictures or representations, be themselves perceivable or no? If they are, then *they* are ideas, and we have gained our point: but if you say they are not, I appeal to any one whether it be sense to assert a colour is like something which is invisible; hard or soft, is like something which is intangible; and so of the rest.

Some there are who make a distinction betwixt *primary* and *secondary* qualities. By the former they mean extension, figure, motion, rest, solidity or impenetrability, and number; by the latter they denote all other sensible qualities, as colours, sounds, tastes, and so forth. The ideas we have of these last they acknowledge not to be the resemblances of anything existing without the mind, or unperceived: but they will have our ideas of the *primary qualities* to be patterns or images of things which exist without the mind, in an unthinking substance which they call Matter. By Matter, therefore, we are to understand an inert, senseless substance, in which extension, figure, and motion do actually subsist. But it is evident, from what we have already shewn, that extension, figure and motion are only ideas existing in the mind, and that an idea can be like nothing but another idea; and that consequently neither they nor their archetypes can exist in an unperceiving substance. Hence it is plain that the very notion of what is called *Matter* or *corporeal substance* involves a contradiction in it. . . .

They who assert that figure, motion, and the rest of the primary or original qualities do exist without the mind, in unthinking substances, do at the same time acknowledge that colours, sounds, heat, cold, and suchlike secondary qualities, do not; which they tell us are sensations, existing in the mind alone, that depend on and are occasioned by the different size, texture, and motion of the minute particles of matter. This they take for an undoubted truth, which they can demonstrate beyond all exception. Now, if it be certain that those *original* qualities are inseparably united with the other sensible qualities, and not, even in thought, capable of being abstracted from them, it plainly follows that *they* exist only in the mind. But I desire any one to reflect and try whether he can, by any abstraction of thought, conceive the extension and motion of a body without all other sensible qualities. For my own part, I see evidently that it is not in my power to frame an idea of a body extended and moving, but I must withal give it some colour or other sensible quality, which is acknowledged to exist only in the mind. In short, extension, figure, and motion, abstracted from all other qualities, are inconceivable. Where therefore the other sensible qualities are, there must these be also, to wit, in the mind and nowhere else. . . .

If we inquire into what the most accurate philosophers declare themselves to mean by *material substance,* we shall find them acknowledge they have no other meaning annexed to those sounds but the idea of Being in general, together with the relative notion of its supporting accidents. The general idea of Being appeareth to me the most abstract and incomprehensible of all other; and as for its supporting accidents, this . . . cannot be understood in the common sense of those words: it must therefore be taken in some other sense, but what that is they do not explain. So that when I consider the two parts or branches which make the signification of the words *material substance,* I am convinced there is no distinct meaning annexed to them. . . .

But, though it were possible that solid, figured, moveable substances may exist without the mind, corresponding to the ideas we have of bodies, yet how is it possible for us to know this? Either we must know it by Sense or by Reason. As for our senses, by them we have the knowledge only of our sensations, ideas, or those things that are immediately perceived by sense, call them what you will: but they do not inform us that things exist without the mind, or unperceived, like to those which are perceived. This the materialists themselves acknowledge.—It remains therefore that if we have any knowledge at all of external things, it must be by reason inferring their existence from what is immediately perceived by sense. But, what reason can induce us to believe the existence of bodies without the mind, from what we perceive, since the very patrons of Matter themselves do not pretend there is any necessary connection betwixt them and our ideas? I say it is granted on all hands (and what happens in dreams, frensies, and the like, puts it beyond dispute) that it is possible we might be affected with all the ideas we have now, though no bodies existed without resembling them. Hence it is evident the supposition of external bodies is not necessary for the producing our ideas; since it is granted they are produced sometimes, and might possibly be produced always, in the same order we see them in at present, without their concurrence.

But though we might possibly have all our sensations without them, yet perhaps it may be thought easier to conceive and explain the manner of their production, by supposing external bodies in their likeness rather than otherwise; and so it might be at least probable there are such things as bodies that excite their ideas in our minds. But neither can this be said. For, though we give the materialists their external bodies, they by their own confession are never the nearer knowing how our ideas are produced; since they own themselves unable to comprehend in what manner body can act upon spirit, or how it is possible it should imprint any idea in the mind. Hence it is evident the production of ideas or sensations in our minds, can be no reason why we should suppose Matter or corporeal substances; since that is acknowledged to remain equally inexplicable with or without this supposition. If therefore it were possible for bodies to exist without the mind, yet to hold they do so must needs be a very precarious opinion; since it is to suppose, without any reason at all, that God has created innumerable beings that are entirely useless, and serve to no manner of purpose.

In short, if there were external bodies, it is impossible we should ever come to know it; and if there were not, we might have the very same reasons to think there were that we have now. Suppose—what no one can deny possible—an intelligence, without the help of external bodies, to be affected with the same train of sensations or ideas that you are, imprinted in the same order and with like vividness in his mind. I ask whether that intelligence hath not all the reason to believe the existence of Corporeal Substances, represented by his ideas, and exciting them in his mind, that you can possibly have for believing the same thing? Of this there can be no question. Which one consideration were enough to make any reasonable person suspect the strength of whatever arguments he may think himself to have, for the existence of bodies without the mind. . . .

22 IS A CAUSE ALWAYS NECESSARY?

DAVID HUME (1711-1776)

. . . 'Tis a general maxim in philosophy, that *whatever begins to exist, must have a cause of existence.* This is commonly taken for granted in all reasonings, without any proof given or demanded. 'Tis suppos'd to be founded on intuition, and to be one of those maxims, which tho' they may be deny'd with the lips, 'tis impossible for men in their hearts really to doubt of. But if we examine this maxim . . . we shall discover in it no mark of any such intuitive certainty; but on the contrary shall find, that 'tis of a nature quite foreign to that species of conviction. . . .

. . . Here is an argument, which proves at once, that the foregoing proposi-

SOURCE: From Bk. I, Part III, sec. 3 of *A Treatise of Human Nature* (1739). The title of this selection has been supplied by the editors. Compare with selections 13, 24, and 58.

tion is neither intuitively nor demonstrably certain. We can never demonstrate the necessity of a cause to every new existence, or new modification of existence, without shewing at the same time the impossibility there is, that any thing can ever begin to exist without some productive principle; and where the latter proposition cannot be prov'd, we must despair of ever being able to prove the former. Now that the latter proposition is utterly incapable of a demonstrative proof, we may satisfy ourselves by considering, that as all distinct ideas are separable from each other, and as the ideas of cause and effect are evidently distinct, 'twill be easy for us to conceive any object to be non-existent this moment, and existent the next, without conjoining to it the distinct idea of a cause or productive principle. The separation, therefore, of the idea of a cause from that of a beginning of existence, is plainly possible for the imagination; and consequently the actual separation of these objects is so far possible, that it implies no contradiction or absurdity; and is therefore incapable of being refuted by any reasoning from mere ideas; without which 'tis impossible to demonstrate the necessity of a cause.

Accordingly we shall find upon examination, that every demonstration, which has been produc'd for the necessity of a cause, is fallacious and sophistical. All the points of time and place, say some philosophers, in which we can suppose any object to begin to exist, are in themselves equal; and unless there be some cause, which is peculiar to one time and to one place, and which by that means determines and fixes the existence, it must remain in eternal suspence; and the object can never begin to be, for want of something to fix its beginning. But I ask; Is there any more difficulty in supposing the time and place to be fix'd without a cause, than to suppose the existence to be determin'd in that manner? The first question that occurs on this subject is always, *whether* the object shall exist or not: The next, *when* and *where* it shall begin to exist. If the removal of a cause be intuitively absurd in the one case, it must be so in the other: And if that absurdity be not clear without a proof in the one case, it will equally require one in the other. The absurdity, then, of the one supposition can never be a proof of that of the other; since they are both upon the same footing, and must stand or fall by the same reasoning.

The second argument, which I find us'd on this head, labours under an equal difficulty. Every thing, 'tis said, must have a cause; for if any thing wanted a cause, *it* would produce *itself;* that is, exist before it existed; which is impossible. But this reasoning is plainly unconclusive; because it supposes, that in our denial of a cause we still grant what we expressly deny, *viz.,* that there must be a cause; which therefore is taken to be the object itself; and *that,* no doubt, is an evident contradiction. But to say that any thing is produc'd, or to express myself more properly, comes into existence, without a cause, is not to affirm, that 'tis itself its own cause; but on the contrary, in excluding all external causes, excludes *a fortiori* the thing itself which is created. An object, that exists absolutely without any cause, certainly is not its own cause; and when you assert, that the one follows from the other, you suppose the very point in question, and take it for granted, that 'tis utterly impossible any thing can ever begin to exist without a cause, but that upon the exclusion of one productive principle, we must still have recourse to another.

'Tis exactly the same case with the third argument, which has been employ'd to demonstrate the necessity of a cause. Whatever is produc'd without any cause, is produc'd by *nothing;* or in other words, has nothing for its cause. But nothing can never be a cause, no more than it can be something, or equal to two right angles. By the same intuition, that we perceive nothing not to be equal to two right angles, or not to be something, we perceive, that it can never be a cause; and consequently must perceive, that every object has a real cause of its existence.

I believe it will not be necessary to employ many words in shewing the weakness of this argument, after what I have said of the foregoing. They are all of them founded on the same fallacy, and are deriv'd from the same turn of thought. 'Tis sufficient only to observe, that when we exclude all causes we really do exclude them, and neither suppose nothing nor the object itself to be the causes of the existence; and consequently can draw no argument from the absurdity of these suppositions to prove the absurdity of that exclusion . If every thing must have a cause, it follows, that upon the exclusion of other causes we must accept of the object itself or of nothing as causes. But 'tis the very point in question, whether every thing must have a cause or not; and therefore, according to all just reasoning, it ought never to be taken for granted.

They are still more frivolous, who say, that every effect must have a cause, because 'tis imply'd in the very idea of effect. Every effect necessarily presupposes a cause; effect being a relative term, of which cause is the correlative. But this does not prove, that every being must be preceded by a cause; no more than it follows, because every husband must have a wife, that therefore every man must be marry'd. The true state of the question is, whether every object, which begins to exist, must owe its existence to a cause; and this I assert neither to be intuitively nor demonstratively certain, and hope to have prov'd it sufficiently by the foregoing arguments. . . .

23 CRIME AND FREE WILL

CLARENCE DARROW (1857-1938)

... That man is the product of heredity and environment and that he acts as his machine responds to outside stimuli and nothing else, seem amply proven by the evolution and history of man. But, quite aside from this, logic and philosophy must lead to the same conclusions. This is not a universe where acts result from chance. Law is everywhere supreme. Every process of nature and life is a continuous sequence of cause and effect. ...

All the teaching of the world is based on the theory that there is no free will. Why else should children be trained with so much care? Why should they be taught what is right and what is wrong? Why should so much pains be taken in forming habits? To what effect is the storing of knowledge in the brain of the child, except that it may be taught to avoid the wrong and to do the right? Man's every action is caused by motive. Whether his action is wise or unwise, the motive was at least strong enough to move him. If two or more motives pulled in opposite directions, he could not have acted from the weakest but must have obeyed the strongest. The same motives applied to some other machine might have produced an opposite result, but to his particular structure it was all-controlling. How any special motive will affect any special machine must depend upon the relative strength of the motive and make of the machine. It is for this reason that intelligent people have always taken so much pains to fortify the machine, so that it would respond to what they believed was right. To say that one could ever act from the weakest motive would bring chaos and chance into a world of method and order. Even punishment could have no possible effect to deter the criminal after release, or to influence others by the example of the punishment. As well might the kernel of corn refuse to grow upward to the sunlight, and grow downward instead.

Before any progress can be made in dealing with crime the world must fully realize that crime is only a part of conduct; that each act, criminal or otherwise, follows a cause; that given the same conditions the same result will

SOURCE: From *Crime: Its Cause and Treatment* by Clarence Darrow, pp. 34–36. Copyright 1922, 1950 by the publishers, Thomas Y. Crowell Company, New York, and used with their permission. The title of this selection has been supplied by the editors. Compare with selections 11, 24, section IV of 47, and 58.

follow forever and ever; that all punishment for the purpose of causing suffering, or growing out of hatred, is cruel and anti-social; that however much society may feel the need of confining the criminal, it must first of all understand that the act had an all-sufficient cause for which the individual was in no way responsible, and must find the cause of his conduct, and, so far as possible, remove the cause.

24 FREE WILL
JOHN STUART MILL (1806-1873)

1. The question, whether the law of causality applies in the same strict sense to human actions as to other phenomena, is the celebrated controversy concerning the freedom of the will; which, from at least as far back as the time of Pelagius, has divided both the philosophical and religious world. The affirmative opinion is commonly called the doctrine of Necessity, as asserting human volitions and actions to be necessary and inevitable. The negative maintains that the will *is not determined,* like other phenomena, by antecedents, but determines itself; that our volitions are not, properly speaking, the effects of causes, or at least have no causes which they uniformly and implicitly obey. . . .

The former of these opinions is that which I consider the true one; but the misleading terms in which it is often expressed, and the indistinct manner in which it is usually apprehended, have both obstructed its reception, and perverted its influence when received. The metaphysical theory of free-will, as held by philosophers (for the practical feeling of it, common in a greater or less degree to all mankind, is in no way inconsistent with the contrary theory), was invented because the supposed alternative of admitting human actions to be *necessary* was deemed inconsistent with every one's instinctive consciousness, as well as humiliating to the pride and even degrading to the moral nature of man. Nor do I deny that the doctrine, as sometimes held, is open to these imputations; for the misapprehension in which I shall be able to show that they originate, unfortunately is not confined to the opponents of the doctrine, but is participated in by many, perhaps we might say by most, of its supporters.

SOURCE: Part of chapter 2 of Book VI of *A System of Logic* (1843). The title of this selection has been supplied by the editors. Compare with selections 6, 11, 22, and 26.

2. Correctly conceived, the doctrine called Philosophical Necessity is simply this: that, given the motives which are present to an individual's mind, and given likewise the character and disposition of the individual, the manner in which he will act might be unerringly inferred; that if we knew the person thoroughly, and knew all the inducements which are acting upon him, we could foretell his conduct with as much certainty as we can predict any physical event. This proposition I take to be a mere interpretation of universal experience, a statement in words of what every one is internally convinced of. No one who believed that he knew thoroughly the circumstances of any case, and the characters of the different persons concerned, would hesitate to foretell how all of them would act. Whatever degree of doubt he may in fact feel, arises from the uncertainty whether he really knows the circumstances, or the character of some one or other of the persons, with the degree of accuracy required; but by no means from thinking that if he did know these things, there could be any uncertainty what the conduct would be. Nor does this full assurance conflict in the smallest degree with what is called our feeling of freedom. We do not feel ourselves the less free, because those to whom we are intimately known are well assured how we shall will to act in a particular case. We often, on the contrary, regard the doubt what our conduct will be, as a mark of ignorance of our character, and sometimes even resent it as an imputation. The religious metaphysicians who have asserted the freedom of the will, have always maintained it to be consistent with divine foreknowledge of our actions: and if with divine, then with any other foreknowledge. We may be free, and yet another may have reason to be perfectly certain what use we shall make of our freedom. It is not, therefore, the doctrine that our volitions and actions are invariable consequents of our antecedent states of mind, that is either contradicted by our consciousness, or felt to be degrading.

But the doctrine of causation, when considered as obtaining between our volitions and their antecedents, is almost universally conceived as involving more than this. Many do not believe, and very few practically feel, that there is nothing in causation but invariable, certain, and unconditional sequence. There are few to whom mere constancy of succession appears a sufficiently stringent bond of union for so peculiar a relation as that of cause and effect. Even if the reason repudiates, the imagination retains, the feeling of some more intimate connection, of some peculiar tie, or mysterious constraint exercised by the antecedent over the consequent. Now this it is which, considered as applying to the human will, conflicts with our consciousness, and revolts our feelings. We are certain that, in the case of our volitions, there is not this mysterious constraint. We know that we are not compelled, as by a magical spell, to obey any particular motive. We feel, that if we wished to prove that we have the power of resisting the motive, we could do so (that wish being, it needs scarcely be observed, a *new antecedent);* and it would be humiliating to our pride, and (what is of more importance) paralyzing to our desire of excellence, if we thought otherwise. But neither is any such mysterious compulsion now supposed, by the best philosophical authorities, to be exercised by any other cause over its effect. Those who think that causes draw their effects after them by a mystical tie, are right in believing that the relation between volitions and their antecedents is of another nature. But they should go farther, and admit that this is also true of all other effects and their antecedents. If such a tie is considered to be involved in the word Necessity, the doctrine is not true of human actions; but neither is it then true of inanimate objects. It would be more correct to say that matter is not bound by necessity, than that mind is so.

That the free-will metaphysicians, being mostly of the school which rejects Hume's . . . analysis of Cause and Effect, should miss their way for want of the light which that analysis affords, can not surprise us. The wonder is, that the necessitarians, who usually admit that philosophical theory, should in practice equally lose sight of it. The very same misconception of the doctrine called Philosophical Necessity, which prevents the opposite party from recognizing its truth, I believe to exist more or less obscurely in the minds of most necessitarians, however they may in words disavow it. I am much mistaken if they habitually feel that the necessity which they recognize in actions is but uniformity of order, and capability of being predicted. They have a feeling as if there were at bottom a stronger tie between the volitions and their causes; as if, when they asserted that the will is governed by the balance of motives, they meant something more cogent than if they had only said, that whoever knew the motives, and our habitual susceptibilities to them, could predict how we should will to act. They commit, in opposition to their own scientific system, the very same mistake which their adversaries commit in obedience to theirs; and in consequence do really in some instances suffer those depressing consequences which their opponents erroneously impute to the doctrine itself.

3. I am inclined to think that this error is almost wholly an effect of the associations with a word, and that it would be prevented, by forbearing to employ, for the expression of the simple fact of causation, so extremely inappropriate a term as Necessity. That word, in its other acceptations, involves much more than mere uniformity of sequence: it implies irresistibleness. Applied to the will, it only means that the given cause will be followed by the effect, subject to all possibilities of counteraction by other causes; but in common use it stands for the operation of those causes exclusively which

are supposed too powerful to be counteracted at all. When we say that all human actions take place of necessity, we only mean that they will certainly happen if nothing prevents; when we say that dying of want, to those who can not get food, is a necessity, we mean that it will certainly happen whatever may be done to prevent it. The application of the same term to the agencies on which human actions depend, as is used to express those agencies of nature which are really uncontrollable, can not fail, when habitual, to create a feeling of uncontrollableness in the former also. This, however, is a mere illusion. There are physical sequences which we call necessary, as death for want of food or air; there are others which, though as much cases of causation as the former, are not said to be necessary, as death from poison, which an antidote, or the use of the stomach-pump, will sometimes avert. It is apt to be forgotten by people's feelings, even if remembered by their understandings, that human actions are in this last predicament; they are never (except in some cases of mania) ruled by any one motive with such absolute sway that there is no room for the influence of any other. The causes, therefore, on which action depends, are never uncontrollable; and any given effect is only necessary provided that the causes tending to produce it are not controlled. That whatever happens, could not have happened otherwise, unless something had taken place which was capable of preventing it, no one surely needs hesitate to admit. But to call this by the name Necessity is to use the term in a sense so different from its primitive and familiar meaning, from that which it bears in the common occasions of life, as to amount almost to a play upon words. The associations derived from the ordinary sense of the term will adhere to it in spite of all we can do; and though the doctrine of Necessity, as stated by most who hold it is very remote from fatalism, it is probable that most necessitarians are fatalists, more or less, in their feelings.

A fatalist believes, or half believes (for nobody is a consistent fatalist), not only that whatever is about to happen will be the infallible result of the causes which produce it (which is the true necessitarian doctrine), but moreover that there is no use in struggling against it; that it will happen, however we may strive to prevent it. Now, a necessitarian, believing that our actions follow from our characters, and that our characters follow from our organization, our education, and our circumstances, is apt to be, with more or less of consciousness on his part, a fatalist as to his own actions, and to believe that his nature is such, or that his education and circumstances have so moulded his character, that nothing can now prevent him from feeling and acting in a particular way, or at least that no effort of his own can hinder it. In the words of the sect which in our own day has most perseveringly inculcated and most perversely misunderstood this great doctrine, his character is formed *for* him, and not *by* him; therefore his wishing that it had been formed differently is of no use; he has no power to alter it. But this is a grand error. He has, to a certain extent, a power to alter his character. Its being, in the ultimate resort, formed for him, is not inconsistent with its being, in part, formed *by* him as one of the intermediate agents. His character is formed by his circumstances (including among these his particular organization); but his own desire to mould it in a particular way, is one of those circumstances, and by no means one of the least influential. We can not, indeed, directly will to be different from what we are. But neither did those who are supposed to have formed our characters directly will that we should be what we are. Their will had no direct power except over their own actions. They made us what they did make us, by willing, not the end, but the requisite means; and we, when our habits are not too inveterate, can, by similarly willing the requisite means, make ourselves different. If they could place us under the influence of certain circumstances, we, in like manner, can place ourselves under the influence of other circumstances. We are exactly as capable of making our own character, if we will, as others are of making it for us.

Yes (answers the Owenite),* but these words, *"if we will,"* surrender the whole point: since the will to alter our own character is given us, not by any efforts of ours, but by circumstances which we can not help, it comes to us either from external causes, or not at all. Most true: if the Owenite stops here, he is in a position from which nothing can expel him. Our character is formed by us as well as for us; but the wish which induces us to attempt to form it is formed for us; and how? Not, in general, by our organization, nor wholly by our education, but by our experience; experience of the painful consequences of the character we previously had; or by some strong feeling of admiration or aspiration, accidentally aroused. But to think that we have no power of altering our character, and to think that we shall not use our power unless we desire to use it, are very different things, and have a very different effect on the mind. A person who does not wish to alter his character, can not be the person who is supposed to feel discouraged or paralyzed by thinking himself unable to do it. The depressing effect of the fatalist doctrine can only be felt where there *is* a wish to do what that doctrine represents as impossible. It is of no consequence what we think forms our character, when we have no desire of our own about forming it; but it is of great consequence that we should not be prevented from forming such a desire by thinking the attainment impracticable, and that if we have the desire, we should know that the work is not so irrevocably done as to be incapable of being altered.

*A follower of Robert Owen (1771–1858), English reformer and author of an influential book which argued that all human actions have definite causes.

And indeed, if we examine closely, we shall find that this feeling, of our being able to modify our own character *if we wish,* is itself the feeling of moral freedom which we are conscious of. A person feels morally free who feels that his habits or his temptations are not his masters, but he theirs; who, even in yielding to them, knows that he could resist; that were he desirous of altogether throwing them off, there would not be required for that purpose a stronger desire than he knows himself to be capable of feeling. It is of course necessary, to render our consciousness of freedom complete, that we should have succeeded in making our character all we have hitherto attempted to make it; for if we have wished and not attained, we have, to that extent, not power over our own character; we are not free. Or at least, we must feel that our wish, if not strong enough to alter our character, is strong enough to conquer our character when the two are brought into conflict in any particular case of conduct. And hence it is said with truth, that none but a person of confirmed virtue is completely free.

The application of so improper a term as Necessity to the doctrine of cause and effect in the matter of human character, seems to me one of the most signal instances in philosophy of the abuse of terms, and its practical consequences one of the most striking examples of the power of language over our associations. The subject will never be generally understood until that objectionable term is dropped. The free-will doctrine, by keeping in view precisely that portion of the truth which the word Necessity puts out of sight, namely the power of the mind to co-operate in the formation of its own character, has given to its adherents a practical feeling much nearer to the truth than has generally (I believe) existed in the minds of necessitarians. The latter may have had a stronger sense of the importance of what human beings can do to shape the characters of one another; but the free-will doctrine has, I believe, fostered in its supporters a much stronger spirit of self-culture. . . .

25 A DEFENCE OF FREE WILL
C. ARTHUR CAMPBELL (1897-   )

... The problem of free will gets its urgency for the ordinary educated man by reason of its close connection with the conception of moral responsibility. When we regard a man as morally responsible for an act, we regard him as a legitimate object of moral praise or blame in respect of it. But it seems plain that a man cannot be a legitimate object of moral praise or blame for an act unless in willing the act he is in some important sense a "free" agent. Evidently free will in some sense, therefore, is a precondition of moral responsibility. Without doubt it is the realisation that any threat to freedom is thus a threat to moral responsibility—with all that that implies—combined with the knowledge that there are a variety of considerations, philosophic, scientific, and theological, tending to place freedom in jeopardy, that gives to the problem of free will its perennial and universal appeal. And it is therefore in close connection with the question of the conditions of moral responsibility that any discussion of the problem must proceed, if it is not to be academic in the worst sense of the term.

We raise the question at once, therefore, what are the conditions, in respect of freedom, which must attach to an act in order to make it a morally responsible act? It seems to me that the fundamental conditions are two. . . .

The first condition is the universally recognised one that the act must be *self*-caused, *self*-determined. But it is important to accept this condition in its full rigour. The agent must be not merely *a* cause but the *sole* cause of that for which he is deemed morally responsible. If entities other than the self have also a causal influence upon an act, then that act is not one for which we can say without qualification that the *self* is morally responsible. If in respect of it we hold the self responsible at all, it can only be for some feature of the act—assuming the possibility of disengaging such a feature—of which the self *is* the sole cause. I do not see how this conclusion can be evaded. But it has awkward implications which have led not a few people to abandon the notion of individual moral responsibility altogether.

SOURCE: Part of "In Defence of Free Will," an Inaugural Address delivered in the University of Glasgow on April 26th, 1938. Reprinted with the kind permission of the author and the publishers, Jackson, Son & Company, publishers to the University of Glasgow. The title of this selection has been supplied by the editors. Compare with selections 23 and 24.

This first condition, however, is quite clearly not sufficient. It is possible to conceive an act of which the agent is the sole cause, but which is at the same time an act *necessitated* by the agent's nature. . . . In the case of such an act, where the agent could not do otherwise than he did, we must all agree, I think, that it would be inept to say that he *ought* to have done otherwise and is thus morally blameworthy, or *ought not* to have done otherwise and is thus morally praiseworthy. It is perfectly true that we do sometimes hold a person morally responsible for an act, even when we believe that he, being what he now is, virtually could not do otherwise. But underlying that judgement is always the assumption that the person has *come* to be what he now is in virtue of past acts of will in which he *was* confronted by real alternatives, by genuinely open possibilities: and, strictly speaking, it is in respect of these *past* acts of his that we praise or blame the agent *now*. For ultimate analysis, the agent's power of alternative action would seem to be an inexpugnable condition of his liability to moral praise or blame, i.e. of his moral responsibility.

We may lay down, therefore, that an act is a "free" act in the sense required for moral responsibility only if the agent (a) is the sole cause of the act; and (b) could exert his causality in alternative ways. . . . The doctrine which demands, and asserts, the fulfilment of both conditions is the doctrine we call "Libertarianism." . . .

And now, the conditions of free will being defined in these general terms, we have to ask whether human beings are in fact capable of performing free acts; and if so, where precisely such acts are to be found. In order to prepare the way for an answer, it is desirable, I think, that we should get clear at once about the significance of a certain very familiar, but none the less formidable, criticism of free will which . . . the Libertarian has to meet. This is the criticism which bases itself upon the facts of heredity on the one hand and of environment on the other. I may briefly summarise the criticism as follows.

Every historic self has an hereditary nature consisting of a group of inborn propensities, in range more or less common to the race, but specific to the individual in their respective strengths. With this equipment the self just *happens* to be born. Strictly speaking, it antedates the existence of the self proper, i.e. the existence of the self-conscious subject, and it is itself the effect of a series of causes leading back to indefinitely remote antiquity. It follows, therefore, that any of the self's choices that manifests the influence of his hereditary nature is not a choice of which *he*, the actual historic self, is the sole cause. The choice is determined, at least in part, by factors external to the self. The same thing holds good of "environment." Every self is born and bred in a particular physical and social environment, not of his own choosing, which plays upon him in innumerable ways, encouraging this propensity, discouraging that, and so on. Clearly any of the self's choices that manifests the influence of environmental factors is likewise a choice which is determined, at least in part, by factors external to the self. But if we thus grant, as seems inevitable, that heredity and environment are external influences, where shall we find a choice in the whole history of a self that is not subject to external influence? Surely we must admit that every particular act of choice bears the marks of the agent's hereditary nature and environmental nurture; in which case a free act, in the sense of an act determined solely by the self, must be dismissed as a mere chimaera. . . .

The externality of these influences is taken for granted in our reflective practical judgements upon persons. On those occasions when we are in real earnest about giving a critical and considered estimate of a man's moral calibre—as, e.g. in any serious biographical study—we impose upon ourselves as a matter of course the duty of enquiring with scrupulous care into his hereditary propensities and environmental circumstances, with a view to discovering how far his conduct is influenced by these factors. And having traced these influences, we certainly do not regard the result as having no bearing on the question of the man's moral responsibility for his conduct. On the contrary, the very purpose of the enquiry is to enable us, by due appreciation of the *external* influences that affect his conduct, to gain as accurate a view as possible of that which can justly be attributed to the man's own *self-determination*. The allowances that we all of us do in practice make for hereditary and environmental influences in passing judgement on our fellows would be meaningless if we did not suppose these influences to be in a real sense "external" to the self. . . .

We know now that condition (a) is not fulfilled by any act in respect of which inheritance or environment exerts a causal influence. For that type of influence has been shown to be in a real sense external to the self. The free act of which we are in search has therefore got to be one into which influences of this kind do not enter at all. . . .

. . . Our reflective practical judgements on persons, while fully recognising the externality of the influence of heredity and environment, do nevertheless presuppose throughout that there *is something* in conduct which is genuinely self-determined; something which the agent contributes solely on his own initiative, unaffected by external influences; something for which, accordingly, he may justly be held morally responsible. That conviction may, of course, be a false one. But the fact of its wide-spread existence can hardly be without significance for our problem.

Let us proceed, then, by following up this clue. Let us ask, why do human beings so obstinately persist in believing that there is an indissoluble core of purely *self*-originated activity which even heredity and environment are powerless to affect? There can be little doubt, I think, of the answer in general terms. They do so, at bottom, because they feel certain of the existence of such activity from their immediate practical experience of themselves. Nor can there be in the end much doubt, I think, in what function of the self that activity is to be located. There seems to me to be one, and only one, function of the self with respect to which the agent can even pretend to have an assurance of that absolute self-origination which is here at issue. But to render precise the nature of that function is obviously of quite paramount importance: and we can do so, I think, only by way of a somewhat thorough analysis—which I now propose to attempt—of the experiential situation in which it occurs, *viz.* the situation of "moral temptation."

It is characteristic of that situation that in it I am aware of an end A which I believe to be morally right, and also of an end B, incompatible with A, towards which, in virtue of that system of conative dispositions which constitutes my "character" as so far formed, I entertain a strong desire. There may be, and perhaps must be, desiring elements in my nature which are directed to A also. But what gives to the situation its specific character as one of moral temptation is that the urge of our desiring nature towards the right end, A, is felt to be *relatively* weak. We are sure that if our desiring nature is permitted to issue directly in action, it is end B that we shall choose. That is what is meant by saying, as William James does, that end B is "in the line of least resistance" relatively to our conative dispositions. The expression is, of course, a metaphorical one, but it serves to describe, graphically enough, a situation of which we all have frequent experience, *viz.* where we recognise a specific end as that towards which the "set" of our desiring nature most strongly inclines us, and which we shall indubitably choose if no inhibiting factor intervenes.

But inhibiting factors, we should most of us say, *may* intervene: and that in two totally different ways which it is vital to distinguish clearly. The inhibiting factor may be of the nature of another desire (or aversion), which operates by changing the balance of the desiring situation. Though at one stage I desire B, which I believe to be wrong, more strongly than I desire A, which I believe to be right, it may happen that before action is taken I become aware of certain hitherto undiscerned consequences of A which I strongly desire, and the result may be that now not B but A presents itself to me as the end in the line of least resistance. Moral temptation is here overcome by the simple process of ceasing to be a moral temptation.

That is one way, and probably by far the commoner way, in which an inhibiting factor intervenes. But it is certainly not regarded by the self who is confronted by moral temptation as the *only* way. In such situations we all believe, rightly or wrongly, that even although B *continues* to be in the line of least resistance, even although, in other words, the situation remains one with the characteristic marks of moral temptation, we *can* nevertheless align ourselves with A. We can do so, we believe, because we have the power to introduce a new energy, to make what we call an "effort of will," whereby we are able to act contrary to the felt balance of mere desire, and to achieve the higher end despite the fact that it continues to be in the line of greater resistance relatively to our desiring nature. The self in practice believes that it has this power; and believes, moreover, that the decision rests solely with its self, here and now, whether this power be exerted or not.

Now the objective validity or otherwise of this belief is not at the moment in question. I am here merely pointing to its existence as a psychological fact. No amount of introspective analysis, so far as I can see, even tends to disprove that we do as a matter of fact believe, in situations of moral temptation, that it rests with our self absolutely to decide whether we exert the effort of will which will enable us to rise to duty, or whether we shall allow our desiring nature to take its course.

I have now to point out, further, how this act of moral decision, at least in the significance which it has for the agent himself, fulfils in full the two conditions which we found it necessary to lay down at the beginning for the kind of "free" act which moral responsibility presupposes.

For obviously it is, in the first place, an act which the agent believes he could perform in alternative ways. He believes that it is genuinely open to him to put forth effort—in varying degrees, if the situation admits of that—or withhold it altogether. And when he *has* decided—in whatever way—he remains convinced that these alternative courses were really open to him.

It is perhaps a little less obvious, but, I think, equally certain, that the agent believes the second condition to be fulfilled likewise, i.e. that the act of decision is determined *solely* by his self. It appears less obvious, because we all realise that formed character has a great deal to do with the choices that we make; and formed character is, without a doubt, partly dependent on the external factors of heredity and environment. But it is crucial here that we should not misunderstand the precise nature of the influence which formed character brings to bear upon the choices that constitute conduct. No one denies that it determines, at least largely, what things we desire, and again how greatly we desire them. It may thus fairly be said to determine the felt balance of desires in the situation of moral temptation. But all that that amounts to is that formed character prescribes the nature of the situation *within* which the act of moral decision takes place. It does not in the least follow that it has any influence whatsoever in determining the act of decision itself—the decision as to whether we shall exert effort or take the easy course of following the bent of our desiring nature: take, that is to say, the course which, in virtue of the determining influence of our character as so far formed, we feel to be in the line of least resistance.

When one appreciates this, one is perhaps better prepared to recognise the fact that the agent himself in the situation of moral temptation does not, and indeed could not, regard his formed character as having any influence whatever upon his act of decision as such. For the very nature of that decision, as it presents itself to him, is as to whether he will or will not permit his formed character to dictate his action. In other words, the agent distinguishes sharply between the self which makes the decision, and the self which, as formed character, determines not the decision but the situation within which the decision takes place. Rightly or wrongly, the agent believes that through his act of decision he can oppose and transcend his own formed character in the interest of duty. We are therefore obliged to say, I think, that the agent *cannot* regard his formed character as in any sense a determinant of the act of decision as such. The act is felt to be a genuinely creative act, originated by the self *ad hoc,* and by the self alone. . . .

Now in considering the claim to truth of this belief of our practical consciousness, we should begin by noting that the onus of proof rests upon the critic who rejects this belief. Until cogent evidence to the contrary is adduced, we are entitled to put our trust in a belief which is so deeply embedded in our experience as practical beings as to be, I venture to say, ineradicable from it. Anyone who doubts whether it is ineradicable may be invited to think himself imaginatively into a situation of moral temptation as we have above described it, and then to ask himself whether in that situation he finds it possible to *disbelieve* that his act of decision has the characteristics in question. I have no misgivings about the answer. It is possible to disbelieve only when we are thinking abstractly about the situation; not when we are living through it, either actually or in imagination. This fact certainly establishes a strong *prima facie* presumption in favour of the Libertarian position. Nevertheless I agree that we shall have to weigh carefully several criticisms of high authority before we can feel justified in asserting free will as an ultimate and unqualified truth. . . .

I shall begin with one which, though it is a simple matter to show its irrelevance to the Libertarian doctrine as I have stated it, is so extremely popular that it cannot safely be ignored.

The charge made is that the Libertarian view is incompatible with the *predictability* of human conduct. For we do make rough predictions of people's conduct, on the basis of what we know of their character, every day of our lives, and there can be no doubt that the practice, within certain limits, is amply justified by results. Indeed if it were not so, social life would be reduced to sheer chaos. The close relationship between character and conduct which prediction postulates really seems to be about as certain as anything can be. But the Libertarian view, it is urged, by ascribing to the self a mysterious power of decision uncontrolled by character, and capable of issuing in acts inconsistent with character, denies that continuity between character and conduct upon which prediction depends. If Libertarianism is true, prediction is impossible. But prediction *is* possible, therefore Libertarianism is untrue.

My answer is that the Libertarian view is perfectly compatible with prediction within certain limits, and that there is no empirical evidence at all that prediction is in fact possible beyond these limits. The following considerations will, I think, make the point abundantly clear.

(1) There is no question, on our view, of a free will that can will just anything at all. The range of possible choices is limited by the agent's character in every case; for nothing can be an object of possible choice which is not suggested by either the agent's desires or his moral ideals, and these depend on "character" for us just as much as for our opponents. We have, indeed explicitly recognised at an earlier stage that character determines the situation within which the act of moral decision takes place, although not the act of moral decision itself. This consideration obviously furnishes a broad basis for at least approximate predictions.

(2) There is *one* experiential situation, and *one only,* on our view, in which there is any possibility of the act of will not being in accordance with character; *viz.* the situation in which the course which formed character prescribes is a course in conflict with the agent's moral ideal: in other words, the situation of moral temptation. Now this is a situation of comparative rarity. Yet with respect to all other situations in life we are in full agreement with those who hold that conduct is the response of the agent's formed character to the given situation. Why should it not be so? There could be no reason, on our view any more than on another, for the agent even to consider deviating from the course which his formed character prescribes and he most strongly desires, *unless* that course is believed by him to be incompatible with what is right.

(3) Even within that one situation which is relevant to free will, our view can still recognise a certain basis for prediction. In that situation our character as so far formed prescribes a course opposed to duty, and an effort of will is required if we are to deviate from that course. But of course we are all aware that a greater effort of will is required in proportion to the degree in which we have to transcend our formed character in order to will the right. Such action is, as we say, "harder." But if action is "harder" in proportion as it involves deviation from formed character, it seems reasonable to suppose that, on the whole, action will be of rarer occurrence in that same

proportion: though perhaps we may not say that at any level of deviation it becomes flatly impossible. It follows that even with respect to situations of moral temptation we may usefully employ our knowledge of the agent's character as a clue to prediction. It will be a clue of limited, but of by no means negligible, value. It will warrant us in predicting, e.g., of a person who has become enslaved to alcohol, that he is unlikely, even if fully aware of the moral evil of such slavery, to be successful immediately and completely in throwing off its shackles. Predictions of this kind we all make often enough in practice. And there seems no reason at all why a Libertarian doctrine should wish to question their validity.

Now when these three considerations are borne in mind, it becomes quite clear that the doctrine we are defending is compatible with a very substantial measure of predictability indeed. And I submit that there is not a jot of empirical evidence that any larger measure than this obtains in fact.

Let us pass on then to consider a much more interesting and, I think, more plausible criticism. It is constantly objected against the Libertarian doctrine that it is fundamentally *unintelligible*. Libertarianism holds that the act of moral decision is the *self's* act, and yet insists at the same time that it is not influenced by any of those determinate features in the self's nature which go to constitute its "character." But, it is asked, do not these two propositions contradict one another? Surely a *self*-determination which is determination by something other than the self's *character* is a contradiction in terms? What meaning is there in the conception of a "self" in abstraction from its "character"? If you really wish to maintain, it is urged, that the act of decision is not determined by the self's character, you ought to admit frankly that it is not determined by the *self* at all. But in that case, of course, you will not be advocating a freedom which lends any kind of support to moral responsibility; indeed very much the reverse.

Now this criticism, and all of its kind, seem to me to be the product of a simple, but extraordinarily pervasive, error: the error of confining one's self to the categories of the external observer in dealing with the actions of human agents. Let me explain.

It is perfectly true that the stand-point of the external observer, which we are obliged to adopt in dealing with physical processes, does not furnish us with even a glimmering of a notion of what can be meant by an entity which acts causally and yet not through any of the determinate features of its character. So far as we confine ourselves to external observation, I agree that this notion must seem to us pure nonsense. But then we are *not* obliged to confine ourselves to external observation in dealing with the human agent. Here, though here alone, we have the inestimable advantage of being able to apprehend operations from the *inside,* from the stand-point of *living* experience. But if we do adopt this internal stand-point—surely a proper stand-point, and one which we should be only too glad to adopt if we could in the case of other entities—the situation is entirely changed. We find that we not merely can, but constantly do, attach meaning to a causation which is the self's causation but is yet not exercised by the self's character. We have seen as much already in our analysis of the situation of moral temptation. When confronted by such a situation, we saw, we are certain that it lies with our *self* to decide whether we shall let our character as so far formed dictate our action or whether we shall by effort oppose its dictates and rise to duty. We are certain, in other words, that the act is *not* determined by our *character,* while we remain equally certain that the act *is* determined by our *self.*

Or look, for a further illustration . . . to the experience of effortful willing itself, where the act of decision has found expression in the will to rise to duty. In such an experience we are certain that it is our self which makes the effort. But we are equally certain that the effort does not flow from that system of conative dispositions which we call our formed character; for the very function that the effort has for us is to enable us to act against the "line of least resistance," i.e. to act in a way *contrary* to that to which our formed character inclines us.

I conclude, therefore, that those who find the Libertarian doctrine of the self's causality in moral decision inherently unintelligible find it so simply because they restrict themselves, quite arbitrarily, to an inadequate stand-point: a stand-point from which, indeed, a genuinely creative activity, if it existed, never *could* be apprehended. . . .

26 HISTORY AND DETERMINISM
JOHN STUART MILL (1806-1873)

1. . . . The collective series of social phenomena, in other words, the course of history, is subject to general laws, which philosophy may possibly detect. . . .

Among the impediments to the general acknowledgment, by thoughtful minds, of the subjection of historical facts to scientific laws, the most fundamental continues to be that which is grounded on the doctrine of Free Will,

SOURCE: From Bk. VI, ch. 11 of *A System of Logic* (1843). The title of this selection has been supplied by the editors. Compare with selections 24 and 27.

or, in other words, on the denial that the law of invariable Causation holds true of human volitions; for if it does not, the course of history, being the result of human volitions, cannot be a subject of scientific laws, since the volitions on which it depends can neither be foreseen nor reduced to any canon of regularity even after they have occurred. I have discussed this question, as far as seemed suitable to the occasion, in a former chapter, and I only think it necessary to repeat that the doctrine of the Causation of human actions, improperly called the doctrine of Necessity, affirms no mysterious *nexus* or overruling fatality; it asserts only that men's actions are the joint result of the general laws and circumstances of human nature, and of their own particular characters, those characters again being the consequence of the natural and artificial circumstances that constituted their education, among which circumstances must be reckoned their own conscious efforts. Any one who is willing to take (if the expression may be permitted) the trouble of thinking himself into the doctrine as thus stated, will find it, I believe, not only a faithful interpretation of the universal experience of human conduct, but a correct representation of the mode in which he himself, in every particular case, spontaneously interprets his own experience of that conduct.

But if this principle is true of individual man, it must be true of collective man. If it is the law of human life, the law must be realised in history. The experience of human affairs when looked at *en masse,* must be in accordance with it if true, or repugnant to it if false. . . .

The facts of statistics, since they have been made a subject of careful recordation and study, have yielded conclusions, some of which have been very startling to persons not accustomed to regard moral actions as subject to uniform laws. The very events which in their own nature appear most capricious and uncertain, and which in any individual case no attainable degree of knowledge would enable us to foresee, occur, when considerable numbers are taken into the account, with a degree of regularity approaching to mathematical. What act is there which all would consider as more completely dependent on individual character, and on the exercise of individual free will, than that of slaying a fellow-creature? Yet in any large country, the number of murders, in proportion to the population, varies (it has been found) very little from one year to another, and in its variations never deviates widely from a certain average. What is still more remarkable, there is a similar approach to constancy in the proportion of these murders annually committed with every particular kind of instrument. There is a like approximation to identity, as between one year and another, in the comparative number of legitimate and illegitimate births. The same thing is found true of suicides, accidents, and all other social phenomena of which the registration is sufficiently perfect; one of the most curiously illustrative examples being the fact, ascertained by the registers of the London and Paris post-offices, that the number of letters posted which the writers have forgotten to direct is nearly the same, in proportion to the whole number of letters posted, in one year as in another. . . .

This singular degree of regularity *en masse,* combined with the extreme of irregularity in the cases composing the mass, is a felicitous verification *a posteriori* of the law of causation in its application to human conduct. Assuming the truth of that law, every human action, every murder, for instance, is the concurrent result of two sets of causes. On the one part, the general circumstances of the country and its inhabitants; the moral, educational, economical, and other influences operating on the whole people, and constituting what we term the state of civilisation. On the other part, the great variety of influences special to the individual: his temperament, and other peculiarities of organisation, his parentage, habitual associates, temptations, and so forth. If we now take the whole of the instances which occur within a sufficiently large field to exhaust all the combinations of these special influences, or, in other words, to eliminate chance; and if all these instances have occurred within such narrow limits of time that no material change can have taken place in the general influences constituting the state of civilisation of the country, we may be certain that if human actions are governed by invariable laws, the aggregate result will be something like a constant quantity. The number of murders committed within that space and time being the effect partly of general causes which have not varied, and partly of partial causes the whole round of whose variations has been included, will be, practically speaking, invariable.

Literally and mathematically invariable it is not, and could not be expected to be; because the period of a year is too short to include *all* the possible combinations of partial causes, while it is, at the same time, sufficiently long to make it probable that in some years, at least, of every series, there will have been introduced new influences of a more or less general character; such as a more vigorous or a more relaxed police; some temporary excitement from political or religious causes; or some incident generally notorious, of a nature to act morbidly on the imagination. That in spite of these unavoidable imperfections in the data, there should be so very trifling a margin of variation in the annual results, is a brilliant confirmation of the general theory.

? The same considerations which thus strikingly corroborate the evidence of the doctrine that historical facts are the invariable effects of causes, tend equally to clear that doctrine from various misapprehensions. . . . Some persons, for instance, seemingly imagine the doctrine to imply, not merely that the total number of murders committed in a given space and time is entirely the effect of the general circumstances of society, but that every particular murder is so too; that the individual murderer is, so to speak, a mere instrument in the hands of general causes; that he himself has no option, or, if he has, and chose to exercise it, some one else would be necessitated to take his place; that if any one of the actual murderers had abstained from the crime, some person who would otherwise have remained innocent would have committed an extra murder to make up the average. Such a corollary would certainly convict any theory which necessarily led to it of absurdity. It is obvious, however, that each particular murder depends, not on the general state of society only, but on that combined with causes special to the case, which are generally much more powerful; and if these special causes, which have greater influence than the general ones in causing every particular murder, have no influence on the number of murders in a given period, it is because the field of observation is so extensive as to include all possible combinations of the special causes—all varieties of individual character and individual temptation compatible with the general state of society. The collective experiment, as it may be termed, exactly separates the effect of the general from that of the special causes, and shows the net result of the former; but it declares nothing at all respecting the amount of influence of the special causes, be it greater or smaller, since the scale of the experiment extends to the number of cases within which the effects of the special causes balance one another, and disappear in that of the general causes.

I will not pretend that all the defenders of the theory have always kept their language free from this same confusion, and have shown no tendency to exalt the influence of general causes at the expense of special. I am of opinion, on the contrary, that they have done so in a very great degree, and by so doing have encumbered their theory with difficulties, and laid it open to objections which do not necessarily affect it. Some, for example . . . have inferred, or allowed it to be supposed that they inferred, from the regularity in the recurrence of events which depend on moral qualities, that the moral qualities of mankind are little capable of being improved, or are of little importance in the general progress of society, compared with intellectual or economic causes. But to draw this inference is to forget that the statistical tables from which the invariable averages are deduced were compiled from facts occurring within narrow geographical limits, and in a small number of successive years; that is, from a field the whole of which was under the operation of the same general causes, and during too short a time to allow of much change therein. All moral causes but those common to the country generally have been eliminated by the great number of instances taken; and those which are common to the whole country have not varied considerably in the short space of time comprised in the observations. If we admit the supposition that they have varied; if we compare one age with another, or one country with another, or even one part of a country with another, differing in position and character as to the moral elements, the crimes committed within a year give no longer the same, but a widely different numerical aggregate. And this cannot but be the case; for inasmuch as every single crime committed by an individual mainly depends on his moral qualities, the crimes committed by the entire population of the country must depend in an equal degree on their collective moral qualities. To render this element inoperative upon the large scale it would be necessary to suppose that the general moral average of mankind does not vary from country to country, or from age to age; which is not true, and even if it were true, could not possibly be proved by any existing statistics. I do not on this account the less agree in the opinion . . . that the intellectual element in mankind, including in that expression the nature of their beliefs, the amount of their knowledge, and the development of their intelligence, is the predominant circumstance in determining their progress. But I am of this opinion, not because I regard their moral or economical condition either as less powerful or less variable agencies, but because these are in a great degree the consequences of the intellectual condition, and are, in all cases, limited by it . . . The intellectual changes are the most conspicuous agents in history, not from their superior force, considered in themselves, but because practically they work with the united power belonging to all three.

3. There is another distinction often neglected in the discussion of this subject, which it is extremely important to observe. The theory of the subjection of social progress to invariable laws is often held in conjunction with the doctrine that social progress cannot be materially influenced by the exertions of individual persons or by the acts of governments. But though these opinions are often held by the same persons, they are two very different opinions, and the confusion between them is the eternally recurring error of confounding Causation with Fatalism. Because whatever happens will be the effect of causes, human volitions among the rest, it does not follow that volitions, even those of peculiar individuals, are not of great efficacy as causes. If any one in a storm at sea, because about the same number of persons in every year perish by shipwreck, should conclude that it was useless for him to attempt to save his own life, we should call him a Fatalist, and should remind him that the efforts of shipwrecked persons to save their lives are so far from being immaterial, that the average amount of those efforts is one of the causes on which the ascertained annual number of deaths by shipwreck depend. However universal the laws of social development may be, they cannot be more universal or more rigorous than those of the physical agencies of nature; yet

human will can convert these into instruments of its designs, and the extent to which it does so makes the chief difference between savages and the most highly civilised people. Human and social facts, from their more complicated nature, are not less, but more, modifiable than mechanical and chemical facts; human agency, therefore, has still greater power over them. And accordingly, those who maintain that the evolution of society depends exclusively, or almost exclusively, on general causes, always include among these the collective knowledge and intellectual development of the race. But if of the race, why not also of some powerful monarch or thinker, or of the ruling portion of some political society, acting through its government? Though the varieties of character among ordinary individuals neutralise one another on any large scale, exceptional individuals in important positions do not in any given age neutralise one another; there was not another Themistocles, or Luther, or Julius Caesar, of equal powers and contrary dispositions, who exactly balances the given Themistocles, Luther, and Caesar, and prevented them from having any permanent effect. Moreover, for aught that appears, the volitions of exceptional persons, or the opinions and purposes of the individuals who at some particular time compose a government, may be indispensable links in the chain of causation by which even the general causes produce their effects; and I believe this to be the only tenable form of the theory.

Lord Macaulay, in a celebrated passage of one of his early essays (let me add that it was one which he did not himself choose to reprint), gives expression to the doctrine of the absolute inoperativeness of great men, more unqualified, I should think, than has been given to it by any writer of equal abilities. He compares them to persons who merely stand on a loftier height, and thence receive the sun's rays a little earlier than the rest of the human race. "The sun illuminates the hills while it is still below the horizon, and truth is discovered by the highest minds a little before it becomes manifest to the multitude. This is the extent of their superiority. They are the first to catch and reflect a light which, without their assistance, must in a short time be visible to those who lie far beneath them." If this metaphor is to be carried out, it follows that if there had been no Newton the world would not only have had the Newtonian system, but would have had it equally soon, as the sun would have risen just as early to spectators in the plain if there had been no mountain at hand to catch still earlier rays. And so it would be if truths, like the sun, rose by their own proper motion, without human effort, but not otherwise. I believe that if Newton had not lived, the world must have waited for the Newtonian philosophy until there had been another Newton or his equivalent. No ordinary man, and no succession of ordinary men, could have achieved it. I will not go the length of saying that what Newton did in a single life might not have been done in successive steps by some of those who followed him, each singly inferior to him in genius. But even the least of those steps required a man of great intellectual superiority. Eminent men do not merely see the coming light from the hill-top; they mount on the hill-top and evoke it; and if no one had ever ascended thither, the light, in many cases, might never have risen upon the plain at all. Philosophy and religion are abundantly amenable to general causes; yet few will doubt that had there been no Socrates, no Plato, and no Aristotle, there would have been no philosophy for the next two thousand years, nor in all probability then; and that if there had been no Christ and no St. Paul, there would have been no Christianity.

The point in which, above all, the influence of remarkable individuals is decisive, is in determining the celerity of the movement. In most states of society it is the existence of great men which decides even whether there shall be any progress. It is conceivable that Greece, or that Christian Europe, might have been progressive in certain periods of their history through general causes only; but if there had been no Mahomet, would Arabia have produced Avicenna or Averroes, or Caliphs of Bagdad or of Cordova? In determining, however, in what manner and order the progress of mankind shall take place, if it take place at all, much less depends on the character of individuals. There is a sort of necessity established in this respect by the general laws of human nature, by the constitution of the human mind. Certain truths cannot be discovered or inventions made unless certain others have been made first; certain social improvements, from the nature of the case, can only follow, and not precede, others. The order of human progress, therefore, may to a certain extent have definite laws assigned to it; while as to its celerity, or even as to its taking place at all, no generalisation, extending to the human species generally, can possibly be made, but only some very precarious approximate generalisations, confined to the small portion of mankind in whom there has been anything like consecutive progress within the historical period, and deduced from their special position, or collected from their particular history. Even looking to the *manner* of progress, the order of succession of social states, there is no need of great flexibility in our generalisations. The limits of variation in the possible development of social, as of animal life, are a subject of which little is yet understood, and are one of the great problems in social science. It is, at all events, a fact that different portions of mankind, under the influence of different circumstances, have developed themselves in a more or less different manner and into different forms; and among these determining circumstances, the individual character of their great speculative thinkers or practical organisers may well have been one. Who can tell how profoundly the whole subsequent history of China may have been influenced by the

HISTORY AND DETERMINISM

individuality of Confucius? and of Sparta (and hence of Greece and the world) by that of Lycurgus?

Concerning the nature and extent of what a great man under favourable circumstances can do for mankind, as well as of what a government can do for a nation, many different opinions are possible; and every shade of opinion on these points is consistent with the fullest recognition that there are invariable laws of historical phenomena. Of course the degree of influence which has to be assigned to these more special agencies makes a great difference in the precision which can be given to the general laws, and in the confidence with which predictions can be grounded on them. Whatever depends on the peculiarities of individuals, combined with the accident of the positions they hold, is necessarily incapable of being foreseen. Undoubtedly, these casual combinations might be eliminated like any others by taking a sufficiently large cycle: the peculiarities of a great historical character make their influence felt in history sometimes for several thousand years, but is is highly probable that they will make no difference at all at the end of fifty millions. Since, however, we cannot obtain an average of the vast length of time necessary to exhaust all the possible combinations of great men and circumstances, as much of the law of evolution of human affairs as depends upon this average is and remains inaccessible to us; and within the next thousand years, which are of considerably more importance to us than the whole remainder of the fifty millions, the favourable and unfavourable combinations which will occur will be to us purely accidental. We cannot foresee the advent of great men. Those who introduce new speculative thoughts or great practical conceptions into the world cannot have their epoch fixed beforehand. What science can do is this. It can trace through past history the general causes which had brought mankind into that preliminary state, which, when the right sort of great man appeared, rendered them accessible to his influence. If this state continues, experience renders it tolerably certain that in a longer or shorter period the great man will be produced, provided that the general circumstances of the country and people are (which very often they are not) compatible with his existence; of which point also science can in some measure judge. It is in this manner that the results of progress, except as to the celerity of their production, can be, to a certain extent, reduced to regularity and law. And the belief that they can be so is equally consistent with assigning very great, or very little efficacy, to the influence of exceptional men, or of the acts of governments. And the same may be said of all other accidents and disturbing causes.

4. It would nevertheless be a great error to assign only a trifling importance to the agency of eminent individuals, or of governments. It must not be

concluded that the influence of either is small because they cannot bestow what the general circumstances of society, and the course of its previous history, have not prepared it to receive. Neither thinkers nor governments effect all that they intend, but in compensation they often produce important results which they did not in the least foresee. Great men and great actions are seldom wasted: they send forth a thousand unseen influences, more effective than those which are seen; and though nine out of every ten things done, with a good purpose, by those who are in advance of their age, produce no material effect, the tenth thing produces effects twenty times as great as any one would have dreamed of predicting from it. Even the men who for want of sufficiently favourable circumstances left no impress at all upon their own age have often been of the greatest value to posterity. Who could appear to have lived more entirely in vain than some of the early heretics? They were burnt or massacred, their writings extirpated, their memory anathematised, and their very names and existence left for seven or eight centuries in the obscurity of musty manuscripts—their history to be gathered, perhaps, only from the sentences by which they were condemned. Yet the memory of these men—men who resisted certain pretensions or certain dogmas of the Church in the very age in which the unanimous assent of Christendom was afterwards claimed as having been given to them, and asserted as the ground of their authority—broke the chain of tradition, established a series of precedents for resistance, inspired later Reformers with the courage, and armed them with the weapons, which they needed when mankind were better prepared to follow their impulse. . . .

If a government can do much, even when it seems to have done little, in causing positive improvement, still greater are the issues dependent on it in the way of warding off evils, both internal and external, which else would stop improvement altogether. A good or a bad counsellor, in a single city at a particular crisis, has affected the whole subsequent fate of the world. It is as certain as any contingent judgment respecting historical events can be, that if there had been no Themistocles there would have been no victory of Salamis; and had there not, where would have been all our civilisation? . . . Historical science authorises not absolute, but only conditional predictions. General causes count for much, but individuals also "produce great changes in history, and colour its whole complexion long after their death. . . ."

. . . The whole stream of Grecian history . . . is one series of examples how often events on which the whole destiny of subsequent civilisation turned were dependent on the personal character for good or evil of some one individual. It must be said, however, that Greece furnishes the most extreme example of this nature to be found in history, and is a very exaggerated specimen of the general tendency. It has happened only that once, and will probably never happen again, that the fortunes of mankind depended upon keeping a certain order of things in existence in a single town, or a country scarcely larger than Yorkshire; capable of being ruined or saved by a hundred causes, of very slight magnitude in comparison with the general tendencies of human affairs. Neither ordinary accidents nor the characters of individuals can ever again be so vitally important as they then were. The longer our species lasts and the more civilised it becomes, the more . . . does the influence of past generations over the present, and of mankind *en masse* over every individual in it, predominate over other forces: and though the course of affairs never ceases to be susceptible of alteration both by accidents and by personal qualities, the increasing preponderance of the collective agency of the species over all minor causes is constantly bringing the general evolution of the race into something which deviates less from a certain and preappointed track. Historical science, therefore, is always becoming more possible; not solely because it is better studied, but because, in every generation, it becomes better adapted for study.

27 ECONOMIC DETERMINISM AND HISTORICAL DEVELOPMENT

FRIEDRICH ENGELS (1820-1895)

1. What we understand by the economic conditions which we regard as the determining basis of the history of society are the methods by which human beings in a given society produce their means of subsistence and exchange the products among themselves (in so far as division of labor exists). Thus the *entire technique* of production and transport is here included. According to our conception this technique also determines the method of exchange and, further, the division of products and with it, after the dissolution of tribal society, the division into classes also and hence the relations of lordship and servitude and with them the state, politics, law, etc. Under economic condi-

SOURCE: From a letter to Heinz Starkenburg, January 25, 1894. Reprinted from pp. 516–519 of *The Selected Correspondence of Karl Marx and Friedrich Engels,* 1846–1895 (1942), with the kind permission of the International Publishers Co., New York. The title of this selection has been supplied by the editors. Compare with selection 26.

tions are further included the geographical basis in which they operate and those remnants of earlier stages of economic development which have actually been transmitted and have survived—often only through tradition or the force of inertia; also of course the external milieu which surrounds this form of society.

If, as you say, technique largely depends on the state of science, science depends far more still on the *state* and the *requirements* of technique. If society has a technical need, that helps science forward more than ten universities. The whole of hydrostatics (Torricelli, etc.,) was called forth by the necessity for regulating the mountain streams of Italy in the sixteenth and seventeenth centuries. We have only known anything reasonable about electricity since its technical applicability was discovered. But unfortunately it has become the custom in Germany to write the history of the sciences as if they had fallen from the skies.

2. We regard economic conditions as the factor which ultimately determines historical development. But race is itself an economic factor. Here, however, two points must not be overlooked:

(a) Political, juridical, philosophical, religious, literary, artistic, etc., development is based on economic development. But all these react upon one another and also upon the economic base. It is not that the economic position is the *cause and alone active,* while everything else only has a passive effect. There is, rather, interaction on the basis of the economic necessity, which *ultimately* always asserts itself. The state, for instance, exercises an influence by tariffs, free trade, good or bad fiscal system; and even deadly inanition and impotence of the German petty bourgeois, arising from the miserable economic position of Germany from 1648 to 1830 and expressing itself at first in pietism, then in sentimentality and cringing servility to princes and nobles, was not without economic effect. It was one of the greatest hindrances to recovery and was not shaken until the revolutionary and Napoleonic wars made the chronic misery an acute one. So it is not, as people try here and there conveniently to imagine, that the economic position produces an automatic effect. Men make their history themselves, only in given surroundings which condition it and on the basis of actual relations already existing, among which the economic relations, however much they may be influenced by the other political and ideological ones, are still ultimately the decisive ones, forming the red thread which runs through them and alone leads to understanding.

(b) Men make their history themselves, but not as yet with a collective will or according to a collective plan or even in a definitely defined, given society. Their efforts clash, and for that very reason all such societies are governed by *necessity,* which is supplemented by and appears under the forms of *accident*. The necessity which here asserts itself amidst all accident is again ultimately economic necessity. This is where the so-called great men come in for treatment. That such and such a man and precisely that man arises at that particular time in that given country is of course pure accident. But cut him out and there will be a demand for a substitute, and this substitute will be found, good or bad, but in the long run he will be found. That Napoleon, just that particular Corsican, should have been the military dictator whom the French Republic, exhausted by its own war, had rendered necessary, was an accident; but that, if a Napoleon had been lacking, another would have filled the place, is proved by the fact that the man has always been found as soon as he became necessary: Caesar, Augustus, Cromwell, etc. While Marx discovered the materialist conception of history, Thierry, Mignet, Guizot, and all the English historians up to 1850 are the proof that it was being striven for, and the discovery of the same conception by Morgan proved that the time was ripe for it and that indeed it *had* to be discovered.

So with all the other accidents, and apparent accidents, of history. The further the particular sphere which we are investigating is removed from the economic sphere and approaches that of pure abstract ideology, the more shall we find it exhibiting accidents in its development, the more will its curve run in a zig-zag. But if you plot the average axis of the curve, you will find that the axis of this curve will approach more and more nearly parallel to the axis of the curve of economic development the longer the period considered and the wider the field dealt with. . . .

28 EXISTENTIALISM

JEAN-PAUL SARTRE (1905-   )

I should like on this occasion to defend existentialism against some charges which have been brought against it.

First, it has been charged with inviting people to remain in a kind of desperate quietism because, since no solutions are possible, we should have to consider action in this world as quite impossible. We should then end up in a philosophy of contemplation; and since contemplation is a luxury, we

SOURCE: The greater part of the essay *Existentialism,* from the beginning, p. 11, to p. 47, translated from the French by Bernard Frechtman (New York: Philosophical Library, 1947). Reprinted by permission of the publishers, The Philosophical Library, Inc.

come in the end to a bourgeois philosophy. The communists in particular have made these charges.

On the other hand, we have been charged with dwelling on human degradation, with pointing up everywhere the sordid, shady, and slimy, and neglecting the gracious and beautiful, the bright side of human nature; for example, according to Mlle. Mercier, a Catholic critic, with forgetting the smile of the child. Both sides charge us with having ignored human solidarity, with considering man as an isolated being. The communists say that the main reason for this is that we take pure subjectivity, the *Cartesian I think,* as our starting point; in other words, the moment in which man becomes fully aware of what it means to him to be an isolated being; as a result, we are unable to return to a state of solidarity with the men who are not ourselves, a state which we can never reach in the *cogito.*

From the Christian standpoint, we are charged with denying the reality and seriousness of human undertakings, since, if we reject God's commandments and the eternal verities, there no longer remains anything but pure caprice, with everyone permitted to do as he pleases and incapable, from his own point of view, of condemning the points of view and acts of others.

I shall try today to answer these different charges. Many people are going to be surprised at what is said here about humanism. We shall try to see in what sense it is to be understood. In any case, what can be said from the very beginning is that by existentialism we mean a doctrine which makes human life possible and, in addition, declares that every truth and every action implies a human setting and a human subjectivity.

As is generally known, the basic charge against us is that we put the emphasis on the dark side of human life. Someone recently told me of a lady who, when she let slip a vulgar word in a moment of irritation, excused herself by saying, "I guess I'm becoming an existentialist." Consequently, existentialism is regarded as something ugly; that is why we are said to be naturalists; and if we are, it is rather surprising that in this day and age we cause so much more alarm and scandal than does naturalism, properly so called. The kind of person who can take in his stride such a novel as Zola's *The Earth* is disgusted as soon as he starts reading an existentialist novel; the kind of person who is resigned to the wisdom of the ages—which is pretty sad—finds us even sadder. Yet, what can be more disillusioning than saying "true charity begins at home" or "a scoundrel will always return evil for good"?

We know the commonplace remarks made when this subject comes up, remarks which always add up to the same thing: we shouldn't struggle against the powers-that-be; we shouldn't resist authority; we shouldn't try to rise above our station; any action which doesn't conform to authority is romantic; any effort not based on past experience is doomed to failure; experience shows that man's bent is always toward trouble, that there must be a strong hand to hold him in check, if not, there will be anarchy. There are still people who go on mumbling these melancholy old saws, the people who say, "It's only human!" whenever a more or less repugnant act is pointed out to them, the people who glut themselves on *chansons réalistes;* these are the people who accuse existentialism of being too gloomy, and to such an extent that I wonder whether they are complaining about it, not for its pessimism, but much rather its optimism. Can it be that what really scares them in the doctrine I shall try to present here is that it leaves to man a possibility of choice? To answer this question, we must re-examine it on a strictly philosophical plane. What is meant by the term *existentialism?*

Most people who use the word would be rather embarrassed if they had to explain it, since, now that the word is all the rage, even the work of a musician or painter is being called existentialist. A gossip columnist in *Clartés* signs himself *The Existentialist,* so that by this time the word has been so stretched and has taken on so broad a meaning, that it no longer means anything at all. It seems that for want of an advance-guard doctrine analogous to surrealism, the kind of people who are eager for scandal and flurry turn to this philosophy which in other respects does not at all serve their purposes in this sphere.

Actually, it is the least scandalous, the most austere of doctrines. It is intended strictly for specialists and philosophers. Yet it can be defined easily. What complicates matters is that there are two kinds of existentialist; first, those who are Christian, among whom I would include Jaspers and Gabriel Marcel, both Catholic; and on the other hand the atheistic existentialists, among whom I class Heidegger, and then the French existentialists and myself. What they have in common is that they think that existence precedes essence, or, if you prefer, that subjectivity must be the starting point.

Just what does that mean? Let us consider some object that is manufactured, for example, a book or a paper-cutter: here is an object which has been made by an artisan whose inspiration came from a concept. He referred to the concept of what a paper-cutter is and like-wise to a known method of production, which is part of the concept, something which is, by and large, a routine. Thus, the paper-cutter is at once an object produced in a certain way and, on the other hand, one having a specific use; and one can not postulate a man who produces a paper-cutter but does not know what it is used for. Therefore, let us say that, for the paper-cutter, essence—that is, the ensemble of both the production routines and the properties which enable it to be both produced and defined—precedes existence. Thus, the presence of the paper-cutter or book in front of me is determined. Therefore, we have here a technical view of the world whereby it can be said that production precedes existence.

When we conceive God as the Creator, He is generally thought of as a superior sort of artisan. Whatever doctrine we may be considering, whether one like that of Descartes or that of Leibnitz, we always grant that will more or less follows understanding or, at the very least, accompanies it, and that when God creates He knows exactly what He is creating. Thus, the concept of man in the mind of God is comparable to the concept of paper-cutter in the mind of the manufacturer, and, following certain techniques and a conception, God produces man, just as the artisan, following a definition and a technique, makes a paper-cutter. Thus, the individual man is the realization of a certain concept in the divine intelligence.

In the eighteenth century, the atheism of the *philosophes* discarded the idea of God, but not so much for the notion that essence precedes existence. To a certain extent, this idea is found everywhere; we find it in Diderot, in Voltaire, and even in Kant. Man has a human nature; this human nature, which is the concept of the human, is found in all men, which means that each man is a particular example of a universal concept, man. In Kant, the result of this universality is that the wild-man, the natural man, as well as the bourgeois, are circumscribed by the same definition and have the same basic qualities. Thus, here too the essence of man precedes the historical existence that we find in nature.

Atheistic existentialism, which I represent, is more coherent. It states that if God does not exist, there is at least one being in whom existence precedes essence, a being who exists before he can be defined by any concept, and that this being is man, or, as Heidegger says, human reality. What is meant here by saying that existence precedes essence? It means that, first of all, man exists, turns up, appears on the scene, and, only afterwards, defines himself. If man, as the existentialist conceives him, is indefinable, it is because at first he is nothing. Only afterward will he be something, and he himself will have made what he will be. Thus, there is no human nature, since there is no God to conceive it. Not only is man what he conceives himself to be, but he is also only what he wills himself to be after this thrust toward existence.

Man is nothing else but what he makes of himself. Such is the first principle of existentialism. It is also what is called subjectivity, the name we are labeled with when charges are brought against us. But what do we mean by this, if not that man has a greater dignity than a stone or table? For we mean that man first exists, that is, that man first of all is the being who hurls himself toward a future and who is conscious of imagining himself as being in the future. Man is at the start a plan which is aware of itself, rather than a patch of moss, a piece of garbage, or a cauliflower; nothing exists prior to this plan; there is nothing in heaven; man will be what he will have planned to be. Not what he will want to be. Because by the word "will" we generally mean a conscious decision, which is subsequent to what we have already made of ourselves. I may want to belong to a political party, write a book, get married; but all that is only a manifestation of an earlier, more spontaneous choice that is called "will." But if existence really does precede essence, man is responsible for what he is. Thus, existentialism's first move is to make every man aware of what he is and to make the full responsibility of his existence rest on him. And when we say that a man is responsible for himself, we do not only mean that he is responsible for his own individuality, but that he is responsible for all men.

The word subjectivism has two meanings, and our opponents play on the two. Subjectivism means, on the one hand, that an individual chooses and makes himself; and, on the other, that it is impossible for man to transcend human subjectivity. The second of these is the essential meaning of existentialism. When we say that man chooses his own self, we mean that every one of us does likewise; but we also mean by that that in making this choice he also chooses all men. In fact, in creating the man that we want to be, there is not a single one of our acts which does not at the same time create an image of man as we think he ought to be. To choose to be this or that is to affirm at the same time the value of what we choose, because we can never choose evil. We always choose the good, and nothing can be good for us without being good for all.

If, on the other hand, existence precedes essence, and if we grant that we exist and fashion our image at one and the same time, the image is valid for everybody and for our whole age. Thus, our responsibility is much greater than we might have supposed, because it involves all mankind. If I am a workingman and choose to join a Christian trade-union rather than be a communist, and if by being a member I want to show that the best thing for man is resignation, that the kingdom of man is not of this world, I am not only involving my own case—I want to be resigned for everyone. As a result, my action has involved all humanity. To take a more individual matter, if I want to marry, to have children; even if this marriage depends solely on my own circumstances or passion or wish, I am involving all humanity in monogamy and not merely myself. Therefore, I am responsible for myself and for everyone else. I am creating a certain image of man of my own choosing. In choosing myself, I choose man.

This helps us understand what the actual content is of such rather grandiloquent words as anguish, forlornness, despair. As you will see, it's all quite simple.

First, what is meant by anguish? The existentialists say at once that man is anguish. What that means is this: the man who involves himself and who realizes that he is not only the person he chooses to be, but also a lawmaker who is, at the same time, choosing all mankind as well as himself, can not help escape the feeling of his total and deep responsibility. Of course, there are many people who are not anxious; but we claim that they are hiding their anxiety, that they are fleeing from it. Certainly, many people believe that when they do something, they themselves are the only ones involved, and when someone says to them, "What if everyone acted that way?" they shrug their shoulders and answer, "Everyone doesn't act that way." But really, one should always ask himself, "What would happen if everybody looked at things that way?" There is no escaping this disturbing thought except by a kind of double-dealing. A man who lies and makes excuses for himself by saying "not everybody does that," is someone with an uneasy conscience, because the act of lying implies that a universal value is conferred upon the lie.

Anguish is evident even when it conceals itself. This is the anguish that Kierkegaard called the anguish of Abraham. You know the story: an angel has ordered Abraham to sacrifice his son; if it really were an angel who has come and said, "You are Abraham, you shall sacrifice your son," everything would be all right. But everyone might first wonder, "Is it really an angel, and am I really Abraham? What proof do I have?"

There was a madwoman who had hallucinations; someone used to speak to her on the telephone and give her orders. Her doctor asked her, "Who is it who talks to you?" She answered, "He says it's God." What proof did she really have that it was God? If an angel comes to me, what proof is there that it's an angel? And if I hear voices, what proof is there that they come from heaven and not from hell, or from the subconscious, or a pathological condition? What proves that they are addressed to me? What proof is there that I have been appointed to impose my choice and my conception of man on humanity? I'll never find any proof or sign to convince me of that. If a voice addresses me, it is always for me to decide that this is the angel's voice; if I consider that such an act is a good one, it is I who will choose to say that it is good rather than bad.

Now, I'm not being singled out as an Abraham, and yet at every moment I'm obliged to perform exemplary acts. For every man, everything happens as if all mankind had its eyes fixed on him and were guiding itself by what he does. And every man ought to say to himself, "Am I really the kind of man who has the right to act in such a way that humanity might guide itself by my actions?" And if he does not say that to himself, he is masking his anguish.

There is no question here of the kind of anguish which would lead to quietism, to inaction. It is a matter of a simple sort of anguish that anybody who has had responsibilities is familiar with. For example, when a military officer takes the responsibility for an attack and sends a certain number of men to death, he chooses to do so, and in the main he alone makes the choice. Doubtless, orders come from above, but they are too broad; he interprets them, and on this interpretation depend the lives of ten or fourteen or twenty men. In making a decision he can not help having a certain anguish. All leaders know this anguish. That doesn't keep them from acting; on the contrary, it is the very condition of their action. For it implies that they envisage a number of possibilities, and when they choose one, they realize that it has value only because it is chosen. We shall see that this kind of anguish, which is the kind that existentialism describes, is explained, in addition, by a direct responsibility to the other men whom it involves. It is not a curtain separating us from action, but is part of action itself.

When we speak of forlornness, a term Heidegger was fond of, we mean only that God does not exist and that we have to face all the consequences of this. The existentialist is strongly opposed to a certain kind of secular ethics which would like to abolish God with the least possible expense. About 1880, some French teachers tried to set up a secular ethics which went something like this: God is a useless and costly hypothesis; we are discarding it; but, meanwhile, in order for there to be an ethics, a society, a civilization, it is essential that certain values be taken seriously and that they be considered as having an *a priori* existence. It must be obligatory, *a priori,* to be honest, not to lie, not to beat your wife, to have children, etc., etc. So we're going to try a little device which will make it possible to show that values exist all the same, inscribed in a heaven of ideas, though otherwise God does not exist. In other words—and this, I believe, is the tendency of everything called reformism in France—nothing will be changed if God does not exist. We shall find ourselves with the same norms of honesty, progress, and humanism, and we shall have made of God an outdated hypothesis which will peacefully die off by itself.

The existentialist, on the contrary, thinks it very distressing that God does not exist, because all possibility of finding values in a heaven of ideas disappears along with Him; there can no longer be an *a priori* Good, since there is no infinite and perfect consciousness to think it. Nowhere is it written that the Good exists, that we must be honest, that we must not lie; because the fact is we are on a plane where there are only men. Dostoievsky said, "If God didn't exist, everything would be possible." That is the very starting point of existentialism. Indeed, everything is permissible if God does not exist, and as a result man is forlorn, because neither within him nor without does he find anything to cling to. He can't start making excuses for himself.

If existence really does precede essence, there is no explaining things away by reference to a fixed and given human nature. In other words, there is no determinism, man is free, man is freedom. On the other hand, if God does not exist, we find no values or commands to turn to which legitimize our conduct. So, in the bright realm of values, we have no excuse behind us, nor justification before us. We are alone, with no excuses.

That is the idea I shall try to convey when I say that man is condemned to be free. Condemned, because he did not create himself, yet, in other respects is free; because, once thrown into the world, he is responsible for everything he does. The existentialist does not believe in the power of passion. He will never agree that a sweeping passion is a ravaging torrent which fatally leads a man to certain acts and is therefore an excuse. He thinks that man is responsible for his passion.

The existentialist does not think that man is going to help himself by finding in the world some omen by which to orient himself. Because he thinks that man will interpret the omen to suit himself. Therefore, he thinks that man, with no support and no aid, is condemned every moment to invent man. Ponge, in a very fine article, has said, "Man is the future of man." That's exactly it. But if it is taken to mean that this future is recorded in heaven, that God sees it, then it is false, because it would really no longer be a future. If it is taken to mean that, whatever a man may be, there is a future to be forged, a virgin future before him, then this remark is sound. But then we are forlorn.

To give you an example which will enable you to understand forlornness better, I shall cite the case of one of my students who came to see me under the following circumstances: his father was on bad terms with his mother, and, moreover, was inclined to be a collaborationist; his older brother had been killed in the German offensive of 1940, and the young man, with somewhat immature but generous feelings, wanted to avenge him. His mother lived alone with him, very much upset by the half-treason of her husband and the death of her older son; the boy was her only consolation.

The boy was faced with the choice of leaving for England and joining the Free French Forces—that is, leaving his mother behind—or remaining with his mother and helping her to carry on. He was fully aware that the woman lived only for him and that his going off—and perhaps his death—would plunge her into despair. He was also aware that every act that he did for his mother's sake was a sure thing, in the sense that it was helping her to carry on, whereas every effort he made toward going off and fighting was an uncertain move which might run aground and prove completely useless; for example, on his way to England he might, while passing through Spain, be detained indefinitely in a Spanish camp; he might reach England or Algiers and be stuck in an office at a desk job. As a result, he was faced with two very different kinds of action: one, concrete, immediate, but concerning only one individual; the other concerned an incomparably vaster group, a national collectivity, but for that very reason was dubious, and might be interrupted en route. And, at the same time, he was wavering between two kinds of ethics. On the one hand, an ethics of sympathy, of personal devotion; on the other, a broader ethics, but one whose efficacy was more dubious. He had to choose between the two.

Who could help him choose? Christian doctrine? No. Christian doctrine says, "Be charitable, love your neighbor, take the more rugged path, etc., etc." But which is the more rugged path? Whom should he love as a brother? The fighting man or his mother? Which does the greater good, the vague act of fighting in a group, or the concrete one of helping a particular human being to go on living? Who can decide *a priori*? Nobody. No book of ethics can tell him. The Kantian ethics says, "Never treat any person as a means, but as an end." Very well, if I stay with my mother, I'll treat her as an end and not as a means; but by virtue of this very fact, I'm running the risk of treating the people around me who are fighting, as means; and, conversely, if I go to join those who are fighting, I'll be treating them as an end, and, by doing that, I run the risk of treating my mother as a means.

If values are vague, and if they are always too broad for the concrete and specific case that we are considering, the only thing left for us is to trust our instincts. That's what this young man tried to do; and when I saw him, he said, "In the end, feeling is what counts. I ought to choose whichever pushes me in one direction. If I feel that I love my mother enough to sacrifice everything else for her—my desire for vengeance, for action, for adventure—then I'll stay with her. If, on the contrary, I feel that my love for my mother isn't enough, I'll leave."

But how is the value of a feeling determined? What gives his feeling for his mother value? Precisely the fact that he remained with her. I may say that I like so-and-so well enough to sacrifice a certain amount of money for him, but I may say so only if I've done it. I may say "I love my mother well enough to remain with her" if I have remained with her. The only way to determine the value of this affection is, precisely, to perform an act which confirms and defines it. But, since I require this affection to justify my act, I find myself caught in a vicious circle.

On the other hand, Gide has well said that a mock feeling and a true feeling are almost indistinguishable; to decide that I love my mother and will remain with her, or to remain with her by putting on an act, amount somewhat to the same thing. In other words, the feeling is formed by the acts one performs; so, I can not refer to it in order to act upon it. Which means that I can neither seek within myself the true condition which will impel me to act, nor apply to a system of ethics for concepts which will permit me to act. You will say, "At least, he did go to a teacher for advice." But if you seek advice from a priest, for example, you have chosen this priest; you already knew, more or less, just about what advice he was going to give you. In other words, choosing your adviser is involving yourself. The proof of this is that if you are a Christian, you will say, "Consult a priest." But some priests are collaborating, some are just marking time, some are resisting. Which to choose? If the young man chooses a priest who is resisting or collaborating, he has already decided on the kind of advice he's going to get. Therefore, in coming to see me he knew the answer I was going to give him, and I had only one answer to give: "You're free, choose, that is, invent." No general ethics can show you what is to be done; there are no omens in the world. The Catholics will reply, "But there are." Granted—but, in any case, I myself choose the meaning they have.

When I was a prisoner, I knew a rather remarkable young man who was a Jesuit. He had entered the Jesuit order in the following way: he had had a number of very bad breaks; in childhood, his father died, leaving him in poverty, and he was a scholarship student at a religious institution where he was constantly made to feel that he was being kept out of charity; then, he failed to get any of the honors and distinctions that children like; later on, at about eighteen, he bungled a love affair; finally, at twenty-two, he failed in military training, a childish enough matter, but it was the last straw.

This young fellow might well have felt that he had botched everything. It was a sign of something, but what? He might have taken refuge in bitterness or despair. But he very wisely looked upon all this as a sign that he was not made for secular triumphs, and that only the triumphs of religion, holiness, and faith were open to him. He saw the hand of God in all this, and so he entered the order. Who can help seeing that he alone decided what the sign meant?

Some other interpretation might have been drawn from this series of setbacks; for example, that he might have done better to turn carpenter or revolutionist. Therefore, he is fully responsible for the interpretation. Forlornness implies that we ourselves choose our being. Forlornness and anguish go together.

As for despair, the term has a very simple meaning. It means that we shall confine ourselves to reckoning only with what depends upon our will, or on the ensemble of probabilities which make our action possible. When we want something, we always have to reckon with probabilities. I may be counting on the arrival of a friend. The friend is coming by rail or street-car; this supposes that the train will arrive on schedule, or that the street-car will not jump the track. I am left in the realm of possibility; but possibilities are to be reckoned with the ensemble of these possibilities, and no further. The moment the possibilities I am considering are not rigorously involved by my action, I ought to disengage myself from them, because no God, no scheme, can adapt the world and its possibilities to my will. When Descartes said, "Conquer yourself rather than the world," he meant essentially the same thing.

The Marxists to whom I have spoken reply, "You can rely on the support of others in your action, which obviously has certain limits because you're not going to live forever. That means: rely on both what others are doing elsewhere to help you, in China, in Russia, and what they will do later on, after your death, to carry on the action and lead it to its fulfillment, which will be the revolution. You even *have* to rely upon that, otherwise you're immoral." I reply at once that I will always rely on fellow-fighters insofar as these comrades are involved with me in a common struggle, in the unity of a party or a group in which I can more or less make my weight felt; that is, one whose ranks I am in as a fighter and whose movements I am aware of at every moment. In such a situation, relying on the unity and will of the party is exactly like counting on the fact that the train will arrive on time or that the car won't jump the track. But, given that man is free and that there is no human nature for me to depend on, I can not count on men whom I do not know by relying on human goodness or man's concern for the good of society. I don't know what will become of the Russian revolution; I may make an example of it to the extent that at the present time it is apparent that the proletariat plays a part in Russia that it plays in no other nation. But I can't swear that this will inevitably lead to a triumph of the proletariat. I've got to limit myself to what I see.

Given that men are free and that tomorrow they will freely decide what man will be, I can not be sure that, after my death, fellow-fighters will carry on my work to bring it to its maximum perfection. Tomorrow, after my death, some men may decide to set up Fascism, and the others may be cowardly and muddled enough to let them do it. Fascism will then be the human reality, so much the worse for us.

Actually, things will be as man will have decided they are to be. Does that mean that I should abandon myself to quietism? No. First, I should involve myself; then, act on the old saw, "Nothing ventured, nothing gained." Nor does it mean that I shouldn't belong to a party, but rather that I shall have no illusions and shall do what I can. For example, suppose I ask myself, "Will socialization, as such, ever come about?" I know nothing about it. All I know is that I'm going to do everything in my power to bring it about. Beyond that, I can't count on anything. Quietism is the attitude of people who say, "Let others do what I can't do." The doctrine I am presenting is the very opposite of quietism, since it declares, "There is no reality except in action." Moreover, it goes further, since it adds, "Man is nothing else than his plan; he exists only to the extent that he fulfills himself; he is therefore nothing else than the ensemble of his acts, nothing else than his life."

According to this, we can understand why our doctrine horrifies certain people. Because often the only way they can bear their wretchedness is to think, "Circumstances have been against me. What I've been and done doesn't show my true worth. To be sure, I've had no great love, no great friendship, but that's because I haven't met a man or woman who was worthy. The books I've written haven't been very good because I haven't had the proper leisure. I haven't had children to devote myself to because I didn't find a man with whom I could have spent my life. So there remains with me, unused and quite viable, a host of propensities, inclinations, possibilities, that one wouldn't guess from the mere series of things I've done."

Now, for the existentialist there is really no love other than one which manifests itself in a person's being in love. There is no genius other than one which is expressed in works of art; the genius of Proust is the sum of Proust's works; the genius of Racine is his series of tragedies. Outside of that, there is nothing. Why say that Racine could have written another tragedy, when he didn't write it? A man is involved in life, leaves his impress on it, and outside of that there is nothing. To be sure, this may seem a harsh thought to someone whose life hasn't been a success. But, on the other hand, it prompts people to understand that reality alone is what counts, that dreams, expectations, and hopes warrant no more than to define a man as a disappointed dream, as miscarried hopes, as vain expectations. In other words, to define him negatively and not positively. However, when we say, "You are nothing else than your life," that does not imply that the artist will be judged solely on the basis of his works of art; a thousand other things will contribute toward summing him up. What we mean is that a man is nothing else than a series of undertakings, that he is the sum, the organization, the ensemble of the relationships which make up these undertakings.

When all is said and done, what we are accused of, at bottom, is not our pessimism, but an optimistic toughness. If people throw up to us our works of fiction in which we write about people who are soft, weak, cowardly, and sometimes even downright bad, it's not because these people are soft, weak, cowardly, or bad; because if we were to say, as Zola did, that they are that way because of heredity, the workings of environment, society, because of biological or psychological determinism, people would be reassured. They would say, "Well, that's what we're like, no one can do anything about it." But when the existentialist writes about a coward, he says that this coward is responsible for his cowardice. He's not like that because he has a cowardly heart or lung or brain; he's not like that on account of his physiological make-up; but he's like that because he has made himself a coward by his acts. There's no such thing as a cowardly constitution; there are nervous constitutions; there is poor blood, as the common people say, or strong constitutions. But the man whose blood is poor is not a coward on that account, for what makes cowardice is the act of renouncing or yielding. A constitution is not an act; the coward is defined on the basis of the acts he performs. People feel, in a vague sort of way, that this coward we're talking about is guilty of being a coward, and the thought frightens them. What people would like is that a coward or a hero be born that way.

One of the complaints most frequently made about *The Ways of Freedom** can be summed up as follows: "After all, these people are so spineless, how are you going to make heroes out of them?" This objection almost makes me laugh, for it assumes that people are born heroes. That's what people really want to think. If you're born cowardly, you may set your mind perfectly at rest; there's nothing you can do about it; you'll be cowardly all your life, whatever you may do. If you're born a hero, you may set your mind just as much at rest; you'll be a hero all your life; you'll drink like a hero and eat like a hero. What the existentialist says is that the coward makes himself cowardly, that the hero makes himself heroic. There's always a possibility for the coward not to be cowardly any more and for the hero to stop being heroic. What counts is total involvement; some one particular action or set of circumstances is not total involvement.

Thus, I think we have answered a number of the charges concerning existentialism. You see that it can not be taken for a philosophy of quietism, since it defines man in terms of action; nor for a pessimistic description of man —there is no doctrine more optimistic, since man's destiny is within himself; nor for an attempt to discourage man from acting, since it tells him that the only hope is in his acting and that action is the only thing that enables a man to live. Consequently, we are dealing here with an ethics of action and involvement.

Nevertheless, on the basis of a few notions like these, we are still charged with immuring man in his private subjectivity. There again we're very much misunderstood. Subjectivity of the individual is indeed our point of departure, and this for strictly philosophic reasons. Not because we are bourgeois, but because we want a doctrine based on truth and not a lot of fine theories, full of hope but with no real basis. There can be no other truth to take off from than this: *I think; therefore, I exist.* There we have the absolute truth of consciousness becoming aware of itself. Every theory which takes man out of the moment in which he becomes aware of himself is, at its very beginning, a theory which confounds truth, for outside the Cartesian *cogito*, all views are only probable, and a doctrine of probability which is not bound to a truth dissolves into thin air. In order to describe the probable, you must have a firm hold on the true. Therefore, before there can be any truth whatsoever, there

---

**Les Chemins de la Liberté*, M. Sartre's projected trilogy of novels, two of which, *L'Age de Raison (The Age of Reason)* and *Le Sursis (The Reprieve)* have already appeared.—Translator's note.

must be an absolute truth; and this one is simple and easily arrived at; it's on everyone's doorstep; it's a matter of grasping it directly.

Secondly, this theory is the only one which gives man dignity, the only one which does not reduce him to an object. The effect of all materialism is to treat all men, including the one philosophizing, as objects, that is, as an ensemble of determined reactions in no way distinguished from the ensemble of qualities and phenomena which constitute a table or a chair or a stone. We definitely wish to establish the human realm as an ensemble of values distinct from the material realm. But the subjectivity that we have thus arrived at, and which we have claimed to be truth, is not a strictly individual subjectivity, for we have demonstrated that one discovers in the *cogito* not only himself, but others as well.

The philosophies of Descartes and Kant to the contrary, through the *I think* we reach our own self in the presence of others, and the others are just as real to us as our own self. Thus, the man ho becomes aware of himself through the *cogito* also perceives all others, and he perceives them as the condition of his own existence. He realizes that he can not be anything (in the sense that we say that someone is witty or nasty or jealous) unless others recognize it as such. In order to get any truth about myself, I must have contact with another person. The other is indispensable to my own existence, as well as to my knowledge about myself. This being so, in discovering my inner being I discover the other person at the same time, like a freedom placed in front of me which thinks and wills only for or against me. Hence, let us at once announce the discovery of a world which we shall call intersubjectivity; this is the world in which man decides what he is and what others are.

Besides, if it is impossible to find in every man some universal essence which would be human nature, yet there does exist a universal human condition. It's not by chance that today's thinkers speak more readily of man'sw-condition than of his nature. By condition they mean, more or less definitely, the *a priori* limits which outline man's fundamental situation in the universe. Historical situations vary; a man may be born a slave in a pagan society or a feudal lord or a proletarian. What does not vary is the necessity for him to exist in the world, to be at work there, to be there in the midst of other people, and to be mortal there. The limits are neither subjective nor objective, or, rather, they have an objective and a subjective side. Objective because they are to be found everywhere and are recognizable everywhere; subjective because they are *lived* and are nothing if man does not live them, that is, freely determine his existence with reference to them. And though the configurations may differ, at least none of them are completely strange to me, because they all appear as attempts either to pass beyond these limits or recede from them or deny them or adapt to them. Consequently, every configuration, however individual it may be, has a universal value.

Every configuration, even the Chinese, the Indian, or the Negro, can be understood by a Westerner. "Can be understood" means that by virtue of a situation that he can imagine, a European of 1945 can, in like manner, push himself to his limits and reconstitute within himself the configuration of the Chinese, the Indian, or the African. Every configuration has universality in the sense that every configuration can be understood by every man. This does not at all mean that this configuration defines man forever, but that it can be met with again. There is always a way to understand the idiot, the child, the savage, the foreigner, provided one has the necessary information.

In this sense, we may say that there is a universality of man; but it is not given, it is perpetually being made. I build the universal in choosing myself; I build it in understanding the configuration of every other man, whatever age he might have lived in. This absoluteness of choice does not do away with the relativeness of each epoch. At heart, what existentialism shows is the connection between the absolute character of free involvement, by virtue of which every man realizes himself in realizing a type of mankind, an involvement always comprehensible in any age whatsoever and by any person whosoever, and the relativeness of the cultural ensemble which may result from such a choice; it must be stressed that the relativity of Cartesianism and the absolute character of Cartesian involvement go together. In this sense, you may, if you like, say that each of us performs an absolute act in breathing, eating, sleeping, or behaving in any way whatever. There is no difference between being free, like a configuration, like an existence which chooses its essence, and being absolute. There is no difference between being an absolute temporarily localized, that is, localized in history, and being universally comprehensible. . . .

29 THE ELIMINATION OF METAPHYSICS
ALFRED JULES AYER (1910-)

The traditional disputes of philosophers are, for the most part, as unwarranted as they are unfruitful. The surest way to end them is to establish beyond question what should be the purpose and method of a philosophical enquiry. And this is by no means so difficult a task as the history of philosophy would lead one to suppose. For if there are any questions which science leaves it to philosophy to answer, a straightforward process of elimination must lead to their discovery.

We may begin by criticising the metaphysical thesis that philosophy affords us knowledge of a reality transcending the world of science and common sense. Later on, when we come to define metaphysics and account for its existence, we shall find that it is possible to be a metaphysician without believing in a transcendent reality; for we shall see that many metaphysical utterances are due to the commission of logical errors, rather than to a conscious desire on the part of their authors to go beyond the limits of experience. But it is convenient for us to take the case of those who believe that it is possible to have knowledge of a transcendent reality as a starting-point for our discussion. The arguments which we use to refute them will subsequently be found to apply to the whole of metaphysics.

One way of attacking a metaphysician who claimed to have knowledge of a reality which transcended the phenomenal world would be to enquire from what premises his propositions were deduced. Must he not begin, as other men do, with the evidence of his senses? And if so, what valid process of reasoning can possibly lead him to the conception of a transcendent reality? Surely from empirical premises nothing whatsoever concerning the properties, or even the existence, of anything super-empirical can legitimately be inferred. But this objection would be met by a denial on the part of the metaphysician that his assertions were ultimately based on the evidence of his senses. He would say that he was endowed with a faculty of intellectual

SOURCE: The whole of chapter 1 from *Language, Truth and Logic* by A. J. Ayer (first published 1936; 2nd ed., 1946). Victor Gollancz Ltd., London, 1946. Reprinted through the permission of the publisher. Compare with selections 20, 34, and 45.

intuition which enabled him to know facts that could not be known through sense-experience. And even if it could be shown that he was relying on empirical premises, and that his venture into a non-empirical world was therefore logically unjustified, it would not follow that the assertions which he made concerning this non-empirical world could not be true. For the fact that a conclusion does not follow from its putative premise is not sufficient to show that it is false. Consequently one cannot overthrow a system of transcendent metaphysics merely by criticising the way in which it comes into being. What is required is rather a criticism of the nature of the actual statements which comprise it. And this is the line of argument which we shall, in fact, pursue. For we shall maintain that no statement which refers to a "reality" transcending the limits of all possible sense-experience can possibly have any literal significance; from which it must follow that the labours of those who have striven to describe such a reality have all been devoted to the production of nonsense.

It may be suggested that this is a proposition which has already been proved by Kant. But although Kant also condemned transcendent metaphysics, he did so on different grounds. For he said that the human understanding was so constituted that it lost itself in contradictions when it ventured out beyond the limits of possible experience and attempted to deal with things in themselves. And thus he made the impossibility of a transcendent metaphysic not, as we do, a matter of logic, but a matter of fact. He asserted, not that our minds could not conceivably have had the power of penetrating beyond the phenomenal world, but merely that they were in fact devoid of it. And this leads the critic to ask how, if it is possible to know only what lies within the bounds of sense-experience, the author can be justified in asserting that real things do exist beyond, and how he can tell what are the boundaries beyond which the human understanding may not venture, unless he succeeds in passing them himself. As Wittgenstein says, "in order to draw a limit to thinking, we should have to think both sides of this limit,"[1] a truth to which Bradley gives a special twist in maintaining that the man who is ready to prove that metaphysics is impossible is a brother metaphysician with a rival theory of his own.[2]

Whatever force these objections may have against the Kantian doctrine, they have none whatsoever against the thesis that I am about to set forth. It cannot here be said that the author is himself overstepping the barrier he maintains to be impassable. For the fruitlessness of attempting to transcend the limits of possible sense-experience will be deduced, not from a psycho-

---
[1] *Tractatus Logico-Philosophicus,* Preface.
[2] Bradley, *Appearance and Reality,* 2nd ed., p. 1.

logical hypothesis concerning the actual constitution of the human mind, but from the rule which determines the literal significance of language. Our charge against the metaphysician is not that he attempts to employ the understanding in a field where it cannot profitably venture, but that he produces sentences which fail to conform to the conditions under which alone a sentence can be literally significant. Nor are we ourselves obliged to talk nonsense in order to show that all sentences of a certain type are necessarily devoid of literal significance. We need only formulate the criterion which enables us to test whether a sentence expresses a genuine proposition about a matter of fact, and then point out that the sentences under consideration fail to satisfy it. And this we shall now proceed to do. We shall first of all formulate the criterion in somewhat vague terms, and then give the explanations which are necessary to render it precise.

The criterion which we use to test the genuineness of apparent statements of fact is the criterion of verifiability. We say that a sentence is factually significant to any given person, if, and only if, he knows how to verify the proposition which it purports to express—that is, if he knows what observations would lead him, under certain conditions, to accept the proposition as being true, or reject it as being false. If, on the other hand, the putative proposition is of such a character that the assumption of its truth, or falsehood, is consistent with any assumption whatsoever concerning the nature of his future experience, then, as far as he is concerned, it is, if not a tautology, a mere pseudo-proposition. The sentence expressing it may be emotionally significant to him; but it is not literally significant. And with regard to questions the procedure is the same. We enquire in every case what observations would lead us to answer the question, one way or the other; and, if none can be discovered, we must conclude that the sentence under consideration does not, as far as we are concerned, express a genuine question, however strongly its grammatical appearance may suggest that it does.

As the adoption of this procedure is an essential factor in the argument of this book, it needs to be examined in detail.

In the first place, it is necessary to draw a distinction between practical verifiability, and verifiability in principle. Plainly we all understand, in many cases believe, propositions which we have not in fact taken steps to verify. Many of these are propositions which we could verify if we took enough trouble. But there remain a number of significant propositions, concerning matters of fact, which we could not verify even if we chose; simply because we lack the practical means of placing ourselves in the situation where the relevant observations could be made. A simple and familiar example of such a proposition is the proposition that there are mountains on the farther side of the moon.[3] No rocket has yet been invented which would enable me to go and look at the farther side of the moon, so that I am unable to decide the matter by actual observation. But I do know what observations would decide it for me, if, as is theoretically conceivable, I were once in a position to make them. And therefore I say that the proposition is verifiable in principle, if not in practice, and is accordingly significant. On the other hand, such a metaphysical pseudo-proposition as "the Absolute enters into, but is itself incapable of, evolution and progress,"[4] is not even in principle verifiable. For one cannot conceive of an observation which would enable one to determine whether the Absolute did, or did not, enter into evolution and progress. Of course it is possible that the author of such a remark is using English words in a way in which they are not commonly used by English-speaking people, and that he does, in fact, intend to assert something which could be empirically verified. But until he makes us understand how the proposition that he wishes to express would be verified, he fails to communicate anything to us. And if he admits, as I think the author of the remark in question would have admitted, that his words were not intended to express either a tautology or a proposition which was capable, at least in principle, of being verified, then it follows that he has made an utterance which has no literal significance even for himself.

A further distinction which we must make is the distinction between the "strong" and the "weak" sense of the term "verifiable." A proposition is said to be verifiable, in the strong sense of the term, if, and only if, its truth could be conclusively established in experience. But it is verifiable, in the weak sense, if it is possible for experience to render it probable. In which sense are we using the term when we say that a putative proposition is genuine only if it is verifiable?

It seems to me that if we adopt conclusive verifiability as our criterion of significance, as some positivists have proposed,[5] our argument will prove too much. Consider, for example, the case of general propositions of law—such propositions, namely, as "arsenic is poisonous"; "all men are mortal"; "a body tends to expand when it is heated." It is of the very nature of these propositions that their truth cannot be established with certainty by any finite series of observations. But if it is recognised that such general propositions of law are designed to cover an infinite number of cases, then it must be

[3] This example has been used by Professor Schlick to illustrate the same point.
[4] A remark taken at random from *Appearance and Reality*, by F. H. Bradley.
[5] e.g. M. Schlick, "Positivismus und Realismus," *Erkenntnis*, Vol. I, 1930. F. Waismann, "Logische Analyse des Warscheinlichkeitsbegriffs," *Erkenntnis*, Vol. I, 1930.

admitted that they cannot, even in principle, be verified conclusively. And then, if we adopt conclusive verifiability as our criterion of significance, we are logically obliged to treat these general propositions of law in the same fashion as we treat the statements of the metaphysician.

In face of this difficulty, some positivists[6] have adopted the heroic course of saying that these general propositions are indeed pieces of nonsense, albeit an essentially important type of nonsense. But here the introduction of the term "important" is simply an attempt to hedge. It serves only to mark the authors' recognition that their view is somewhat too paradoxical, without in any way removing the paradox. Besides, the difficulty is not confined to the case of general propositions of law, though it is there revealed most plainly. It is hardly less obvious in the case of propositions about the remote past. For it must surely be admitted that, however strong the evidence in favour of historical statements may be, their truth can never become more than highly probable. And to maintain that they also constituted an important, or unimportant, type of nonsense would be unplausible, to say the very least. Indeed, it will be our contention that no proposition, other than a tautology, can possibly be anything more than a probable hypothesis. And if this is correct, the principle that a sentence can be factually significant only if it expresses what is conclusively verifiable is self-stultifying as a criterion of significance. For it leads to the conclusion that it is impossible to make a significant statement of fact at all.

Nor can we accept the suggestion that a sentence should be allowed to be factually significant if, and only if, it expresses something which is definitely confutable by experience.[7] Those who adopt this course assume that, although no finite series of observations is ever sufficient to establish the truth of a hypothesis beyond all possibility of doubt, there are crucial cases in which a single observation, or series of observations, can definitely confute it. But, as we shall show later on, this assumption is false. A hypothesis cannot be conclusively confuted any more than it can be conclusively verified. For when we take the occurrence of certain observations as proof that a given hypothesis is false, we presuppose the existence of certain conditions. And though, in any given case, it may be extremely improbable that this assumption is false, it is not logically impossible. We shall see that there need be no self-contradiction in holding that some of the relevant circumstances are other than we have taken them to be, and consequently that the hypothesis

---

[6] e.g. M. Schlick, "Die Kausalität in der gegenwärtigen Physik," *Naturwissenschaft*, Vol. 19, 1931.
[7] This has been proposed by Karl Popper in his *Logik der Forschung*. [1934; translated into English under the title *The Logic of Scientific Discovery*, 1959—Eds.]

has not really broken down. And if it is not the case that any hypothesis can be definitely confuted, we cannot hold that the genuineness of a proposition depends on the possibility of its definite confutation.

Accordingly, we fall back on the weaker sense of verification. We say that the question that must be asked about any putative statement of fact is not, Would any observations make its truth or falsehood logically certain? but simply, Would any observations be relevant to the determination of its truth or falsehood? And it is only if a negative answer is given to this second question that we conclude that the statement under consideration is nonsensical.

To make our position clearer, we may formulate it in another way. Let us call a proposition which records an actual or possible observation an experiential proposition. Then we may say that it is the mark of a genuine factual proposition, not that it should be equivalent to an experiential proposition, or any finite number of experiential propositions, but simply that some experiential propositions can be deduced from it in conjunction with certain other premises without being deducible from those other premises alone.[8]

This criterion seems liberal enough. In contrast to the principle of conclusive verifiability, it clearly does not deny significance to general propositions or to propositions about the past. Let us see what kinds of assertion it rules out.

A good example of the kind of utterance that is condemned by our criterion as being not even false but nonsensical would be the assertion that the world of sense-experience was altogether unreal. It must, of course, be admitted that our senses do sometimes deceive us. We may, as the result of having certain sensations, expect certain other sensations to be obtainable which are, in fact, not obtainable. But, in all such cases, it is further sense-experience that informs us of the mistakes that arise out of sense-experience. We say that the senses sometimes deceive us, just because the expectations to which our sense-experiences give rise do not always accord with what we subsequently experience. That is, we rely on our senses to substantiate or confute the judgments which are based on our sensations. And therefore the fact that our perceptual judgements are sometimes found to be erroneous has not the slightest tendency to show that the world of sense-experience is unreal. And, indeed, it is plain that no conceivable observation, or series of observations, could have any tendency to show that the world revealed to us by sense-experience was unreal. Consequently, anyone who condemns the sensible world as a world of mere appearance, as opposed to reality, is saying some-

---

[8]This is an over-simplified statement, which is not literally correct. I give what I believe to be the correct formulation in the Introduction, p. 13. [Not reprinted here.—Eds.]

thing which, according to our criterion of significance, is literally nonsensical.

An example of a controversy which the application of our criterion obliges us to condemn as fictitious is provided by those who dispute concerning the number of substances that there are in the world. For it is admitted both by monists, who maintain that reality is one substance, and by pluralists, who maintain that reality is many, that it is impossible to imagine any empirical situation which would be relevant to the solution of their dispute. But if we are told that no possible observation could give any probability either to the assertion that reality was one substance or to the assertion that it was many, then we must conclude that neither assertion is significant. We shall see later on[9] that there are genuine logical and empirical questions involved in the dispute between monists and pluralists. But the metaphysical question concerning "substance" is ruled out by our criterion as spurious.

A similar treatment must be accorded to the controversy between realists and idealists, in its metaphysical aspect. A simple illustration which I have made use of in a similar argument elsewhere,[10] will help to demonstrate this. Let us suppose that a picture is discovered and the suggestion made that it was painted by Goya. There is a definite procedure for dealing with such a question. The experts examine the picture to see in what way it resembles the accredited works of Goya, and to see if it bears any marks which are characteristic of a forgery; they look up contemporary records for evidence of the existence of such a picture, and so on. In the end, they may still disagree, but each one knows what empirical evidence would go to confirm or discredit his opinion. Suppose, now, that these men have studied philosophy, and some of them proceed to maintain that this picture is a set of ideas in the perceiver's mind, or in God's mind, others that it is objectively real. What possible experience could any of them have which would be relevant to the solution of this dispute one way or the other? In the ordinary sense of the term "real," in which it is opposed to "illusory," the reality of the picture is not in doubt. The disputants have satisfied themselves that the picture is real, in this sense, by obtaining a correlated series of sensations of sight and sensations of touch. Is there any similar process by which they could discover whether the picture was real, in the sense in which the term "real" is opposed to "ideal"? Clearly there is none. But, if that is so, the problem is fictitious according to our criterion. This does not mean that the realist-idealist controversy may be dismissed without further ado. For it can legitimately be regarded as a dispute concerning the analysis of existential propositions, and so as involving a logical problem which, as we shall see, can be definitively

[9]In Chapter VIII.
[10]Vide "Demonstration of the Impossibility of Metaphysics," *Mind*, 1934, p. 339.

THE ELIMINATION OF METAPHYSICS

solved.[11] What we have just shown is that the question at issue between idealists and realists becomes fictitious when, as is often the case, it is given a metaphysical interpretation.

There is no need for us to give further examples of the operation of our criterion of significance. For our object is merely to show that philosophy, as a genuine branch of knowledge, must be distinguished from metaphysics. We are not now concerned with the historical question how much of what has traditionally passed for philosophy is actually metaphysical. We shall, however, point out later on that the majority of the "great philosophers" of the past were not essentially metaphysicians, and thus reassure those who would otherwise be prevented from adopting our criterion by considerations of piety.

As to the validity of the verification principle, in the form in which we have stated it, a demonstration will be given in the course of this book. For it will be shown that all propositions which have factual content are empirical hypotheses; and that the function of an empirical hypothesis is to provide a rule for the anticipation of experience.[12] And this means that every empirical hypothesis must be relevant to some actual, or possible, experience, so that a statement which is not relevant to any experience is not an empirical hypothesis, and accordingly has no factual content. But this is precisely what the principle of verifiability asserts.

It should be mentioned here that the fact that the utterances of the metaphysician are nonsensical does not follow simply from the fact that they are devoid of factual content. It follows from that fact, together with the fact that they are not *a priori* propositions. And in assuming that they are not *a priori* propositions, we are once again anticipating the conclusions of a later chapter in this book.[13] For it will be shown there that *a priori* propositions, which have always been attractive to philosophers on account of their certainty, owe this certainty to the fact that they are tautologies. We may accordingly define a metaphysical sentence as a sentence which purports to express a genuine proposition, but does, in fact, express neither a tautology nor an empirical hypothesis. And as tautologies and empirical hypotheses form the entire class of significant propositions, we are justified in concluding that all metaphysical assertions are nonsensical. Our next task is to show how they come to be made.

The use of the term "substance," to which we have already referred, provides us with a good example of the way in which metaphysics mostly

---

[11]Vide Chapter VIII.
[12]Vide Chapter V.
[13]Chapter IV.

comes to be written. It happens to be the case that we cannot, in our language, refer to the sensible properties of a thing without introducing a word or phrase which appears to stand for the thing itself as opposed to anything which may be said about it. And, as a result of this, those who are infected by the primitive superstition that to every name a single real entity must correspond assume that it is necessary to distinguish logically between the thing itself and any, or all, of its sensible properties. And so they employ the term "substance" to refer to the thing itself. But from the fact that we happen to employ a single word to refer to a thing, and make that word the grammatical subject of the sentences in which we refer to the sensible appearances of the thing, it does not by any means follow that the thing itself is a "simple entity," or that it cannot be defined in terms of the totality of its appearances. It is true that in talking of "its" appearances we appear to distinguish the thing from the appearances, but that is simply an accident of linguistic usage. Logical analysis shows that what makes these "appearances" the "appearances of" the same thing is not their relationship to an entity other than themselves, but their relationship to one another. The metaphysician fails to see this because he is misled by a superficial grammatical feature of his language.

A simpler and clearer instance of the way in which a consideration of grammar leads to metaphysics is the case of the metaphysical concept of Being. The origin of our temptation to raise questions about Being, which no conceivable experience would enable us to answer, lies in the fact that, in our language, sentences which express existential propositions and sentences which express attributive propositions may be of the same grammatical form. For instance, the sentences "Martyrs exist" and "Martyrs suffer" both consist of a noun followed by an intransitive verb, and the fact that they have grammatically the same appearance leads one to assume that they are of the same logical type. It is seen that in the proposition "Martyrs suffer," the members of a certain species are credited with a certain attribute, and it is sometimes assumed that the same thing is true of such a proposition as "Martyrs exist." If this were actually the case, it would, indeed, be as legitimate to speculate about the Being of martyrs as it is to speculate about their suffering. But, as Kant pointed out,[14] existence is not an attribute. For, when we ascribe an attribute to a thing, we covertly assert that it exists: so that if existence were itself an attribute, it would follow that all positive existential propositions were tautologies, and all negative existential propositions self-contradictory; and this is not the case.[15] So that those who raise questions

[14] Vide *The Critique of Pure Reason*, "Transcendental Dialectic," Book II, Chapter iii, section 4.
[15] This argument is well stated by John Wisdom, *Interpretation and Analysis*, pp. 62, 63.

about Being which are based on the assumption that existence is an attribute are guilty of following grammar beyond the boundaries of sense.

A similar mistake has been made in connection with such propositions as "Unicorns are fictitious." Here again the fact that there is a superficial grammatical resemblance between the English sentences "Dogs are faithful" and "Unicorns are fictitious," and between the corresponding sentences in other languages, creates the assumption that they are of the same logical type. Dogs must exist in order to have the property of being faithful, and so it is held that unless unicorns in some way existed they could not have the property of being fictitious. But, as it is plainly self-contradictory to say that fictitious objects exist, the device is adopted of saying that they are real in some non-empirical sense—that they have a mode of real being which is different from the mode of being of existent things. But since there is no way of testing whether an object is real in this sense, as there is for testing whether it is real in the ordinary sense, the assertion that fictitious objects have a special non-empirical mode of real being is devoid of all literal significance. It comes to be made as a result of the assumption that being fictitious is an attribute. And this is a fallacy of the same order as the fallacy of supposing that existence is an attribute, and it can be exposed in the same way.

In general, the postulation of real non-existent entities results from the superstition, just now referred to, that, to every word or phrase that can be the grammatical subject of a sentence, there must somewhere be a real entity corresponding. For as there is no place in the empirical world for many of these "entities," a special non-empirical world is invoked to house them. To this error must be attributed, not only the utterances of a Heidegger, who bases his metaphysics on the assumption that "Nothing" is a name which is used to denote something peculiarly mysterious,[16] but also the prevalence of such problems as those concerning the reality of propositions and universals whose senselessness, though less obvious, is no less complete.

These few examples afford a sufficient indication of the way in which most metaphysical assertions come to be formulated. They show how easy it is to write sentences which are literally nonsensical without seeing that they are nonsensical. And thus we see that the view that a number of the traditional "problems of philosophy" are metaphysical, and consequently fictitious, does not involve any incredible assumptions about the psychology of philosophers.

Among those who recognise that if philosophy is to be accounted a genuine branch of knowledge it must be defined in such a way as to distinguish it from

---

[16] Vide *Was ist Metaphysik,* by Heidegger: criticised by Rudolf Carnap in his "Überwindung der Metaphysik durch logische Analyse der Sprache," *Erkenntnis,* Vol. II, 1932.

metaphysics, it is fashionable to speak of the metaphysician as a kind of misplaced poet. As his statements have no literal meaning, they are not subject to any criteria of truth or falsehood: but they may still serve to express, or arouse, emotion, and thus be subject to ethical or aesthetic standards. And it is suggested that they may have considerable value, as means of moral inspiration, or even as works of art. In this way, an attempt is made to compensate the metaphysician for his extrusion from philosophy.[17]

I am afraid that this compensation is hardly in accordance with his deserts. The view that the metaphysician is to be reckoned among the poets appears to rest on the assumption that both talk nonsense. But this assumption is false. In the vast majority of cases the sentences which are produced by poets do have literal meaning. The difference between the man who uses language scientifically and the man who uses it emotively is not that the one produces sentences which are incapable of arousing emotion, and the other sentences which have no sense, but that the one is primarily concerned with the expression of true propositions, the other with the creation of a work of art. Thus, if a work of science contains true and important propositions, its value as a work of science will hardly be diminished by the fact that they are inelegantly expressed. And similarly, a work of art is not necessarily the worse for the fact that all the propositions comprising it are literally false. But to say that many literary works are largely composed of falsehoods, is not to say that they are composed of pseudo-propositions. It is, in fact, very rare for a literary artist to produce sentences which have no literal meaning. And where this does occur, the sentences are carefully chosen for their rhythm and balance. If the author writes nonsense, it is because he considers it most suitable for bringing about the effects for which his writing is designed.

The metaphysician, on the other hand, does not intend to write nonsense. He lapses into it through being deceived by grammar, or through committing errors of reasoning, such as that which leads to the view that the sensible world is unreal. But it is not the mark of a poet simply to make mistakes of this sort. There are some, indeed, who would see in the fact that the metaphysician's utterances are senseless a reason against the view that they have aesthetic value. And, without going so far as this, we may safely say that it does not constitute a reason for it.

It is true, however, that although the greater part of metaphysics is merely the embodiment of humdrum errors, there remain a number of metaphysical passages which are the work of genuine mystical feeling; and they may more plausibly be held to have moral or aesthetic value. But, as far as we are

---

[17]For a discussion of this point, see also C. A. Mace, "Representation and Expression," *Analysis*, Vol. I, No. 3; and "Metaphysics and Emotive Language," *Analysis*, Vol. II, Nos. 1 and 2.

concerned, the distinction between the kind of metaphysics that is produced by a philosopher who has been duped by grammar, and the kind that is produced by a mystic who is trying to express the inexpressible, is of no great importance: what is important to us is to realise that even the utterances of the metaphysician who is attempting to expound a vision are literally senseless; so that henceforth we may pursue our philosophical researches with as little regard for them as for the more inglorious kind of metaphysics which comes from a failure to understand the workings of our language.

PART V
PHILOSOPHY OF RELIGION

30 RELIGION
GEORGE SANTAYANA
(1863-1952)

Experience has repeatedly confirmed that well-known maxim of Bacon's, that "a little philosophy inclineth man's mind to atheism, but depth in philosophy bringeth men's minds about to religion." In every age the most comprehensive thinkers have found in the religion of their time and country something they could accept, interpreting and illustrating that religion so as to give it depth and universal application. Even the heretics and atheists, if they have had profundity, turn out after a while to be forerunners of some new orthodoxy. What they rebel against is a religion alien to their nature; they are atheists only by accident, and relatively to a convention which inwardly offends them, but they yearn mightily in their own souls after the religious acceptance of a world interpreted in their own fashion. So it appears in the end that their atheism and loud protestation were in fact the hastier part of their thought, since what emboldened them to deny the poor world's faith was that they were too impatient to understand it. Indeed, the enlightenment common to young wits and worm-eaten old satirists, who plume themselves on detecting the scientific ineptitude of religion—something which the blindest half see—is not nearly enlightened enough: it points to notorious facts incompatible with religious tenets literally taken, but it leaves unexplored the habits of thought from which those tenets sprang, their original meaning, and their true function. Such studies would bring the sceptic face to face with the mystery and pathos of mortal existence. They would make him understand why religion is so profoundly moving and in a sense so profoundly just. There must needs be something humane and necessary in an influence that has become the most general sanction of virtue, the chief occasion for art and philosophy, and the source, perhaps, of the best human happiness. If nothing, as Hooker said, is "so malapert as a splenetic religion," a sour irreligion is almost as perverse.

SOURCE: Reprinted with the permission of Charles Scribner's Sons from *Reason in Religion,* pages 3-6, by George Santayana (volume III of *The Life of Reason*). Copyright 1905 Charles Scribner's Sons: renewal copyright 1933. Permission to reprint also granted by Constable and Company Ltd., London. The title of this selection has been supplied by the editors. Compare with selection 35.

At the same time, when Bacon penned the sage epigram we have quoted he forgot to add that the God to whom depth in philosophy brings back men's minds is far from being the same from whom a little philosophy estranges them. It would be pitiful indeed if mature reflection bred no better conceptions than those which have drifted down the muddy stream of time, where tradition and passion have jumbled everything together. Traditional conceptions, when they are felicitous, may be adopted by the poet, but they must be purified by the moralist and disintegrated by the philosopher. Each religion, so dear to those whose life it sanctifies, and fulfilling so necessary a function in the society that has adopted it, necessarily contradicts every other religion, and probably contradicts itself. What religion a man shall have is a historical accident, quite as much as what language he shall speak. In the rare circumstances where a choice is possible, he may, with some difficulty, make an exchange; but even then he is only adopting a new convention which may be more agreeable to his personal temper but which is essentially as arbitrary as the old.

The attempt to speak without speaking any particular language is not more hopeless than the attempt to have a religion that shall be no religion in particular. A courier's or a dragoman's speech may indeed be often unusual and drawn from disparate sources, not without some mixture of personal originality; but that private jargon will have a meaning only because of its analogy to one or more conventional languages and its obvious derivation from them. So travellers from one religion to another, people who have lost their spiritual nationality, may often retain a neutral and confused residuum of belief, which they may egregiously regard as the essence of all religion, so little may they remember the graciousness and naturalness of that ancestral accent which a perfect religion should have. Yet a moment's probing of the conceptions surviving in such minds will show them to be nothing but vestiges of old beliefs, creases which thought, even if emptied of all dogmatic tenets, has not been able to smooth away at its first unfolding. Later generations, if they have any religion at all, will be found either to revert to ancient authority, or to attach themselves spontaneously to something wholly novel and immensely positive, to some faith promulgated by a fresh genius and passionately embraced by a converted people. Thus every living and healthy religion has a marked idiosyncrasy. Its power consists in its special and surprising message and in the bias which that revelation gives to life. The vistas it opens and the mysteries it propounds are another world to live in; and another world to live in—whether we expect ever to pass wholly into it or no—is what we mean by having a religion. . . .

31 THE NECESSARY EXISTENCE OF GOD

ST. ANSELM (1033-1109)

... Lord, I acknowledge and I thank thee that thou hast created me in this thine image, in order that I may be mindful of thee, may conceive of thee, and love thee; but that image has been so consumed and wasted away by vices, and obscured by the smoke of wrong-doing, that it cannot achieve that for which it was made, except thou renew it, and create it anew. I do not endeavor, O Lord, to penetrate thy sublimity, for in no wise do I compare my understanding with that; but I long to understand in some degree thy truth, which my heart believes and loves. For I do not seek to understand that I may believe, but I believe in order to understand. For this also I believe,—that unless I believed, I should not understand. . . .

And so, Lord, do thou, who dost give understanding to faith, give me, so far as thou knowest it to be profitable, to understand that thou art as we believe; and that thou art that which we believe. And, indeed, we believe that thou art a being than which nothing greater can be conceived. Or is there no such nature, since the fool hath said in his heart, there is no God? . . . But, at any rate, this very fool, when he hears of this being of which I speak—a being than which nothing greater can be conceived—understands what he hears, and what he understands is in his understanding; although he does not understand it to exist.

For, it is one thing for an object to be in the understanding, and another to understand that the object exists. When a painter first conceives of what he will afterwards perform, he has it in his understanding, but he does not yet understand it to be, because he has not yet performed it. But after he has made the painting, he both has it in his understanding, and he understands that it exists, because he has made it.

Hence, even the fool is convinced that something exists in the understanding, at least, than which nothing greater can be conceived. For, when he hears

SOURCE: Part of chapter 1, and chapters 2 through 4 of the *Proslogium,* translated from the Latin by Sidney Norton Deane, Open Court Publishing Co., 1903; reprinted with the kind permission of the publisher. The title of this selection has been supplied by the editors. See also selections 32 and 33.

of this, he understands it. And whatever is understood, exists in the understanding. And assuredly that, than which nothing greater can be conceived, cannot exist in the understanding alone. For, suppose it exists in the understanding alone: then it can be conceived to exist in reality; which is greater.

Therefore, if that, than which nothing greater can be conceived, exists in the understanding alone, the very being, than which nothing greater can be conceived, is one, than which a greater can be conceived. But obviously this is impossible. Hence, there is no doubt that there exists a being, than which nothing greater can be conceived, and it exists both in the understanding and in reality. . . .

And it assuredly exists so truly, that it cannot be conceived not to exist. For, it is possible to conceive of a being which cannot be conceived not to exist; and this is greater than one which can be conceived not to exist. Hence, if that, than which nothing greater can be conceived, can be conceived not to exist, it is not that, than which nothing greater can be conceived. But this is an irreconcilable contradiction. There is, then, so truly a being than which nothing greater can be conceived to exist, that it cannot even be conceived not to exist; and this being thou art, O Lord, our God.

So truly, therefore, dost thou exist, O Lord, my God, that thou canst not be conceived not to exist; and rightly. For, if a mind could conceive of a being better than thee, the creature would rise above the Creator; and this is most absurd. And, indeed, whatever else there is, except thee alone, can be conceived not to exist. To thee alone, therefore, it belongs to exist more truly than all other beings, and hence in a higher degree than all others. For, whatever else exists does not exist so truly, and hence in a less degree it belongs to it to exist. Why, then, has the fool said in his heart, there is no God . . . since it is so evident, to a rational mind, that thou dost exist in the highest degree of all? Why, except that he is dull and a fool? . . .

But how has the fool said in his heart what he could not conceive; or how is it that he could not conceive what he said in his heart? Since it is the same to say in the heart, and to conceive.

But, if really, nay, since really, he both conceived, because he said in his heart; and did not say in his heart, because he could not conceive; there is more than one way in which a thing is said in the heart or conceived. For, in one sense, an object is conceived, when the word signifying it is conceived; and in another, when the very entity, which the object is, is understood.

In the former sense, then, God can be conceived not to exist; but in the latter, not at all. For no one who understands what fire and water are can conceive fire to be water, in accordance with the nature of the facts themselves, although this is possible according to the words. So, then, no one who understands what God is can conceive that God does not exist; although he says these words in his heart, either without any, or with some foreign, signification. For, God is that than which a greater cannot be conceived. And he who thoroughly understands this, assuredly understands that this being so truly exists, that not even in concept can it be nonexistent. Therefore, he who understands that God so exists, cannot conceive that he does not exist.

I thank thee, gracious Lord, I thank thee; because what I formerly believed by thy bounty, I now so understand by thine illumination, that if I were unwilling to believe that thou dost exist, I should not be able not to understand this to be true.

32 REASON, FAITH, AND GOD'S EXISTENCE
ST. THOMAS AQUINAS
(1225–1274)

I. On The Way In Which Divine Truth Is To Be Made Known
. . . There is a twofold mode of truth in what we profess about God. Some truths about God exceed all the ability of the human reason. Such is the truth that God is triune. But there are some truths which the natural reason also is able to reach. Such are that God exists, that He is one, and the like. In fact, such truths about God have been proved demonstratively by the philosophers, guided by the light of the natural reason.

That there are certain truths about God that totally surpass man's ability appears with the greatest evidence. Since, indeed, the principle of all knowledge that the reason perceives about some thing is the understanding of the very substance of that being . . . it is necessary that the way in which we understand the substance of a thing determines the way in which we know what belongs to it. Hence, if the human intellect comprehends the substance of some thing, for example, that of a stone or of a triangle, no intelligible characteristic belonging to that thing surpasses the grasp of the human reason. But this does not happen to us in the case of God. For the human intellect

SOURCE: Part I is from *On the Truth of the Catholic Faith: Summa Contra Gentiles*, Book 1, chapters 3, 7, 10, and 11; translated from the Latin by Anton C. Pegis. Copyright 1955 by Doubleday and Co., Inc. Reprinted by permission of the publisher. Part II is from *Summa Theologica*, Part 1, Question 2, Article 3; translated by Julius R. Weinberg especially for this volume. The title of this selection has been supplied by the editors. Compare with selections 31, 34, and 36.

is not able to reach a comprehension of the divine substance through its natural power. For, according to its manner of knowing in the present life, the intellect depends on the sense for the origin of knowledge; and so those things that do not fall under the senses cannot be grasped by the human intellect except in so far as the knowledge of them is gathered from sensible things. Now, sensible things cannot lead the human intellect to the point of seeing in them the nature of the divine substance; for sensible things are effects that fall short of the power of their cause. Yet, beginning with sensible things, our intellect is led to the point of knowing about God that He exists, and other such characteristics that must be attributed to the First Principle. There are, consequently, some intelligible truths about God that are open to the human reason; but there are others that absolutely surpass its power. . . .

That the Truth of Reason Is Not Opposed to the Truth of the Christian Faith. Now, although the truth of the Christian faith . . . surpasses the capacity of the reason, nevertheless that truth that the human reason is naturally endowed to know cannot be opposed to the truth of the Christian faith. For that with which the human reason is naturally endowed is clearly most true; so much so, that it is impossible for us to think of such truths as false. Nor is it permissible to believe as false that which we hold by faith, since this is confirmed in a way that is so clearly divine. Since, therefore, only the false is opposed to the true, as is clearly evident from an examination of their definitions, it is impossible that the truth of faith should be opposed to those principles that the human reason knows naturally.

Furthermore, that which is introduced into the soul of the student by the teacher is contained in the knowledge of the teacher—unless his teaching is fictitious, which it is improper to say of God. Now, the knowledge of the principles that are known to us naturally has been implanted in us by God; for God is the Author of our nature. These principles, therefore, are also contained by the divine Wisdom. Hence, whatever is opposed to them is opposed to the divine Wisdom, and, therefore, cannot come from God. That which we hold by faith as divinely revealed, therefore, cannot be contrary to our natural knowledge. . . .

From this we evidently gather the following conclusion: whatever arguments are brought forward against the doctrines of faith are conclusions incorrectly derived from the first and self-evident principles imbedded in nature. Such conclusions do not have the force of demonstration; they are arguments that are either probable or sophistical. And so, there exists the possibility to answer them. . . .

The Opinion of Those Who Say That the Existence of God, Being Self-Evident, Cannot be Demonstrated. There are some persons to whom the inquiry seeking to demonstrate that God exists may perhaps appear superfluous. These are the persons who assert that the existence of God is self-evident, in such wise that its contrary cannot be entertained in the mind. It thus appears that the existence of God cannot be demonstrated, as may be seen from the following arguments.

Those propositions are said to be self-evident that are known immediately upon the knowledge of their terms. Thus, as soon as you know the nature of a *whole* and the nature of a *part,* you know immediately that every whole is greater than its part. The proposition *God exists* is of this sort. For by the name *God* we understand something than which a greater cannot be thought. This notion is formed in the intellect by one who hears and understands the name *God.* As a result, God must exist already at least in the intellect. But He cannot exist solely in the intellect, since that which exists both in the intellect and in reality is greater than that which exists in the intellect alone. Now, as the very definition of the name points out, nothing can be greater than God. Consequently, the proposition that God exists is self-evident, as being evident from the very meaning of the name God.

Again, it is possible to think that something exists whose non-existence cannot be thought. Clearly, such a being is greater than the being whose non-existence can be thought. Consequently, if God Himself could be thought not to be, then something greater than God could be thought. This, however, is contrary to the definition of the name God. Hence, the proposition that God exists is self-evident.

Furthermore, those propositions ought to be the most evident in which the same thing is predicated of itself, for example, *man is man,* or whose predicates are included in the definition of their subjects, for example, *man is an animal.* Now, in God . . . it is pre-eminently the case that His being is His essence, so that to the question *what is He?* and to the question *is He?* the answer is one and the same. Thus, in the proposition *God exists,* the predicate is consequently either identical with the subject or at least included in the definition of the subject. Hence, that God exists is self-evident. . . .

These, then, and others like them are the arguments by which some think that the proposition *God exists* is so self-evident that its contrary cannot be entertained by the mind. . . .

A Refutation of the Abovementioned Opinion and a Solution of the Arguments. In part, the above opinion arises from the custom by which from their earliest days people are brought up to hear and to call upon the name of God. Custom, and especially custom in a child, comes to have the force of nature. As a result, what the mind is steeped in from childhood it clings to very firmly, as something known naturally and self-evidently.

In part, however, the above opinion comes about because of a failure to distinguish between that which is self-evident in an absolute sense and that which is self-evident in relation to us. For assuredly that God exists is, absolutely speaking, self-evident, since what God is is His own being. Yet, because we are not able to conceive in our minds that which God is, that God exists remains unknown in relation to us. So, too, that every whole is greater than its part is, absolutely speaking, self-evident; but it would perforce be unknown to one who could not conceive the nature of a whole. . . .

And, contrary to the point made by the *first* argument, it does not follow immediately that, as soon as we know the meaning of the name *God,* the existence of God is known. It does not follow first because it is not known to all, even including those who admit that God exists, that God is that than which a greater cannot be thought. After all, many ancients said that this world itself was God. . . . What is more, granted that everyone should understand by the name *God* something than which a greater cannot be thought, it will still not be necessary that there exist in reality something than which a greater cannot be thought. For a thing and the definition of a name are posited in the same way. Now, from the fact that that which is indicated by the name *God* is conceived by the mind, it does not follow that God exists save only in the intellect. Hence, that than which a greater cannot be thought will likewise not have to exist save only in the intellect. From this it does not follow that there exists in reality something than which a greater cannot be thought. No difficulty, consequently, befalls anyone who posits that God does not exist. For that something greater can be thought than anything given in reality or in the intellect is a difficulty only to him who admits that there is something than which a greater cannot be thought in reality.

Nor, again, is it necessary, as the *second* argument advanced, that something greater than God can be thought if God can be thought not to be. For that He can be thought not to be does not arise either from the imperfection or the uncertainty of His own being, since this is in itself most manifest. It arises, rather, from the weakness of our intellect, which cannot behold God Himself except through His effects and which is thus led to know His existence through reasoning.

This enables us to solve the *third* argument as well. For just as it is evident to us that a whole is greater than a part of itself, so to those seeing the divine essence in itself it is supremely self-evident that God exists because His essence is His being. But, because we are not able to see His essence, we arrive at the knowledge of His being, not through God Himself, but through His effects. . . .

II. [Five Arguments for God's Existence]

. . . The existence of God can be demonstrated in five ways.

The first and more obvious way is taken from the consideration of motion.

Now it is certain and evident to sense that something is in motion in this world. But everything which is in motion is moved by another thing. For nothing is in motion save as it is in potency to that to which it is moved. This is because to move is to lead something from potency into act, and a thing can be led from potency to act only by something in act. For example, that which is actually hot such as fire makes wood which is potentially hot to be actually hot. Thus, by so doing, it moves and alters the wood. Now it is impossible that the same thing be simultaneously in act and potency in the same respect. For this is possible only according to diverse respect. For that which is actually hot can not simultaneously be potentially hot; at that time it is potentially cold. Hence, it is impossible that something be both mover and moved in the same respect. That is, it is impossible that something move itself. Therefore, everything which is in motion is moved by something else. Hence, if that by which something is moved is also moved, it is necessary that it be moved by another and the last mentioned by still another. But this can not go on to infinity, because if it did there would be no first moving thing and hence no other moving thing. This is because secondary movers only move because they have been moved by a first mover, just as a stick only moves something because it has been moved by the hand. Therefore, it is necessary to arrive at some first moving thing which is moved by nothing. Everyone understands this to be God.

The second way is taken from the nature of an efficient cause. For we discover in these sensible things that there is an order of efficient causes. Now, it is neither observed nor is it even possible that something be its own efficient cause. For if anything were its own efficient cause, it would exist prior to itself which is impossible. However, it is not possible that in efficient causes we proceed to infinity, because in all ordered efficient causes the first is the cause of the intermediary and the intermediary is the cause of the last, regardless of whether there is only one or there are many intermediaries. Now, if the cause has been taken away, the effect is removed. Hence, if there had not been a first among efficient causes, there will be neither intermediary causes nor an ultimate effect. But if there is an infinite process among efficient causes, there will be no first efficient cause. Hence there will be neither an ultimate effect nor intermediary efficient causes. Now this is obviously false. Hence it is necessary to posit some first efficient cause which everyone calls God.

The third way is taken from the possible and the necessary which is as follows: We discover among things some which are able to exist and not exist. For some things are found to be generated and corrupted and thus they are able to exist and not exist. Now, it is impossible that all such things always exist because what is able not to exist will at some time not exist. Hence, if all things are capable of not existing, at some time nothing will exist. And if this were so, nothing would now exist because what does not exist only begins to exist through something which does exist. If, therefore, nothing existed it would be impossible for anything to begin to exist. Thus nothing would exist. Now this is obviously false. Hence, not all beings are merely possible, but something necessary must exist among things. However, every necessary being either has some cause of its necessity or it does not. Now it is not possible to proceed to infinity among necessary things which have a cause of their necessity (just as has been proved in the case of efficient causes). Hence it is necessary to posit something which is necessary through itself and which does not have the cause of its necessity elsewhere, but which is the cause of the necessity in other things. Everyone calls this something God.

The fourth way is taken from the degrees which are found among things. For among things some are found to be more or less good, or true, or noble, etc. But greater and less are asserted of divers things according as they approximate in diverse ways something which is greatest, as the greater heat is that which more closely approaches the greatest in heat. Hence there is something which is truest and best and noblest, and hence the greatest being. For those things which are most true are to the greatest extent beings, as [Aristotle says] in the 2nd book of the *Metaphysics*. Now that which is said to be greatest in any genus is the cause of all things which are in that genus, as fire in any genus is the cause of all things which are in that genus, as fire which is most hot, is the cause of all hot things, as is said in the same text of the *Metaphysics*. Hence there is something which is the cause of being and goodness and any other perfection in all beings. This we call God.

The fifth way is taken from the governance of things. For we see that some things which lack intelligence (namely natural bodies) act because of some purpose. The evidence for this is that they always, or for the most part, act in the same way so that they attain that which is best. Hence it is not by chance but rather by intention that these things proceed toward an end. However, those things which do not have intelligence only tend to an end by being directed by something which knows and understands (as in the case of the arrow and the archer). Hence there is some intelligent being by which all natural things are ordered to an end. This we call God. . . .

33 ON EVIL AND THE ARGUMENT FROM DESIGN

DAVID HUME (1711-1776)

[I. The Argument From Design]

... Not to lose any time in circumlocutions, said Cleanthes, addressing himself to Demea, much less in replying to the pious declamations of Philo; I shall briefly explain how I conceive this matter. Look round the world; contemplate the whole and every part of it: you will find it to be nothing but one great machine, subdivided into an infinite number of lesser machines, which again admit of subdivisions, to a degree beyond what human senses and faculties can trace and explain. All these various machines, and even their most minute parts, are adjusted to each other with an accuracy, which ravishes into admiration all men, who have ever contemplated them. The curious adapting of means to ends, throughout all nature, resembles exactly, though it much exceeds, the productions of human contrivance; of human design, thought, wisdom, and intelligence. Since therefore the effects resemble each other, we are led to infer, by all the rules of analogy, that the causes also resemble; and that the Author of Nature is somewhat similar to the mind of men; though possessed of much larger faculties, proportioned to the grandeur of the work, which he has executed. By this argument *a posteriori,* and by this argument alone, do we prove at once the existence of a Deity, and his similarity to human mind and intelligence.

I shall be so free, Cleanthes, said Demea, as to tell you, that from the beginning, I could not approve of your conclusion concerning the similarity of the Deity to men; still less can I approve of the mediums, by which you endeavor to establish it. What! No demonstration of the being of a God! No abstract arguments! No proofs *a priori!* Are these, which have hitherto been so much insisted on by philosophers, all fallacy, all sophism? Can we reach no farther in this subject than experience and probability? I will not say, that this is betraying the cause of a deity: but surely, by this affected candor, you

SOURCE: From Hume's *Dialogues Concerning Natural Religion* (1779), Parts II and X. This work consists of a discussion among three philosophers, named Cleanthes, Demea, and Philo, concerning the foundations of religious belief. The title of this selection has been supplied by the editors. Compare Part I with selections 31 and 32; compare Part II with selection 35.

give advantage to atheists, which they never could obtain, by the mere dint of argument and reasoning.

What I chiefly scruple in this subject, said Philo, is not so much, that all religious arguments are by Cleanthes reduced to experience, as that they appear not to be even the most certain and irrefragable of that inferior kind. That a stone will fall, that fire will burn, that the earth has solidity, we have observed a thousand and a thousand times; and when any new instance of this nature is presented, we draw without hesitation the accustomed inference. The exact similarity of the cases gives us a perfect assurance of a similar event; and a stronger evidence is never desired nor sought after. But wherever you depart, in the least, from the similarity of the cases, you diminish proportionably the evidence; and may at last bring it to a very weak *analogy,* which is confessedly liable to error and uncertainty. After having experienced the circulation of the blood in human creatures, we make no doubt that it takes place in Titius and Maevius: but from its circulation in frogs and fishes, it is only a presumption, though a strong one, from analogy, that it takes place in men and other animals. The analogical reasoning is much weaker, when we infer the circulation of sap in vegetables from our experience that the blood circulates in animals; and those, who hastily followed that imperfect analogy, are found, by more accurate experiments, to have been mistaken.

If we see a house, Cleanthes, we conclude, with the greatest certainty, that it had an architect or builder; because this is precisely that species of effect, which we have experienced to proceed from that species of cause. But surely you will not affirm, that the universe bears such a resemblance to a house, that we can with the same certainty infer a similar cause, or that the analogy is here entire and perfect. The dissimilitude is so striking, that the utmost you can here pretend to is a guess, a conjecture, a presumption concerning a similar cause; and how that pretension will be received in the world, I leave you to consider.

It would surely be very ill received, replied Cleanthes; and I should be deservedly blamed and detested, did I allow, that the proofs of a Deity amounted to no more than a guess or conjecture. But is the whole adjustment of means to ends in a house and in the universe so slight a resemblance? The economy of final causes? The order, proportion, and arrangement of every part? Steps of a stair are plainly contrived, that human legs may use them in mounting; and this inference is certain and infallible. Human legs are also contrived for walking and mounting; and this inference, I allow, is not altogether so certain, because of the dissimilarity which you remark; but does it, therefore, deserve the name only of presumption or conjecture?

Good God! cried Demea, interrupting him, where are we? Zealous defenders of religion allow, that the proofs of a Deity fall short of perfect evidence!

And you, Philo, on whose assistance I depended, in proving the adorable mysteriousness of the Divine Nature, do you assent to all these extravagant opinions of Cleanthes? For what other name can I give them? . . .

You seem not to apprehend, replied Philo, that I argue with Cleanthes in his own way; and by showing him the dangerous consequences of his tenets, hope at last to reduce him to our opinion. . . . Now, according to this method of reasoning, Demea, it follows (and is, indeed, tacitly allowed by Cleanthes himself) that order, arrangement, or the adjustment of final causes is not, of itself, any proof of design, but only so far as it has been experienced to proceed from that principle. For aught we can know *a priori,* matter may contain the source or spring of order originally, within itself, as well as mind does; and there is no more difficulty in conceiving, that the several elements, from an internal unknown cause, may fall into the most exquisite arrangement, than to conceive that their ideas, in the great, universal mind, from a like internal, unknown cause, fall into that arrangement. The equal possibility of both these suppositions is allowed. But by experience we find (according to Cleanthes), that there is a difference between them. Throw several pieces of steel together, without shape or form; they will never arrange themselves so as to compose a watch: stone, and mortar, and wood, without an architect, never erect a house. But the ideas in a human mind, we see, by an unknown, inexplicable economy, arrange themselves so as to form the plan of a watch or house. Experience, therefore, proves, that there is an original principle of order in mind, not in matter. From similar effects we infer similar causes. The adjustment of means to ends is alike in the universe, as in a machine of human contrivance. The causes, therefore, must be resembling. . . .

That all inferences, Cleanthes, concerning fact, are founded on experience, and that all experimental reasonings are founded on the supposition, that similar causes prove similar effects, and similar effects similar causes; I shall not, at present, much dispute with you. But observe, I entreat you, with what extreme caution all just reasoners proceed in the transferring of experiments to similar cases. Unless the cases be exactly similar, they repose no perfect confidence in applying their past observation to any particular phenomenon. Every alteration of circumstances occasions a doubt concerning the event; and it requires new experiments to prove certainly, that the new circumstances are of no moment or importance. A change in bulk, situation, arrangement, age, disposition of the air, or surrounding bodies; any of these particulars may be attended with the most unexpected consequences: and unless the objects be quite familiar to us, it is the highest temerity to expect with assurance, after any of these changes, an event similar to that which before fell under our observation. The slow and deliberate steps of philosophers, here, if anywhere, are distinguished from the precipitate march of the vulgar, who, hurried on by the smallest similitudes, are incapable of all discernment or consideration.

But can you think, Cleanthes, that your usual phlegm and philosophy have been preserved in so wide a step as you have taken, when you compared to the universe, houses, ships, furniture, machines; and from their similarity in some circumstances inferred a similarity in their causes? Thought, design, intelligence, such as we discover in men and other animals, is no more than one of the springs and principles of the universe, as well as heat or cold, attraction or repulsion, and a hundred others, which fall under daily observation. It is an active cause, by which some particular parts of nature, we find, produce alterations on other parts. But can a conclusion, with any propriety, be transferred from parts to the whole? Does not the great disproportion bar all comparison and inference? From observing the growth of a hair, can we learn anything concerning the generation of a man? Would the manner of a leaf's blowing, even though perfectly known, afford us any instruction concerning the vegetation of a tree?

But allowing that we were to take the *operations* of one part of nature upon another for the foundation of our judgment concerning the *origin* of the whole (which never can be admitted), yet why select so minute, so weak, so bounded a principle as the reason and design of animals is found to be upon this planet? What peculiar privilege has this little agitation of the brain which we call *thought*, that we must thus make it the model of the whole universe? Our partiality in our own favor does indeed present it on all occasions; but sound philosophy ought carefully to guard against so natural an illusion. . . .

[II. Evil]

. . . The whole earth, believe me, Philo, is cursed and polluted [said Demea]. A perpetual war is kindled amongst all living creatures. Necessity, hunger, want, stimulate the strong and courageous: fear, anxiety, terror, agitate the weak and infirm. The first entrance into life gives anguish to the new-born infant and to its wretched parent: weakness, impotence, distress, attend each stage of that life: and 'tis at last finished in agony and horror.

Observe too, says Philo, the curious artifices of nature, in order to embitter the life of every living being. The stronger prey upon the weaker, and keep them in perpetual terror and anxiety. The weaker too, in their turn, often prey upon the stronger, and vex and molest them without relaxation. Consider that innumerable race of insects, which either are bred on the body of each animal, or flying about infix their stings in him. These insects have others still less than themselves, which torment them. And thus on each hand, before and behind, above and below, every animal is surrounded with enemies, which incessantly seek his misery and destruction.

Man alone, said Demea, seems to be, in part, an exception to this rule. For by combination in society, he can easily master lions, tigers, and bears, whose greater strength and agility naturally enable them to prey upon him.

On the contrary, it is here chiefly, cried Philo, that the uniform and equal maxims of nature are most apparent. Man, it is true, can, by combination, surmount all his *real* enemies, and become master of the whole animal creation: but does he not immediately raise up to himself *imaginary* enemies, the demons of his fancy, who haunt him with superstitious terrors, and blast every enjoyment of life? His pleasure, as he imagines, becomes, in their eyes, a crime: his food and repose give them umbrage and offense: his very sleep and dreams furnish new materials to anxious fear: and even death, his refuge from every other ill, presents only the dread of endless and innumerable woes. Nor does the wolf molest more the timid flock, than superstition does the anxious breast of wretched mortals.

Besides, consider, Demea; this very society, by which we surmount those wild beasts, our natural enemies; what new enemies does it not raise to us? What woe and misery does it not occasion? Man is the greatest enemy of man. Oppression, injustice, contempt, contumely, violence, sedition, war, calumny, treachery, fraud; by these they mutually torment each other: and they would soon dissolve that society which they had formed, were it not for the dread of still greater ills, which must attend their separation.

But though these external insults, said Demea, from animals, from men, from all the elements, which assault us, form a frightful catalogue of woes, they are nothing in comparison of those, which arise within ourselves, from the distempered condition of our mind and body. How many lie under the lingering torment of diseases? . . . The disorders of the mind . . . though more secret, are not perhaps less dismal and vexatious. Remorse, shame, anguish, rage, disappointment, anxiety, fear, dejection, despair; who has ever passed through life without cruel inroads from these tormentors: How many have scarcely ever felt any better sensations? Labor and poverty, so abhorred by everyone, are the certain lot of the far greater number; and those few privileged persons, who enjoy ease and opulence, never reach contentment or true felicity. All the goods of life united would not make a very happy man: but all the ills united would make a wretch indeed; and anyone of them almost (and who can be free from everyone), nay often the absence of one good (and who can possess all), is sufficient to render life ineligible.

Were a stranger to drop, on a sudden, into this world, I would show him, as a specimen of its ills, an hospital full of diseases, a prison crowded with malefactors and debtors, a field of battle strewed with carcasses, a fleet floundering in the ocean, a nation languishing under tyranny, famine, or pestilence. To turn the gay side of life to him, and give him a notion of its pleasures; whither should I conduct him? to a ball, to an opera, to court? He might justly think, that I was only showing him a diversity of distress and sorrow....

... Ask youself, ask any of your acquaintance, whether they would live over again the last ten or twenty years of their lives. No! but the next twenty, they say, will be better:

> And from the dregs of life, hope to receive
> What the first sprightly running could not give.

Thus at last they find (such is the greatest of human misery; it reconciles even contradictions) that they complain, at once, of the shortness of life, and of its vanity and sorrow.

And is it possible, Cleanthes, said Philo, that after all these reflections, and infinitely more, which might be suggested, you can still persevere in your anthropomorphism, and assert the moral attributes of the Deity, his justice, benevolence, mercy, and rectitude, to be of the same nature with these virtues in human creatures? His power we allow infinite: whatever he wills is executed: but neither man nor any other animal is happy: therefore he does not will their happiness. His wisdom is infinite: he is never mistaken in choosing the means to any end: but the course of nature tends not to human or animal felicity: therefore it is not established for that purpose. Through the whole compass of human knowledge, there are no inferences more certain and infallible than these. In what respect, then, do his benevolence and mercy resemble the benevolence and mercy of men?

Epicurus's old questions are yet unanswered.

Is he willing to prevent evil, but not able? then is he impotent. Is he able, but not willing? then is he malevolent. Is he both able and willing? whence then is evil? ...

34 THE POSSIBILITY OF RELIGIOUS KNOWLEDGE

ALFRED JULES AYER (1910-   )

... This mention of God brings us to the question of the possibility of religious knowledge. We shall see that this possibility has already been ruled out by our treatment of metaphysics. But, as this a point of considerable interest, we may be permitted to discuss it at some length.

It is now generally admitted, at any rate by philosophers, that the existence of a being having the attributes which define the god of any non-animistic religion cannot be demonstratively proved. To see that this is so, we have only to ask ourselves what are the premises from which the existence of such a god could be deduced. If the conclusion that a god exists is to be demonstratively certain, then these premises must be certain; for, as the conclusion of a deductive argument is already contained in the premises, any uncertainty there may be about the truth of the premises is necessarily shared by it. But we know that no empirical proposition can ever be anything more than probable. It is only *a priori* propositions that are logically certain. But we cannot deduce the existence of a god from an *a priori* proposition. For we know that the reason why *a priori* propositions are certain is that they are tautologies. And from a set of tautologies nothing but a further tautology can be validly deduced. It follows that there is no possibility of demonstrating the existence of a god.

What is not so generally recognised is that there can be no way of proving that the existence of a god, such as the God of Christianity, is even probable. Yet this also is easily shown. For if the existence of such a god were probable, then the proposition that he existed would be an empirical hypothesis. And in that case it would be possible to deduce from it, and other empirical hypotheses, certain experiential propositions which were not deducible from those other hypotheses alone. But in fact this is not possible. It is sometimes claimed, indeed, that the existence of a certain sort of regularity in nature

SOURCE: From chapter 6, pp. 114–20, of *Language, Truth and Logic* by A. J. Ayer (first published 1936; 2nd ed., 1946). Victor Gollancz Ltd., London, 1946. Reprinted through the permission of the publisher. The title of this selection has been supplied by the editors. Compare with selections 29, 31, and 38.

constitutes sufficient evidence for the existence of a god. But if the sentence "God exists" entails no more than that certain types of phenomena occur in certain sequences, then to assert the existence of a god will be simply equivalent to asserting that there is the requisite regularity in nature; and no religious man would admit that this was all he intended to assert in asserting the existence of a god. He would say that in talking about God, he was talking about a transcendent being who might be known through certain empirical manifestations, but certainly could not be defined in terms of those manifestations. But in that case the term "god" is a metaphysical term. And if "god" is a metaphysical term, then it cannot be even probable that a god exists. For to say that "God exists" is to make a metaphysical utterance which cannot be either true or false. And by the same criterion, no sentence which purports to describe the nature of a transcendent god can possess any literal significance.

It is important not to confuse this view of religious assertions with the view that is adopted by atheists, or agnostics.[1] For it is characteristic of an agnostic to hold that the existence of a god is a possibility in which there is no good reason either to believe or disbelieve; and it is characteristic of an atheist to hold that it is at least probable that no god exists. And our view that all utterances about the nature of God are nonsensical, so far from being identical with, or even lending any support to, either of these familiar contentions, is actually incompatible with them. For if the assertion that there is a god is nonsensical, then the atheist's assertion that there is no god is equally nonsensical, since it is only a significant proposition that can be significantly contradicted. As for the agnostic, although he refrains from saying either that there is or that there is not a god, he does not deny that the question whether a transcendent god exists is a genuine question. He does not deny that the two sentences "There is a transcendent god" and "There is no transcendent god" express propositions one of which is actually true and the other false. All he says is that we have no means of telling which of them is true, and therefore ought not to commit ourselves to either. But we have seen that the sentences in question do not express propositions at all. And this means that agnosticism also is ruled out.

Thus we offer the theist the same comfort as we gave to the moralist. His assertions cannot possibly be valid, but they cannot be invalid either. As he says nothing at all about the world, he cannot justly be accused of saying anything false, or anything for which he has insufficient grounds. It is only when the theist claims that in asserting the existence of a transcendent god he is expressing a genuine propostion that we are entitled to disagree with him.

[1] This point was suggested to me by Professor H. H. Price.

It is to be remarked that in cases where deities are identified with natural objects, assertions concerning them may be allowed to be significant. If, for example, a man tells me that the occurrence of thunder is alone both necessary and sufficient to establish the truth of the proposition that Jehovah is angry, I may conclude that, in his usage of words, the sentence "Jehovah is angry" is equivalent to "It is thundering." But in sophisticated religions, though they may be to some extent based on men's awe of natural process which they cannot sufficiently understand, the "person" who is supposed to control the empirical world is not himself located in it; he is held to be superior to the empirical world, and so outside it; and he is endowed with super-empirical attributes. But the notion of a person whose essential attributes are non-empirical is not an intelligible notion at all. We may have a word which is used as if it named this "person," but, unless the sentences in which it occurs express propositions which are empirically verifiable, it cannot be said to symbolize anything. And this is the case with regard to the word "god," in the usage in which it is intended to refer to a transcendent object. The mere existence of the noun is enough to foster the illusion that there is a real, or at any rate a possible entity corresponding to it. It is only when we enquire what God's attributes are that we discover that "God," in this usage, is not a genuine name.

It is common to find belief in a transcendent god conjoined with belief in an after-life. But, in the form which it usually takes, the content of this belief is not a genuine hypothesis. To say that men do not ever die, or that the state of death is merely a state of prolonged insensibility, is indeed to express a significant proposition, though all the available evidence goes to show that it is false. But to say there is something imperceptible inside a man, which is his soul or his real self, and that it goes on living after he is dead, is to make a metaphysical assertion which has no more factual content than the assertion that there is a transcendent god.

It is worth mentioning that, according to the account which we have given of religious assertions, there is no logical ground for antagonism between religion and natural science. As far as the question of truth or falsehood is concerned, there is no opposition between the natural scientist and the theist who believes in a transcendent god. For since the religious utterances of the theist are not genuine propositions at all, they cannot stand in any logical relation to the propositions of science. Such antagonism as there is between religion and science appears to consist in the fact that science takes away one of the motives which make men religious. For it is acknowledged that one of the ultimate sources of religious feeling lies in the inability of men to determine their own destiny; and science tends to destroy the feeling of awe with which men regard an alien world, by making them believe that they can understand and anticipate the course of natural phenomena, and even to some extent control it. The fact that it has recently become fashionable for physicists themselves to be sympathetic towards religion is a point in favour of this hypothesis. For this sympathy towards religion marks the physicists' own lack of confidence in the validity of their hypotheses, which is a reaction on their part from the anti-religious dogmatism of nineteenth-century scientists, and a natural outcome of the crisis through which physics has just passed.

It is not within the scope of this enquiry to enter more deeply into the causes of religious feeling, or to discuss the probability of the continuance of religious belief. We are concerned only to answer those questions which arise out of our discussion of the possibility of religious knowledge. The point which we wish to establish is that there cannot be any transcendent truths of religion. For the sentences which the theist uses to express such "truths" are not literally significant.

An interesting feature of this conclusion is that it accords with what many theists are accustomed to say themselves. For we are often told that the nature of God is a mystery which transcends the human understanding. But to say that something transcends the human understanding is to say that it is unintelligible. And what is unintelligible cannot significantly be described. Again, we are told that God is not an object of reason but an object of faith. This may be nothing more than than an admission that the existence of God must be taken on trust, since it cannot be proved. But it may also be an assertion that God is the object of a purely mystical intuition, and cannot therefore be defined in terms which are intelligible to the reason. And I think there are many theists who would assert this. But if one allows that it is impossible to define God in intelligible terms, then one is allowing that it is impossible for a sentence both to be significant and to be about God. If a mystic admits that the object of his vision is something which cannot be described, then he must also admit that he is bound to talk nonsense when he describes it.

For his part, the mystic may protest that his intuition does reveal truths to him, even though he cannot explain to others what these truths are; and that we who do not possess this faculty of intuition can have no ground for denying that it is a cognitive faculty. For we can hardly maintain *a priori* that there are no ways of discovering true propositions except those which we ourselves employ. The answer is that we set no limit to the number of ways in which one may come to formulate a true proposition. We do not in any way deny that a synthetic truth may be discovered by purely intuitive methods as well as by the rational method of induction. But we do say that every synthetic proposition, however it may have been arrived at, must be subject to the test of actual experience. We do not deny *a priori* that the mystic is

THE POSSIBILITY OF RELIGIOUS KNOWLEDGE

able to discover truths by his own special methods. We wait to hear what are the propositions which embody his discoveries, in order to see whether they are verified or confuted by our empirical observations. But the mystic, so far from producing propositions which are empirically verified, is unable to produce any intelligible propositions at all. And therefore we say that his intuition has not revealed to him any facts. It is no use his saying that he has apprehended facts but is unable to express them. For we know that if he really had acquired any information, he would be able to express it. He would be able to indicate in some way or other how the genuineness of his discovery might be empirically determined. The fact that he cannot reveal what he "knows," or even himself devise an empirical test to validate his "knowledge," shows that his state of mystical intuition is not a genuinely cognitive state. So that in describing his vision the mystic does not give us any information about the external world; he merely gives us indirect information about the condition of his own mind.

These considerations dispose of the argument from religious experience, which many philosophers still regard as a valid argument in favour of the existence of a god. They say that it is logically possible for men to be immediately acquainted with God, as they are immediately acquainted with a sense-content, and that there is no reason why one should be prepared to believe a man when he says that he is seeing a yellow patch, and refuse to believe him when he says that he is seeing God. The answer to this is that if the man who asserts that he is seeing God is merely asserting that he is experiencing a peculiar kind of sense-content, then we do not for a moment deny that his assertion may be true. But, ordinarily, the man who says that he is seeing God is saying not merely that he is experiencing a religious emotion, but also that there exists a transcendent being who is the object of this emotion; just as the man who says that he sees a yellow patch is ordinarily saying not merely that his visual sense-field contains a yellow sense-content, but also that there exists a yellow object to which the sense-content belongs. And it is not irrational to be prepared to believe a man when he asserts the existence of a yellow object, and to refuse to believe him when he asserts the existence of a transcendent god. For whereas the sentence "There exists here a yellow-coloured material thing" expresses a genuine synthetic proposition which could be empirically verified, the sentence "There exists a transcendent god" has, as we have seen, no literal significance.

We conclude, therefore, that the argument from religious experience is altogether fallacious. The fact that people have religious experiences is interesting from the psychological point of view, but it does not in any way imply that there is such a thing as religious knowledge, any more than our having moral experiences implies that there is such a thing as moral knowledge. The theist, like the moralist, may believe that his experiences are cognitive experiences, but, unless he can formulate his "knowledge" in propositions that are empirically verifiable, we may be sure that he is deceiving himself. It follows that those philosophers who fill their books with assertions that they intuitively "know" this or that moral or religious "truth" are merely providing material for the psycho-analyst. For no act of intuition can be said to reveal a truth about any matter of fact unless it issues in verifiable propositions. And all such propositions are to be incorporated in the system of empirical propositions which constitutes science.

35 THE WILL TO BELIEVE
WILLIAM JAMES (1842–1910)

1. ... Let us give the name of *hypothesis* to anything that may be proposed to our belief; and just as the electricans speak of live and dead wires, let us speak of any hypothesis as either *live* or *dead*. A live hypothesis is one which appeals as a real possibility to him to whom it is proposed. If I ask you to believe in the Mahdi, the notion makes no electric connection with your nature—it refuses to scintillate with any credibility at all. As an hypothesis it is completely dead. To an Arab, however (even if he be not one of the Mahdi's followers), the hypothesis is among the mind's possibilities: it is alive. This shows that deadness and liveness in an hypothesis are not intrinsic properties, but relations to the individual thinker. They are measured by his willingness to act irrevocably. Practically, that means belief; but there is some believing tendency wherever there is willingness to act at all.

Next, let us call the decision between two hypotheses an *option*. Options may be of several kinds. They may be—first, *living* or *dead*; secondly, *forced* or *avoidable*; thirdly, *momentous* or *trivial*; and for our purposes we may call an option a *genuine* option when it is of the forced, living, and momentous kind.

(1) A living option is one in which both hypotheses are live ones. If I say to you: "Be a theosophist or be a Mohammedan," it is probably a dead option, because for you neither hypothesis is likely to be alive. But if I say: "Be an agnostic or be a Christian," it is otherwise: trained as you are, each hypothesis makes some appeal, however small, to your belief.

SOURCE: From *The Will to Believe and Other Essays* (1897). Compare with selections 15, 36, and 37.

(2) Next, if I say to you: "Choose between going out with your umbrella or without it," I do not offer you a genuine option, for it is not forced. You can easily avoid it by not going out at all. Similarly, if I say, "Either love me or hate me," "Either call my theory true or call it false," your option is avoidable. You may remain indifferent to me, neither loving nor hating, and you may decline to offer any judgment as to my theory. But if I say, "Either accept this truth or go without it," I put on you a forced option, for there is no standing place outside of the alternative. Every dilemma based on a complete logical disjunction, with no possibility of not choosing, is an option of this forced kind.

(3) Finally, if I were Dr. Nansen and proposed to you to join my North Pole expedition, your option would be momentous; for this would probably be your only similar opportunity, and your choice now would either exclude you from the North Pole sort of immortality altogether or put at least the chance of it into your hands. He who refuses to embrace a unique opportunity loses the prize as surely as if he tried and failed. *Per contra,* the option is trivial when the opportunity is not unique, when the stake is insignificant, or when the decision is reversible if it later prove unwise. Such trivial options abound in the scientific life. A chemist finds an hypothesis live enough to spend a year in its verification: he believes in it to that extent. But if his experiments prove inconclusive either way, he is quit for his loss of time, no vital harm being done. It will facilitate our discussion if we keep all these distinctions in mind. . . .

2. . . . The thesis I defend is . . . this: *Our passional nature not only lawfully may, but must, decide an option between propositions, whenever it is a genuine option that cannot by its nature be decided on intellectual grounds; for to say, under such circumstances, "Do not decide, but leave the question open," is itself a passional decision—just like deciding yes or no—and is attended with the same risk of losing the truth.* . . .

3. . . . Wherever the option between losing truth and gaining it is not momentous, we can throw the chance of *gaining truth* away, and at any rate save ourselves from any chance of *believing falsehood,* by not making up our minds at all till objective evidence has come. In scientific questions, this is almost always the case; and even in human affairs in general, the need of acting is seldom so urgent that a false belief to act on is better than no belief at all. Law courts, indeed, have to decide on the best evidence attainable for the moment, because a judge's duty is to make law as well as to ascertain it, and (as a learned judge once said to me) few cases are worth spending much time over: the great thing is to have them decided on *any* acceptable principle, and got out of the way. But in our dealings with objective nature

we obviously are recorders, not makers, of the truth; and decisions for the mere sake of deciding promptly and getting on to the next business would be wholly out of place. Throughout the breadth of physical nature facts are what they are quite independently of us, and seldom is there any such hurry about them that the risks of being duped by believing a premature theory need be faced. The questions here are always trivial options, the hypotheses are hardly living (at any rate not living for us spectators), the choice between believing truth or falsehood is seldom forced. The attitude of sceptical balance is therefore the absolutely wise one if we would escape mistakes. What difference, indeed, does it make to most of us whether we have or have not a theory of the Röntgen rays, whether we believe or not in mind-stuff, or have a conviction about the causality of conscious states? It makes no difference. Such options are not forced on us. On every account it is better not to make them, but still keep weighing reasons *pro et contra* with an indifferent hand.

I speak, of course, here of the purely judging mind. For purposes of discovery such indifference is to be less highly recommended, and science would be far less advanced than she is if the passionate desires of individuals to get their own faiths confirmed had been kept out of the game. . . . If you want an absolute duffer in an investigation, you must, after all, take the man who has no interest whatever in its results: he is the warranted incapable, the positive fool. The most useful investigator, because the most sensitive observer, is always he whose eager interest in one side of the question is balanced by an equally keen nervousness lest he become deceived. Science has organized this nervousness into a regular *technique,* her so-called method of verification; and she has fallen so deeply in love with the method that one may even say she has ceased to care for truth by itself at all. It is only truth as technically verified that interests her. The truth of truths might come in merely affirmative form, and she would decline to touch it. Such truth as that, she might repeat with Clifford, would be stolen in defiance of her duty to mankind. Human passions, however, are stronger than technical rules. *"Le coeur a ses raisons,"* as Pascal says, *"que la raison ne connait pas"* *; and however indifferent to all but the bare rules of the game the umpire, the abstract intellect, may be, the concrete players who furnish him the materials to judge of are usually, each one of them, in love with some pet "live hypothesis" of his own. Let us agree, however, that wherever there is no forced option, the dispassionately judicial intellect with no pet hypothesis, saving us, as it does, from dupery at any rate, ought to be our ideal.

The question next arises: Are there not somewhere forced options in our speculative questions, and can we (as men who may be interested at least as

*The heart has its reasons, that reason does not know.

much in positively gaining truth as in merely escaping dupery) always wait with impunity till the coercive evidence shall have arrived? It seems *a priori* improbable that the truth should be so nicely adjusted to our needs and powers as that. In the great boarding-house of nature, the cakes and the butter and the syrup seldom come out so even and leave the plates so clean. Indeed, we should view them with scientific suspicion if they did.

4. *Moral questions* immediately present themselves as questions whose solution cannot wait for sensible proof. A moral question is a question not of what sensibly exists, but of what is good, or would be good if it did exist. Science can tell us what exists; but to compare the *worths,* both of what exists and of what does not exist, we must consult not science, but what Pascal calls our heart. Science herself consults her heart when she lays it down that the infinite ascertainment of fact and correction of false belief are the supreme goods for man. Challenge the statement, and science can only repeat it oracularly, or else prove it by showing that such ascertainment and correction bring men all sorts of other goods which man's heart in turn declares. The question of having moral beliefs at all or not having them is decided by our will. Are our moral preferences true or false, or are they only odd biological phenomena, making things good or bad for *us,* but in themselves indifferent? How can your pure intellect decide? If your heart does not *want* a world of moral reality, your head will assuredly never make you believe in one. Mephistophelian scepticism, indeed, will satisfy the head's play-instincts much better than any rigorous idealism can. Some men (even at the student age) are so naturally cool-hearted that the moralistic hypothesis never has for them any pungent life, and in their supercilious presence the hot young moralist always feels strangely ill at ease. The appearance of knowingness is on their side, of *naivete* and gullibility on his. Yet, in the articulate heart of him, he clings to it that he is not a dupe, and that there is a realm in which (as Emerson says) all their wit and intellectual superiority is no better than the cunning of a fox. Moral scepticism can no more be refuted or proved by logic than intellectual scepticism can. When we stick to it that there *is* truth (be it of either kind), we do so with our whole nature, and resolve to stand or fall by the results. The sceptic with his whole nature adopts the doubting attitude; but which of us is the wiser, Omniscience only knows.

Turn now from these wide questions of good to a certain class of questions of fact, questions concerning personal relations, states of mind between one man and another. *Do you like me or not?*—for example. Whether you do or not depends, in countless instances, on whether I meet you half-way, am willing to assume that you must like me, and show you trust and expectation. The previous faith on my part in your liking's existence is in such cases what makes your liking come. But if I stand aloof, and refuse to budge an inch until I have objective evidence . . . ten to one your liking never comes. How many women's hearts are vanquished by the mere sanguine insistence of some man that they *must* love him! He will not consent to the hypothesis that they cannot. The desire for a certain kind of truth here brings about that special truth's existence; and so it is in innumerable cases of other sorts. Who gains promotions, boons, appointments, but the man in whose life they are seen to play the part of live hypotheses, who discounts them, sacrifices other things for their sake before they have come, and takes risks for them in advance? His faith acts on the powers above him as a claim, and creates its own verification.

A social organism of any sort whatever, large or small, is what it is because each member proceeds to his own duty with a trust that the other members will simultaneously do theirs. Wherever a desired result is achieved by the co-operation of many independent persons, its existence as a fact is a pure consequence of the precursive faith in one another of those immediately concerned. A government, an army, a commercial system, a ship, a college, an athletic team, all exist on this condition, without which not only is nothing achieved, but nothing is even attempted. A whole train of passengers (individually brave enough) will be looted by a few highwaymen, simply because the latter can count on one another, while each passenger fears that if he makes a movement of resistance, he will be shot before any one else backs him up. If we believed that the whole carfull would rise at once with us, we should each severally rise, and trainrobbing would never be attempted. There are, then, cases where a fact cannot come at all unless a preliminary faith exists in its coming. *And where faith in a fact can help create the fact,* that would be an insane logic which should say that faith running ahead of scientific evidence is the "lowest kind of immorality" into which a thinking being can fall. Yet such is the logic by which our scientific absolutists pretend to regulate our lives!

5. In truths dependent on our personal action, then, faith based on desire is certainly a lawful and possibly an indispensable thing.

But now, it will be said, these are all childish human cases, and have nothing to do with great cosmical matters, like the question of religious faith. Let us then pass on to that. Religions differ so much in their accidents that in discussing the religious question we must make it very generic and broad. What then do we now mean by the religious hypothesis? Science says things are; morality says some things are better than other things; and religion says essentially two things.

First, she says that the best things are the more eternal things, the overlapping things, the things in the universe that throw the last stone, so to speak, and say the final word. "Perfection is eternal"—this phrase of Charles Secretan seems a good way of putting this first affirmation of religion, an affirmation which obviously cannot yet be verified scientifically at all.

The second affirmation of religion is that we are better off even now if we believe her first affirmation to be true.

Now, let us consider what the logical elements of this situation are *in case the religious hypothesis in both its branches be really true.* (Of course, we must admit that possibility at the outset. If we are to discuss the question at all, it must involve a living option. If for any of you religion be a hypothesis that cannot, by any living possibility, be true, then you need go no farther. I speak to the "saving remnant" alone.) So proceeding, we see, first, that religion offers itself as a *momentous* option. We are supposed to gain, even now, by our belief, and to lose by our non-belief, a certain vital good. Secondly, religion is a *forced* option, so far as that good goes. We cannot escape the issue by remaining sceptical and waiting for more light, because, although we do avoid error in that way *if religion be untrue,* we lose the good, *if it be true,* just as certainly as if we positively chose to disbelieve. It is as if a man should hesitate indefinitely to ask a certain woman to marry him because he was not perfectly sure that she would prove an angel after he brought her home. Would he not cut himself off from that particular angel-possibility as decisively as if he went and married some one else? Scepticism, then, is not avoidance of option; it is option of a certain particular kind of risk. *Better risk loss of truth than chance of error*—that is your faith-vetoer's exact position. He is actively playing his stake as much as the believer is; he is backing the field against the religious hypothesis, just as the believer is backing the religious hypothesis against the field. To preach scepticism to us as a duty until "sufficient evidence" for religion be found, is tantamount therefore to telling us, when in presence of the religious hypothesis, that to yield to our fear of its being error is wiser and better than to yield to our hope that it may be true. It is not intellect against all passions, then; it is only intellect with one passion laying down its law. And by what, forsooth, is the supreme wisdom of this passion warranted? Dupery for dupery, what proof is there that dupery through hope is so much worse than dupery through fear? I, for one, can see no proof; and I simply refuse obedience to the scientist's command to imitate his kind of option, in a case where my own stake is important enough to give me the right to choose my own form of risk. If religion be true and the evidence for it be still insufficient, I do not wish, by putting your extinguisher upon my nature (which feels to me as if it had after all some business in this matter), to forfeit my sole chance in life of getting upon the winning side—that chance depending, of course, on my willingness to run the risk of acting as if my passional need of taking the world religiously might be prophetic and right.

All this is on the supposition that it really may be prophetic and right, and that, even to us who are discussing the matter, religion is a live hypothesis which may be true. Now, to most of us religion comes in a still further way that makes a veto on our active faith even more illogical. The more perfect and more eternal aspect of the universe is represented in our religions as having personal form. The universe is no longer a mere *It* to us, but a *Thou,* if we are religious; and any relation that may be possible from person to person might be possible here. For instance, although in one sense we are passive portions of the universe, in another we show a curious autonomy, as if we were small active centres on our own account. We feel, too, as if the appeal of religion to us were made to our own active good-will, as if evidence might be forever witheld from us unless we met the hypothesis half-way. To take a trivial illustration: just as a man who in a company of gentlemen made no advances, asked a warrant for every concession, and believed no one's word without proof, would cut himself off by such churlishness from all the social rewards that a more trusting spirit would earn—so here, one who should shut himself up in snarling logicality and try to make the gods extort his recognition willy-nilly, or not get it at all, might cut himself off forever from his only opportunity of making the gods' acquaintance. This feeling, forced on us we know not whence, that by obstinately believing that there are gods (although not to do so would be so easy both for our logic and our life) we are doing the universe the deepest service we can, seems part of the living essence of the religious hypothesis. If the hypothesis *were* true in all its parts, including this one, then pure intellectualism, with its veto on our making willing advances, would be an absurdity; and some participation of our sympathetic nature would be logically required. I, therefore, for one, cannot see my way to accepting the agnostic rules for truth-seeking, or wilfully agree to keep my willing nature out of the game. I cannot do so for this plain reason, that *a rule of thinking which would absolutely prevent me from acknowledging certain kinds of truth if those kinds of truth were really there, would be an irrational rule.* That for me is the long and short of the formal logic of the situation, no matter what the kinds of truth might materially be.

I confess I do not see how this logic can be escaped. But sad experience makes me fear that some of you may still shrink from radically saying with me, *in abstracto,* that we have the right to believe at our own risk any hypothesis that is live enough to tempt our will. I suspect, however, that if this is so, it is because you have got away from the abstract logical point of view altogether, and are thinking (perhaps without realizing it) of some particular religious hypothesis which for you is dead. The freedom to "believe what we will" you apply to the case of some patent superstition; and the faith you think of is the faith defined by the schoolboy when he said, "Faith is when you believe something that you know ain't true." I can only repeat that this is misapprehension. *In concreto,* the freedom to believe can only cover living options which the intellect of the individual cannot by itself resolve; and living options never seem absurdities to him who has them to consider. When I look at the religious question as it really puts itself to concrete men, and when I think of all the possibilities which both practically and theoretically it involves, then this command that we shall put a stopper on our heart, instincts, and courage, and *wait*—acting of course meanwhile more or less as if religion were *not* true—till doomsday, or till such time as our intellect and senses working together may have raked in evidence enough—this command, I say, seems to me the queerest idol ever manufactured in the philosophic cave. Were we scholastic absolutists, there might be more excuse. If we had an infallible intellect with its objective certitudes, we might feel ourselves disloyal to such a perfect organ of knowledge in not trusting to it exclusively, in not waiting for its releasing word. But if we are empiricists, if we believe that no bell in us tolls to let us know for certain when truth is in our grasp, then it seems a piece of idle fantasticality to preach so solemnly our duty of waiting for the bell. Indeed we *may* wait if we will—I hope you do not think that I am denying that—but if we do so, we do so at our peril as much as if we believed. In either case we *act,* taking our life in our hands. No one of us ought to issue vetoes to the other, nor should we bandy words of abuse. We ought, on the contrary, delicately and profoundly to respect one another's mental freedom: then only shall we bring about the intellectual republic; then only shall we have that spirit of inner tolerance without which all our outer tolerance is soulless, and which is empiricism's glory; then only shall we live and let live, in speculative as well as in practical things. . . .

36 FAITH, BELIEF, AND ACTION
WILLIAM JAMES (1842-1910)

. . . There is one element of our active nature which . . . philosophers as a rule have with great insincerity tried to huddle out of sight in their pretension to found systems of absolute certainty. I mean the element of faith. Faith means belief in something concerning which doubt is still theoretically possible; and as the test of belief is willingness to act, one may say that faith is the readiness to act in a cause the prosperous issue of which is not certified to us in advance. It is in fact the same moral quality which we call courage in practical affairs. . . .

The necessity of faith as an ingredient in our mental attitude is strongly insisted on by the scientific philosophers of the present day; but by a singularly arbitrary caprice they say that it is only legitimate when used in the interests of one particular proposition—the proposition, namely that the course of nature is uniform. That nature will follow tomorrow the same laws that she follows today is, they all admit, a truth which no man can *know;* but in the interests of cognition as well as of action we must postulate or assume it. . . .

With regard to all other possible truths, however, a number of our most influential contemporaries think that an attitude of faith is not only illogical but shameful. Faith in a religious dogma for which there is no outward proof, but which we are tempted to postulate for our emotional interests, just as we postulate the uniformity of nature for our intellectual interests, is branded by Professor Huxley as "the lowest depth of immorality." Citations of this kind from leaders of the modern *Aufklärung** might be multiplied almost indefinitely. Take Professor Clifford's article on the "Ethics of Belief."** He calls it "guilt" and "sin" to believe even the truth without "scientific evidence." But what is the use of being a genius, unless *with the same scientific evidence* as other men, one can reach more truth than they? Why does Clifford fearlessly proclaim his belief in the conscious-automaton theory, although the "proofs" before him are the same which make Mr. Lewes reject it? . . . Simply

SOURCE: Excerpted from "The Sentiment of Rationality," in *The Will to Believe* (1897). The title of this selection has been supplied by the editors. Compare with selection 35.
*Enlightenment.
**Selection 15 of this volume.

because, like every human being of the slightest mental originality, he is peculiarly sensitive to evidence that bears in some one direction. It is utterly hopeless to try to exorcise such sensitiveness by calling it the disturbing subjective factor, and branding it as the root of all evil. . . . Pretend what we may, the whole man within us is at work when we form our philosophical opinions. Intellect, will, taste, and passion co-operate just as they do in practical affairs; and lucky it is if the passion be not something as petty as a love of personal conquest over the philosopher across the way. The absurd abstraction of an intellect verbally formulating all its evidence and carefully estimating the probability thereof by a vulgar fraction by the size of whose denominator and numerator alone it is swayed, is ideally as inept as it is actually impossible. It is almost incredible that men who are themselves working philosophers should pretend that any philosophy can be, or ever has been, constructed without the help of personal preference, belief, or divination. . . .

If I am born with such a superior general reaction to evidence that I can guess right and act accordingly, and gain all that comes of right action, while my less gifted neighbor (paralyzed by his scruples and waiting for more evidence which he dares not anticipate, much as he longs to) still stands shivering on the brink, by what law shall I be forbidden to reap the advantages of my superior native sensitiveness? Of course I yield to my belief in such a case as this or distrust it, alike at my peril, just as I do in any of the great practical decisions of life. If my inborn faculties are good, I am a prophet; if poor, I am a failure: nature spews me out of her mouth, and there is an end to me. In the total game of life we stake our persons all the while; and if in its theoretic part our persons will help us to a conclusion, surely we should also stake them here, however inarticulate they may be.

But in being myself so very articulate in proving what to all readers with a sense for reality will seem a platitude, am I not wasting words? We cannot live or think at all without some degree of faith. Faith is synonymous with working hypothesis. The only difference is that while some hypotheses can be refuted in five minutes, others may defy ages. A chemist who conjectures that a certain wall-paper contains arsenic, and has faith enough to lead him to take the trouble to put some of it into a hydrogen bottle, finds out by the results of his action whether he was right or wrong. But theories like that of Darwin, or that of the kinetic constitution of matter, may exhaust the labors of generations in their corroboration, each tester of their truth proceeding in this simple way—that he acts as if it were true, and expects the result to disappoint him if his assumption is false. The longer disappointment is delayed, the stronger grows his faith in his theory. . . .

Now, I wish to show what to my knowledge has never been clearly pointed out, that belief (as measured by action) not only does and must continually outstrip scientific evidence, but that there is a certain class of truths of whose reality belief is a factor as well as a confessor; and that as regards this class of truths faith is not only licit and pertinent, but essential and indispensable. The truths cannot become true till our faith has made them so.

Suppose, for example, that I am climbing in the Alps, and have had the ill-luck to work myself into a position from which the only escape is by a terrible leap. Being without similar experience, I have no evidence of my ability to perform it successfully; but hope and confidence in myself make me sure I shall not miss my aim, and nerve my feet to execute what without those subjective emotions would perhaps have been impossible. But suppose that, on the contrary, the emotions of fear and mistrust preponderate; or suppose that, having just read the *Ethics of Belief,* I feel it would be sinful to act upon an assumption unverified by previous experience—why, then I shall hesitate so long that at last, exhausted and trembling, and launching myself in a moment of despair, I miss my foothold and roll into the abyss. In this case (and it is one of an immense class) the part of wisdom clearly is to believe what one desires; for the belief is one of the indispensable preliminary conditions of the realization of its object. *There are then cases where faith creates its own verification.* Believe, and you shall be right, for you shall save yourself; doubt, and you shall again be right, for you shall perish. The only difference is that to believe is greatly to your advantage.

The future movements of the stars or the facts of past history are determined now once for all, whether I like them or not. They are given irrespective of my wishes, and in all that concerns truths like these subjective preference should have no part; it can only obscure the judgment. But in every fact into which there enters an element of personal contribution on my part, as soon as this personal contribution demands a certain degree of subjective energy which, in its turn, calls for a certain amount of faith in the result—so that, after all, the future fact is conditioned by my present faith in it—how trebly asinine would it be for me to deny myself the use of the subjective method, the method of belief based on desire! . . .

The highest good can be achieved only by our getting our proper life; and that can come about only by help of a moral energy born of the faith that in some way or other we shall succeed in getting it if we try pertinaciously enough. This world *is* good, we must say, since it is what we make it—and we shall make it good. How can we exclude from the cognition of a truth a faith which is involved in the creation of the truth? . . . All depends on the character of the personal contribution. . . . Wherever the facts to be formulated contain such a contribution, we may logically, legitimately, and inexpugnably believe what we desire. The belief creates its verification. The thought becomes literally father to the fact, as the wish was father to the thought. . . .

The essential thing to notice is that our active preference is a legitimate part of the game—that it is our plain business as men to try one of the keys, and the one in which we most confide. If then the proof exist not till I have acted, and I must needs in acting run the risk of being wrong, how can the popular science professors be right in objurgating in me as infamous a "credulity" which the strict logic of the situation requires? If this really be a moral universe; if by my acts I be a factor of its destinies; if to believe where I may doubt be itself a moral act analogous to voting for a side not yet sure to win—by what right shall they close in upon me and steadily negate the deepest conceivable function of my being by their preposterous command that I shall stir neither hand nor foot, but remain balancing myself in eternal and insoluble doubt? Why, doubt itself is a decision of the widest practical reach, if only because we may miss by doubting what goods we might be gaining by espousing the winning side. But more than that! It is often practically impossible to distinguish doubt from dogmatic negation. If I refuse to stop a murder because I am in doubt whether it be not justifiable homicide, I am virtually abetting the crime. If I refuse to bale out a boat because I am in doubt whether my efforts will keep her afloat, I am really helping to sink her. If in the mountain precipice I doubt my right to risk a leap, I actively connive at my destruction. He who commands himself not to be credulous of God, of duty, of freedom, of immortality, may again and again be indistinguishable from him who dogmatically denies them. Scepticism in moral matters is an active ally of immorality. Who is not for is against. The universe will have no neutrals in these questions. In theory as in practice, dodge or hedge, or talk as we like about a wise scepticism, we are really doing volunteer military service for one side or the other. . . .

37 RELIGION AND THE WILL TO BELIEVE

MORRIS R. COHEN (1880-1947)

... I have spoken of the dark side of religion and have thus implied that there is another side. But if this implication puts me out of the class of those who are unqualified opponents of all that has been called religion, I do not wish to suggest that I am merely an advocate, or that I have any doubts as to the justice of the arguments that I have advanced. Doubtless some of my arguments may turn out to be erroneous, but at present I hold them all in good faith. I believe that this dark side of religion is a reality, and it is my duty on this occasion to let those who follow me do justice to the other side. But if what I have said has any merit, those who wish to state the bright side of religion must take account of and not ignore the realities which I have tried to indicate. This means that the defense of religion must be stated in a spirit of sober regard for truth, and not as a more or less complacent apology for beliefs which we are determined not to abandon. Anyone can, by assuming his faith to be the truth, argue from it more or less plausibly and entirely to his own satisfaction. But that is seldom illuminating or strengthening. The real case for religion must show compelling reasons why, despite the truths that I have sought to display, men who do not believe in religion should change their views. If this be so, we must reject such apologies for religion as Balfour's *Foundations of Belief*. One who accepts the Anglican Church may regard such a book as a sufficient defense. But in all essentials it is a subtle and urbane, but none the less complacent, begging of all the serious questions in the case. For similar reasons also I think we must reject the apology for religion advanced by my revered and beloved teacher William James.

Let us take up his famous essay on "The Will to Believe." Consider in the first place his argument that science (which is organized reason) is inapplicable in the realm of religion, because to compare values or worths "we must consult not science but what Pascal calls our heart" . . . But if it were true

SOURCE: From the essay "The Dark Side of Religion," in *The Faith of a Liberal* (New York: Henry Holt and Company, 1946), pp. 357–361. Reprinted by the kind permission of Harry N. Rosenfield, administrator of the estate of Morris R. Cohen. The title of this selection has been supplied by the editors. Compare with selection 35.

that science and reason have no force in matters of religion, why argue at all? Why all these elaborate reasons in defense of religion? Is it not because the arguments of men like Voltaire and Huxley did have influence that men like DeMaistre and James tried to answer them? Who, the latter ask, ever heard of anyone's changing his religion because of an argument? It is not necessary for me to give a list of instances from my own knowledge. Let us admit that few men confess themselves defeated or change their views in the course of any one argument. Does this prove that arguments have no effect? Do not men frequently use against others the very arguments which at first they professed to find unconvincing? The fact is that men do argue about religion, and it is fatuous for those who argue on one side to try also to discredit *all* rational arguments. It seems more like childish weakness to kick against a game or its rules when you are losing in it. And it is to the great credit of the Catholic Church that it has categorically condemned fideism or the effort to eliminate reason from religion. Skepticism against reason is not a real or enduring protection to religion. Its poison, like that of the Nessus shirt, finally destroys the faith that puts it on. Genuine faith in the truth is confident that it can prove itself to universal reason.

Let us look at the matter a little closer.

James argues that questions of belief are decided by our will. Now it is true that one can say: "I do not wish to argue. I want to continue in the belief that I have." But is not the one who says this already conscious of a certain weakness in his faith which might well be the beginning of its disintegration? The man who has a robust faith in his friend does not say, "I want to believe that he is honest," but "I know that he is honest, and any doubt about it is demonstrably false or unreasonable." To be willing to put your case and its evidence before the court of reason is to show real confidence in it.

But James argues that certain things are beloved not on the basis of rational or scientific weighing of evidence, but on the compulsion of our passional nature. This is true. But reflection may ease the passional compulsion. And why not encourage such reflection?

The history of the last few generations has shown that many have lost their faith in Christianity because of reflection induced by Darwinism. Reflection on the inconsistencies of the Mosaic chronology and cosmology has shown that these do not differ from other mythologies; and this has destroyed the belief of many in the plenary inspiration of the Bible. It is therefore always possible to ask: Shall I believe a given religious proposition as the absolute truth, or shall I suspend final decision until I have further evidence? I must go to church or stay out. But I may do the latter at least without hiding from myself the inadequacy of my knowledge or of the evidence. In politics I vote for X or Y without necessarily getting myself into the belief that my act is anything more than a choice of probabilities. I say : Better vote for X than Y; although if I knew more (for which there is no time) I might vote the other way. In science I choose on the basis of all the available evidence but expressly reserve the possibility that future evidence may make me change my view. It is difficult to make such reservations within any religious system. But it is possible to remain permanently skeptical or agnostic with regard to religion itself and its absolute claims.

The momentous character of the choice in regard to religion may be dissolved by reflection which develops detachment or what James calls light-heartedness. What is the difference between believing in one religion or in another or in none? A realization of the endless variety of religious creeds, of the great diversity of beliefs that different people hold to be essential to our salvation, readily liberates us from the compulsion to believe in every Mullah that comes along or else fear eternal damnation. James draws a sharp distinction between a living and a nonliving issue. To him, I suppose, the question of whether to accept Judaism, Islam, or Buddhism was not a living one. But the question whether to investigate so-called psychical phenomena as proofs of immortality was a living one. But surely reflection may change the situation, and a student of religion may come to feel that James' choice was arbitrary and untenable.

The intensification of the feeling that religious issues are important comes about through the assumption that my eternal salvation depends upon my present choice, or—at most—on what I do during the few moments of my earthly career. There is remarkably little evidence for this assumption. If our life is eternal, we may have had more chances before and we may have more later. Why assume that the whole of an endless life is determined by an infinitesimal part of it? From this point of view, men like Jonathan Edwards, to whom eternal Hell is always present and who makes an intense religious issue out of every bite of food, appear to be just unbalanced, and in need of more play in the sunshine and fresh air and perhaps a little more sleep. I mention Jonathan Edwards because his life and teachings enable us to turn the tables on religion by what James regards as the great pragmatic argument in its favor. Accept it, James says, and you will be better off at once. . . . As most religions condemn forever those who do not follow them, it is as risky to accept any one as none at all. And it is possible to take the view that they are all a little bit ungracious, too intense, and too sure of what in our uncertain life cannot be proved. Let us better leave them all alone and console ourselves with the hypothesis—a not altogether impossible one—that the starry universe and whatever gods there be do not worry about us at all, and will not resent our enjoying whatever humane and enlightened comfort and whatever vision of truth and beauty our world offers us. Let us cultivate our little garden. The pretended certainties of religion do not really offer much more. This is of course not a refutation of religion, or of the necessity which reflective minds find to grapple with it. But it indicates that there may be more wisdom and courage as well as more faith in honest doubt than in most of the creeds.

38 HONEST TO GOD
JOHN A. T. ROBINSON (1919-   )

1.

The Bible speaks of a God 'up there'. No doubt its picture of a three-decker universe, of 'the heaven above, the earth beneath and the waters under the earth', was once taken quite literally. No doubt also its more sophisticated writers, if pressed, would have been the first to regard this as symbolic language to represent and convey spiritual realities. Yet clearly they were not pressed. Or at any rate they were not oppressed by it. Even such an educated man of the world as St Luke can express the conviction of Christ's ascension —the conviction that he is not merely alive but reigns in the might and right of God—in the crudest terms of being 'lifted up' into heaven, there to sit down at the right hand of the Most High.[1] He feels no need to offer any apology for this language, even though he of all New Testament writers was commending Christianity to what Schleiermacher called its 'cultured despisers'. This is the more remarkable because, in contrast, he leaves his readers in no doubt that what we might regard as the scarcely more primitive notions of God entertained by the Athenians,[2] that the deity lives in temples made by man and needs to be served by human hands, were utterly superseded by Christianity.

Moreover, it is the two most mature theologians of the New Testament, St John and the later Paul, who write most uninhibitedly of this 'going up' and 'coming down'.

> No one has ascended into heaven but he who descended from heaven, the Son of man.[3]

SOURCE: From *Honest to God*, by John A. T. Robinson (London: SCM Press Ltd., 1963), pp. 11–18, 21–2, 29, and 45–57. Published in the U. S. A., 1963, by The Westminster Press, Philadelphia. © SCM Press, Ltd., London, 1963. Used by permission. Permission to reprint the quotations from *The Shaking of the Foundations* by Paul Tillich was granted by Charles Scribner's Sons, New York.
[1] Acts 1.9–11.
[2] Acts 17.22–31.
[3] John 3.13.

Do you take offence at this? Then what if you were to see the Son of man ascending where he was before?[4]

In saying, 'He ascended', what does it mean but that he had also descended into the lower parts of the earth? He who descended is he who also ascended far above all the heavens, that he might fill all things.[5]

They are able to use this language without any sense of constraint because it had not become an embarrassment to them. Everybody accepted what it meant to speak of a God up there, even though the groundlings might understand it more grossly than the gnostics. For St Paul, no doubt, to be 'caught up to the third heaven'[6] was as much a metaphor as it is to us (though for him a considerably more precise metaphor). But he could use it to the spiritually sophisticated at Corinth with no consciousness that he must 'demythologize' if he were to make it acceptable.

For the New Testament writers the idea of a God 'up there' created no embarrassment—because it had not yet become a difficulty. For us too it creates little embarrassment—because, for the most part, it has ceased to be a difficulty. We are scarcely even conscious that the majority of the words for what we value most are still in terms of height, though as Edwyn Bevan observed in his Gifford Lectures,[7] 'The proposition: Moral and spiritual worth is greater or less in ratio to the distance outwards from the earth's surface, would certainly seem to be, if stated nakedly like that, an odd proposition.' Yet it is one that we have long ago found it unnecessary to explain away. We may indeed continue to have to tell our children that heaven is not in fact over their heads nor God literally 'above the bright blue sky'. Moreover, whatever we may accept with the top of our minds, most of us still retain deep down the mental image of 'an old man in the sky'. Nevertheless, for most of us most of the time the traditional language of a three-storeyed universe is not a serious obstacle. It does not worry us intellectually, it is not an 'offence' to faith, because we have long since made a remarkable transposition, of which we are hardly aware. In fact, we do not realize how crudely spatial much of the Biblical terminology is, for we have ceased to perceive it that way. It is as though when reading a musical score what we actually saw was not the notes printed but the notes of the key into which mentally we were transposing it. There are some notes, as it were, in the Biblical score which still strike us in the old way (the Ascension story, for instance) and which we

---

[4] John 6.61f.
[5] Eph. 4.9f.
[6] II Cor. 12.2.
[7] *Symbolism and Belief* (1938), p. 30. Chs. II and III on 'Height' are a *locus classicus* for the conception of God 'up there.'

have to make a conscious effort to transpose, but in general we assimilate the language without trouble.

For in place of a God who is literally or physically 'up there' we have accepted, as part of our mental furniture, a God who is spiritually or metaphysically 'out there'. There are, of course, those for whom he is almost literally 'out there'. They may have accepted the Copernican revolution in science, but until recently at any rate they have still been able to think of God as in some way 'beyond' outer space. In fact the number of people who instinctively seem to feel that it is no longer possible to believe in God in the space-age shows how crudely physical much of this thinking about a God 'out there' has been. Until the last recesses of the cosmos had been explored or were capable of being explored (by radio-telescope if not by rocketry), it was still possible to locate God mentally in some *terra incognita*. But now it seems there is no room for him, not merely in the inn, but in the entire universe: for there are no vacant places left. In reality, of course, our new view of the universe has made not the slightest difference. Indeed, the limit set to 'space' by the speed of light (so that beyond a certain point—not all that much further than our present range—everything recedes over the horizon of visibility) is even more severe. And there is nothing to stop us, if wish to, locating God 'beyond' it. And there he would be quite invulnerable—in a 'gap' science could never fill. But in fact the coming of the space-age has destroyed this crude projection of God—and for that we should be grateful. For if God is 'beyond', he is not *literally* beyond anything.

But the idea of a God spiritually or metaphysically 'out there' dies very much harder. Indeed, most people would be seriously disturbed by the thought that it should need to die at all. For it *is* their God, and they have nothing to put in its place. And for the words 'they' and 'their' it would be more honest to substitute 'we' and 'our'. For it is the God of our own upbringing and conversation, the God of our fathers and of our religion, who is under attack. Every one of us lives with some mental picture of a God 'out there', a God who 'exists' above and beyond the world he made, a God 'to' whom we pray and to whom we 'go' when we die. In traditional Christian theology, the doctrine of the Trinity witnesses to the self-subsistence of this divine Being outside us and apart from us. The doctrine of creation asserts that at a moment of time this God called 'the world' into existence over against himself. The Biblical record describes how he proceeds to enter into contact with those whom he has made, how he establishes a 'covenant' with them, how he 'sends' to them his prophets, and how in the fullness of time he 'visits' them in the person of his Son, who must one day 'come again' to gather the faithful to himself.

This picture of a God 'out there' coming to earth like some visitor from outer space underlies every popular presentation of the Christian drama of salvation, whether from the pulpit or the presses. Indeed, it is noticeable that those who have been most successful in communicating it in our day—Dorothy Sayers, C. S. Lewis, J. B. Phillips—have hesitated least in being boldly anthropomorphic in the use of this language. They have not, of course, taken it literally, any more than the New Testament writers take literally the God 'up there', but they have not apparently felt it any embarrassment to the setting forth of the Gospel. This is sufficient testimony to the fact that there is a ready-made public for whom this whole frame of reference still presents no difficulties, and their very achievement should make us hesitate to pull it down or call it in question.

Indeed, the last thing I want to do is to appear to criticize from a superior position. I should like to think that it were possible to use this mythological language of the God 'out there' and make the same utterly natural and unself-conscious transposition as I have suggested we already do with the language of the God 'up there'. Indeed, unless we become used to doing this and are able to take this theological notation, as it were, in our stride, we shall cut ourselves off from the classics of the Christian faith, just as we should be unable to read the Bible were we to stumble at *its* way of describing God. I believe, however, that we may have to pass through a century or more of reappraisal before this becomes possible and before this language ceases to be an offence to faith for a great many people. No one wants to live in such a period, and one could heartily wish it were not necessary. But the signs are that we are reaching the point at which the whole conception of a God 'out there', which has served us so well since the collapse of the three-decker universe, is itself becoming more of a hindrance than a help.

In a previous age there came a moment when the three-decker likewise proved an embarrassment, even as a piece of mental furniture. But in this case there was a considerable interval between the time when it ceased to be taken literally as a model of the universe and the time when it ceased to perform a useful function as a metaphor. An illustration of this is to be seen in the doctrine of hell. In the old scheme, hell was 'down there'. By Shakespeare's time no one thought of it as literally under the earth, but still in *Hamlet* it is lively and credible enough as a metaphor. But a localized hell gradually lost more and more of its purchase over the imagination, and revivalist attempts to stoke its flames did not succeed in restoring its power. The tragedy in this instance is that no effective translation into terms of the God 'out there' was found for the Devil and his angels, the pit and the lake of fire. This element therefore tended to drop out of popular Christianity altogether—much to the detriment of the depth of the Gospel.

But the point I wish to make here is that the supersession of the old scheme was a gradual one. After it had been discredited scientifically, it continued to serve theologically as an acceptable frame of reference. The image of a God 'up there' survived its validity as a literal description of reality by many centuries. But today I believe we may be confronted by a double crisis. The final psychological, if not logical, blow delivered by modern science and technology to the idea that there might *literally* be a God 'out there' has *coincided* with an awareness that the *mental* picture of such a God may be more of a stumbling-block than an aid to belief in the Gospel. There is a double pressure to discard this entire construction, and with it any belief in God at all.

Moreover, it is not merely a question of the speed of adjustment required. The abandonment of a God 'out there' represents a much more radical break than the transition to this concept from that of a God 'up there'. For this earlier transposition was largely a matter of verbal notation, of a change in spatial metaphor, important as this undoubtedly was in liberating Christianity from a flat-earth cosmology. But to be asked to give up any idea of a Being 'out there' at all will appear to be an outright denial of God. For, to the ordinary way of thinking, to believe in God means to be convinced of the existence of such a supreme and separate Being. 'Theists' are those who believe that such a Being exists, 'atheists' those who deny that he does.

But suppose such a super-Being 'out there' is really only a sophisticated version of the Old Man in the sky? Suppose belief in God does not, indeed cannot, mean being persuaded of the 'existence' of some entity, even a supreme entity, which might or might not be there, like life on Mars? Suppose the atheists are right—but that this is no more the end or denial of Christianity than the discrediting of the God 'up there', which must in its time have seemed the contradiction of all that the Bible said? Suppose that all such atheism does is to destroy an idol, and that we can and must get on without a God 'out there' at all? Have we seriously faced the possibility that to abandon such an idol may in the future be the only way of making Christianity meaningful, except to the few remaining equivalents of flat-earthers (just as to have clung earlier to the God 'up there' would have made it impossible in the modern world for any but primitive peoples to believe the Gospel)? Perhaps after all the Freudians are right, that such a God—the God of traditional popular theology—*is* a projection, and perhaps we are being called to live without that projection in any form.

That is not an attractive proposition: inevitably it feels like being orphaned. And it is bound to be misunderstood and resisted as a denial of the Gospel, as a betrayal of what the Bible says (though actually the Bible speaks in literal terms of a God whom we have already abandoned). And it will encounter the opposition not only of the fundamentalists but of 90 per cent of Church people. Equally it will be resented by most unthinking non-churchgoers, who tend to be more jealous of the beliefs they have rejected and deeply shocked that they should be betrayed. Above all, there is the large percentage of oneself that finds this revolution unacceptable and wishes it were unnecessary.

This raises again the insistent question, Why? Is it really necessary to pass through this Copernican revolution? Must we upset what most people happily believe—or happily choose not to believe? And have we anything to put in its place? . . .

2.

At this stage, to indicate what I am talking about, let me instance three pieces of writing, all brief, which contain ideas that immediately found lodgement when I first read them and which have since proved seminal not only for me but for many of this generation.

The first of these in date for me (though not in composition) was a sermon by Paul Tillich, which appeared in his collection *The Shaking of the Foundations,* published in England in 1949.[8] It was called 'The Depth of Existence' and it opened my eyes to the transformation that seemed to come over so much of the traditional religious symbolism when it was transposed from the heights to the depths. God, Tillich was saying, is not a projection 'out there', an Other beyond the skies, of whose existence we have to convince ourselves, but the Ground of our very being.

> The name of this infinite and inexhaustible depth and ground of all being is *God.* That depth is what the word *God* means. And if that word has not much meaning for you, translate it, and speak of the depths of your life, of the source of your being, of your ultimate concern, of what you take seriously without any reservation. Perhaps, in order to do so, you must forget everything traditional that you have learned about God, perhaps even that word itself. For if you know that God means depth, you know much about him. You cannot then call yourself an atheist or unbeliever. For you cannot think or say: Life has no depth! Life is shallow. Being itself is surface only. If you could say this in complete seriousness, you would be an atheist; but otherwise you are not. He who knows about depth knows about God.[9]

I remember at the time how these words lit up for me. I did what I have never done before or since: I simply read Tillich's sermon, in place of an address of my own, to the students I was then teaching. I do not remember looking at the words again till I came to write this, but they formed one of

---

[8] Now available in a Pelican edition (1962), to which the page references are given. [Also available in a Scribner Library paperback edition—Eds.]
[9] *Op. cit.* pp. 63f.

the streams below the surface that were to collect into the underground river of which I have since become conscious. I shall return to them, as to the other influences I mention in this chapter, subsequently. Here it is enough to say they seemed to speak of God with a new and indestructible relevance and made the traditional language of a God that came in from outside both remote and artificial. . . .

3.

Traditional Christian theology has been based upon the proofs for the existence of God. The presupposition of these proofs, psychologically if not logically, is that God might or might not exist. They argue from something which everyone admits exists (the world) to a Being beyond it who could or could not be there. The purpose of the argument is to show that he must be there, that his being is 'necessary'; but the presupposition behind it is that there is an entity or being 'out there' whose existence is problematic and has to be demonstrated. Now such an entity, even if it could be proved beyond dispute, would not be God: it would merely be a further piece of existence, that might conceivably not have been there— or a demonstration would not have been required.

Rather, we must start the other way round. God is, by definition, ultimate reality. And one cannot argue whether ultimate reality *exists*. One can only ask what ultimate reality is like—whether, for instance, in the last analysis what lies at the heart of things and governs their working is to be described in personal or impersonal catgories. Thus, the fundamental theological question consists not in establishing the 'existence' of God as a separate entity but in pressing through in ultimate concern to what Tillich calls 'the ground of our being'. . . .

4.

The break with traditional thinking to which I believe we are now summoned is considerably more radical than that which enabled Christian theology to detach itself from a literal belief in a localized heaven. The translation from the God 'up there' to the God 'out there', though of liberating psychological significance, represented, as I have said, no more than a change of direction in spatial symbolism. Both conceptions presuppose fundamentally the same relationship between 'God' on the one hand and 'the world' on the other: God is a Being existing in his own right to whom the world is related in the sort of way the earth is to the sun. Whether the sun is 'above' a flat earth or 'beyond' a round one does not fundamentally affect the picture. But suppose there is no Being out there at all? Suppose, to use our analogy, the skies are empty?

Now it would again be possible to present the transposition with which we are concerned as simply a change in spatial metaphor. I quoted earlier the passage from Tillich in which he proposes replacing the images of 'height' by those of 'depth' in order to express the truth of God. And there is no doubt that this simple substitution can make much religious language suddenly appear more relevant. For we are familiar today with depth psychology, and with the idea that ultimate truth is deep or profound. Moreover, while 'spiritual wickedness in high places', and all the mythology of angelic powers which the Biblical writers associate with it, seems to the modern man a fantastic phantasmagoria, similar, equally mythological, language when used by Freud of conflicts in the unconscious appears perfectly acceptable.

And the change of symbolism has real and not merely apparent psychological significance. For the category of 'depth' has richer associations than that of height. As Tillich points out:

> 'Deep' in its spiritual use has two meanings: it means either the opposite of 'shallow', or the opposite of 'high'. Truth is deep and not shallow; suffering is depth and not height. Both the light of truth and the darkness of suffering are deep. There is a depth in God, and there is a depth out of which the psalmist cries to God.[10]

And this double meaning may explain why 'depth' seems to speak to us of concern while 'height' so often signifies unconcern. The Epicurean gods, serene in their empyrean above the cares and distractions of this world, are the epitome of 'sublime' indifference. And Browning's supreme affirmation of optimism, 'God's in his heaven: all's right with the world', strikes the modern man somewhat more cynically. For if God is 'above it all' he cannot really be involved.

Yet we are not here dealing simply with a change of symbolism, important as that may be. This is not just the old system in reverse, with a God 'down under' for a God 'up there'. When Tillich speaks of God in 'depth', he is not speaking of another Being *at all*. He is speaking of 'the infinite and inexhaustible depth and ground of all being', of our ultimate concern, of what we take seriously without reservation. And after the passage I quoted earlier[11] he goes on to make the same point in relation not only to the depths of our personal life but to the deepest springs of our social and historical existence:

> The name of this infinite and inexhaustible ground of history is *God*. That is what the word means, and it is that to which the words *Kingdom of God* and *Divine Providence* point. And if these words do not have much meaning for you, translate them, and speak of the depth of history, of the ground and aim of our social life, and of what you take seriously without reservation in your moral and

---

[10] *The Shaking of the Foundations,* p. 60.
[11] *Op. cit.,* pp. 63 f [p. 250 above—Eds.]

political activities. Perhaps you should call this depth *hope*, simply hope. For if you find hope in the ground of history, you are united with the great prophets who were able to look into the depth of their times, who tried to escape it, because they could not stand the horror of their visions, and who yet had the strength to look to an even deeper level and there to discover hope.[12]

What Tillich is meaning by God is the exact opposite of any *deus ex machina*, a supernatural Being to whom one can turn away from the world and who can be relied upon to intervene from without. God is not 'out there'. He is in Bonhoeffer's words 'the "beyond" in the midst of our life', a depth of reality reached 'not on the borders of life but at its centre',[13] not by any flight of the alone to the alone, but, in Kierkegaard's fine phrase, by 'a deeper immersion in existence'. For the word 'God' denotes the ultimate depth of all our being, the creative ground and meaning of all our existence.

So conditioned for us is the word 'God' by associations with a Being out there that Tillich warns us that to make the necessary transposition, 'you must forget everything traditional that you have learned about God, perhaps even that word itself'.[14] Indeed, the line between those who believe in God and those who do not bears little relation to their profession of the existence or non-existence of such a Being. It is a question, rather, of their openness to the holy, the sacred, in the unfathomable depths of even the most secular relationship. As Martin Buber puts it of the person who professedly denies God,

> When he, too, who abhors the name, and believes himself to be godless, gives his whole being to addressing the *Thou* of his life, as a *Thou* that cannot be limited by another, he addresses God.[15]

For in the conditioned he has seen and responded to the unconditional. He has touched the hem of the eternal.

The difference between the two ways of thought can perhaps best be expressed by asking what is meant by speaking of a *personal* God. Theism, as the term was understood in the previous chapter, understands by this a supreme Person, a self-existent subject of infinite goodness and power, who enters into a relationship with us comparable with that of one human personality with another. The theist is concerned to argue the existence of such a Being as the creator and most sufficient explanation of the world as we know it. Without a Person 'out there', the skies would be empty, the heavens as brass, and the world without hope or compassion.

But the way of thinking we are seeking to expound is not concerned to

---
[12]*Op. cit.*, pp. 65 f.
[13]Dietrich Bonhoeffer, *Letters and Papers from Prison*, ed. E. Bethge (1953; 2nd ed., 1956), p. 124.
[14]*Op. cit.*, p. 64.
[15]*I and Thou* (1937), p. 76; cf. Tillich, *The Protestant Era* (1951), p. 65.

posit, nor, like the antitheists, to depose, such a Being at all. In fact it would not naturally use the phrase 'a personal God'; for this in itself belongs to an understanding of theology and of what theological statements are about which is alien to it. For this way of thinking, to say that 'God is personal' is to say that 'reality at its very deepest level is personal', that personality is of *ultimate* significance in the constitution of the universe, that in personal relationships we touch the final meaning of existence as nowhere else. 'To predicate personality of God', says Feuerbach, 'is nothing else than to declare personality as the absolute essence'.[16] To believe in God as love means to believe that in pure personal relationship we encounter, not merely what ought to be, but what is, the deepest, veriest truth about the structure of reality. This, in face of all the evidence, is a tremendous act of faith. But it is not the feat of persuading oneself of the existence of a super-Being beyond this world endowed with personal qualities. Belief in God is the trust, the well-nigh incredible trust, that to give ourselves to the uttermost in love is not to be confounded but to be 'accepted', that Love is the ground of our being, to which ultimately we 'come home'.

If this is true, then theological statements are not a description of 'the highest Being' but an analysis of the depths of personal relationships—or, rather, an analysis of the depths of *all* experience 'interpreted by love'. Theology, as Tillich insists, is about 'that which concerns us ultimately'.[17] A statement is 'theological' not because it relates to a particular Being called 'God', but because it asks *ultimate* questions about the meaning of existence: it asks what, at the level of *theos,* at the level of its deepest mystery, is the reality and significance of our life. A veiw of the world which affirms this reality and significance in personal categories is *ipso facto* making an affirmation about the *ultimacy* of personal relationships: it is saying that *God,* the final truth and reality 'deep down things', *is* love. And the specifically Christian view of the world is asserting that the final definition of this reality, from which 'nothing can separate us', since it is the very ground of our being, is 'the love of God in Christ Jesus our Lord'.[18]

Man and God. If statements about God are statements about the 'ultimacy' of personal relationships, then we must agree that in a real sense Feuerbach was right in wanting to translate 'theology' into 'anthropology'. He was concerned to restore the divine attributes from heaven to earth, whence, he believed, they had been filched and projected on to a perfect Being, an

---

[16] *The Essence of Christianity* (Eng. tr. 1854, from the second ed. of 1843), p. 97.
[17] *Systematic Theology,* vol. i, p. 15.
[18] Rom. 8.39.

imaginary Subject before whom impoverished man falls in worship. Feuerbach believed that true religion consists in acknowledging the divinity of the attributes, not in transferring them to an illegitimate subject (dubbed by his Marxist disciple Bakunin 'the mirage of God'). 'The true atheist', he wrote, 'is not the man who denies God, the subject; it is the man for whom the attributes of divinity, such as love, wisdom and justice, are nothing. And denial of the subject is by no means necessarily denial of the attributes'.[19] This is, of course, very near to the position we have been taking; and Bultmann, in answer to a challenge from Karl Barth, says, 'I would heartily agree: I *am* trying to substitute anthropology for theology, for I am interpreting theological affirmations as assertions about human life'.[20]

Yet it is also clear that we are here on very dangerous ground. For, to Feuerbach, to say that 'theology is nothing else than anthropology' means that 'the knowledge of God is nothing else than a knowledge of man'.[21] And his system runs out into the deification of man, taken to its logical conclusion in the Superman of Nietzsche and Auguste Comte's Religion of Humanity.

The same ambiguity is to be found in the deeply Christian humanism of Professor John Macmurray, whose thought follows similar lines. At the beginning of his Gifford Lectures he says, 'The conception of a deity is the conception of a personal ground of all that we experience,[22] and he concludes them with a chapter, 'The Personal Universe',[23] which argues a position close to that for which we have been contending. But both in these lectures and even more in his earlier book, *The Structure of Religious Experience*, he makes statements which leave one wondering whether there is anything distinctive about religion at all. For instance, 'Religion is about fellowship and community',[24] and, 'The task of religion is the maintenance and extension of human community'.[25] The question inevitably arises, if theology is translated into anthropology, why do we any longer need the category of God? Is it not 'semantically superfluous'? Is not the result of destroying 'supranaturalism' simply to end up with naturalism, as the atheists asserted?

The dilemma can be stated in another passage of Macmurray. The question of God is the question of transcendence. It is precisely this that the location of God 'up there' or 'out there' was to express and safeguard and which its

---

[19] *Op. cit.*, p. 21. I have preferred, for this quotation, the translation in H. de Lubac, *op. cit.*, p. 11.
[20] *Kerygma and Myth*, vol. i, p. 107.
[21] *Op. cit.*, p. 206.
[22] *The Self as Agent* (1957), p. 17.
[23] *Persons in Relation* (1961), Ch. X.
[24] *The Structure of Religious Experience* (1936), p. 30 f.
[25] *Op. cit.*, p. 43.

denial appears to imperil. But for Macmurray transcendence is a category that applies equally to humanity:

> We are both transcendent of experience and immanent in it. This union of transcendence and immanence is . . . the full fact about human personality. . . . We are accustomed to find it applied in theology to God, and it is usually assumed to be a peculiar and distinguishing attribute of Deity. We see now that this is a mistake. The union of immanence and transcendence is a peculiar and defining characteristic of all personality, human or divine; but it is primarily a natural, empirical fact of common human experience. Religious reflection applies it to God as a defining characteristic of universal personality because it finds it in experience as a given fact of all finite personal experience.[26]

Macmurray here denies that transcendence is distinctively an attribute of God: he asserts it as a feature of all our experience. I believe that he is wrong in what he denies, but right in what he asserts. Contrary to what he says, our experience of God *is* distinctively and characteristically an awareness of the transcendent, the numinous, the unconditional. Yet that is a feature of *all* our experience—*in depth*. Statements about God are acknowledgements of the transcendent, unconditional element in all our relationships, and supremely in our relationships with other persons. Theological statements are indeed affirmations about human existence—but they are affirmations about the ultimate ground and depth of that existence. It is not enough to say that 'religion is about human fellowship and community', any more than one can simply reverse the Biblical statement and say that 'love *is* God'. And that, significantly, is what Feuerbach thought St John should have said.[27] But it is what the Apostle rather carefully refuses to do. He is clear that *apart from* the relationship of love there is no knowledge of God: 'He who does not love does not know God; for God is love.'[28] And conversely: 'He who abides in love abides in God, and God abides in him.'[29] But the premise of this last sentence is not, as we might logically expect, 'Love is God', but, 'God is love'.[30] The most he will say the other way round is that 'love is *of* God'.[31] It is *ek theou:* it has God as its source and ground. For it is precisely his thesis[32] that our convictions about love and its ultimacy are not projections from human love; rather, our sense of the sacredness of love derives from the fact that in this relationship as nowhere else there is disclosed and laid

---

[26] *Op. cit.,* pp. 27 f.
[27] *Op. cit.,* p. 261; cf, p. 47: 'Love is God himself, and apart from it there is no God.'
[28] I John 4.8.
[29] I John 4.16.
[30] *Ibid.*
[31] I John 4.7.
[32] I John 4.10, 19.

bare the divine Ground of all our being. And this revelation for St John finds its focus and final vindication in the fact of Jesus Christ—'the humanity of God'[33]—rather than in the divinity of Man.

To assert that *'God* is love' is to believe that in love one comes into touch with the most fundamental reality in the universe, that Being itself ultimately has this character. It is to say, with Buber, that 'Every particular *Thou* is a glimpse through to the eternal *Thou*',[34] that it is 'between man and man'[35] that we meet God, not, with Feuerbach, that 'man with man—the unity of *I* and *Thou*—*is* God'.[36] Nevertheless, as Bonhoeffer insists, 'God is the "beyond" *in the midst*';[37] 'The transcendent is not infinitely remote but close at hand'.[38] For the eternal *Thou* is met only *in, with and under* the finite *Thou,* whether in the encounter with other persons or in the reponse to the natural order.

Yet the eternal *Thou* is not to be equated with the finite *Thou,* nor God with man or nature. That is the position of naturalism, whether pantheistic or humanistic. And, Tillich insists, it is necessary to push 'beyond naturalism and supranaturalism'.[39] The naturalist critique of supranaturalism is valid. It has torn down an idol and Christianity must not be found clinging to it. But equally Christianity must challenge the assumption of naturalism that God is merely a redundant name for nature or for humanity. John Wren-Lewis observes that the naturalist critique of supranaturalism itself points to depths, divine depths, in experience for which it fails to account. He claims that Freud's own analysis of religion indicates as much:

> For it is an integral part of his argument that fantasies about spiritual forces in the occult world are really 'projections' or 'displacements' of elements in our experience of personal relationships which we seek to avoid recognizing, but it is hard to see why the common projections made by the human race should have a numinous, transcendental character *unless there is something numinous and transcendental in the experience of personal relationships themselves.*[40]

---

[33] The title of Karl Barth's book (1961) and of the central lecture in it (pp. 37–65). Feuerbach interestingly enough also uses the phrase 'the human nature of God' (*op. cit.,* p. 49), but as always with a subtly different twist.
[34] *I and Thou,* p. 75.
[35] *Between Man and Man* (1947), pp. 30, 203–5; cf. *I and Thou,* p. 39.
[36] *Philosophie der Zukunft,* p. 62.
[37] *Op. cit.,* p. 124 (italics mine).
[38] *Op. cit.,* p. 175.
[39] *Systematic Theology,* vol. ii, p. 5.
[40] 'The Decline of Magic in Art and Politics,' *The Critical Quarterly,* Spring 1960, p. 18. I should add that there is much in Wren-Lewis's writings (for instance, in his subsequent elaboration of this last sentence or in his article 'Modern Philosophy and the Doctrine of the Trinity' in *The Philosophical Quarterly,* vol. v (1955), pp. 214–224, which makes me doubt whether in the last analysis he himself is not expounding the thesis 'love is God'. At any rate he certainly does not guard himself adequately against this interpretation.

The necessity for the name 'God' lies in the fact that our being has depths which naturalism, whether evolutionary, mechanistic, dialectical or humanistic, cannot or will not recognize. And the nemesis which has overtaken naturalism in our day has revealed the peril of trying to suppress them. As Tillich puts it,

> Our period has decided for a *secular* world. That was a great and much-needed decision. . . . It gave consecration and holiness to our daily life and work. Yet it excluded those deep things for which religion stands: the feeling for the inexhaustible mystery of life, the grip of an ultimate meaning of existence, and the invincible power of an unconditional devotion. These things *cannot* be excluded. If we try to expel them in their divine images, they re-emerge in daemonic images. Now, in the old age of our secular world, we have seen the most horrible manifestations of these daemonic images; we have looked more deeply into the mystery of evil than most generations before us; we have seen the unconditional devotion of millions to a satanic image; we feel our period's sickness unto death.[41]

There are depths of revelation, intimations of eternity, judgements of the holy and the sacred, awarenesses of the unconditional, the numinous and the ecstatic, which cannot be explained in purely naturalistic categories without being reduced to something else. There is the 'Thus saith the Lord' heard by prophet, apostle and martyr for which naturalism cannot account. But neither can it discount it merely by pointing to the fact that 'the Lord' is portrayed in the Bible in highly mythological terms, as one who 'inhabits eternity' or 'walks in the garden in the cool of the evening'. The question of God is the question *whether this depth of being is a reality or an illusion,* not whether a Being exists beyond the bright blue sky, or anywhere else. Belief in God is a matter of 'what you take seriously without any reservation', of what for you is *ultimate* reality.

The man who acknowledges the transcendence of God is the man who *in* the conditioned relationships of life recognizes the unconditional and responds to it in unconditional personal relationship. In Tillich's words again,

> To call God transcendent in this sense does not mean that one must establish a 'superworld' of divine objects. It does mean that, within itself, the finite world points beyond itself. In other words, it is self-transcendent.[42]

This, I believe, is Tillich's great contribution to theology—the reinterpretation of transcendence in a way which preserves its reality while detaching it from the projection of supranaturalism. 'The Divine, as he sees it, does not inhabit

---

[41] *The Shaking of the Foundations,* p. 181.
[42] *Systematic Theology,* vol. ii, p. 8.

a transcendent world *above nature;* it is found in the "ecstatic" character of *this* world, as its transcendent Depth and Ground.'[43] Indeed, as a recent commentator has observed, supranaturalism for Tillich actually represents 'a loss of transcendence':

> It is the attempt to understand and express God's relation to the world by a literalization of this-worldly categories. . . . The result is a God who *exists* as a being, *above* the world. . . . Thus God is described as an entity within the subject-object structures of the spatial-temporal world.[44]

Or, as Tillich puts it himself:

> To criticise such a conditioning of the unconditional, even if it leads to atheistic consequences, is more religious, because it is more aware of the unconditional character of the divine, than a theism that bans God into the supranatural realm.[45]

Nevertheless, the abandonment of any idea of a God 'out there' will inevitably appear a denial of his 'otherness' and the negation of much in the Biblical assertion of what Kierkegaard called 'the infinite qualitative difference between God and man'. It will be valuable therefore to look again at what the Bible is saying about the nature of God and see how it can retain, and indeed regain, its deepest significance in the light of this reinterpretation. . . .

---

[43] W. M. Horton, 'Tillich's Role in Contemporary Theology' in *The Theology of Paul Tillich* (ed. C. W. Kegley and R. W. Bretall, 1952, p. 37). In his 'Reply to Interpretation and Criticism' in the same volume, Tillich describes his own position as 'self-transcending or ecstatic naturalism' (p. 341).
[44] E. Farley, *The Transcendence of God* (1962), p. 77.
[45] *The Protestant Era*, p. 92.

PART VI
ETHICS AND VALUES

39 THE RING OF GYGES
PLATO (427-347 B.C.)

... Imagine two men, one just, the other unjust, given full license to do whatever they like, and then follow them to observe where each will be led by his desires. We shall catch the just man taking the same road as the unjust; he will be moved by self-interest, the end which it is natural to every creature to pursue as good, until forcibly turned aside by law and custom to respect the principle of equality.

Now, the easiest way to give them that complete liberty of action would be to imagine them possessed of the talisman found by Gyges, the ancestor of the famous Lydian. The story tells how he was a shepherd in the King's service. One day there was a great storm, and the ground where his flock was feeding was rent by an earthquake. Astonished at the sight, he went down into the chasm and saw, among other wonders of which the story tells, a brazen horse, hollow, with windows in its sides. Peering in, he saw a dead body, which seemed to be of more than human size. It was naked save for a gold ring, which he took from the finger and made his way out. When the shepherds met, as they did every month, to send an account to the King of the state of his flocks, Gyges came wearing the ring. As he was sitting with the others, he happened to turn the bezel of the ring inside his hand. At once he became invisible, and his companions, to his surprise, began to speak of him as if he had left them. Then, as he was fingering the ring, he turned the bezel outwards and became visible again. With that, he set about testing the ring to see if it really had this power, and always with the same result: according as he turned the bezel inside or out he vanished and reappeared. After this discovery he contrived to be one of the messengers sent to the court. There he seduced the Queen, and with her help murdered the King and seized the throne.

Now suppose there were two such magic rings, and one were given to the

SOURCE: From *The Republic of Plato* (about 387 B. C.) translated (from the Greek) by Francis MacDonald Cornford. Oxford University Press, 1941. Reprinted by permission. The title of this selection has been supplied by the editors. The selection is from Book II, 359-60. It is part of an argument presented by Glaucon, a character in the dialogue, in an attempt to stimulate Socrates, the narrator of the imaginary conversation, to specify exactly what justice is and how justice is better than injustice, in every way.

just man, the other to the unjust. No one, it is commonly believed, would have such iron strength of mind as to stand fast in doing right or keep his hands off other men's goods, when he could go to the market-place and fearlessly help himself to anything he wanted, enter houses and sleep with any woman he chose, set prisoners free and kill men at his pleasure, and in a word go about among men with the powers of a god. He would behave no better than the other; both would take the same course. Surely this would be strong proof that men do right only under compulsion; no individual thinks of it as good for him personally, since he does wrong whenever he finds he has the power. Every man believes that wrongdoing pays him personally much better, and, according to this theory, that is the truth. Granted full license to do as he liked, people would think him a miserable fool if they found him refusing to wrong his neighbours or to touch their belongings, though in public they would keep up a pretence of praising his conduct, for fear of being wronged themselves. . . .

40 ON THE GOOD
ARISTOTLE (384–322 B.C.)

Every art and every kind of inquiry, and likewise every act and purpose, seems to aim at some good; and so it has been well said that the good is that at which everything aims. . . . If then in what we do there be some end which we wish for on its own account, choosing all the others as means to this, but not every end without exception as a means to something else (for so we should go on *ad infinitum,* and desire would be left void and objectless), this evidently will be the good or the best of all things. And surely from a practical point of view it much concerns us to know this good; for then, like archers shooting at a definite mark, we shall be more likely to attain what we want. . . .

We see that there are many ends. But some of these are chosen only as means, as wealth, flutes, and the whole class of instruments. And it is plain that not all ends are final. But the best of all things must, we conceive, be something final. If then there be only one final end, this will be what we are seeking—or if there be more than one, then the most final of them.

SOURCE: From Aristotle's *Nicomachean Ethics,* Bk. I, chs. 1, 2, 7, and 8, translated from the Greek by F. H. Peters (1906). Reprinted by permission of the publishers, Routledge & Kegan Paul Ltd., London. The title of this selection has been supplied by the editors. Compare with selections 39, 41, and 46.

ON THE GOOD

Now that which is pursued as an end in itself is more final than that which is pursued as means to something else, and that which is never chosen as means than that which is chosen both as an end in itself and as means, and that is strictly final which is always chosen as an end in itself and never as means. Happiness seems more than anything else to answer to this description; for we always choose it for itself, and never for the sake of something else; while honor and pleasure and reason, and all virtue or excellence, we choose partly indeed for themselves (for, apart from any result, we should choose each of them), but partly also for the sake of happiness, supposing that they will help to make us happy. But no one chooses happiness for the sake of these things, or as a means to anything else at all.

We seem to be led to the same conclusion when we start from the notion of self-sufficiency. The final good is thought to be self-sufficing (or all-sufficing). In applying this term we do not regard a man as an individual leading a solitary life, but we also take account of parents, children, wife, and, in short, friends and fellow-citizens generally, since man is naturally a social being. Some limit must indeed be set to this; for if you go on to parents and descendants and friends of friends, you will never come to a stop. But this we will consider further on: for the present we will take self-sufficing to mean what by itself makes life desirable and in want of nothing. And happiness is believed to answer to this description.

And further, happiness is believed to be the most desirable thing in the world, and that not merely as one among other good things; if it were merely one among other good things (so that other things could be added to it), it is plain that the addition of the least of other goods must make it more desirable: for the addition becomes a surplus of good, and of two goods the greater is always more desirable. Thus it seems that happiness is something final and self-sufficing, and is the end of all that man does.

But perhaps . . . though no one will dispute the statement that happiness is the best thing in the world, yet a still more precise definition of it is needed.

This will best be gained, I think, by asking, What is the function of man? For as the goodness and the excellence of a piper or a sculptor, or the practiser of any art, and generally of those who have any function or business to do, lies in that function, so man's good would seem to lie in his function, if he has one. But can we suppose that, while a carpenter, or a cobbler has a function and a business of his own, man has no business of his own, man has no business and no function assigned to him by nature? Nay, surely as his several members, eye and hand and foot, plainly have each its own function, so we must suppose that man also has some function over and above all these. What then is it?

Life evidently he has in common even with the plants, but we want that which is peculiar to him. We must exclude, therefore, the life of mere nutrition and growth. Next to this comes the life of sense; but this too he plainly shares with horses and cattle and all kinds of animals. There remains then the life whereby he acts—the life of his rational nature, with its two sides or divisions, one rational as obeying reason, the other rational as having and exercising reason. But as this expression is ambiguous, we must be understood to mean thereby the life that consists in the exercise of the faculties; for this seems to be more properly entitled to the name. The function of man, then, is exercise of his vital faculties (or soul) on one side in obedience to reason, and on the other side with reason.

But what is called the function of a man of any profession and the function of a man who is good in that profession are generically the same, e.g., of a harper and of a good harper; and this holds in all cases without exception, only that in the case of the latter his superior excellence at his work is added; for we say a harper's function is to harp, and a good harper's to harp well. Man's function then being, as we say, a kind of life—that is to say, exercise of his faculties and action of various kinds with reason—the good man's function is to do this well and beautifully (or nobly). But the function of anything is done well when it is done in accordance with the proper excellence of that thing. Putting all this together, then, we find that the good of man is exercise of his faculties in accordance with excellence or virtue, or, if there be more than one, in accordance with the best and most complete virtue.

But there must also be a full term of years for this exercise; for one swallow or one fine day does not make a spring, nor does one day or any small space of time make a blessed or happy man. . . .

But I think we may say that it makes no small difference whether the good be conceived as the mere possession of something, or as its use—as a mere habit or trained faculty, or as the exercise of that faculty. For the habit or faculty may be present, and yet issue in no good result, as when a man is asleep, or in any other way hindered from his function; but with its exercise this is not possible, for it must show itself in acts and in good acts. And as in the Olympic games it is not the fairest and strongest who receive the crown, but those who contend (for among these are the victors), so in life, too, the winners are those who not only have all the excellences, but manifest these in deed.

And, further, the life of these men is in itself pleasant. For pleasure is an affection of the soul, and each man takes pleasure in that which he is said to love—he who loves horses in horses, he who loves sight-seeing in sight-seeing, and in the same way he who loves justice in acts of justice, and generally the lover of excellence or virtue in virtuous acts or the manifestation of excellence. And while with most men there is a perpetual conflict between the several things in which they find pleasure, since these are not naturally pleasant, those who love what is noble take pleasure in that which is naturally pleasant. For the manifestations of excellence are naturally pleasant, so that they are both pleasant to them and pleasant in themselves. Their life, then, does not need pleasure to be added to it as an appendage, but contains pleasure in itself. . . .

41 REASON, PASSION, AND MORALS

DAVID HUME (1711-1776)

I. Of The Influencing Motives Of The Will

Nothing is more usual in philosophy, and even in common life, than to talk of the combat of passion and reason, to give the preference to reason, and to assert that men are only so far virtuous as they conform themselves to its dictates. Every rational creature, 'tis said, is oblig'd to regulate his actions by reason; and if any other motive or principle challenge the direction of his conduct, he ought to oppose it, 'till it be entirely subdu'd, or at least brought to a conformity with that superior principle. On this method of thinking the greatest part of moral philosophy, ancient and modern, seems to be founded; nor is there an ampler field, as well for metaphysical arguments, as popular declamations, than this suppos'd pre-eminence of reason above passion. The eternity, invariableness, and divine origin of the former have been display'd to the best advantage: The blindness, unconstancy and deceitfulness of the latter have been as strongly insisted on. In order to shew the fallacy of all this philosophy, I shall endeavour to prove *first*, that reason alone can never be a motive to any action of the will; and *secondly*, that it can never oppose passion in the direction of the will.

The understanding exerts itself after two different ways, as it judges from demonstration or probability; as it regards the abstract relations of our ideas, or those relations of objects, of which experience only gives us information. I believe it scarce will be asserted, that the first species of reasoning alone is ever the cause of any action. As its proper province is the world of ideas, and as the will always places us in that of realities, demonstration and volition

SOURCE: From *A Treatise of Human Nature* (1739–1740), Bk. II, Part III, Section 3, and Book III, Part I, Section 1. The title of this selection has been supplied by the editors. Compare with selections 13, 43, and especially 47.

seem, upon that account, to be totally remov'd, from each other. Mathematics, indeed, are useful in all mechanical operations, and arithmetic in almost every art and profession: But 'tis not of themselves they have any influence. Mechanics are the art of regulating the motions of bodies *to some design'd end or purpose;* and the reason why we employ arithmetic in fixing the proportions of numbers, is only that we may discover the proportions of their influence and operation. A merchant is desirous of knowing the sum total of his accounts with any person: Why? but that he may learn what sum will have the same *effects* in paying his debt, and going to market, as all the particular articles taken together. Abstract or demonstrative reasoning, therefore, never influences any of our actions, but only as it directs our judgment concerning causes and effects; which leads us to the second operation of the understanding.

'Tis obvious, that when we have the prospect of pain or pleasure from any object, we feel a consequent emotion of aversion or propensity, and are carry'd to avoid or embrace what will give us this uneasiness or satisfaction. 'Tis also obvious, that this emotion rests not here, but making us cast our view on every side, comprehends whatever objects are connected with its original one by the relation of cause and effect. Here then reasoning takes place to discover this relation; and according as our reasoning varies, our actions receive a subsequent variation. But 'tis evident in this case, that the impulse arises not from reason, but is only directed by it. 'Tis from the prospect of pain or pleasure that the aversion or propensity arises towards any object: And these emotions extend themselves to the causes and effects of that object, as they are pointed out to us by reason and experience. It can never in the least concern us to know, that such objects are causes, and such others effects, if both the causes and effects be indifferent to us. Where the objects themselves do not affect us, their connexion can never give them any influence; and 'tis plain, that as reason is nothing but the discovery of this connexion, it cannot be by its means that the objects are able to affect us.

Since reason alone can never produce any action, or give rise to volition, I infer, that the same faculty is as incapable of preventing volition, or of disputing the preference with any passion or emotion. This consequence is necessary. 'Tis impossible reason cou'd have the latter effect of preventing volition, but by giving an impulse in a contrary direction to our passion; and that impulse, had it operated alone, wou'd have been able to produce volition. Nothing can oppose or retard the impulse of passion, but a contrary impulse; and if this contrary impulse ever arises from reason, that latter faculty must have an original influence on the will, and must be able to cause, as well as hinder any act of volition. But if reason has no original influence, 'tis impossible it can withstand any principle, which has such an efficacy, or ever keep the mind in suspence a moment. Thus it appears, that the principle, which opposes our passion, cannot be the same with reason, and is only call'd so in an improper sense. We speak not strictly and philosophically when we talk of the combat of passion and of reason. Reason is, and ought only to be the slave of the passions, and can never pretend to any other office than to serve and obey them. As this opinion may appear somewhat extraordinary, it may not be improper to confirm it by some other considerations.

A passion is an original existence, or, if you will, modification of existence, and contains not any representative quality, which renders it a copy of any other existence or modification. When I am angry, I am actually possest with the passion, and in that emotion have no more a reference to any other object, than when I am thirsty, or sick, or more than five foot high. 'Tis impossible, therefore, that this passion can be oppos'd by, or be contradictory to truth and reason; since this contradiction consists in the disagreement of ideas, consider'd as copies, with those objects, which they represent.

What may at first occur on this head, is, that as nothing can be contrary to truth or reason, except what has a reference to it, and as the judgments of our understanding only have this reference, it must follow, that passions can be contrary to reason only so far as they are *accompany'd* with some judgment or opinion. According to this principle, which is so obvious and natural, 'tis only in two senses, that any affection can be call'd unreasonable. First, when a passion, such as hope or fear, grief or joy, despair or security, is founded on the supposition of the existence of objects, which really do not exist. Secondly, when in exerting any passion in action, we chuse means insufficient for the design'd end, and deceive ourselves in our judgment of causes and effects. Where a passion is neither founded on false suppositions, nor chuses means insufficient for the end, the understanding can neither justify nor condemn it. 'Tis not contrary to reason to prefer the destruction of the whole world to the scratching of my finger. 'Tis not contrary to reason for me to chuse my total ruin, to prevent the least uneasiness of an *Indian* or person wholly unknown to me. 'Tis as little contrary to reason to prefer even my acknowledg'd lesser good to my greater, and have a more ardent affection for the former than the latter. A trivial good may, from certain circumstances, produce a desire superior to what arises from the greatest and most valuable enjoyment; nor is there any thing more extraordinary in this, than in mechanics to see one pound weight raise up a hundred by the advantage of its situation. In short, a passion must be accompany'd with some false judgment, in order to its being unreasonable; and even then 'tis not the passion, properly speaking, which is unreasonable, but the judgment.

The consequences are evident. Since a passion can never, in any sense, be call'd unreasonable, but when founded on a false supposition, or when it chuses means insufficient for the design'd end, 'tis impossible that reason and passion can ever oppose each other, or dispute for the government of the will and actions. The moment we perceive the falshood of any supposition, or the insufficiency of any means our passions yield to our reason without any opposition. I may desire any fruit as of an excellent relish; but whenever you convince me of my mistake, my longing ceases. I may will the performance of certain actions as means of obtaining any desir'd good; but as my willing of these actions is only secondary, and founded on the supposition, that they are causes of the propos'd effect; as soon as I discover the falshood of that supposition, they must become indifferent to me.

'Tis natural for one, that does not examine objects with a strict philosophic eye, to imagine, that those actions of the mind are entirely the same, which produce not a different sensation, and are not immediately distinguishable to the feeling and perception. Reason, for instance, exerts itself without producing any sensible emotion; and except in the more sublime disquisitions of philosophy, or in the frivolous subtiltes of the schools, scarce ever conveys any pleasure or uneasiness. Hence it proceeds, that every action of the mind, which operates with the same calmness and tranquillity, is confounded with reason by all those, who judge of things from the first view and appearance. Now 'tis certain, there are certain calm desires and tendencies, which, tho' they be real passions, produce little emotion in the mind, and are more known by their effects than by the immediate feeling or sensation. These desires are of two kinds; either certain instincts originally implanted in our natures, such as benevolence and resentment, the love of life, and kindness to children; or the general appetite to good, and aversion to evil, consider'd merely as such. When any of these passions are calm, and cause no disorder in the soul, they are very readily taken for the determinations of reason, and are suppos'd to proceed from the same faculty, with that, which judges of truth and falshood. Their nature and principles have been suppos'd the same, because their sensations are not evidently different.

Beside these calm passions, which often determine the will, there are certain violent emotions of the same kind, which have likewise a great influence on that faculty. When I receive any injury from another, I often feel a violent passion of resentment, which makes me desire his evil and punishment, independent of all considerations of pleasure and advantage to myself. When I am immediately threaten'd with any grievous ill, my fears, apprehensions, and aversions rise to a great height, and produce a sensible emotion.

The common error of metaphysicians has lain in ascribing the direction of the will entirely to one of these principles, and supposing the other to have no influence. Men often act knowingly against their interest: For which reason the view of the greatest possible good does not always influence them. Men often counter-act a violent passion in prosecution of their interests and designs: 'Tis not therefore the present uneasiness alone, which determines them. In general we may observe, that both these principles operate on the will; and where they are contrary, that either of them prevails, according to the *general* character or *present* disposition of the person. What we call strength of mind, implies the prevalence of the calm passions above the violent; tho' we may easily observe, there is no man so constantly possess'd of this virtue, as never on any occasion to yield to the sollicitations of passion and desire. From these variations of temper proceeds the great difficulty of deciding concerning the actions and resolutions of men, where there is any contrariety of motives and passions.

II. Of Virtue and Vice in General

. . . Those who affirm that virtue is nothing but a conformity to reason; that there are eternal fitnesses and unfitnesses of things, which are the same to every rational being that considers them; that the immutable measures of right and wrong impose an obligation, not only on human creatures, but also on the Deity himself: All these systems concur in the opinion, that morality, like truth, is discern'd merely by ideas, and by their juxtaposition and comparison. In order, therefore, to judge of these systems, we need only consider, whether it be possible, from reason alone, to distinguish betwixt moral good and evil, or whether there must concur some other principles to enable us to make that distinction.

If morality had naturally no influence on human passions and actions, 'twere in vain to take such pains to inculcate it; and nothing wou'd be more fruitless than that multitude of rules and precepts, with which all moralists abound. Philosophy is commonly divided into *speculative* and *practical;* and as morality is always comprehended under the latter division, 'tis supposed to influence our passions and actions, and to go beyond the calm and indolent judgments of the understanding. And this is confirm'd by common experience, which informs us, that men are often govern'd by their duties, and are deter'd from some actions by the opinion of injustice, and impell'd to others by that of obligation.

Since morals, therefore, have an influence on the actions and affections, it follows, that they cannot be deriv'd from reason; and that because reason alone, as we have already prov'd, can never have any such influence. Morals excite passions, and produce or prevent actions. Reason of itself is utterly impotent in this particular. The rules of morality, therefore, are not conclusions of our reason.

No one, I believe, will deny the justness of this inference; nor is there any other means of evading it, than by denying that principle, on which it is founded. As long as it is allow'd, that reason has no influence on our passions and actions, 'tis in vain to pretend, that morality is discover'd only by a deduction of reason. An active principle can never be founded on an inactive; and if reason be inactive in itself, it must remain so in all its shapes and appearances, whether it exerts itself in natural or moral subjects, whether it considers the powers of external bodies, or the actions of rational beings.

It would be tedious to repeat all the arguments, by which I have prov'd that reason is perfectly inert, and can never either prevent or produce any action or affection. 'Twill be easy to recollect what has been said upon that subject. I shall only recall on this occasion one of these arguments, which I shall endeavour to render still more conclusive, and more applicable to the present subject.

Reason is the discovery of truth or falshood. Truth or falshood consists in an agreement or disagreement either to the *real* relations of ideas, or to *real* existence and matter of fact. Whatever, therefore, is not susceptible of this agreement or disagreement, is incapable of being true or false, and can never be an object of our reason. Now 'tis evident our passions, volitions, and actions, are not susceptible of any such agreement or disagreement; being original facts and realities, compleat in themselves, and implying no reference to other passions, volitions, and actions. 'Tis impossible, therefore, they can be pronounced either true or false, and be either contrary or conformable to reason.

This argument is of double advantage to our present purpose. For it proves *directly,* that actions do not derive their merit from a conformity to reason, nor their blame from a contrariety to it; and it proves the same truth more *indirectly,* by shewing us, that as reason can never immediately prevent or produce any action by contradicting or approving of it, it cannot be the source of moral good and evil, which are found to have that influence. Actions may be laudable or blameable; but they cannot be reasonable or unreasonable: Laudable or blameable, therefore, are not the same with reasonable or unreasonable. The merit and demerit of actions frequently contradict, and sometimes controul our natural propensities. But reason has no such influence. Moral distinctions, therefore, are not the offspring of reason. Reason is wholly inactive, and can never be the source of so active a principle as conscience, or a sense of morals. . . .

Nor does this reasoning only prove, that morality consists not in any relations, that are the objects of science; but if examin'd, will prove with equal certainty, that it consists not in any *matter of fact,* which can be discover'd by the understanding. This is the *second* part of our argument; and if it can be made evident, we may conclude, that morality is not an object of reason.

But can there be any difficulty in proving, that vice and virtue are not matters of fact, whose existence we can infer by reason? Take any action allow'd to be vicious: Wilful murder, for instance. Examine it in all lights, and see if you can find that matter of fact, or real existence, which you call *vice*. In whichever way you take it, you find only certain passions, motives, volitions and thoughts. There is no other matter of fact in the case. The vice entirely escapes you, as long as you consider the object. You never can find it, till you turn your reflexion into your own breast, and find a sentiment of disapprobation, which arises in you, towards this action. Here is a matter of fact; but 'tis the object of feeling, not of reason. It lies in yourself, not in the object. So that when you pronounce any action or character to be vicious, you mean nothing, but that from the constitution of your nature you have a feeling or sentiment of blame from the contemplation of it. Vice and virtue, therefore, may be compar'd to sounds, colours, heat and cold, which, according to modern philosophy, are not qualities in objects, but perceptions in the mind: And this discovery in morals, like that other in physics, is to be regarded as a considerable advancement of the speculative sciences; tho', like that too, it has little or no influence on practice. Nothing can be more real, or concern us more, than our own sentiments of pleasure and uneasiness; and if these be favourable to virtue, and unfavourable to vice, no more can be requisite to the regulation of our conduct and behaviour.

I cannot forbear adding to these reasonings an observation, which may, perhaps, be found of some importance. In every system of morality, which I have hitherto met with, I have always remark'd, that the author proceeds for some time in the ordinary way of reasoning, and establishes the being of a God, or makes observations concerning human affairs; when of a sudden I am surpriz'd to find, that instead of the usual copulations of propositions, *is,* and *is not,* I meet with no proposition that is not connected with an *ought,* or an *ought not.* This change is imperceptible; but is, however, of the last consequence. For as this *ought,* or *ought not,* expresses some new relation or affirmation, 'tis necessary that it shou'd be observ'd and explain'd; and at the same time that a reason should be given, for what seems altogether inconceivable, how this new relation can be a deduction from others, which are entirely different from it. But as authors do not commonly use this precaution, I shall presume to recommend it to the readers; and am persuaded, that this small attention wou'd subvert all the vulgar systems of morality, and let us see, that the distinction of vice and virtue is not founded merely on the relations of objects, nor is perceiv'd by reason.

42 HEDONISTIC UTILITARIANISM
JEREMY BENTHAM (1748-1832)

I. Of the Principle of Utility

1. Nature has placed mankind under the governance of two sovereign masters, *pain* and *pleasure*. It is for them alone to point out what we ought to do, as well as to determine what we shall do. On the one hand the standard of right and wrong, on the other the chain of causes and effects, are fastened to their throne. They govern us in all we do, in all we say, in all we think: every effort we can make to throw off our subjection, will serve but to demonstrate and confirm it. In words a man may pretend to abjure their empire: but in reality he will remain subject to it all the while. The *principle of utility* recognises this subjection, and assumes it for the foundation of that system, the object of which is to rear the fabric of felicity by the hands of reason and of law. Systems which attempt to question it, deal in sounds instead of sense, in caprice instead of reason, in darkness instead of light.

But enough of metaphor and declamation: it is not by such means that moral science is to be improved.

2. The principle of utility is the foundation of the present work: it will be proper therefore at the outset to give an explicit and determinate account of what is meant by it. By the principle of utility is meant that principle which approves or disapproves of every action whatsoever, according to the tendency which it appears to have to augment or diminish the happiness of the party whose interest is in question: or, what is the same thing in other words, to promote or to oppose that happiness. I say of every action whatsoever; and therefore not only of every action of a private individual, but of every measure of government.

3. By utility is meant that property in any object, whereby it tends to produce benefit, advantage, pleasure, good, or happiness, (all this in the present case comes to the same thing) or (what comes again to the same thing) to prevent the happening of mischief, pain, evil, or unhappiness to the party whose interest is considered: if that party be the community in general, then the happiness of the community: if a particular individual, then the happiness of that individual.

SOURCE: From chapters 1, 2, and 4 of *An Introduction to the Principles of Morals and Legislation,* 1789, 2nd edition, 1823. The title of this selection has been supplied by the editors. Compare with selections 40 and 43.

4. The interest of the community is one of the most general expressions that can occur in the phraseology of morals: no wonder that the meaning of it is often lost. When it has a meaning, it is this. The community is a fictitious *body,* composed of the individual persons who are considered as constituting as it were its *members.* The interest of the community then is, what?—the sum of the interests of the several members who compose it.

5. It is in vain to talk of the interest of the community, without understanding what is the interest of the individual. A thing is said to promote the interest, or to be *for* the interest, of an individual, when it tends to add to the sum total of his pleasures: or, what comes to the same thing, to diminish the sum total of his pains.

6. An action then may be said to be comformable to the principle of utility, or, for shortness sake, to utility, (meaning with respect to the community at large) when the tendency it has to augment the happiness of the community is greater than any it has to diminish it. . . .

10. Of an action that is conformable to the principle of utility, one may always say either that it is one that ought to be done, or at least that it is not one that ought not to be done. One may say also, that it is right it should be done; at least that it is not wrong it should be done: that it is a right action; at least that it is not a wrong action. When thus interpreted, the words *ought,* and *right* and *wrong,* and others of that stamp, have a meaning: when otherwise, they have none.

11. Has the rectitude of this principle been ever formally contested? It should seem that it had, by those who have not known what they have been meaning. Is it susceptible of any direct proof? It should seem not: for that which is used to prove every thing else, cannot itself be proved: a chain of proofs must have their commencement somewhere. To give such proof is as impossible as it is needless.

12. Not that there is or ever has been that human creature breathing, however stupid or perverse, who has not on many, perhaps on most occasions of his life, deferred to it. By the natural constitution of the human frame, on most occasions of their lives men in general embrace this principle, without thinking of it: if not for the ordering of their own actions, yet for the trying of their own actions, as well as of those of other men. There have been, at the same time, not many, perhaps, even of the most intelligent, who have been disposed to embrace it purely and without reserve. There are even few who have not taken some occasion or other to quarrel with it, either on account of their not understanding always how to apply it, or on account of some prejudice or other which they were afraid to examine into, or could not bear to part with. For such is the stuff that man is made of: in principle and in practice, in a right track and in a wrong one, the rarest of all human qualities is consistency.

13. When a man attempts to combat the principle of utility, it is with reasons drawn, without his being aware of it, from that very principle itself. His arguments, if they prove any thing, prove not that the principle is *wrong*, but that, according to the applications he supposes to be made of it, it is *misapplied*. Is it possible for a man to move the earth? Yes; but he must first find out another earth to stand upon. . . .

II. Of Principles Adverse to That of Utility

1. If the principle of utility be a right principle to be governed by, and that in all cases, it follows from what has been just observed, that whatever principle differs from it in any case must necessarily be a wrong one. To prove any other principle, therefore, to be a wrong one, there needs no more than just to show it to be what it is, a principle of which the dictates are in some point or other different from those of the principle of utility: to state it is to confute it.

2. A principle may be different from that of utility in two ways: (1) By being constantly opposed to it: this is the case with a principle which may be termed the principle of *asceticism*. (2) By being sometimes opposed to it, and sometimes not, as it may happen: this is the case with another, which may be termed the principle of *sympathy* and *antipathy*.

3. By the principle of asceticism I mean that principle, which, like the principle of utility, approves or disapproves of any action, according to the tendency which it appears to have to augment or diminish the happiness of the party whose interest is in question; but in an inverse manner: approving of actions in as far as they tend to diminish his happiness; disapproving of them in as far as they tend to augment it.

4. It is evident that any one who reprobates any the least particle of pleasure, as such, from whatever source derived, is *pro tanto* a partizan of the principle of asceticism. It is only upon that principle, and not from the principle of utility, that the most abominable pleasure which the vilest of malefactors ever reaped from his crime would be to be reprobated, if it stood alone. The case is, that it never does stand alone; but is necessarily followed by such a quantity of pain (or, what comes to the same thing, such a chance for a certain quantity of pain) that the pleasure in comparison of it, is as nothing: and this is the true and sole, but perfectly sufficient, reason for making it a ground for punishment. . . .

10. The principle of utility is capable of being consistently pursued; and it is but tautology to say, that the more consistently it is pursued, the better it must ever be for human-kind. The principle of asceticism never was, nor ever can be, consistently pursued by any living creature. Let but one tenth part of the inhabitants of this earth pursue it consistently, and in a day's time they will have turned it into a hell.

11. Among principles adverse to that of utility, that which at this day seems to have most influence in matters of government, is what may be called the principle of sympathy and antipathy. By the principle of sympathy and antipathy, I mean that principle which approves or disapproves of certain actions, not on account of their tending to augment the happiness, nor yet on account of their tending to diminish the happiness of the party whose interest is in question, but merely because a man finds himself disposed to approve or disapprove of them: holding up that approbation or disapprobation as a sufficient reason for itself, and disclaiming the necessity of looking out for any extrinsic ground. Thus far in the general department of morals: and in the particular department of politics, measuring out the quantum (as well as determining the ground) of punishment, by the degree of the disapprobation.

12. It is manifest, that this is rather a principle in name than in reality: it is not a positive principle of itself, so much as a term employed to signify the negation of all principle. What one expects to find in a principle is something that points out some external consideration, as a means of warranting and guiding the internal sentiments of approbation and disapprobation: this expectation is but ill fulfilled by a proposition, which does neither more nor less than hold up each of those sentiments as a ground and standard for itself.

13. In looking over the catalogue of human actions (says a partizan of this principle) in order to determine which of them are to be marked with the seal of disapprobation, you need but to take counsel of your own feelings: whatever you find in yourself a propensity to condemn, is wrong for that very reason. For the same reason it is also meet for punishment: in what proportion it is adverse to utility, or whether it be adverse to utility at all, is a matter that makes no difference. In that same *proportion* also is it meet for punishment: if you hate much, punish much: if you hate little, punish little: punish as you hate. If you hate not at all, punish not at all: the fine feelings of the soul are not to be overborne and tyrannized by the harsh and rugged dictates of political utility. . . .

15. It is manifest, that the dictates of this principle will frequently coincide with those of utility, though perhaps without intending any such thing. Probably more frequently than not: and hence it is that the business of penal justice is carried on upon that tolerable sort of footing upon which we see it carried on in common at this day. For what more natural or more general ground of hatred to a practice can there be, than the mischievousness of such practice? What all men are exposed to suffer by, all men will be disposed to hate. It is far yet, however, from being a constant ground: for when a man suffers, it is not always that he knows what it is he suffers by. A man may suffer grievously, for instance, by a new tax, without being able to trace up the cause of his sufferings to the injustice of some neighbour, who has eluded the payment of an old one.

16. The principle of sympathy and antipathy is most apt to err on the side of severity. It is for applying punishment in many cases which deserve none: in many cases which deserve some, it is for applying more than they deserve. There is no incident imaginable, be it ever so trivial, and so remote from mischief, from which this principle may not extract a ground of punishment. Any difference in taste: any difference in opinion: upon one subject as well as upon another. No disagreement so trifling which perseverance and altercation will not render serious. Each becomes in the other's eyes an enemy, and, if laws permit, a criminal. This is one of the circumstances by which the human race is distinguished (not much indeed to its advantage) from the brute creation. . . .

19. There are two things which are very apt to be confounded, but which it imports us carefully to distinguish:—the motive or cause, which, by operating on the mind of an individual, is productive of any act: and the ground or reason which warrants a legislator, or other by-stander, in regarding that act with an eye of approbation. When the act happens, in the particular instance in question, to be productive of effects which we approve of, much more if we happen to observe that the same motive may frequently be productive, in other instances, of the like effects, we are apt to transfer our approbation to the motive itself, and to assume, as the just ground for the approbation we bestow on the act, the circumstance of its originating from that motive. It is in this way that the sentiment of antipathy has often been considered as a just ground of action. Antipathy, for instance, in such or such a case, is the cause of an action which is attended with good effects: but this does not make it a right ground of action in that case, any more than in any other. Still farther. Not only the effects are good, but the agent sees beforehand that they will be so. This may make the action indeed a perfectly right action: but it does not make antipathy a right ground of action. For the same sentiment of antipathy, if implicitly deferred to, may be, and very frequently is, productive of the very worst effects. Antipathy, therefore, can never be a right ground of action. No more, therefore, can resentment, which, as will be seen more particularly hereafter, is but a modification of antipathy. The only right ground of action, that can possibly subsist, is, after all, the consideration of utility, which, if it is a right principle of action, and of approbation, in any one case, is so in every other. Other principles in abundance, that is, other motives, may be the reasons why such and such an act *has* been done: that is, the reasons or causes of its being done: but it is this alone that can be the reason why it might or ought to have been done. Antipathy or resentment requires always to be regulated, to prevent its doing mischief: to be regulated by what? always by the principle of utility. The principle of utility neither requires nor admits of any other regulator than itself. . . .

III. Value of a Lot of Pleasure or Pain, How to be Measured

1. Pleasures then, and the avoidance of pains, are the *ends* which the legislator has in view: it behooves him therefore to understand their *value*. Pleasures and pains are the *instruments* he has to work with: it behooves him therefore to understand their force, which is again, in other words, their value.

2. To a person considered *by himself*, the value of a pleasure or pain considered *by itself*, will be greater or less, according to the four following circumstances:

(1) Its *intensity*.
(2) Its *duration*.
(3) Its *certainty* or *uncertainty*.
(4) Its *propinquity* or *remoteness*.

3. These are the circumstances which are to be considered in estimating a pleasure or a pain considered each of them by itself. But when the value of any pleasure or pain is considered for the purpose of estimating the tendency of any *act* by which it is produced, there are two other circumstances to be taken into the account; these are,

(5) Its *fecundity*, or the chance it has of being followed by sensations of the *same* kind: that is, pleasures, if it be a pleasure: pains, if it be a pain.

(6) Its purity, or the chance it has of *not* being followed by sensations of the *opposite* kind: that is, pains, if it be a pleasure: pleasures, if it be a pain.

These two last, however, are in strictness scarcely to be deemed properties of the pleasure or the pain itself; they are not, therefore, in strictness to be taken into the account of the value of that pleasure or that pain. They are in strictness to be deemed properties only of the act, or other event, by which such pleasure or pain has been produced; and accordingly are only to be taken into the account of the tendency of such act or such event.

4. To a *number* of persons, with reference to each of whom the value of a pleasure or a pain is considered, it will be greater or less, according to seven circumstances: to wit, the six preceding ones; *viz.*

(1) Its *intensity*.
(2) Its *duration*.
(3) Its *certainty* or *uncertainty*.
(4) Its *propinquity* or *remoteness*.
(5) Its *fecundity*.
(6) Its *purity*.

And one other; to wit:

(7) Its *extent;* that is, the number of persons to whom it *extends;* or (in other words) who are affected by it.

5. To take an exact account then of the general tendency of any act, by which the interests of a community are affected, proceed as follows. Begin with any one person of those whose interests seem most immediately to be affected by it: and take an account,

(1) Of the value of each distinguishable *pleasure* which appears to be produced by it in the *first* instance.

(2) Of the value of each *pain* which appears to be produced by it in the *first* instance.

(3) Of the value of each pleasure which appears to be produced by it *after* the first. This constitutes the *fecundity* of the first *pleasure* and the *impurity* of the first *pain.*

(4) Of the value of each *pain* which appears to be produced by it after the first. This constitutes the *fecundity* of the first *pain,* and the *impurity* of the first pleasure.

(5) Sum up all the values of all the *pleasures* on the one side, and those of all the pains on the other. The balance, if it be on the side of pleasure, will give the *good* tendency of the act upon the whole, with respect to the interests of that *individual* person; if on the side of pain, the *bad* tendency of it upon the whole.

(6) Take an account of the *number* of persons whose interests appear to be concerned; and repeat the above process with respect to each. *Sum up* the numbers expressive of the degrees of *good* tendency, which the act has, with respect to each individual, in regard to whom the tendency of it is *good* upon the whole . . . do this again with respect to each individual, in regard to whom the tendency of it is *bad* upon the whole. Take the *balance;* which, if on the side of *pleasure,* will give the general *good tendency* of the act, with respect to the total number or community of individuals concerned; if on the side of pain, the general *evil tendency,* with respect to the same community.

6. It is not to be expected that this process should be strictly pursued previously to every moral judgment, or to every legislative or judicial operation. It may, however, be always kept in view: and as near as the process actually pursued on these occasions approaches to it, so near will such process approach to the character of an exact one. . . .

8. . . . In all this there is nothing but what the practice of mankind, wheresoever they have a clear view of their own interest, is perfectly comformable to. An article of property, an estate in land, for instance, is valuable, on what account? On account of the pleasures of all kinds which it enables a man to produce, and what comes to the same thing the pains of all kinds

which it enables him to avert. But the value of such an article of property is universally understood to rise or fall according to the length or shortness of the time which a man has in it: the certainty of uncertainty of its coming into possession: and the nearness or remoteness of the time at which, if at all, it is to come into possession. . . .

43 THE CATEGORICAL IMPERATIVE

IMMANUEL KANT (1724-1804)

Nothing can possibly be conceived in the world, or even out of it, which can be called good without qualification, except a *good will.* Intelligence, wit, judgment, and the other *talents* of the mind, however they may be named, or courage, resolution, perseverance, as qualities of temperament, are undoubtedly good and desirable in many respects; but these gifts of nature may also become extremely bad and mischievous if the will which is to make use of them, and which, therefore, constitutes what is called *character,* is not good. It is the same with the *gifts of fortune.* Power, riches, honor, even health, and the general well-being and contentment with one's condition which is called *happiness,* inspire pride, and often presumption, if there is not a good will to correct the influence of these on the mind, and with this also to rectify the whole principle of acting, and adapt it to its end. The sight of a being who is not adorned with a single feature of a pure and good will, enjoying unbroken prosperity, can never give pleasure to an impartial rational spectator. Thus a good will appears to constitute the indispensable condition even of being worthy of happiness.

There are even some qualities which are of service to this good will itself, and may facilitate its action, yet which have no intrinsic unconditional value, but always presuppose a good will, and this qualifies the esteem that we justly have for them, and does not permit us to regard them as absolutely good. Moderation in the affections and passions, self-control, and calm deliberation are not only good in many respects, but even seem to constitute part of the

SOURCE: From the first section of the *Fundamental Principles of the Metaphysics of Morals,* 1785, translated from the German by T. K. Abbott (1873). Reprinted by permission of Longmans, Green & Co. Limited, London. The title of this selection has been supplied by the editors. Compare with selections 41 and 47.

intrinsic worth of the person; but they are far from deserving to be called good without qualification, although they have been so unconditionally praised by the ancients. For without the principles of a good will, they may become extremely bad; and the coolness of a villain not only makes him far more dangerous, but also directly makes him more abominable in our eyes than he would have been without it.

A good will is good not because of what it performs or effects, not by its aptness for the attainment of some proposed end, but simply by virtue of the volition—that is, it is good in itself, and considered by itself is to be esteemed much higher than all that can be brought about by it in favor of any inclination, nay, even the sum-total of all inclinations. Even if it should happen that, owing to special disfavor of fortune, or the niggardly provision of a stepmotherly nature, this will should wholly lack power to accomplish its purpose, if with its greatest efforts it should yet achieve nothing, and there should remain only the good will (not, to be sure, a mere wish, but the summoning of all means in our power), then, like a jewel, it would still shine by its own light, as a thing which has its whole value in itself. Its usefulness or fruitlessness can neither add to nor take away anything from this value. It would be, as it were, only the setting to enable us to handle it the more conveniently in common commerce, or to attract to it the attention of those who are not yet connoisseurs, but not to recommend it to true connoisseurs, or to determine its value. . . .

We have then to develop the notion of a will which deserves to be highly esteemed for itself, and is good without a view to anything further, a notion which exists already in the sound natural understanding, requiring rather to be cleared up than to be taught, and which in estimating the value of our actions always takes the first place and constitutes the condition of all the rest. In order to do this, we will take the notion of duty, which includes that of a good will, although implying certain subjective restrictions and hindrances. These, however, far from concealing it or rendering it unrecognizable, rather bring it out by contrast and make it shine forth so much the brighter.

I omit here all actions which are already recognized as inconsistent with duty, although they may be useful for this or that purpose, for with these the question whether they are done *from duty* cannot arise at all, since they even conflict with it. I also set aside those actions which really conform to duty, but to which men have *no* direct *inclination,* performing them because they are impelled thereto by some other inclination. For in this case we can readily distinguish whether the action which agrees with duty is done *from duty* or from a selfish view. It is much harder to make this distinction when the action accords with duty, and the subject has besides a *direct* inclination to it. For example, it is always a matter of duty that a dealer should not overcharge an

THE CATEGORICAL IMPERATIVE 283

inexperienced purchaser; and wherever there is much commerce the prudent tradesman does not overcharge, but keeps a fixed price for everyone, so that a child buys of him as well as any other. Men are thus *honestly* served; but this is not enough to make us believe that the tradesman has so acted from duty and from principles of honesty; his own advantage required it; it is out of the question in this case to suppose that he might besides have a direct inclination in favor of the buyers, so that, as it were, from love he should give no advantage to one over another. Accordingly the action was done neither from duty nor from direct inclination, but merely with a selfish view.

On the other hand, it is a duty to maintain one's life; and, in addition, everyone has also a direct inclination to do so. But on this account the often anxious care which most men take for it has no intrinsic worth, and their maxim has no moral import. They preserve their life *as duty requires,* no doubt, but not *because duty requires.* On the other hand, if adversity and hopeless sorrow have completely taken away the relish for life, if the unfortunate one, strong in mind, indignant at his fate rather than desponding or dejected, wishes for death, and yet preserves his life without loving it—not from inclination or fear, but from duty—then his maxim has a moral worth.

To be beneficent when we can is a duty; and besides this, there are many minds so sympathetically constituted that, without any other motive of vanity or self-interest, they find a pleasure in spreading joy around them, and can take delight in the satisfaction of others so far as it is their own work. But I maintain that in such a case an action of this kind, however proper, however amiable it may be, has nevertheless no true moral worth, but is on a level with other inclinations, for example, the inclination to honor, which, if it is happily directed to that which is in fact of public utility and accordant with duty, and consequently honorable, deserves praise and encouragement, but not esteem. For the maxim lacks the moral import, namely, that such actions be done *from duty,* not from inclination. Put the case that the mind of that philanthropist was clouded by sorrow of his own, extinguishing all sympathy with the lot of others, and that while he still has the power to benefit others in distress, he is not touched by their trouble because he is absorbed with his own; and now suppose that he tears himself out of this dead insensibility and performs the action without any inclination to it, but simply from duty, then first has his action its genuine moral worth. Further still, if nature has put little sympathy in the heart of this or that man, if he, supposed to be an upright man, is by temperament cold and indifferent to the sufferings of others, perhaps because in respect of his own he is provided with the special gift of patience and fortitude, and supposes, or even requires, that others should have the same—and such a man would certainly not be the meanest product of nature—but if nature had not specially framed him for a philanthropist, would he not still find in himself a source from whence to give himself a far higher worth than that of a good-natured temperament could be? Unquestionably. It is just in this that the moral worth of the character is brought out which is incomparably the highest of all, namely, that he is beneficent, not from inclination, but from duty. . . .

An action done from duty derives its moral worth, *not from the purpose* which is to be attained by it, but from the maxim by which it is determined, and therefore does not depend on the realization of the object of the action, but merely on the *principle of volition* by which the action has taken place, without regard to any object of desire. It is clear from what precedes that the purpose which we may have in view in our actions, or their effects regarded as ends and springs of the will, cannot give to actions any unconditional or moral worth. In what, then, can their worth lie if it is not to consist in the will and in reference to its expected effect? It cannot lie anywhere but in the *principle of the will* without regard to the ends which can be attained by the action. . . .

Thus the moral worth of an action does not lie in the effect expected from it, nor in any principle of action which requires to borrow its motive from this expected effect. For all these effects—agreeableness of one's condition, and even the promotion of the happiness of others—could have been also brought about by other causes, so that for this there would have been no need of the will of a rational being; whereas it is in this alone that the supreme and unconditional good can be found. The pre-eminent good which we call moral can therefore consist in nothing else than *the conception of law* in itself, *which certainly is only possible in a rational being,* in so far as this conception, and not the expected effect, determines the will. This is a good which is already present in the person who acts accordingly, and we have not to wait for it to appear first in the result.

But what sort of law can that be the conception of which must determine the will, even without paying any regard to the effect expected from it, in order that this will may be called good absolutely and without qualification? As I have deprived the will of every impulse which could arise to it from obedience to any law, there remains nothing but the universal conformity of its actions to law in general, which alone is to serve the will as a principle, that is, I am never to act otherwise than *so that I could also will that my maxim should become a universal law.* Here, now, it is the simple conformity to law in general, without assuming any particular law applicable to certain actions, that serves the will as its principle, and must so serve it if duty is not to be a vain delusion and a chimerical notion. The common reason of men in its practical judgments perfectly coincides with this, and always has in view the principle here suggested. Let the question be, for example: May I when in distress make a promise with the intention not to keep it? I readily distinguish here between the two significations which the question may have: whether it is prudent or whether it is right to make a false promise? The former may undoubtedly often be the case. I see clearly indeed that it is not enough to extricate myself from a present difficulty by means of this subterfuge, but it must be well considered whether there may not hereafter spring from this lie much greater inconvenience than that from which I now free myself, and as, with all my supposed *cunning,* the consequences cannot be so easily foreseen but that credit once lost may be much more injurious to me than any mischief which I seek to avoid at present, it should be considered whether it would not be more *prudent* to act herein according to a universal maxim, and to make it a habit to promise nothing except with the intention of keeping it. But it is soon clear to me that such a maxim will still only be based on the fear of consequences. Now it is a wholly different thing to be truthful from duty, and to be so from apprehension of injurious consequences. . . . For to deviate from the principle of duty is beyond all doubt wicked; but to be unfaithful to my maxim of prudence may often be very advantageous to me, although to abide by it is certainly safer. The shortest way, however, and an unerring one, to discover the answer to this question whether a lying promise is consistent with duty, is to ask myself, Should I be content that my maxim (to extricate myself from difficulty by a false promise) should hold good as a universal law, for myself as well as for others; and should I be able to say to myself, "Every one may make a deceitful promise when he finds himself in a difficulty from which he cannot otherwise extricate himself?" Then I presently become aware that, while I can will the lie, I can by no means will that lying should be a universal law. For with such a law there would be no promises at all, since it would be in vain to allege my intention in regard to my future actions to those who would not believe this allegation, or if they over-hastily did so, would pay me back in my own coin. Hence my maxim, as soon as it should be made a universal law, would necessarily destroy itself.

I do not, therefore, need any far-reaching penetration to discern what I have to do in order that my will may be morally good. Inexperienced in the course of the world, incapable of being prepared for all its contingencies, I only ask myself: Canst thou also will that thy maxim should be a universal law? If not, then it must be rejected, and that not because of a disadvantage accruing from it to myself or even to others, but because it cannot enter as a principle into a possible universal legislation, and reason extorts from me immediate respect for such legislation. I do not indeed as yet *discern* on what this respect is based . . . but at least I understand this . . . that the necessity of acting from *pure* respect for the practical law is what constitutes duty, to which every other motive must give place because it is the condition of a will being good *in itself,* and the worth of such a will is above everything. . . .

44 ETHICAL ABSOLUTISM AND ETHICAL RELATIVISM
WALTER T. STACE (1886-1967)

There is an opinion widely current nowadays in philosophical circles which passes under the name of "ethical relativity." Exactly what this phrase means or implies is certainly far from clear. But unquestionably it stands as a label for the opinions of a group of ethical philosophers whose position is roughly on the extreme left wing among the moral theorizers of the day. And perhaps one may best understand it by placing it in contrast with the opposite kind of extreme view against which, undoubtedly, it has arisen as a protest. For among moral philosophers one may clearly distinguish a left and a right wing. Those of the left wing are the ethical relativists. They are the revolutionaries, the clever young men, the up to date. Those of the right wing we may call the ethical absolutists. They are the conservatives and the old-fashioned.

Ethical Absolutism
According to the absolutists there is but one eternally true and valid moral code. This moral code applies with rigid impartiality to all men. What is a duty for me must likewise be a duty for you. And this will be true whether you are an Englishman, a Chinaman, or a Hottentot. If cannibalism is an abomination in England or America, it is an abomination in central Africa, notwithstanding that the African may think otherwise. The fact that he sees nothing wrong in his cannibal practices does not make them for him morally right. They are as much contrary to morality for him as they are for us. The only difference is that he is an ignorant savage who does not know this. There is not one law for one man or race of men, another for another. There is not one moral standard for Europeans, another for Indians, another for Chinese. There is but one law, one standard, one morality, for all men. And this standard, this law, is absolute and unvarying.

SOURCE: Reprinted from *The Concept of Morals* (New York: The Macmillan Company, 1937), pp. 1–16, 27–28, 46–48, and 53, by kind permission of the author. The title of this selection has been supplied by the editors.

Moreover, as the one moral law extends its domination over all the corners of the earth, so too it is not limited in its application by any considerations of time or period. That which is right now was right in the centuries of Greece and Rome, nay, in the very ages of the cave man. That which is evil now was evil then. If slavery is morally wicked today, it was morally wicked among the ancient Athenians, notwithstanding that their greatest man accepted it as a necessary condition of human society. Their opinion did not make slavery a moral good for them. It only showed that they were, in spite of their otherwise noble conceptions, ignorant of what is truly right and good in this matter.

The ethical absolutist recognizes as a fact that moral customs and moral ideas differ from country to country and from age to age. This indeed seems manifest and not to be disputed. We think slavery morally wrong, the Greeks thought it morally unobjectionable. The inhabitants of New Guinea certainly have very different moral ideas from ours. But the fact that the Greeks or the inhabitants of New Guinea think something right does not make it right, even for them. Nor does the fact that we think the same things wrong make them wrong. They are *in themselves* either right or wrong. What we have to do is to discover which they are. What anyone thinks makes no difference. It is here just as it is in matters of physical science. We believe the earth to be a globe. Our ancestors may have thought it flat. This does not show that it *was* flat, and is *now* a globe. What it shows is that men having in other ages been ignorant about the shape of the earth have now learned the truth. So if the Greeks thought slavery morally legitimate, this does not indicate that it was for them and in that age morally legitimate, but rather that they were ignorant of the truth of the matter.

The ethical absolutist is not indeed committed to the opinion that his own, or our own, moral code is the true one. Theoretically at least he might hold that slavery is ethically justifiable, that the Greeks knew better than we do about this, that ignorance of the true morality lies with us and not with them. All that he is actually committed to is the opinion that, whatever the true moral code may be, it is always the same for all men in all ages. His view is not at all inconsistent with the belief that humanity has still much to learn in moral matters. If anyone were to assert that in five hundred years the moral conceptions of the present day will appear as barbarous to the people of that age as the moral conceptions of the middle ages appear to us now, he need not deny it. If anyone were to assert that the ethics of Christianity are by no means final, and will be superseded in future ages by vastly nobler moral ideals, he need not deny this either. For it is of the essence of his creed to believe that morality is in some sense objective, not man-made, not produced by human opinion; that its principles are real truths about which men have to learn—just as they have to learn about the shape of the world—about which they may have been ignorant in the past, and about which therefore they may well be ignorant now.

Thus although absolutism is conservative in the sense that it is regarded by the more daring spirits as an out of date opinion, it is not necessarily conservative in the sense of being committed to the blind support of existing moral ideas and institutions. If ethical absolutists are sometimes conservative in this sense too, that is their personal affair. Such conservatism is accidental, not essential to the absolutist's creed. There is no logical reason, in the nature of the case, why an absolutist should not be a communist, an anarchist, a surrealist, or an upholder of free love. The fact that he is usually none of these things may be accounted for in various ways. But it has nothing to do with the sheer logic of his ethical position. The sole opinion to which he is committed is that whatever is morally right (or wrong)—be it free love or monogamy or slavery or cannibalism or vegetarianism—is morally right (or wrong) for all men at all times.

Usually the absolutist goes further than this. He often maintains, not merely that the moral law is the same for all the men of this planet—which is, after all, a tiny speck in space—but that in some way or in some sense it has application everywhere in the universe. He may express himself by saying that it applies to all "rational beings"—which would apparently include angels and the men on Mars (if they are rational). He is apt to think that the moral law is a part of the fundamental structure of the universe. But with this aspect of absolutism we need not, at the moment, concern ourselves. At present we may think of it as being simply the opinion that there is a single moral standard for all human beings.

[*Historical Causes for the Acceptance of Absolutism.*] This brief and rough sketch of ethical absolutism is intended merely to form a background against which we may the more clearly indicate, by way of contrast, the theory of ethical relativity. Up to the present, therefore, I have not given any of the reasons which the absolutist can urge in favour of his case. It is sufficient for my purpose at the moment to state *what* he believes, without going into the question of *why* he believes it. But before proceeding to our next step—the explanation of ethical relativity—I think it will be helpful to indicate some of the historical causes (as distinguished from logical reasons) which have helped in the past to render absolutism a plausible interpretation of morality as understood by European peoples.

Our civilization is a Christian civilization. It has grown up, during nearly two thousand years, upon the soil of Christian monotheism. In this soil our whole outlook upon life, and consequently all our moral ideas, have their roots. They have been moulded by this influence. The wave of religious scepticism which, during the last half century, has swept over us, has altered this fact scarcely at all. The moral ideas even of those who most violently reject the dogmas of Christianity with their intellects are still Christian ideas. This will probably remain true for many centuries even if Christian theology, as a set of intellectual beliefs, comes to be wholly rejected by every educated person. It will probably remain true so long as our civilization lasts. A child cannot, by changing in later life his intellectual creed, strip himself of the early formative moral influences of his childhood, though he can no doubt modify their results in various minor ways. With the outlook on life which was instilled into him in his early days he, in large measure, lives and dies. So it is with a civilization. And our civilization, whatever religious or irreligious views it may come to hold or reject, can hardly escape within its lifetime the moulding influences of its Christian origin. Now ethical absolutism was, in its central ideas, the product of Christian theology.

The connection is not difficult to detect. For morality has been conceived, during the Christian dispensation, as issuing from the will of God. That indeed was its single and all-sufficient source. There would be no point, for the naive believer in the faith, in the philosopher's questions regarding the foundations of morality and the basis of moral obligation. Even to ask such questions is a mark of incipient religious scepticism. For the true believer the author of the moral law is God. What pleases God, what God commands—that is the definition of right. What displeases God, what he forbids, that is the definition of wrong. Now there is, for the Christian monotheist, only one God ruling over the entire universe. And this God is rational, self-consistent. He does not act upon whims. Consequently his will and his commands must be the same everywhere. They will be unvarying for all peoples and in all ages. If the heathen have other moral ideas then ours—inferior ideas—that can only be because they live in ignorance of the true God. If they knew God and his commands, their ethical precepts would be the same as ours.

Polytheistic creeds may well tolerate a number of diverse moral codes. For the God of the western hemisphere might have different views from those entertained by the God of the eastern hemisphere. And the God of the north might issue to his worshippers commands at variance with the commands issued to other peoples by the God of the south. But a monotheistic religion implies a single universal and absolute morality.

This explains why ethical absolutism, until very recently, was not only believed by philosophers but *taken for granted without any argument*. . . .

Ethical Relativism

We can now turn to the consideration of ethical relativity. . . . The revolt of the relativists against absolutism is, I believe, part and parcel of the general revolutionary tendency of our times. In particular it is a result of the decay of belief in the dogmas of orthodox religion. Belief in absolutism was supported, as we have seen, by belief in Christian monotheism. And now that, in an age of widespread religious scepticism, that support is withdrawn, absolutism tends to collapse. Revolutionary movements are as a rule, at any rate in their first onset, purely negative. They attack and destroy. And ethical relativity is, in its essence, a purely negative creed. It is simply a denial of ethical absolutism. That is why the best way of explaining it is to begin by explaining ethical absolutism. If we understand that what the latter asserts the former denies, then we understand ethical relativity.

Any ethical position which denies that there is a single moral standard which is equally applicable to all men at all times may fairly be called a species of ethical relativity. There is not, the relativist asserts, merely one moral law, one code, one standard. There are many moral laws, codes, standards. What morality ordains in one place or age may be quite different from what morality ordains in another place or age. The moral code of Chinamen is quite different from that of Europeans, that of African savages quite different from both. Any morality, therefore, is relative to the age, the place, and the circumstances in which it is found. It is in no sense absolute.

This does not mean merely—as one might at first sight be inclined to suppose—that the very same kind of action which is *thought* right in one country and period may be *thought* wrong in another. This would be a mere platitude, the truth of which everyone would have to admit. Even the absolutist would admit this—would even wish to emphasize it—since he is well aware that different peoples have different sets of moral ideas, and his whole point is that some of these sets of ideas are false. What the relativist means to assert is, not this platitude, but that the very same kind of action which *is* right in one country and period may *be* wrong in another. And this, far from being a platitude, is a very startling assertion.

It is very important to grasp thoroughly the difference between the two ideas. For there is reason to think that many minds tend to find ethical relativity attractive because they fail to keep them clearly apart. It is so very obvious that moral ideas differ from country to country and from age to age. And it is so very easy, if you are mentally lazy, to suppose that to say this means the same as to say that no universal moral standard exists,—or in other words that it implies ethical relativity. We fail to see that the word "standard" is used in two different senses. It is perfectly true that, in one sense, there are many variable moral standards. We speak of judging a man by the standard of his time. And this implies that different times have different standards. And this, of course, is quite true. But when the word "standard" is used in this sense it means simply the set of moral ideas current during the period in question. It means what people *think* right, whether as a matter of fact it *is* right or not. On the other hand when the absolutist asserts that there exists a single universal moral "standard," he is not using the word in this sense at all. He means by "standard" what *is* right as distinct from what people merely think right. His point is that although what people think right varies in different countries and periods, yet what actually is right is everywhere and always the same. And it follows that when the ethical relativist disputes the position of the absolutist and denies that any universal moral standard exists he too means by "standard" what actually is right. But it is exceedingly easy, if we are not careful, to slip loosely from using the word in the first sense to using it in the second sense; and to suppose that the variability of moral beliefs is the same thing as the variability of what really is moral. And unless we keep the two senses of the word "standard" distinct, we are likely to think the creed of ethical relativity much more plausible than it actually is.

The genuine relativist, then, does not merely mean that Chinamen may think right what Frenchmen think wrong. He means that what is wrong for the Frenchman may *be* right for the Chinaman. And if one enquires how, in those circumstances, one is to know what actually is right in China or in France, the answer comes quite glibly. What is right in China is the same as what people think right in China; and what is right in France is the same as what people think is right in France. So that, if you want to know what is moral in any particular country or age all you have to do is to ascertain what are the moral ideas current in that age or country. Those ideas are, *for that age or country,* right. Thus what is morally right is identified with what is thought to be morally right, and the distinction which we made above between these two is simply denied. To put the same thing in another way, it is denied that there can be or ought to be any distinction between the two senses of the word "standard." There is only one kind of standard of right and wrong, namely, the moral ideas current in any particular age or country.

Moral right *means* what people think morally right. It has no other meaning. What Frenchmen think right is, therefore, right *for Frenchmen*. And evidently one must conclude—though I am not aware that relativists are anxious to draw one's attention to such unsavoury but yet absolutely necessary conclusions from their creed—that cannibalism is right for people who believe in it, that human sacrifice is right for those races which practice it, and that burning widows alive was right for Hindus until the British stepped in and compelled the Hindus to behave immorally by allowing their widows to remain alive.

When it is said that, according to the ethical relativist, what is thought right in any social group is right for that group, one must be careful not to misinterpret this. The relativist does not, of course, mean that there actually is an objective moral standard in France and a different objective standard in England, and that French and British opinions respectively give us correct information about these different standards. His point is rather that there are no objectively true moral standards at all. There is no single universal objective standard. Nor are there a variety of local objective standards. All standards are subjective. People's subjective feelings about morality are the only standards which exist.

To sum up. The ethical relativist consistently denies, it would seem, whatever the ethical absolutist asserts. For the absolutist there is a single universal moral standard. For the relativist there is no such standard. There are only local, ephemeral, and variable standards. For the absolutist there are two senses of the word "standard." Standards in the sense of sets of current moral ideas are relative and changeable. But the standard in the sense of what is actually morally right is absolute and unchanging. For the relativist no such distinction can be made. There is only one meaning of the word standard, namely, that which refers to local and variable sets of moral ideas. Or if it is insisted that the word must be allowed two meanings, then the relativist will say that there is at any rate no actual example of a standard in the absolute sense, and that the word as thus used is an empty name to which nothing in reality corresponds; so that the distinction between the two meanings becomes empty and useless. Finally—though this is merely saying the same thing in another way—the absolutist makes a distinction between what is actually right and what is thought right. The relativist rejects this distinction and identifies what is moral with what is thought moral by certain human beings or groups of human beings. . . .

[*Arguments in Favor of Ethical Relativity.*] . . . The first [argument] is that which relies upon the actual varieties of moral "standards" found in the world. It was easy enough to believe in a single absolute morality in older times when there was no anthropology, when all humanity was divided clearly into two groups, Christian peoples and the "heathen." Christian peoples knew and possessed the one true morality. The rest were savages whose moral ideas could be ignored. But all this is changed. Greater knowledge has brought greater tolerance. We can no longer exalt our own morality as alone true, while dismissing all other moralities as false or inferior. The investigations of anthropologists have shown that there exist side by side in the world a bewildering variety of moral codes. On this topic endless volumes have been written, masses of evidence piled up. Anthropologists have ransacked the Melanesian Islands, the jungles of New Guinea, the steppes of Siberia, the deserts of Australia, the forests of central Africa, and have brought back with them countless examples of weird, extravagant, and fantastic "moral" customs with which to confound us. We learn that all kinds of horrible practices

ETHICAL ABSOLUTISM 293

are, in this, that, or the other place, regarded as essential to virtue. We find that there is nothing, or next to nothing, which has always and everywhere been regarded as morally good by all men. Where then is our universal morality? Can we, in face of all this evidence, deny that it is nothing but an empty dream?

This argument, taken by itself, is a very weak one. It relies upon a single set of facts—the variable moral customs of the world. But this variability of moral ideas is admitted by both parties to the dispute, and is capable of ready explanation upon the hypothesis of either party. The relativist says that the facts are to be explained by the non-existence of any absolute moral standard. The absolutist says that they are to be explained by human ignorance of what the absolute moral standard is. And he can truly point out that men have differed widely in their opinions about all manner of topics including the subject-matters of the physical sciences—just as much as they differ about morals. And if the various different opinions which men have held about the shape of the earth do not prove that it has no one real shape, neither do the various opinions which they have held about morality prove that there is no one true morality.

Thus the facts can be explained equally plausibly on either hypothesis. There is nothing in the facts themselves which compels us to prefer the relativistic hypothesis to that of the absolutist. And therefore the argument fails to prove the relativist conclusion. If that conclusion is to be established, it must be by means of other considerations.

This is the essential point. But I will add some supplementary remarks. The work of the anthropologists, upon which ethical relativists seem to rely so heavily, has as a matter of fact added absolutely nothing *in principle* to what has always been known about the variability of moral ideas. Educated people have known all along that the Greeks tolerated sodomy, which in modern times has been regarded in some countries as an abominable crime; that the Hindus thought it a sacred duty to burn their widows; that trickery, now thought despicable, was once believed to be a virtue; that terrible torture was thought by our own ancestors only a few centuries ago to be a justifiable weapon of justice; that it was only yesterday that western peoples came to believe that slavery is immoral. Even the ancients knew very well that moral customs and ideas vary—witness the writings of Herodotus. Thus the principle of the variability of moral ideas was well understood long before modern anthropology was ever heard of. Anthropology has added nothing to the knowledge of this principle except a mass of new and extreme examples of it drawn from very remote sources. But to multiply examples of a principle already well known and universally admitted adds nothing to the argument which is built upon that principle. The discoveries of the anthropologists have no doubt been of the highest importance in their own sphere. But in my considered opinion they have thrown no new light upon the special problems of the moral philosopher.

Although the multiplication of examples has no logical bearing on the argument, it does have an immense *psychological* effect upon people's minds. These masses of anthropological learning are impressive. They are propounded in the sacred name of "science." If they are quoted in support of ethical relativity—as they often are—people *think* that they must prove something important. They bewilder and over-awe the simple-minded, batter down their resistance, make them ready to receive humbly the doctrine of ethical relativity from those who have acquired a reputation by their immense learning and their claims to be "scientific." Perhaps this is why so much ado is made by ethical relativists regarding the anthropological evidence. But we must refuse to be impressed. We must discount all this mass of evidence about the extraordinary moral customs of remote peoples. Once we have admitted—as everyone who is instructed must have admitted these last two thousand years without any anthropology at all—the principle that moral ideas vary, all this new evidence adds nothing to the argument. And the argument itself proves nothing for the reasons already given. . . .

[Another] argument in favour of ethical relativity . . . consists in alleging that no one has ever been able to discover upon what foundation an absolute morality could rest, or from what source a universally binding moral code could derive its authority.

If, for example, it is an absolute and unalterable moral rule that all men ought to be unselfish, from whence does this *command* issue? For a command it certainly is, phrase it how you please. There is no difference in meaning between the sentence "You ought to be unselfish" and the sentence "Be unselfish." Now a command implies a commander. An obligation implies some authority which obliges. Who is this commander, what this authority? Thus the vastly difficult question is raised of *the basis of moral obligation.* Now the argument of the relativist would be that it is impossible to find any basis for a universally binding moral law; but that it is quite easy to discover a basis for morality if moral codes are admitted to be variable, ephemeral, and relative to time, place, and circumstance.

. . . I am assuming that it is no longer possible to solve this difficulty by saying naively that the universal moral law is based upon the uniform commands of God to all men. There will be many, no doubt, who will dispute this. But I am not writing for them. I am writing for those who feel the necessity of finding for morality a basis independent of particular religious dogmas. And I shall therefore make no attempt to argue the matter.

The problem which the absolutist has to face, then, is this. The religious basis of the one absolute morality having disappeared, can there be found for it any other, any secular, basis? If not, then it would seem that we cannot any longer believe in absolutism. We shall have to fall back upon belief in a variety of perhaps mutually inconsistent moral codes operating over restricted areas and limited periods. No one of these will be better, or more true, than any other. Each will be good and true for those living in those areas and periods. We shall have to fall back, in a word, on ethical relativity. . . .

[*Arguments Against Ethical Relativity.*]. . . Ethical relativity, in asserting that the moral standards of particular social groups are the only standards which exist, renders meaningless all propositions which attempt to compare these standards with one another in respect of their moral worth. And this is a very serious matter indeed. We are accustomed to think that the moral ideas of one nation or social group may be "higher" or "lower" than those of another. We believe, for example, that Christian ethical ideals are nobler than those of the savage races of central Africa. Probably most of us would think that the Chinese moral standards are higher than those of the inhabitants of New Guinea. In short we habitually compare one civilization with another and judge the sets of ethical ideas to be found in them to be some better, some worse. The fact that such judgments are very difficult to make with any justice, and that they are frequently made on very superficial and prejudiced grounds, has no bearing on the question now at issue. The question is whether such judgments have any *meaning*. We habitually assume that they have.

But on the basis of ethical relativity they can have none whatever. For the relativist must hold that there is no *common* standard which can be applied to the various civilizations judged. Any such comparison of moral standards implies the existence of some superior standard which is applicable to both. And the existence of any such standard is precisely what the relativist denies. According to him the Christian standard is applicable only to Christians, the Chinese standard only to Chinese, the New Guinea standard only to the inhabitants of New Guinea.

What is true of comparisons between the moral standards of different races will also be true of comparisons between those of different ages. It is not unusual to ask such questions as whether the standard of our own day is superior to that which existed among our ancestors five hundred years ago. And when we remember that our ancestors employed slaves, practiced barbaric physical tortures, and burnt people alive, we may be inclined to think that it is. At any rate we assume that the question is one which has meaning and is capable of rational discussion. But if the ethical relativist is right, whatever we assert on this subject must be totally meaningless. For here again there is no common standard which could form the basis of any such judgments.

This in its turn implies that the whole notion of moral *progress* is a sheer delusion. Progress means an advance from lower to higher, from worse to better. But on the basis of ethical relativity it has no meaning to say that the standards of this age are better (or worse) than those of a previous age. For there is no common standard by which both can be measured. . . .

If these arguments are valid, the ethical relativist cannot really maintain that there is anywhere to be found a moral standard binding upon anybody against his will. And he cannot maintain that, even within the social group, there is a common standard as between individuals. And if that is so, then even judgments to the effect that one man is morally better than another become meaningless. All moral valuation thus vanishes. There is nothing to prevent each man from being a rule unto himself. The result will be moral chaos and the collapse of all effective standards. . . .

45 THE EMOTIVE MEANING OF ETHICAL TERMS
CHARLES L. STEVENSON
(1906-)

I

Ethical questions first arise in the form "is so and so good?" or "is this alternative better than that?" These questions are difficult partly because we don't quite know what we are seeking. We are asking, "is there a needle in the haystack?" without even knowing just what a needle is. So the first thing to do is to examine the questions themselves. We must try to make them clearer, either by defining the terms in which they are expressed or by any other method that is available.

The present essay is concerned wholly with this preliminary step of making ethical questions clear. In order to help answer the question "is X good?" we must *substitute* for it a question that is free from ambiguity and confusion.

It is obvious that in substituting a clearer question we must not introduce

SOURCE: Reprinted from *Mind,* vol. XLVI (1937), pp. 14–31, by consent of the author and Basil Blackwell, publisher of *Mind.* By request of the author the text followed here is the text of the essay as it appears in the author's collection *Facts and Values* (New Haven: Yale University Press, 1963), where he "remedied a few irregularities in style, and changed one of the examples," and added some footnotes.

some utterly different kind of question. It won't do (to take an extreme instance of a prevalent fallacy) to substitute for "is X good?" the question "is X pink with yellow trimmings?" and then point out how easy the question really is. This would beg the original question, not help answer it. On the other hand, we must not expect the substituted question to be strictly "identical" with the original one. The original question may embody hypostatization, anthropomorphism, vagueness, and all the other ills to which our ordinary discourse is subject. If our substituted question is to be clearer it must remove these ills. The questions will be identical only in the sense that a child is identical with the man he later becomes. Hence we must not demand that the substitution strike us, on immediate introspection, as making no change in meaning.

Just how, then, must the substituted question be related to the original? Let us assume (inaccurately) that it must result from replacing "good" by some set of terms that define it. The question then resolves itself to this: How must the defined meaning of "good" be related to its original meaning?

I answer that it must be *relevant*. A defined meaning will be called "relevant" to the original meaning under these circumstances: Those who have understood the definition must be able to say all that they then want to say by using the term in the defined way. They must never have occasion to use the term in the old, unclear sense. (If a person did have to go on using the word in the old sense, then to this extent his meaning would not be clarified and the philosophical task would not be completed.) It frequently happens that a word is used so confusedly and ambiguously that we must give it *several* defined meanings, rather than one. In this case only the whole set of defined meanings will be called "relevant," and any one of them will be called "partially relevant." This is not a rigorous treatment of *relevance*, by any means, but it will serve for the present purposes.

Let us now turn to our particular task—that of giving a relevant definition of "good." Let us first examine some of the ways in which others have attempted to do this.

The word "good" has often been defined in terms of *approval*, or similar psychological attitudes. We may take as typical examples: "good" means *desired by me* (Hobbes); and "good" means *approved by most people* (Hume, in effect).[1] It will be convenient to refer to definitions of this sort as

---

[1] The definition ascribed to Hume is oversimplified, but not, I think, in a way that weakens the force of the observations that I am about to make. Perhaps the same should be said of Hobbes.
A more accurate account of Hume's Ethics is given in *Ethics and Language* (New Haven, 1944), pp. 273-76.

"interest theories," following R. B. Perry, although neither "interest" nor "theory" is used in the most usual way.[2]

Are definitions of this sort relevant?

It is idle to deny their *partial relevance*. The most superficial inquiry will reveal that "good" is exceedingly ambiguous. To maintain that "good" is *never* used in Hobbes' sense, and never in Hume's, is only to manifest an insensitivity to the complexities of language. We must recognize, perhaps, not only these senses, but a variety of similar ones, differing both with regard to the kind of interest in question and with regard to the people who are said to have the interest.

But that is a minor matter. The essential question is not whether interest theories are *partially* relevant, but whether they are *wholly* relevant. This is the only point for intelligent dispute. Briefly: Granted that some senses of "good" may relevantly be defined in terms of interest, is there some *other* sense which is *not* relevantly so defined? We must give this question careful attention. For it is quite possible that when philosophers (and many others) have found the question "is X good?" so difficult, they have been grasping for this *other* sense of "good" and not any sense relevantly defined in terms of interest. If we insist on defining "good" in terms of interest, and answer the question when thus interpreted, we may be begging *their* question entirely. Of course this *other* sense of "good" may not exist, or it may be a complete confusion; but that is what we must discover.

Now many have maintained that interest theories are *far* from being completely relevant. They have argued that such theories neglect the very sense of "good" that is most typical of ethics. And certainly, their arguments are not without plausibility.

Only—what *is* this typical sense of "good"? The answers have been so vague and so beset with difficulties that one can scarcely determine.

There are certain requirements, however, with which the typical sense has been expected to comply—requirements which appeal strongly to our common sense. It will be helpful to summarize these, showing how they exclude the interest theories:

In the first place, we must be able sensibly to *disagree* about whether something is "good." This condition rules out Hobbes' definition. For con-

---

[2] In *General Theory of Value* (New York, 1926) Perry used "interest" to refer to any sort of favoring or disfavoring, or any sort of disposition to be for or against something. And he used "theory" where he might, alternatively, have used "proposed definition," or "proposed analysis of a common sense meaning."

In most of the (chronologically) later essays in the present volume the term "interest" systematically gives place to the term "attitude." The purpose of the change was solely to provide a more transparent terminology: it was not intended to repudiate Perry's *conception* of interest.

sider the following argument: "This is good." "That isn't so; it's not good." As translated by Hobbes, this becomes: "I desire this." "That isn't so, for *I* don't." The speakers are not contradicting one another, and think they are only because of an elementary confusion in the use of pronouns. The definition, "good" means *desired by my community,* is also excluded, for how could people from different communities disagree?[3]

In the second place, "goodness" must have, so to speak, a magnetism. A person who recognizes X to be "good" must ipso facto acquire a stronger tendency to act in its favor than he otherwise would have had. This rules out the Humian type of definition. For according to Hume, to recognize that something is "good" is simply to recognize that the majority approve of it. Clearly, a man may see that the majority approve of X without having, himself, a stronger tendency to favor it. This requirement excludes any attempt to define "good" in terms of the interest of people *other* than the speaker.[4]

In the third place, the "goodness" of anything must not be verifiable solely by use of the scientific method. "Ethics must not be psychology." This restriction rules out all of the traditional interest theories without exception. It is so sweeping a restriction that we must examine its plausibility. What are the methodological implications of interest theories which are here rejected?

According to Hobbes' definition a person can prove his ethical judgments with finality by showing that he is not making an introspective error about his desires. According to Hume's definition one may prove ethical judgments (roughly speaking) by taking a vote. *This* use of the empirical method, at any rate, seems highly remote from what we usually accept as proof and reflects on the complete relevance of the definitions that imply it.

But are there not more complicated interest theories that are immune from such methodological implications? No, for the same factors appear; they are only put off for a while. Consider, for example, the definition: "X is good" means *most people would approve of X if they knew its nature and consequences.* How, according to this definition, could we prove that a certain X was good? We should first have to find out, empirically, just what X was like and what its consequences would be. To this extent the empirical method as required by the definition seems beyond intelligent objection. But what remains? We should next have to discover whether most people would approve of the sort of thing we had discovered X to be. This could not be determined by popular vote—but only because it would be too difficult to explain to the voters, beforehand, what the nature and consequences of X really were.

[3] See G. E. Moore, *Philosophical Studies* (New York, 1922), pp. 332–34.
[4] See G. C. Field, *Moral Theory* (London, 1921) pp. 52, 56–57.

Apart from this, voting would be a pertinent method. We are again reduced to counting noses as a *perfectly final* appeal.

Now we need not scorn voting entirely. A man who rejected interest theories as irrelevant might readily make the following statement: "If I believed that X would be approved by the majority, when they knew all about it, I should be strongly *led* to say that X was good." But he would continue: "*Need* I say that X was good, under the circumstances? Wouldn't my acceptance of the alleged 'final proof' result simply from my being democratic? What about the more aristocratic people? They would simply say that the approval of most people, even when they knew all about the object of their approval, simply had nothing to do with the goodness of anything, and they would probably add a few remarks about the low state of people's interests." It would indeed seem, from these considerations, that the definition we have been considering has presupposed democratic ideals from the start; it has dressed up democratic propaganda in the guise of a definition.

The omnipotence of the empirical method, as implied by interest theories and others, may be shown unacceptable in a somewhat different way. G. E. Moore's familiar objection about the open question is chiefly pertinent in this regard. No matter what set of scientifically knowable properties a thing may have (says Moore, in effect), you will find, on careful introspection, that it is an open question to ask whether anything having these properties is *good*. It is difficult to believe that this recurrent question is a totally confused one, or that it seems open only because of the ambiguity of "good." Rather, we must be using some sense of "good" which is not definable, relevantly, in terms of anything scientifically knowable. That is, the scientific method is not sufficient for ethics.[5]

These, then, are the requirements with which the "typical" sense of "good" is expected to comply: (I) goodness must be a topic for intelligent disagreement; (2) it must be "magnetic"; and (3) it must not be discoverable solely through the scientific method.

2

I can now turn to my proposed analysis of ethical judgments. First let me present my position dogmatically, showing to what extent I vary from tradition.

I believe that the three requirements given above are perfectly sensible, that there is some *one* sense of "good" which satisfies all three requirements, and that no traditional interest theory satisfies them all. But this does not imply

---

[5]See G. E. Moore, *Principia Ethica* (Cambridge, 1903), ch. 1. I am simply trying to preserve the spirit of Moore's objection and not the exact form of it.

that "good" must be explained in terms of a Platonic Idea, or of a categorical imperative, or of a unique, unanalyzable property. On the contrary, the three requirements can be met by a *kind* of interest theory. *But we must give up a presupposition that all the traditional interest theories have made.*

Traditional interest theories hold that ethical statements are *descriptive* of the existing state of interests—that they simply *give information* about interests. (More accurately, ethical judgments are said to describe what the state of interests is, was, or will be, or to indicate what the state of interests *would* be under specified circumstances.) It is this emphasis on description, on information, which leads to their incomplete relevance. Doubtless there is always *some* element of description in ethical judgments, but this is by no means all. Their major use is not to indicate facts but to *create an influence.* Instead of merely describing people's interests they *change or intensify* them. They *recommend* an interest in an object, rather than state that the interest already exists.

For instance: When you tell a man that he ought not to steal, your object is not merely to let him know that people disapprove of stealing. You are attempting, rather, to get *him* to disapprove of it. Your ethical judgment has a quasi-imperative force which, operating through suggestion and intensified by your tone of voice, readily permits you to begin to *influence,* to *modify,* his interests. If in the end you do not succeed in getting *him* to disapprove of stealing, you will feel that you have failed to convince him that stealing is wrong. You will continue to feel this, even though he fully acknowledges that you disapprove of it and that almost everyone else does. When you point out to him the consequences of his actions—consequences which you suspect he already disapproves of—these *reasons* which support your ethical judgment are simply a means of facilitating your influence. If you think you can change his interests by making vivid to him how others will disapprove of him, you will do so, otherwise not. So the consideration about other people's interest is just an additional means you may employ in order to move him and is not a part of the ethical judgment itself. Your ethical judgment does not merely describe interests to him, it directs his very interests. The difference between the traditional interest theories and my view is like the difference between describing a desert and irrigating it.

Another example: A munitions maker declares that war is a good thing. If he merely meant that he approved of it, he would not have to insist so strongly nor grow so excited in his argument. People would be quite easily convinced that he approved of it. If he merely meant that most people approved of war, or that most people would approve of it if they knew the consequences, he would have to yield his point if it were proved that this was not so. But he would not do this, nor does consistency require it. He is not *describing* the state of people's approval; he is trying to *change* it by his influence. If he found that few people appoved of war, he might insist all the more strongly that it was good, for there would be more changing to be done.

This example illustrates how "good" may be used for what most of us would call bad purposes. Such cases are as pertinent as any others. I am not indicating the *good* way of using "good." i am not influencing people but am describing the way this influence sometimes goes on. If the reader wishes to say that the munitions maker's influence is bad—that is, if the reader wishes to awaken people's disapproval of the man, and to make him disapprove of his own actions—I should at another time be willing to join in this undertaking. But this is not the present concern. I am not using ethical terms but am indicating how they *are* used. The munitions maker, in his use of "good," illustrates the persuasive character of the word just as well as does the unselfish man who, eager to encourage in each of us a desire for the happiness of all, contends that the supreme good is peace.

Thus ethical terms are *instruments* used in the complicated interplay and readjustment of human interests. This can be seen plainly from more general observations. People from widely separated communities have different moral attitudes. Why? To a great extent because they have been subject to different social influences. Now clearly this influence does not operate through sticks and stones alone; words play a great part. People praise one another to encourage certain inclinations and blame one another to discourage others. Those of forceful personalities issue commands which weaker people, for complicated instinctive reasons, find it difficult to disobey, quite apart from fears of consequences. Further influence is brought to bear by writers and orators. Thus social influence is exerted, to an enormous extent, by means that have nothing to do with physical force or material reward. The ethical terms facilitate such influence. Being suited for use in *suggestion,* they are a means by which men's attitudes may be led this way or that. The reason, then, that we find a greater similarity in the moral attitudes of one community than in those of different communities is largely this: ethical judgments propagate themselves. One man says "this is good"; this may influence the approval of another person, who then makes the same ethical judgment, which in turn influences another person, and so on. In the end, by a process of mutual influence, people take up more or less the same attitudes. Between people of widely separated communities, of course, the influence is less strong; hence different communities have different attitudes.

These remarks will serve to give a general idea of my point of view. We must now go into more detail. There are several questions which must be answered: How does an ethical sentence acquire its power of influencing people—why is it suited to suggestion? Again, what has this influence to do with the *meaning* of ethical terms? And finally, do these considerations really lead us to a sense of "good" which meets the requirements mentioned in the preceding section?

Let us deal first with the question about *meaning*. This is far from an easy question, so we must enter into a preliminary inquiry about meaning in general. Although a seeming digression this will prove indispensable.

3

Broadly speaking, there are two different *purposes* which lead us to use language. On the one hand we use words (as in science) to record, clarify, and communicate *beliefs*. On the other hand we use words to give vent to our feelings (interjections), or to create moods (poetry), or to incite people to actions or attitudes (oratory).

The first use of words I shall call "descriptive," the second, "dynamic." Note that the distinction depends solely upon the *purpose* of the *speaker*.

When a person says "hydrogen is the lightest known gas," his purpose *may* be simply to lead the hearer to believe this, or to believe that the speaker believes it. In that case the words are used descriptively. When a person cuts himself and says "damn," his purpose is not ordinarily to record, clarify, or communicate any belief. The word is used dynamically. The two ways of using words, however, are by no means mutually exclusive. This is obvious from the fact that our purposes are often complex. Thus when one says "I want you to close the door," part of his purpose, ordinarily, is to lead the hearer to believe that he has this want. To that extent the words are used descriptively. But the major part of one's purpose is to lead the hearer to *satisfy* the want. To that extent the words are used dynamically.

It very frequently happens that the same sentence may have a dynamic use on one occasion and not on another, and that it may have different dynamic uses on different occasions. For instance: A man says to a visiting neighbor, "I am loaded down with work." His purpose may be to let the neighbor know how life is going with him. This would *not* be a dynamic use of words. He may make the remark, however, in order to drop a hint. This *would* be dynamic usage (as well as descriptive). Again, he may make the remark to arouse the neighbor's sympathy. This would be a *different* dynamic usage from that of hinting.

Or again, when we say to a man, "of course you won't make those mistakes any more," we *may* simply be making a prediction. But we are more likely to be using "suggestion," in order to encourage him and hence *keep* him from making mistakes. The first use would be descriptive, the second, mainly dynamic.

From these examples it will be clear that we can not determine whether words are used dynamically or not merely by reading the dictionary—even assuming that everyone is faithful to dictionary meanings. Indeed, to know whether a person is using a word dynamically we must note his tone of voice, his gestures, the general circumstances under which he is speaking, and so on.

We must now proceed to an important question: What has the dynamic use of words to do with their *meaning*? One thing is clear—we must not define "meaning" in a way that would make meaning vary with dynamic usage. If we did, we should have no use for the term. All that we could say about such "meaning" would be that it is very complicated and subject to constant change. So we must certainly distinguish between the dynamic use of words and their meaning.

It does not follow, however, that we must define "meaning" in some nonpsychological fashion. We must simply restrict the psychological field. Instead of identifying meaning with *all* the psychological causes and effects that attend a word's utterance, we must identify it with those that it has a *tendency* (causal property, dispositional property) to be connected with. The tendency must be of a particular kind, moreover. It must exist for all who speak the language; it must be persistent and must be realizable more or less independently of determinate circumstances attending the word's utterance. There will be further restrictions dealing with the interrelations of word in different contexts. Moreover, we must include, under the psychological responses which the words tend to produce, not only immediately introspectable experiences but *dispositions* to react in a given way with appropriate stimuli. I hope to go into these matters in a subsequent essay.[6] Suffice it now

---

[6]The "subsequent essay" became, instead, Chapter 3 of *Ethics and Language*, which among other points defends those that follow:

(1) When used in a generic sense that emphasizes what C. W. Morris calls the *pragmatic* aspects of language, the term "meaning" designates a tendency of words to express or evoke states of mind in the people who use the words. The tendency is of a special kind, however, and many qualifications are needed (including some that bear on syntax) to specify its nature.

(2) When the states of mind in question are cognitive, the meaning can conveniently be called *descriptive;* and when they are feelings, emotions, or attitudes, the meanings can conveniently be called *emotive*.

(3) The states of mind (in a rough and tentative sense of that term) are normally quite complicated. They are not necessarily images or feelings but may in their turn be further tendencies—tendencies to respond to various stimuli that may subsequently arise. A word may have a constant meaning, accordingly, even though it is accompanied, at various times that it is used, by different images or feelings.

(4) Emotive meaning is sometimes more than a by-product of descriptive meaning. When a term has both sorts of meaning, for example, a change in its descriptive meaning may not be attended by a change in emotive meaning.

(5) When a speaker's use of emotive terms evokes an attitude in a hearer (as it sometimes may not, since it has only a *tendency* to do so), it must not be conceived as merely adding to the hearer's attitude in the way that a spark might add its heat to the atmosphere. For a more appropriate analogy, in many cases, we must think rather of a spark that ignites tinder.

to say that I think "meaning" may be thus defined in a way to include "propositional" meaning as an important kind.

The definition will readily permit a distinction between meaning and dynamic use. For when words are accompanied by dynamic purposes, it does not follow that they *tend* to be accompanied by them in the way mentioned above. E.g. there need be no tendency realizable more or less independently of the determinate circumstances under which the words are uttered.

There will be a kind of meaning, however, in the sense above defined, which has an intimate relation to dynamic usage. I refer to "emotive" meaning (in a sense roughly like that employed by Ogden and Richards).[7] The emotive meaning of a word is a tendency of a word, arising through the history of its usage, to produce (result from) *affective* responses in people. It is the immediate aura of feeling which hovers about a word.[8] Such tendencies to produce affective responses cling to words very tenaciously. It would be difficult, for instance, to express merriment by using the interjection "alas." Because of the persistence of such affective tendencies (among other reasons) it becomes feasible to classify them as "meanings."

Just *what* is the relation between emotive meaning and the dynamic use of words? Let us take an example. Suppose that a man tells his hostess, at the end of a party, that he thoroughly enjoyed himself, and suppose that he was in fact bored. If we consider his remark an innocent one, are we likely to remind him, later, that he "lied" to his hostess? Obviously not, or at least, not without a broad smile; for although he told her something that he believed to be false, and with the intent of making her believe that it was true—those being the ordinary earmarks of a lie—the expression, "you lied to her," would be emotively too strong for our purposes. It would seem to be a reproach, even if we intended it not to be a reproach. So it will be evident that such words as "lied" (and many parallel examples could be cited) become suited, on account of their emotive meaning, to a certain kind of dynamic use—so well suited, in fact, that the hearer is likely to be misled when we use them

---

[7] See C. K. Ogden and I. A. Richards, *The Meaning of Meaning* (2nd ed. London, 1927). On p. 125 there is a passage on ethics which is the source of the ideas embodied in this essay.
[8] In *Ethics and Language* the phrase "aura of feeling" was expressly repudiated. If the present essay had been more successful in anticipating the analysis given in that later work, it would have introduced the notion of emotive meaning in some such way as this:

The emotive meaning of a word or phrase is a strong and persistent tendency, built up in the course of linguistic history, to give direct expression (quasi-interjectionally) to certain of the speaker's feelings or emotions or attitudes; and it is also a tendency to evoke (quasi-imperatively) corresponding feelings, emotions, or attitudes in those to whom the speaker's remarks are addressed. It is the emotive meaning of a word, accordingly, that leads us to characterize it as *laudatory* or *derogatory*—that rather generic characterization being of particular importance when we are dealing with terms like "good" and "bad" or "right" and "wrong." But emotive meanings are of great variety: they may yield terms that express or evoke horror, amazement, sadness, sympathy, and so on.

in any other way. The more pronounced a word's emotive meaning is, the less likely people are to use it purely descriptively. Some words are suited to encourage people, some to discourage them, some to quiet them, and so on.

Even in these cases, of course, the dynamic purposes are not to be identified with any sort of meaning; for the emotive meaning accompanies a word much more persistently than do the dynamic purposes. But there is an important contingent relation between emotive meaning and dynamic purpose: the former assists the latter. Hence if we define emotively laden terms in a way that neglects their emotive meaning, we become seriously confused. *We lead people to think that the terms defined are used dynamically less often than they are.*

4

Let us now apply these remarks in defining "good." This word may be used morally or nonmorally. I shall deal with the nonmoral usage almost entirely, but only because it is simpler. The main points of the analysis will apply equally well to either usage.

As a preliminary definition let us take an inaccurate approximation. It may be more misleading than helpful but will do to begin with. Roughly, then, the sentence "X is good" means *we like X*. ("We" includes the hearer or hearers.)

At first glance this definition sounds absurd. If used, we should expect to find the following sort of conversation: A. "This is good." B. "But I *don't* like it. What led you to believe that I did?" The unnaturalness of B's reply, judged by ordinary word usage, would seem to cast doubt on the relevance of my definition.

B's unnaturalness, however, lies simply in this: he is assuming that "we like it" (as would occur implicitly in the use of "good") is being used descriptively. This will not do. When "we like it" is to take the place of "this is good," the former sentence must be used not purely descriptively, but dynamically. More specifically, it must be used to promote a very subtle (and for the nonmoral sense in question, a very easily resisted) kind of *suggestion*. To the extent that "we" refers to the hearer it must have the dynamic use, essential to suggestion, of leading the hearer to *make* true what is said, rather than merely to believe it. And to the extent that "we" refers to the speaker, the sentence must have not only the descriptive use of indicating belief about the speaker's interest, but the quasi-interjectory, dynamic function of giving direct expression to the interest. (This immediate expression of feelings assists in the process of suggestion. It is difficult to disapprove in the face of another's enthusiasm.)

For an example of a case where "we like this" is used in the dynamic way that "this is good" is used, consider the case of a mother who says to her several children, "one thing is certain, *we all like to be neat.*" If she really believed this, she would not bother to say so. But she is not using the words descriptively. She is *encouraging* the children to like neatness. By telling them that they like neatness, she will lead them to *make* her statement true, so to speak. If, instead of saying "we all like to be neat" in this way, she had said "it's a good thing to be neat," the effect would have been approximately the same.

But these remarks are still misleading. Even when "we like it" is used for suggestion, it is not quite like "this is good." The latter is more subtle. With such a sentence as "this is a good book," for example, it would be practically impossible to use instead "we like this book." When the latter is used it must be accompanied by so exaggerated an intonation, to prevent its becoming confused with a descriptive statement, that the force of suggestion becomes stronger and ludicrously more overt than when "good" is used.

The definition is inadequate, further, in that the definiens has been restricted to dynamic usage. Having said that dynamic usage was different from meaning, I should not have to mention it in giving the *meaning* of "good."

It is in connection with this last point that we must return to emotive meaning. The word "good" has a laudatory emotive meaning that fits it for the dynamic use of suggesting favorable interest. But the sentence "we like it" has no such emotive meaning. Hence my definition has neglected emotive meaning entirely. Now to neglect emotive meaning serves to foster serious confusions, as I have previously intimated; so I have sought to make up for the inadequacy of the definition by letting the restriction about dynamic usage take the place of emotive meaning. What I should do, of course, is to find a definiens whose emotive meaning, like that of "good," simply does *lead* to dynamic usage.

Why did I not do this? I answer that it is not possible if the definition is to afford us increased clarity. No two words, in the first place, have quite the same emotive meaning. The most we can hope for is a rough approximation. But if we seek for such an approximation for "good," we shall find nothing more than synonyms, such as "desirable" or "valuable"; and these are profitless because they do not clear up the connection between "good" and favorable interest. If we reject such synonyms, in favor of nonethical terms, we shall be highly misleading. For instance "this is good" has something like the meaning of "I *do* like this; do so as well." But this is certainly not accurate. For the imperative makes an appeal to the conscious efforts of the hearer. Of course he cannot like something just by trying. He must be led to like it through suggestion. Hence an ethical sentence differs from an imperative in that it enables one to make changes in a much more subtle, less fully conscious way. Note that the ethical sentence centers the hearer's attention not on his interests but on the object of interest, and thereby facilitates suggestion. Because of its sublety, moreover, an ethical sentence readily permits counter-suggestion and leads to the give and take situation that is so characteristic of arguments about values.

Strictly speaking, then, it is impossible to define "good" in terms of favorable interest if emotive meaning is not to be distorted. Yet it is possible to say that "this is good" is *about* the favorable interest of the speaker and the hearer or hearers, and that it has a laudatory emotive meaning which fits the words for use in suggestion. This is a rough description of meaning, not a definition. But it serves the same clarifying function that a definition ordinarily does, and that, after all, is enough.

A word must be added about the moral use of "good." This differs from the above in that it is about a different kind of interest. Instead of being about what the hearer and speaker *like,* it is about a stronger sort of approval. When a person *likes* something, he is pleased when it prospers and disappointed when it does not. When a person *morally approves* of something he experiences a rich feeling of security when it prospers and is indignant or "shocked" when it does not. These are rough and inaccurate examples of the many factors which one would have to mention in distinguishing the two kinds of interest. In the moral usage, as well as in the nonmoral, "good" has an emotive meaning which adapts it to suggestion.

And now, are these considerations of any importance? Why do I stress emotive meanings in this fashion? Does the omission of them really lead people into errors? I think, indeed, that the errors resulting from such omissions are enormous. In order to see this, however, we must return to the restrictions, mentioned in Section 1, with which the typical sense of "good" has been expected to comply.

5

The first restriction, it will be remembered, had to do with disagreement. Now there is clearly some sense in which people disagree on ethical points, but we must not rashly assume that all disagreement is modeled after the sort that occurs in the natural sciences. We must distinguish between "disagreement in belief" (typical of the sciences) and "disagreement in interest." Disagreement in belief occurs when A believes *p* and B disbelieves it. Disagreement in interest occurs when A has a favorable interest in X and when B has an unfavorable one in it. (For a full-bodied disagreement, neither party is content with the discrepancy.)

Let me give an example of disagreement in interest. A. "Let's go to a cinema tonight." B. "I don't want to do that. Let's go to the symphony." A continues to insist on the cinema, B on the symphony. This is disagreement in a perfectly conventional sense. They cannot agree on where they want to go, and each is trying to redirect the other's interest. (Note that imperatives are used in the example.)

It is disagreement in *interest* which takes place in ethics. When C says "this is good," and D says "no, it's bad," we have a case of suggestion and counter-suggestion. Each man is trying to redirect the other's interest. There obviously need be no domineering, since each may be willing to give ear to the other's influence; but each is trying to move the other none the less. It is in this sense that they disagree. Those who argue that certain interest theories make no provision for disagreement have been misled, I believe, simply because the traditional theories, in leaving out emotive meaning, give the impression that ethical judgments are used descriptively only; and of course when judgments are used purely descriptively, the only disagreement that can arise is disagreement *in belief*. Such disagreement may be disagreement in belief *about* interests, but this is not the same as disagreement *in* interest. My definition does not provide for disagreement in belief about interests any more than does Hobbes'; but that is no matter, for there is no reason to believe, at least on common sense grounds, that this kind of disagreement exists. There is only disagreement *in* interest. (We shall see in a moment that disagreement in interest does not remove ethics from sober argument—that this kind of disagreement may often be resolved through empirical means.)

The second restriction, about "magnetism," or the connection between goodness and actions, requires only a word. This rules out only those interest theories that do *not* include the interest of the speaker in defining "good." My account does include the speaker's interest, hence is immune.

The third restriction, about the empirical method, may be met in a way that springs naturally from the above account of disagreement. Let us put the question in this way: When two people disagree over an ethical matter, can they completely resolve the disagreement through empirical considerations, assuming that each applies the empirical method exhaustively, consistently, and without error?

I answer that sometimes they can and sometimes they cannot, and that at any rate, even when they can, the relation between empirical knowledge and ethical judgments is quite different from the one that traditional interest theories seem to imply.

This can best be seen from an analogy. Let us return to the example where A and B could not agree on a cinema or a symphony. The example differed from an ethical argument in that imperatives were used, rather than ethical judgments, but was analogous to the extent that each person was endeavoring to modify the other's interest. Now how would these people argue the case, assuming that they were too intelligent just to shout at one another?

Clearly, they would give "reasons" to support their imperatives. A might say, "but you know, Garbo is at the Bijou." His hope is that B, who admires Garbo, will acquire a desire to go to the cinema when he knows what film will be there. B may counter, "but Toscanini is guest conductor tonight, in an all-Beethoven program." And so on. Each supports his imperative (*"let's do so and so"*) by reasons which may be empirically established.

To generalize from this: disagreement in interest may be rooted in disagreement in belief. That is to say, people who disagree in interest would often cease to do so if they knew the precise nature and consequences of the object of their interest. To this extent disagreement in interest may be resolved by securing agreement in belief, which in turn may be secured empirically.

This generalization holds for ethics. If A and B, instead of using imperatives, had said, respectively, "it would be *better* to go to the cinema," and "it would be better to go to the symphony," the reasons which they would advance would be roughly the same. They would each give a more thorough account of the object of interest, with the purpose of completing the redirection of interest which was begun by the suggestive force of the ethical sentence. On the whole, of course, the suggestive force of the ethical statement merely exerts enough pressure to start such trains of reasons, since the reasons are much more essential in resolving disagreement in interest than the persuasive effect of the ethical judgment itself.

Thus the empirical method is relevant to ethics simply because our knowledge of the world is a determining factor to our interests. But note that empirical facts are not inductive grounds from which the ethical judgment problematically follows. (This is what traditional interest theories imply.) If someone said "close the door," and added the reason "we'll catch cold," the latter would scarcely be called an inductive ground of the former. Now imperatives are related to the reasons which support them in the same way that ethical judgments are related to reasons.

Is the empirical method *sufficient* for attaining ethical agreement? Clearly not. For empirical knowledge resolves disagreement in interest only to the extent that such disagreement is rooted in disagreement in belief. Not all disagreement in interest is of this sort. For instance: A is of a sympathetic nature and B is not. They are arguing about whether a public dole would be good. Suppose that they discovered all the consequences of the dole. Is it not possible, even so, that A will say that it is good and B that it is bad? The disagreement in interest may arise not from limited factual knowledge but simply from A's sympathy and B's coldness. Or again, suppose in the above argument that A was poor and unemployed and that B was rich. Here again the disagreement might not be due to different factual knowledge. It would be due to the different social positions of the men, together with their predominant self-interest.

When ethical disagreement is not rooted in disagreement in belief, is there *any* method by which it may be settled? If one means by "method" a *rational* method, then there is no method. But in any case there is a "way." Let us consider the above example again, where disagreement was due to A's sympathy and B's coldness. Must they end by saying, "well, it's just a matter of our having different temperaments"? Not necessarily. A, for instance, may try to *change* the temperament of his opponent. He may pour out his enthusiasms in such a moving way—present the sufferings of the poor with such appeal—that he will lead his opponent to see life through different eyes. He may build up by the contagion of his feelings an influence which will modify B's temperament and create in him a sympathy for the poor which did not previously exist. This is often the only way to obtain ethical agreement, if there is any way at all. It is persuasive, not empirical or rational; but that is no reason for neglecting it. There is no reason to scorn it, either, for it is only by such means that our personalities are able to grow, through our contact with others.

The point I wish to stress, however, is simply that the empirical method is instrumental to ethical agreement only to the extent that disagreement in interest is rooted in disagreement in belief. There is little reason to believe that all disagreement is of this sort. Hence the empirical method is not sufficient for ethics. In any case, ethics is not psychology, since psychology does not endeavour to *direct* our interests; it discovers facts about the ways in which interests are or can be directed, but that is quite another matter.

To summarize this section: my analysis of ethical judgments meets the three requirements for the typical sense of "good" that were mentioned in Section 1. The traditional interest theories fail to meet these requirements simply because they neglect emotive meaning. This neglect leads them to neglect dynamic usage, and the sort of disagreement that results from such usage, together with the method of resolving the disagreement. I may add that my analysis answers Moore's objection about the open question. Whatever scientifically knowable properties a thing may have, it *is* always open to question whether a thing having these (enumerated) qualities is good. For to ask whether it is good is to ask for *influence*. And whatever I may know about an object, I can still ask, quite pertinently, to be influenced with regard to my interest in it.

6

And now, have I really pointed out the "typical" sense of "good"? I suppose that many will say "no," claiming that I have simply failed to set down *enough* requirements that this sense must meet, and that my analysis, like all others given in terms of interest, is a way of begging the issue. They will say: "When we ask 'is X good?' we don't want mere influence, mere advice. We decidedly don't want to be influenced through persuasion, nor are we fully content when the influence is supported by a wide scientific knowledge of X. The answer to our question will, of course, modify our interests. But this is only because a unique sort of truth will be revealed to us—a truth that must be apprehended a priori. We want our interests to be guided by this truth and by nothing else. To substitute for this special truth mere emotive meaning and mere factual truth is to conceal from us the very object of our search."

I can only answer that I do not understand. What is this truth to be *about?* For I recollect no Platonic Idea, nor do I know what to *try* to recollect. I find no indefinable property nor do I know what to look for. And the "self-evident" deliverances of reason, which so many philosophers have mentioned, seem on examination to be deliverances of their respective reasons only (if of anyone's) and not of mine.

I strongly suspect, indeed, that any sense of "good" which is expected both to unite itself in synthetic a priori fashion with other concepts and to influence interests as well, is really a great confusion. I extract from this meaning the power of influence alone, which I find the only intelligible part. If the rest is confusion, however, then it certainly deserves more than the shrug of one's shoulders. What I should like to do is to *account* for the confusion—to examine the psychological needs which have given rise to it and show how these needs may be satisfied in another way. This is *the* problem, if confusion is to be stopped at its source. But it is an enormous problem and my reflections on it, which are at present worked out only roughly, must be reserved until some later time.

I may add that if "X is good" has the meaning that I ascribe to it, then it is not a judgment that professional philosophers and only professional philosophers are qualified to make. To the extent that ethics predicates the ethical terms of anything, rather than explains their meaning, it becomes more than a purely intellectual study. Ethical judgments are social instruments. They are used in a cooperative enterprise that leads to a mutual readjustment of human interests. Philosophers have a part in this; but so too do all men.

46 THE CONTINUUM OF ENDS-MEANS

JOHN DEWEY (1859-1952)

Those who have read and enjoyed Charles Lamb's essay on the origin of roast pork have probably not been conscious that their enjoyment of its absurdity was due to perception of the absurdity of any "end" which is set up apart from the means by which it is to be attained and apart from its own further function as means. Nor is it probable that Lamb himself wrote the story as a deliberate travesty of the theories that make such a separation. Nonetheless, that is the whole point of the tale. The story, it will be remembered, is that roast pork was first enjoyed when a house in which pigs were confined was accidentally burned down. While searching in the ruins, the owners touched the pigs that had been roasted in the fire and scorched their fingers. Impulsively bringing their fingers to their mouths to cool them, they experienced a new taste. Enjoying the taste, they henceforth set themselves to building houses, inclosing pigs in them, and then burning the houses down. Now, if ends-in-view are what they are entirely apart from means, and have their value independently of valuation of means, there is nothing absurd, nothing ridiculous, in this procedure, for the end attained, the *de facto* termination, *was* eating and enjoying roast pork, and that was just the end desired. Only when the end attained is estimated in terms of the means employed—the building and burning-down of houses in comparison with other available means by which the desired result in view might be attained—is there anything absurd or unreasonable about the method employed.

The story has a direct bearing upon another point, the meaning of "intrinsic." *Enjoyment* of the taste of roast pork may be said to be immediate, although even so the enjoyment would be a somewhat troubled one, for those who have memory, by the thought of the needless cost at which it was obtained. But to pass from immediacy of enjoyment to something called "intrinsic value" is a leap for which there is no ground. The *value* of enjoyment of an object *as* an attained end is a value of something which in being

SOURCE: Reprinted from chapter 6 of *Theory of Valuation* by John Dewey, Volume II, no. 4 of the *International Encyclopedia of Unified Science,* by permission of The University of Chicago Press. Copyright 1939 by the University of Chicago. Compare with selections 39, 41, and 47.

an end, an outcome, stands in relation to the means of which it is the consequence. Hence if the object in question is prized *as* an end or "final" value, it is valued *in this relation* or as mediated. The first time roast pork was enjoyed, it was *not* an end-value, since by description it was not the result of desire, foresight, and intent. Upon subsequent occasions it was, by description, the outcome of prior foresight, desire, and effort, and hence occupied the position of an end-in-view. There are occasions in which previous effort enhances enjoyment of what is attained. But there are also many occasions in which persons find that, when they have attained something as an end, they have paid too high a price in effort and in sacrifice of other ends. In such situations *enjoyment* of the end attained is itself *valued,* for it is not taken in its immediacy but in terms of its cost—a fact fatal to its being regarded as "an end-in-itself," a self-contradictory term in any case.

The story throws a flood of light upon what is usually meant by the maxim "the end justifies the means" and also upon the popular objection to it. Applied in this case, it would mean that the value of the attained end, the eating of roast pork, was such as to warrant the price paid in the means by which it was attained—destruction of dwelling-houses and sacrifice of the value to which they contribute. The conception involved in the maxim that "the end justifies the means" is basically the same as that in the notion of ends-in-themselves; indeed, from a historical point of view, it is the fruit of the latter, for only the conception that certain things are ends-in-themselves can warrant the belief that the relation of ends-means is unilateral, proceeding exclusively from end to means. When the maxim is compared with empirically ascertained facts, it is equivalent to holding one of two views, both of which are incompatible with the facts. One of the views is that only the specially selected "end" held in view will actually be brought into existence by the means used, something miraculously intervening to prevent the means employed from having their other usual effects; the other (and more probable) view is that, as compared with the importance of the selected and uniquely prized end, other consequences may be completely ignored and brushed aside no matter how intrinsically obnoxious they are. This arbitrary selection of some one part of the attained consequences as *the* end and hence as the warrant of means used (no matter how objectionable are their *other* consequences) is the fruit of holding that *it,* as *the* end, is an end-in-itself, and hence possessed of "value" irrespective of all its existential relations. And this notion is inherent in *every* view that assumes that "ends" can be valued apart from appraisal of the things used as means in attaining them. The sole alternative to the view that *the* end is an arbitrarily selected part of actual consequences which *as* "the end" then justifies the use of means irrespective of the other consequences they produce, is that desires, ends-in-view, and consequences achieved be valued in turn as means of further consequences. The maxim referred to, under the guise of saying that ends, in the sense of actual consequences, provide the warrant for means employed—a correct position—actually says that some fragment of these actual consequences— a fragment arbitrarily selected because the heart has been set upon it— authorizes the use of means to obtain *it,* without the need of foreseeing and weighing other ends as consequences of the means used. It thus discloses in a striking manner the fallacy involved in the position that ends have value independent of appraisal of means involved and independent of their own further causal efficacy.

. . . In all the physical sciences (using 'physical' here as a synonym for *nonhuman*) it is now taken for granted that all "effects" are also "causes," or, stated more accurately, that nothing happens which is *final* in the sense that it is not part of an ongoing stream of events. If this principle, with the accompanying discrediting of belief in objects that are ends but not means, is employed in dealing with distinctive human phenomena, it necessarily follows that the distinction between ends and means is temporal and relational. Every condition that has to be brought into existence in order to serve as means is, *in that connection,* an object of desire and an end-in-view, while the end actually reached is a means to future ends as well as a test of valuations previously made. Since the end attained is a condition of further existential occurrences, it must be appraised as a potential obstacle and potential resource. If the notion of some objects as ends-in-themselves were abandoned, not merely in words but in all practical implications, human beings would for the first time in history be in a position to frame ends-in-view and form desires on the basis of empirically grounded propositions of the temporal relations of events to one another.

At any given time an adult person in a social group has certain ends which are so standardized by custom that they are taken for granted without examination, so that the only problems arising concern the best means for attaining them. In one group money-making would be such an end; in another group, possession of political power; in another group, advancement of scientific knowledge; in still another group, military prowess, etc. But such ends in any case are (i) more or less blank frameworks where the nominal "end" sets limits within which definite ends will fall, the latter being determined by appraisal of things as means; while (ii) as far as they simply express habits that have become established without critical examination of the relation of means and ends, they do not provide a model for a theory of valuation to follow. If a person moved by an experience of intense cold, which is highly objectionable, should momentarily judge it worth while to get warm by burning his house down, all that saves him from an act determined by a "compulsion neurosis" is the intellectual realization of what other consequences would ensue with the loss of his house. It is not necessarily a sign of insanity (as in the case cited) to isolate some event projected as an end out of the context of a world of moving changes in which it will in fact take place. But it is at least a sign of immaturity when an individual fails to view his end as also a moving condition of further consequences, thereby treating it as *final* in the sense in which "final" signifies that the course of events has come to a complete stop. Human beings do indulge in such arrests. But to treat them as models for forming a theory of ends is to substitute a manipulation of ideas, abstracted from the contexts in which they arise and function, for the conclusions of observation of concrete facts. It is a sign either of insanity, immaturity, indurated routine, or of a fanaticism that is a mixture of all three. . . .

The objection always brought against the view set forth is that, according to it, valuation activities and judgments are involved in a hopeless *regressus ad infinitum*. If, so it is said, there is no end which is not in turn a means, foresight has no place at which it can stop, and no end-in-view can be formed except by the most arbitrary of acts—an act so arbitrary that it mocks the claim of being a genuine valuation-proposition.

This objection brings us back to the conditions under which desires take shape and foreseen consequences are projected as ends to be reached. These conditions are those of need, deficit, and conflict. Apart from a condition of tension between a person and environing conditions there is, as we have seen, no occasion for evocation of desire for something else; there is nothing to induce the formation of an end, much less the formation of one end rather than any other out of the indefinite number of ends theoretically possible. Control of transformation of active tendencies into a desire in which a particular end-in-view is incorporated, is exercised by the needs or privations of an actual situation as its requirements are disclosed to observation. The "value" of different ends that suggest themselves is estimated or measured by the capacity they exhibit to guide action in making good, *satisfying*, in its literal sense, existing lacks. Here is the factor which cuts short the process of foreseeing and weighing ends-in-view in their function as means. Sufficient unto the day is the evil thereof and sufficient also is the *good* of that which does away with the existing evil. Sufficient because it is the means of instituting a complete situation or an integrated set of conditions.

. . . A physician has to determine the value of various courses of action and their results in the case of a particular patient. He forms ends-in-view having the value that justifies their adoption, on the ground of what his examination discloses is the "matter" or "trouble" with the patient. He estimates the worth of what he undertakes on the ground of its capacity to produce a condition in which these troubles will not exist, in which, as it is ordinarily put, the patient will be "restored to health." He does not have an idea of health as an absolute end-in-itself, an absolute good by which to determine what to do. On the contrary, he forms his general idea of health as an end and a good (value) for the patient on the ground of what his techniques of examination have shown to be the troubles from which patients suffer and the means by which they are overcome. There is no need to deny that a general and abstract conception of health finally develops. But it is the outcome of a great number of definite, empirical inquiries, not an a priori preconditioning "standard" for carrying on inquiries. . . .

47 THE CONTEXT OF MORAL JUDGMENT
ARTHUR E. MURPHY (1901–1962)

I. The Meaning of "Practical Reason."

" 'Tis not contrary to reason to prefer the destruction of the whole world to the scratching of my finger." In these words and others of similar import, David Hume summed up one of the most important and one of the most disturbing of the doctrines we owe to the development of modern critical philosophy. All of its puzzle, and much of its influence, are due to the fact that it states a substantial truth in a provacative and misleading way, and thus lends to what would otherwise seem to be an indefensible conclusion the support of apparently irrefutable evidence. Is it true or false? The answer depends on what it is understood to say, and that, in turn, on the meaning assigned to the term "reason." If you limit the operations of the mind properly described as "rational" to the tracing out of the implicative relations of ideas, and causal inferences concerning matters of fact, then it will follow that reason, thus employed, can discover nothing in the things it deals with to correspond to what we call their values. It is only when you turn from the object to the subject and survey, not the properties of things themselves, but the "relish" with which they are experienced and enjoyed, that a basis is

SOURCE: The greater part of chapter 1, Part II, of *The Uses of Reason*. Copyright 1943 by The Macmillan Company and used with their permission. Compare with selections 41 and 46. (Additional passages [second edition] used by kind permission of Dr. Frederick H. Ginascol, executor of the Murphy estate.)

found for preferring one to another—even if the one be the scratching of a finger and the other destruction of the world. But this "relish" is an affair of feelings and desires, or, in proper eighteenth century terms, of "the passions" and it is these, therefore, that determine what is good or bad, so far, at least, as "good" and "bad" have an empirically discoverable application. "Reason," identified as above, can tell us whether our estimates of value are logically consistent, and inform us concerning the causal means best suited to further the ends we have in view. The means are properly judged as good, however, only if the end is good, and on this point "reason" has no jurisdiction, for "ultimate ends recommend themselves solely to the affections," or, as a more modern version of the same doctrine would say, to the primary "drives" which determine what the organism desires and on what conditions it can be satisfied. And since the means derive their goodness only from the end they serve, we can see why Hume should conclude that, in the field of morals, "reason is and ought to be the slave of the passions."

What this doctrine says that is true, and will stand the test of critical inspection, is that things are discoverably good or bad, not in their intrinsic characters, but in their capacity to satisfy interests and desires. In Hume's famous instance you may search the geometric properties of a circle as you will, but you will never discover its beauty until you consider it as an object of enjoyment, in its capacity to please aesthetically those who contemplate it. It may be the case, as Miss Millay alleges in a well-known sonnet, that "Euclid alone has looked on Beauty bare," but we shall have to modify the Platonism of this dictum to add that it was not in his capacity as a mathematician that he made this observation. Those less enamoured of the charm of circles than Euclid and Miss Millay can understand the same propositions of geometry and use the same "reason" in exploring their implications. To ask whether, in addition to the beauty that is thus variously enjoyed by appreciative beholders, there is a "real" beauty which inheres in circles quite independently of their capacity to delight aesthetically those who enjoy them—or would enjoy them if their tastes were "developed" in that direction—is to ask a question that we have no means of answering and had better, therefore, leave to those whose interest is literary or edifying rather than philosophical. The value, at least, that *we* find in things and persons is a good that answers to an interest in ourselves, and every command of practical reason, no matter how exalted its pretensions, is cogently addressed only "to whom it may concern." To say, therefore, that reason in morals is "the slave of the passions" *may* mean simply that it is concerned with objects which satisfy desire, and that it is only as affording such satisfaction or capable of doing so that their goodness can responsibly be made out. And, as it is the business of reason, in its practical application, to serve the good, it is *in this sense* its business to serve "the passions" and contribute to their satisfaction. *Apart from* such concern there is no "reason," in the nature of things, to prefer the scratching of a finger to the destruction of the world—or anything to anything else—for the ground of preference, in the possibility of attainable satisfaction, cannot, on this basis, be made out.

But if there is thus a sense in which Hume's statement is true, there is another and no less important one, in which it not merely seems to be, but actually is, false. The burden of the message of the great classical moralists, Greek and Christian alike, was that reason ought not to be, and in a well-ordered life is not, the slave of the passions, but rather controls and directs them to a good, which, apart from its normative influence, they would not have been able to achieve. Did Hume really mean to deny this, as his disciples have denied it since his time? The answer, as in most cases where we are dealing with confused thinking, must be yes and no. As a humane and judicious man he knew how to value what he called the "disinterested" passions, and much of what had traditionally been said of the authority of "reason" in conduct could be restated in his terms, with sympathy taking the place of "reason" and calculation, on a utilitarian basis, operating to liberalize conduct and add foresight to benevolence in a way which, if his terminology did not discourage it, we should naturally describe as rational. Yet the shift in terminology made a real difference, none the less, and one whose effects are still observable. Men do want *ultimate* reasons, and *final* sanctions for conduct, and if they come to believe that there are none, and that the final basis for all our standards of excellence is to be found in "arbitrary" preference and "irrational" instincts, or drives, or will to power, they will be inclined to see in that belief the excuse for arbitrary preferences and irrational claims of a much less innocent sort. There *is* a context in which an arbitrary or irrational action is a wrong action and in which reason is not just an *ad hoc* instrument for finding means to satisfy desires in themselves beyond the range of rational criticism. To suppose that in its use *in this context* the authority of reason was in any way compromised by the Humean discovery that what we are here being reasonable *about* is our desires, and the conditions for their satisfaction, is a mistake, and a disastrous one. Yet it is a mistake that is easily made, once "reason" in general is identified with "reason" in its purely theoretical use, and, in consequence, what is not in *this* sense an affair of reason is handed over to the jurisdiction of "passions" with whose ultimate demands and preferences *mere* reason has nothing to do. Hume, who was in some respects the Bertrand Russell of his time, was at no pains to divorce his theory from this unhappy implication, and later empirical thinkers, encouraged by the prestige of the sciences to limit the properly "objective" and respectable use of reason to the methods of inquiry employed in the physical and social sciences, have for the most part followed in his footsteps. In this way, and with this dubious philosophical benediction, we reach the dichotomy of a reason which has nothing to do with "values," and "values" which, in their *ultimate* basis in non-rational drives, have nothing to do with reason. What it can then mean to be reasonable about values is a further problem to which busy scientists could hardly be expected to give a well-thought-out answer or their popularizers and publicists to take quite seriously. Science, after all, is remaking the world, and will doubtless get around to values in time, if they turn out to be really important.

Philosophers, on the whole, were more far-sighted than this. They saw the necessity, if we are to make sense of morals, of making clear the sense of "reason" in which it properly claims practical authority. The "reason" thus employed will be something other than the purely theoretical faculty which Hume recognized, and its claims will be without cogency save for those who acknowledge the good to which it is directed and the obligations entailed in the pursuit of it. But it will be *reason,* none the less, as distinct from groundless preference or arbitrary demand, and it will be in the name of principles rationally defensible that it speaks. Granting that theoretical reason, dealing with events in space and time in so far as these are causally understandable and predictable, provides no ultimate answer to the question "what ought I to do?" the philosopher therefore looks for further light to *practical* reason, and reaffirms, with its sanction, the truths which he finds that morality requires and science cannot supply. . . .

Evidently what is needed is some reliable way of distinguishing, among claims pertinent to responsible moral judgment, those that are reasonably credible from those that are not. What is wanted, in other words, is a discipline of practical reason that will function in this field as the methods of science do in theirs. . . . The problem . . . remains, for practical purposes, the crucial philosophical problem with which modern thought is confronted. How are we to be reasonable about values in an age when "reason" is the property of specialists for whom the refusal to deal with questions of good and bad is a matter of professional policy, while "values" are officially in the keeping of those more concerned for the most part to justify vested "spiritual" interests than to submit them to any sort of independent examination? Each side finds in the limitations of the other the excuse for its own imperfections. If "reason" can tell us so little about the issues of life as the positivists say, who would not see the wisdom of being unreasonable? And if the custodians of spiritual values are as loose in their thinking and as arbitrary in their premises as they can often be shown to be, who could question the prudence of those who restrict the use of reason to fields in which the difference between sense and nonsense can at least be sensibly made out? So runs the argument, and there seems to be no end to it.

And yet all the while men of good will are trying to be both just and intelligent about their desires and their duties, and to make some sort of sense of their conduct in terms of the goods toward which it might reasonably be directed. Perhaps we should be able to make greater progress in this field if we left the partisans of a scientifically pure reason and the partisans of transcendent values to their interminable task of pointing out each other's mistakes and looked instead for the meaning of practical reason in the use that can be made of reliable information, sound judgment, and enlightened good will in the reasonable direction of conduct. If it should prove to be the case that men can be rational about their conduct in this more specific sense, and that the good thus defined makes sense of activities that without it would be narrow, frustrated and incomplete, we shall not be much disturbed by the refusal of the purists to *call* such rationality a use of "reason" or of the defenders of the "deeper" values to submit their claims to its tests. We, at least, shall know what we are talking about. . . .

When I speak hereafter of "practical reason," I shall mean by it the use of reason in the organization of desires and the adjustment of claims in the pursuit of goods judged to be desirable by methods held to be just and proper to that end. Since we are here concerned to discover not merely what does exist but what would be good if it did exist, and is therefore worth accepting as a goal for action, and what is right, fair or just in the sacrifices those associated in a common action are asked to make for it and the rewards they are to receive on its attainment, it is not surprising that considerations will here be pertinent of which neither a physicist, an astronomer, nor an observer of the behavior of rats (a psychologist) would find it necessary to take account in his own somewhat different investigation. If it is stipulated that nothing is within the sphere of reason which their methods do not recognize as relevant or their instruments record, we shall, in this process, have transcended "reason." But we shall not, for all that, have taken leave of our powers of rational discrimination and sound judgment in so doing. On the contrary, we shall find uses for them, which even the most careful observation of rodent behavior could hardly have elicited. Nor shall we be unduly shocked or upset by the discovery that the good thus discerned is one that is relative to the human interests it organizes and articulates, that, in short, it is their good, and that its rational authority lies not in its supposed disclosure of a "reality" outside this context, but in its capacity to bring the desires that operate within it to a level of just and harmonious satisfaction which, by themselves, they could not have discerned. For, while the good it discloses is *their* good, it is not a good which they can set independently of the light which reason thus employed supplies, and reason is not, in consequence, nor should it be, the slave of the passions, though it is, and ought to be, the spokesman for a good in which the passions find their reasonable satisfaction. In trying to see how reason works here and what the differences are between action that, in a moral sense, is right and reasonable and that which is arbitrary and unjust, we shall (fortunately) need no special powers of insight or appreciation vouchsafed only to the elect. Nothing more is needed than reliable knowledge and good will in the understanding and evaluation of matters of public knowledge and issues of common concern. Nothing less, however, will suffice.

II. Interest and Judgments of Value

How can we be rational about values, when the attitude of reason is one of disinterested, unbiased judgment, and the attitude of valuation is one of interest, preference, bias—a way of being *for* some things and *against* others? If to be disinterested, in the sense in which practical reason requires disinterested judgment, was to be unconcerned, while to have a preference for anything rather than anything else was to be biased in its favor, hence *not* disinterested, there would indeed be a fatal incompatibility between reason and the passions, and to talk of practical reason, as we have done, would be a contradiction in terms. Fortunately for us, and for human nature, no such incompatibility exists. But loose and inaccurate thinking has sometimes led men to suppose its existence, and to maintain in consequence that we can only be rational about things we care nothing or very little about, since in these cases only can a "disinterested" and thus a genuinely rational attitude be expected to prevail. We can reach "objective" judgments about the velocity of light, since no very strong emotions are committed in advance to one conclusion rather than another about it; but to be similarly "objective" in instances about which we care greatly is quite out of the question. This conclusion ministers to a number of interests which have more to lose than to gain by the application of reason to human affairs, and it is not surprising that it has enjoyed a certain popularity. Our first task, therefore, will be to clear up the confusion from which it gains its intellectual respectability and, in the process, to locate more precisely the standpoint from which moral judgments are made and the sense in which they can be, and ought to be, disinterested.

We have agreed that all the goods we can identify in experience possess their goodness in their capacity to satisfy interests, wants, desires. None of these interests is antecedently rational, as conforming to the demands of a reality, discerned by reason, which possesses an inherent excellence of its own and to which it is the business of our desires, so far as they are reasonable, to conform. There may be such a reality, but its inherent excellence, whatever it may consist in, from cosmic immensity to plenitude of Being, becomes a value for us only in so far as we can discern in it a good in which our wills, and minds, and hearts are satisfied. And it is with the good that we can discern that practical reason is reasonably concerned.

But while no interest is antecedently rational, and while reason has no criterion for the good outside that which the satisfaction of human wants itself determines, the satisfaction of our wants can come to be a rational process in so far as we judge the claims of each particular interest from the standpoint of an attainable harmony to which each contributes but in which none has exclusive or unqualified authority. If we wanted only one thing, and wanted it unconditionally, there would be no place for the use of reason in the discovery of the good toward which all our efforts should be directed. Reason would then, and rightly, be the slave, not of the passions, but of that one passion to whose unconditional satisfaction our nature was directed. Nothing is more apparent, however, than that we want many things, and that some of these wants conflict. Moreover, there are things we want if we can have them under some conditions that we should rightly reject under others. Until, therefore, we know on what terms our several interests can be jointly satisfied, and to what the satisfaction of any one among them would commit us, in relation to the others and the conditions of their satisfaction, we simply do not know what we want. Nor can we find out simply by listing our "fundamental drives" and inviting them to fight it out among themselves for mastery. Men want power, they have a "will to power," and they struggle for power. But unless they are maniacs or Nietzschean supermen, and therefore less or more than human, they want power of certain sorts, under specific conditions, and there are other things they want as well as power, concern for which will qualify the kind of power they go after and the way in which they use it when they get it. And short of special revelation of some sort or other, the only way in which they can reliably find out what sort of power they want and what they want to do with it, is by considering the urge for power in its relation to other urges and the possibility of their joint attainment under the conditions in which action can effectively be carried on. This possibility of satisfaction will stand, relatively to competing present urges, as an ideal, something not now actual but attainable and worth attaining; and it will reasonably have authority over them simply in so far as it expresses what is wanted not blindly or at random but with knowledge of the conditions under which a secure and comprehensive satisfaction can actually be achieved. For this we require not only knowledge of the external world but self-knowledge as well, the kind that Socrates invited his fellow Athenians to seek. The reason that judges, in the light of such knowledge, what is worth seeking, or what is good, is the practical reason we have been looking for. Plato summed up the case for the authority of reason in conduct by saying that the good for man is a mixture, and only reason can reliably judge how, and in what measure, the ingredients in this mixture can rightly be combined. The claim of practical reason could hardly be put more simply or more conclusively.

In what sense is a judgment "disinterested" when it is made from the standpoint of this desirable and possible, hence, relatively to present action, ideal goal? Certainly not in the sense that the good it defines is one about which we are or ought to be unconcerned. What we want such an ideal to provide for us is a *ground* for preference, a way of being for or against competing demands for action *reasonably,* not at all a way of being indifferent or merely neutral concerning them. The notion that only in refusing to commit himself is a man "objective," and hence judicious in matters of conduct, is a current inanity that has done much harm. A practically reasonable man is not one without convictions but one who makes up his mind with a just regard for the merits of the case before him. This presupposes that the case has merits (or demerits), and that these can be found out and fairly assessed. What is required for reasonable judgment is the kind of impartiality which consists in freedom from such *antecedent* commitment to one interest or another as would blind a man to the issues involved, or close his mind to relevant information concerning them, or impede a fair estimate of conflicting claims. There is no doubt that it is in some cases very difficult to be thus impartial. But it is no less evident that we frequently do expect men to manifest such impartiality, and regard it as a prerequisite for responsible fair dealing in social relations.

A selection board is not expected to show its impartiality by refusing to prefer any of the applicants among whom it has to choose to any other, that is, by refusing to make a choice. Nor is it supposed to be lacking in concern for (hence "partiality" to) the good to which an "impartial" selection is supposed to contribute. Quite the contrary. What is expected is that it will not prefer one candidate to another save in so far as that preference can be justified by the merits of the applicants, that is, by their reasonably judged capacity to perform the services required of them for the sake of which judgment is pronounced. There is really no mystery about this, nor is the ability to act thus reasonably in a practical situation ordinarily regarded as something too great to demand of frail human nature. If such a board favored one candidate to another because of his wealth, or family connections, it would be deciding arbitrarily, not because its decision was the expression of an interest, but because the interest in question was not one which could stand inspection in the light of its professed intentions and the end for which it was set up.

In such an instance, the difference between a decision that is just or reasonable and one that is arbitrary, or unreasonable, is not that the one is the expression of an interest and the other not, but that the one contributes to and can be justified by a more comprehensive good, in reference to which it is judged, while the other is in conflict with this good. Those interests which can contribute to such a good are said to be reasonable with respect to it, those that oppose it, irrational. The good itself has no cogency apart from the satisfaction it promises for genuine human wants. If there was no use in selecting candidates on their merits, there would be no sense in condemning those who failed to do so. But it is not to be identified with any of these wants apart from the meaning it takes on as one factor in a more inclusive good. And what it can properly claim, as a member of that order, is not to be settled by its initial urgency or allegedly primitive status, but only by its eventual contribution to that way of living which we prefer when we know what we are doing and what, on the whole, we want. In articulating the structure of this way of living reason is not the slave of the passions, nor their rival in a struggle for power, but the spokesman for a good which is their good, but which, without its aid, they could not have discerned.

I do not suggest, of course, that such rationality always or even usually prevails in human conduct. We do not always choose the highest when we see it, and we often have neither the good sense to see it nor the will to look where it is to be found. Hence conduct is very frequently arbitrary and irrational in ways in which it ought not to be—that is, it falls short of a range and level of satisfaction which was possible to it, if it had had the wit to understand and the will to make the most of its opportunities. What is here important is to make out the kind of difference that reason makes where it does operate, and the good to which it is rightly addressed. This good is not beyond the powers of human nature to achieve; if it were it would not define a relevant ideal. But it is one that is reliably attainable only when human nature develops in a particular way, when the interests that move men are judged from the standpoint of their eventual collaboration in a comprehensive good, and the knowledge of the good thus identified becomes a factor in the organization of present conduct toward its effective actualization. Apart from this distinctive aspect of human behavior and the rational use of ideas in the context of activity it defines, there is no way of making sense of the claims of practical reason. It is not surprising, therefore, that those who refuse seriously to consider human behavior under this aspect, preferring to reduce it for scientific or other purposes to a congeries of "drives" or reflexes or "frustrations and aggressions," have been unable to make sense of these claims. Perhaps it was not their business to do so. But it is our business, and we intend to pursue it. If those whose understanding of human nature is restricted, perhaps advisedly, to what can be understood in terms of categories derived from pathology, physiology and animal behavior will proceed with their own affairs, there need be no disagreement between us. If, however, they go on to claim that what they have discovered is "ultimately" all there is in the human animal and that, in consequence, we are merely fooling ourselves when we demand "disinterested" behavior of such an organism, we shall have to reply, with less politeness than pertinence, that on this point they quite literally do not know what they are talking about.

III. Moral Order and Moral Freedom

We have spoken so far of a comprehensive good in which competing interests can attain their reasonable satisfaction, finding in it the measure of fulfillment of which, as elements in an ordered life, they are capable, and of the role of reason in discovering the nature of this good and making it available, as an ideal, in the organization of present conduct. The picture thus presented is true as far as it goes. But there is more to practical reason than that. It is not sufficient to talk of a harmony of interests and a resulting satisfaction. We must go on to ask whose interests are to be harmonized and from what standpoint, and on what level the satisfaction is to be achieved. These are old questions, and they are not easy to answer. Must each man, so far at least as he is reasonable, prefer his own interests to all others, and regard the good of others simply as a means to the end of his own satisfaction? And of what sort are these satisfactions to be? Is it better, as John Stuart Mill declared, to be Socrates dissatisfied than a fool satisfied? And, if it is, how is this betterness to be made out in terms of the satisfaction of interests, which we have so far taken as the goal of reasonable conduct? If we are to understand the use of practical reason, in its application to moral issues, we must answer these questions; for the ordering of satisfactions in the good we accept as our ideal will depend upon our answer, and the reasonable ordering of conduct on the structure of this good.

It is true, indeed it is a truism, that the only interests a man can reasonably be concerned about are his own. But it is no less true, and just as important, to add that he can reasonably be concerned about the interests of others and the claim they make upon him, and can prefer such claims to interests which, if he had had only himself to consider, he would have preferred to satisfy. What the truism says is that he cannot be concerned about the interests of others unless he *is* concerned about them, and unless, in that sense, they are objects of his own interest, in the satisfaction of which he will find at least the satisfaction that comes from getting what one wants even when what one wants, under the circumstances, is the satisfaction of other interests than one's own. This may sound paradoxical, and a paradox has frequently been made of it. But the puzzle arises from a failure to specify the context in which moral judgments are actually made, and the manner in which the preferences that follow such judgment and are guided by it are determined. What a man would want if he had only his own satisfaction to consider is one thing. The interests which, under those circumstances, would reasonably determine his conduct, and the kind of good in which it would eventuate can, with a certain effort of abstractive imagination, be ascertained. If e label such interests *his own* interests and contrast them with the similarly determined interests of others, of which he may have for practical purposes to take account, but only in so far as they serve as instruments or impediments to the satisfaction of "his own" interests as antecedently identified, we shall have a picture of rational conduct in which the end pursued is ego-centric satisfaction and nothing is accounted reasonable in practice that does not serve as a means to this end. It is not a very edifying picture, and it can be used either to justify selfishness as peculiarly rational or to condemn rational action as peculiarly selfish. It has often been used for both purposes. Its plausibility rests on the dictum that the only good a man can reasonably pursue is that which "his own" concerns or interests dictate, and its fallacious import is seen as soon as it is observed that "his own" has here been defined in terms of a situation which excludes from the start the conditions in which moral problems arise and can significantly be solved.

For it is a manifest fact, though a frequently neglected one, that specifically moral problems arise in just those cases in which a man *is* concerned with the interests and the happiness of others beside himself, either because he values their swtisfaction directly as an end worth working for, or because he acknowledges an obligation to respect it. These obligations and values are in this situation *his* concern; they are the objects of his interest; and the good for which he can reasonably work is one in which they must have an appropriate place. To picture them as mere means to a "satisfaction," in which "his own" interests, defined independently of just these concerns, have the dominant place and in respect to which all else functions merely as means, is radically to misrepresent the situation. It is not surprising that the terms of this misrepresentation, masquerading as "rational self-interest," have failed to provide the basis for a sound moral theory.

The object of this concern will, as a rule, be defined by certain approved ways of acting, acknowledged as "right," "fair," or "proper," and felt by the individual to stand as obligations which he is bound to respect in his relations to other people. The keeping of promises, support for aged parents and young children, loyalty to the state and readiness to defend it at grave personal risk in time of war are familiar instances, and there is no society with which we are acquainted, from the most primitive culture to the most developed, in which respect for some such obligations is not a considerable factor in social behavior. To define the good in which men could be satisfied independently of the right ordering of interests in respect to just such obligations would be to define a good which was not their good and in which they could not in fact find satisfaction. It is, therefore, a highly unreasonable procedure, though it is in the name of reason that it is sometimes defended. These rules and obligations are not themselves the product of human reason, save to a minor and limited degree. They include tabus we now regard as cruel and stupid, as well as practices of a more praise-worthy sort. But whether good or bad, from the standpoint of a more reflective morality, they are an essential part of the situation in which men work for the satisfaction of their desires, and they help to determine the structure of any good in which these desires can in fact find satisfaction.

The adjustment of interests that will reasonably satisfy the actual concerns of men must, therefore, have at least the semblance of a moral order—that is, it must be one in which rights and duties are acknowledged and in which decisions, on matters of mutual concern, are regarded as sufficiently warranted only when they can be shown to conform to accredited rules of right action. They may not actually so conform; there is room in such matters for endless hypocrisy and self-deception. And the rules themselves may be blind and arbitrary enough. But so long as they are acknowledged, not merely as threats or commands, conformity to which may or may not be expedient in the furtherance of other interests, but as standards that *ought to be* respected, so that conformity constitutes an obligation which individuals are genuinely concerned to respect, they function as moral rules within the society in question, and men who respect them, in making up their minds, will ask not merely what, on reflection, they want to do, but also, in some instances, what they ought to do. What ought to be done is not necessarily something different from what they antecedently wanted to do. The point is rather that until they have found out what they ought to do, they will not *know* what, on the whole, they want to do. For they want to do what they ought to do, and this is something to be found out, not dictated in advance by the *de facto* urgency of competing interests. There is no doubt, I think, that there are instances in which most men find themselves in this sort of situation. It is no answer to their problem to tell them that they ought to do whatever they want to do, or to "satisfy themselves." That is true enough, so far as it goes, but it will not meet the issue. What they want to do is whatever, under the circumstances, is right and reasonable, and their satisfaction is not to be found short of an adjustment in which other interests than their own demand consideration, not merely as means, but on terms which rules of equity and fair dealing dictate. Practical reason will not have done its work until it has shown us how to meet these situations as reasonably as we can. When Kant insisted that "What ought I to do?" is the basic question for practical reason he was, as usual, keeping his eye on the salient features of the moral situation.

THE CONTEXT OF MORAL JUDGMENT

We have, then, the answer to one of the questions asked some pages back. The interests to be harmonized by practical reason are those with which the individual is himself concerned—they could from the nature of the case be no others. But they are those with which he is concerned not merely as a competitive animal or ego-centric calculator of eventual personal rewards, but as a responsible moral agent. As such he can rightly prefer "his own" interests to others only when and in so far as they are entitled to such preference under rules held to be valid not merely for him, but for all those concerned in the moral community. This reasonable preference is by no means the sole or dominant factor in human conduct—nothing could be plainer than that. But it is one factor in it, and a uniquely valuable one. To leave it out when we are estimating the capacities of human nature as a whole is to turn an abstraction, perhaps legitimate for scientific purposes, into an excuse for moral cynicism. And to leave it out when it is moral behavior itself that is under consideration is a kind of blindness of which, in Bradley's phrase, only "a fool or an advanced thinker" could be guilty.

This goes a long way toward answering our second question as well. On what level, it was asked, is the satisfaction which practical reason recommends as a worthy goal for action to be achieved? The satisfactions of the fool are not those of Socrates, but so long as each is satisfied in his own fashion, who is to judge between them? And if one is satisfied and the other not, was not the first the wiser man, at least from a practical point of view? The answer depends, of course, on the value to be placed on the man who is having the satisfaction—the value, that is, of being the kind of man who can be satisfied in that kind of way. For we are concerned not merely with the satisfaction of interests, but of persons, and it is only when we have taken account of what persons are, and what worth they are capable of possessing, that we can rightly estimate their value. . . .

In the context of moral behavior . . . a "person" is an individual with rights and duties, one who can properly be held responsible for what he does because he is capable of assuming or bearing responsibility, of acting in the name and for the sake of interests that are his, not merely as a biological organism, but as a member of a moral order. He is capable, in G. H. Mead's phrase, of "taking the role of the other," that is, of the other members of the social group in which he functions, and judging his own conduct in terms held to be valid alike for all. If this meant only the passive reflection of group pressures in individual conduct, it would fall considerably short of what I mean by personality. It achieves this level, however, when the "other" is generalized to represent the verdict of justice and right reason, and the acceptance of its obligations is an active commitment to a good which the individual acknowledges as his own.

It was in Kant's moral philosophy that the notion of moral personality, and its central place in rational conduct, received classical statement. What he saw clearly was that when men cooperate freely, through their reasonable acknowledgment of mutual responsibilities, as members of "a kingdom of ends," a level of conduct is achieved which is of peculiar value, a moral order which makes sense of much in human nature that without it would remain frustrated and unfulfilled. We may not agree with him that nothing in this world or out of it is good without qualification but a good will, but when we understand ourselves and our purposes we shall find it hard, I think, to deny that good will, as he understood it, is a great good, and that without it many other goods, which men have mistakenly regarded as more important, would lose their worth as well. A "good will," in this usage, is a will freely, and responsibly, directed to the good attainable in such a community, claiming nothing for itself that this common good does not warrant and acknowledging the equal rights of others who are co-workers for its attainment. In Kant's writings this doctrine is hedged around by crabbed distinctions and scholastic complications, but there are sentences in which it comes to splendid expression, as in the great commandment to which every theory of democracy that makes sense must return for its ultimate moral sanction: "So act as to treat humanity, whether in thine own person or that of another, always as an end, never merely as a means."

This dictum is, of course, the categorical, or unconditional moral imperative which Kant regarded as the fundamental principle of all right conduct. It has often been misunderstood by critics, and there are some among the most modern of them who make their inability to understand it an occasion for self-congratulation. Thus Pareto refers to this principle as "a metaphysical entity," which is "still admired by many good souls," and adds that those who "pretend to know what it is . . . can never make it clear to anyone who insists on remaining in touch with reality." If "remaining in touch with reality" means rejecting all ideals which deal with conduct as it ought to be, then this failure is not very difficult to understand. It is, however, remarkably, and even willfully, simple-minded. For Kant was not ignorant of, and had no intention of denying, the fact that "in reality" we constantly use the services of others as means to our own ends, and that it is quite sensible to do so. What he saw was that there is a level of human relationships on which it is possible not *merely* to use men for our own ends but to share with them in purposes that are mutually understood and honored, and that nothing that comes out of such co-operative action is as much worth attaining as the good will and integrity of the men who freely share in it. Humanity—or human nature—at this level of conduct has a dignity or personal worth that accrues to it not just as a means to some further good, but as an end or fulfilment, the actualization of the excellence of which that nature is capable. The injunction to treat humanity, in respect of this capacity in one's own person and that of others, as an end, not merely as a means, does not seem to me incomprehensible or even obscure. Nor do I find it impossible to understand its obvious implication: that those who reduce a humanity capable of such dignity and freedom to a mere instrument for their own ulterior ends are behaving wrongly. For the integrity of free men is beyond price—its worth is not that of an instrument but of an end. And that, I take it, is what the categorical imperative has to tell us. . . .

The notion that social action on such a level is possible and desirable stands, for those who accept it, as an ideal or norm for present action. It does not describe the way in which men always or even usually behave. It represents a good rarely now achieved and perhaps never fully attainable. But without it, and without the possibility it presents of a life lived at some times and in some measure at the height of its human capacities, we should not know what sense to make of other goods to which we are committed and for which we feel very genuine concern. If it is to maintain itself under reasonable examination as a valid ideal for conduct, the possibility it pictures must be a real one—not the "categorical imperative crying in the wilderness" of Santayana's ironic portrayal. It must, that is to say, be reasonably probable that if we acknowledge its claims and act upon them within the limits set by the specific conditions under which action takes place, we can in fact make actual in some measure the goods it promises. No community humanly attainable may in this sense ever be as good as it ideally ought to be; but if concern for what it ought to be is a considerable factor in the direction of policy, it may be considerably better—nearer to what it ought to be—than it would have been if no such ideal had been acknowledged. That is the way in which norms or ideals work in human conduct, when they work at all, and it is the business of practical reason to judge them in their capacity to fulfil this function.

The good thus realized . . . will still be the good for which our *de facto* concerns and interests provide the material, and the satisfaction it promises will have to be one in which they are satisfied. What is claimed here is that when these concerns are judged as those of a responsible self or person nothing short of such a moral order will satisfy them. It is better to be Socrates dissatisfied than a fool satisfied only if one would rather be a Socrates than a fool, and share in the never finished quest for an excellence that fools would hardly feel the lack of. Socrates, too, might have been satisfied with the pleasures of the fool, but he would have had to be a fool to be thus satisfied. "And suppose a man actually is thus satisfied," the objector queries, "how are you going to prove that he is wrong?" For my own part, I should not attempt to do so. If there is nothing in him that rejects that alternative, if he really can be satisfied in it, then for him it is the best available. A fool's paradise may be a paradise indeed, for a fool. But a man in full possession of his faculties could not live well in it. The principle of moral freedom, like any other moral maxim, is addressed, in the last analysis, to whom it may concern. What I do contend, however, and my confidence in the worth of political freedom rests upon it, is that most men under decently human conditions are by no means such fools as social scientists and cynics frequently take them to be, and that, in consequence, the ideal proposed by practical reason for a just ordering of satisfactions in a community in which each man is respected as a person and no one among them serves merely as a tool or instrument to the satisfactions of others is, for them, a relevant and reasonable ideal. The function of reason here is not to report to fallen human nature a good of which it would otherwise have no inkling, but to bring clarity, comprehensiveness and order to concerns already at work and to enable those who follow it to know themselves and what they are trying to do. It cries not, as Santayana suggests, in the wilderness, but in the hearts and minds of men, and there sometimes and to some extent it finds an answer.

IV. The Good of Freedom

. . . It is beyond my purpose, as it is beyond my powers, to catalogue the various meanings of the term "freedom," each of which may, in its own context, be legitimate and even enlightening. There is one use of it, however, which is directly relevant to our present interest. A man is said to be morally free when his decision on issues that confront him is his own decision and action consequent upon it the expression of his own will, and when he is prepared to accept the responsibility for both decision and action as his own. That does not mean that his choice is arbitrary, capricious or uncaused. On the contrary, he will normally want to show that he had good ground for deciding as he did, and will adduce his concern to act rightly or fairly and his understanding of what, under the circumstances *was* right and fair, as the determining factors in his decision. If, on the other hand, he was shown that his action had resulted from motives fighting it out for supremacy in his consciousness, the most urgent finally winning out and thereby proving its dominance, he would be inclined to say that, on that showing, it was not *he* who had decided at all, but that the decision was something that happened to him, like a toothache or a broken leg. It is no wonder that psychologists who describe human choices in this fashion can make little sense of the notion of moral freedom. The ideas of moral freedom and moral personality are inextricably bound together. A man is acting freely, in this sense, when he decides and acts for himself, makes up his own mind and acts in his own person. A free decision need not be uncaused or self-caused, as has mistakenly been supposed, but it must be caused by the self and therefore not fully determined apart from the specific contribution which the man *as a self* or person makes to its determination.

In the context of moral action, an individual is or becomes a person in so far as he is capable of giving laws to himself, as Rousseau expressed it. That does not mean that he always acts rightly, or is free only when he so acts. What it means is that he acts in such cases as a self or person, and it is to him in this capacity that the action is properly imputed, not to his body, or his fright in early childhood, or the economic system of which he is a part. All these, no doubt, have helped to make him what he is, but what they have helped to bring into being is not just a healthy or twisted body, or a grown-up but still frightened child, or a human by-product of machine industry, but a person capable of reaching his own decisions and demanding for himself and others the right so to decide. The growth of a self, the achievement of human freedom, is one of the most remarkable things that happen in the world, and it is no wonder that much mystery has been made of it. For those who can "rationalize" a process only by reducing it to its causal antecedents, growth is always a mystery, and there will always, I suppose, be those who insist it does not happen because they cannot find the means to understand it. But it does happen, none the less, and is a mystery only for those who insist on interpreting it in other categories than its own. And when it happens men are free, not because they are uninfluenced by anything outside themselves, or insulated causally from their environment, but because what these causes converge upon is a self that acts in its own person, and for ends that it judges to be, under the conditions which the environment sets, the best attainable.

This is a quite special way in which human beings act, and under special conditions. Of a freedom that should function independently of such a way of acting in such conditions we know so little that metaphysicians are at liberty to speculate about it in almost any manner that they please, and skeptics to deny its existence with impunity. But of the freedom which manifests itself in responsible choice we know a good deal, and it is by no means a matter of indifference what we think or say about it. For when we ask what the good of democracy is, or what the reason for preferring a government that preserves the legal right of its citizens to think and to worship as they will, to its totalitarian rival, we shall hardly get an answer that will stand inspection until we reach the point of saying that it is a good thing to foster the conditions in which men are encouraged to make up their own minds on essential issues, because the kind of people who can and will make up their own minds and take the responsibility for their own actions are the kind of people we want and are determined to be. Nothing that a government can offer its citizens

—or subjects—is in the long run worth as much as the character and capacities of men who are men enough to judge it, and themselves, by the best they know and to act as their judgment dictates. No political agency can by legal action create that kind of men. But it can maintain the political conditions under which its citizens have a chance to grow to that stature, and it ought to do so. If any one assures us that he has found out from science, or philosophy, or any other respectable source, that *this* kind of freedom is impossible, or "unreal" or unimportant, we shall want to scrutinize his statements very carefully indeed. We must respect "the facts," wherever we find them, in so far as they *are* facts as they claim to be, and are relevant to the issues we are discussing. . . . We . . . know, at least, what *we* mean by the freedom we value, and why we value it. It is bound up with the capacity for cooperative action on that level of understanding and good will which we rightly regard as of preeminent human value. We cannot give it up without surrendering with it, not only our right to be respected as persons, but our self-respect as well. There is no denying that many have made this surrender. What can be questioned is whether, if they still had the capacity to act as free men, they chose well or wisely in so doing. This is a question not of psychology, or of political science, or of logical analysis, but of morals; it concerns the comparative worth of things and persons, and it is only from a standpoint from which the worth of persons has a meaning and men are valued for what they are, or can become, rather than for what can be got out of them, that an unequivocal answer can be given. Those for whom this standpoint has no cogency and no "reality" will not know what we are talking about when we say that freedom as we understand it is more than a political convenience, that it is in fact a spiritual necessity, one of the things men live by on the only level on which they can with human dignity consent to live, and that its willful surrender is not just a bargain, good or bad under varying conditions, but a betrayal. We cannot argue with them about that, if they have been honest in what they say. But if they go on to claim that, without understanding this, they are competent to say what democracy is and what it is worth to those who honor it, they will be mistaken, nor can the wealth of their factual information compensate here for the poverty of their moral understanding.

The good, then, with which practical reason is concerned, cannot adequately be understood merely as the satisfaction of assorted interests and drives or, when these conflict, of the most primitive or dominant among them. The good that is reasonably sought by free men cannot be less than an *order* of satisfactions, which is also a moral order. You cannot here judge the worth of the satisfaction apart from the worth of the self that is satisfied. Nor is the standard that judges the worth of individuals in terms of their capacity for selfhood in a moral community—a kingdom of ends—an external and transcendent one, imposed from without upon a human nature directed to a different good. It is a standard meaningful for those who can find in it an adequate expression of concerns and aspirations already strongly felt but incapable, apart from the articulation it provides, of understanding themselves and the conditions of their comprehensive satisfaction. These concerns count as basic, not through their primitive urgency or pervasiveness throughout the animal kingdom, but through their centrality in the organization of the kind of life in which men can will and act freely, or as persons. The good they define corresponds, in consequence, not to what the human animal always and everywhere is, nor to anything that could be found out about him by psychological tests of backward children, but to what he can become, and wills to become, when he understands himself and his purposes and can be satisfied with nothing less than the best of which he is capable. It is, in other words, an ideal, and it is in the capacity of human nature, sometimes and under fortunate conditions, to respond to ideals and to act wisely in terms of them, that its cogency is to be sought. It is, once more, not surprising that those who have looked for it elsewhere have failed to find it. . . .

V. The Meaning of Rational Morality

. . . We have been trying in this chapter to specify the context in which and the considerations with respect to which a distinction between good and bad conduct can reasonably be made out. To make this distinction as justly as possible is precisely the task of practical reason, and conduct is reasonable to the extent to which it follows the guidance which, in this matter, a right judgment of the issues of conduct and the worth of the way of living to which they commit us, can supply. To judge wisely of the worth of conduct, we have said, we need to know what we want when we *do* know what we want, when, that is, we adequately understand our own purposes and the conditions of their joint satisfaction. Among these conditions none are more central than those imposed by our concern that rules of fair dealing and equity be observed and that men enjoy not merely what they want, but what they are entitled to. When this concern operates at a distinctively moral level it finds expression in qualities of character which are valued, not only as means to further satisfactions, but as in their own right a fulfilment of the good of which human nature at its best is capable. It is in terms of the worth of persons, thus specified, that the good of freedom can be understood and the centrality of the values bound up with it established. This good, however, is a good of and for individuals who work together in a natural world; it is expressed not in moral self-admiration but in responsible action, and the worth of action is to be determined not only by the excellence of its intention but by the chances that it actually can contribute, more reliably than available alternatives, to the good it professes to seek. No man is as good as he ought to be unless, within the limits of his capacity and condition, he is doing his best, and no man is doing his best unless he has used such intelligence as he has, as well as his "conscience," to guide him in making his action appropriate to and effective in the circumstances of its performance. Bungling is not a moral virtue, and neither is fanaticism. Action that combines good judgment and good will in responsibly shared work for a sharable good comes near enough, for our purposes, to a definition of what we mean by conduct that meets the requirements of rational morality. It is not offered here as a new identification of "the good," for which moral philosophers have traditionally been searching. There are other goods besides the good of moral conduct; and if moral conduct did not aid in the attainment of these other goods, its own excellence would be without root or basis in the world. It is offered simply as an indication of what we are to look for in conduct whose claim to moral excellence can stand rational examination, and what, therefore, we are doing when we apply reason significantly in the field of morals. . . .

48 THE CRITERION OF TASTE
GEORGE SANTAYANA
(1863-1952)

Dogmatism in matters of taste has the same status as dogmatism in other spheres. It is initially justified by sincerity, being a systematic expression of a man's preferences; but it becomes absurd when its basis in a particular disposition is ignored and it pretends to have an absolute or metaphysical scope. Reason, with the order which in every region it imposes on life, is grounded on an animal nature and has no other function than to serve the same; and it fails to exercise its office quite as much when it oversteps its bounds and forgets whom it is serving as when it neglects some part of its legitimate province and serves its master imperfectly, without considering all his interests. . . .

The notorious diversities which human taste exhibits do not become conflicts, and raise no moral problem, until their basis or their function has been

SOURCE: Reprinted with the permission of Charles Scribner's Sons from *Reason in Art*, pp. 191–207 (ch. 10), by George Santayana. Copyright 1905 Charles Scribner's Sons; renewal copyright 1933. Permission to reprint also granted by Constable and Company Limited, London. Compare with selections 49 and 50.

forgotten, and each has claimed a right to assert itself exclusively. This claim is altogether absurd, and we might fail to understand how so preposterous an attitude could be assumed by anybody did we not remember that every young animal thinks himself absolute, and that dogmatism in the thinker is only the speculative side of greed and courage in the brute. The brute cannot surrender his appetites nor abdicate his primary right to dominate his environment. What experience and reason may teach him is merely how to make his self-assertion well balanced and successful. In the same way taste is bound to maintain its preferences but free to rationalise them. After a man has compared his feelings with the no less legitimate feelings of other creatures, he can reassert his own with more complete authority, since now he is aware of their necessary ground in his nature, and of their affinities with whatever other interests his nature enables him to recognise in others and to coordinate with his own.

A criterion of taste is, therefore, nothing but taste itself in its more deliberate and circumspect form. Reflection refines particular sentiments by bringing them into sympathy with all rational life. There is consequently the greatest possible difference in authority between taste and taste, and while delight in drums and eagle's feathers is perfectly genuine and has no cause to blush for itself, it cannot be compared in scope or representative value with delight in a symphony or an epic. The very instinct that is satisfied by beauty prefers one beauty to another; and we have only to question and purge our aesthetic feelings in order to obtain our criterion of taste. This criterion will be natural, personal, autonomous; a circumstance that will give it authority over our own judgment—which is all moral science is concerned about—and will extend its authority over other minds also, in so far as their constitution is similar to ours. In that measure what is a genuine instance of reason in us, others will recognise for a genuine expression of reason in themselves also.

Aesthetic feeling, in different people, may make up a different fraction of life and vary greatly in volume. The more nearly insensible a man is the more incompetent he becomes to proclaim the values which sensibility might have. To beauty men are habitually insensible, even while they are awake and rationally active. Tomes of aesthetic criticism hang on a few moments of real delight and intuition. It is in rare and scattered instants that beauty smiles even on her adorers, who are reduced for habitual comfort to remembering her past favours. An aesthetic glow may pervade experience, but that circumstance is seldom remarked; it figures only as an influence working subterraneously on thoughts and judgments which in themselves take a cognitive or practical direction. Only when the aesthetic ingredient becomes predominant do we exclaim, How beautiful! Ordinarily the pleasures which formal perception gives remain an undistinguished part of our comfort or curiosity.

Taste is formed in those moments when aesthetic emotion is massive and distinct; preferences then grown conscious, judgments then put into words will reverberate through calmer hours; they will constitute prejudices, habits of apperception, secret standards for all other beauties. A period of life in which such intuitions have been frequent may amass tastes and ideals sufficient for the rest of our days. Youth in these matters governs maturity, and while men may develop their early impressions more systematically and find confirmations of them in various quarters, they will seldom look at the world afresh or use new categories in deciphering it. Half our standards come from our first masters, and the other half from our first loves. Never being so deeply stirred again, we remain persuaded that no objects save those we then discovered can have a true sublimity. These high-water marks of aesthetic life may easily be reached under tutelage. It may be some eloquent appreciations read in a book, or some preference expressed by a gifted friend, that may have revealed unsuspected beauties in art or nature; and then, since our own perception was vicarious and obviously inferior in volume to that which our mentor possessed, we shall take his judgments for our criterion, since they were the source and exemplar of all our own. Thus the volume and intensity of some appreciations, especially when nothing of the kind has preceded, makes them authoritative over our subsequent judgments. On those warm moments hang all our cold systematic opinions; and while the latter fill our days and shape our careers it is only the former that are crucial and alive.

A race which loves beauty holds the same place in history that a season of love or enthusiasm holds in an individual life. Such a race has a pre-eminent right to pronounce upon beauty and to bequeath its judgments to duller peoples. We may accordingly listen with reverence to a Greek judgment on that subject, expecting that what might seem to us wrong about it is the expression of knowledge and passion beyond our range; it will suffice that we learn to live in the world of beauty, instead of merely studying its relics, for us to understand, for instance, that imitation is a fundamental principle in art, and that any rational judgment on the beautiful must be a moral and political judgment, enveloping chance aesthetic feelings and determining their value. What most German philosophers, on the contrary, have written about art and beauty has a minimal importance: it treats artifical problems in a grammatical spirit, seldom giving any proof of experience or imagination. What painters say about painting and poets about poetry is better than lay opinion; it may reveal, of course, some petty jealousy or some partial incapacity, because a special gift often carries with it complementary defects in apprehension; yet what is positive in such judgments is founded on knowledge and avoids the romancing into which litterateurs and sentimentalists will gladly wander. The specific values of art are technical values, more permanent and definite than the adventitious analogies on which a stray observer usually bases his views.

THE CRITERION OF TASTE 339

Only a technical education can raise judgments on musical compositions above impertinent autobiography. The Japanese know the beauty of flowers, and tailors and dressmakers have the best sense for the fashions. We ask them for suggestions, and if we do not always take their advice, it is not because the fine effects they love are not genuine, but because they may not be effects which we care to produce.

This touches a second consideration, besides the volume and vivacity of feeling, which enters into good taste. What is voluminous may be inwardly confused or outwardly confusing. Excitement, though on the whole and for the moment agreeable, may verge on pain and may be, when it subsides a little, a cause of bitterness. A thing's attractions may be partly at war with its ideal function. In such a case what, in our haste, we call a beauty becomes hateful on a second view, and according to the key of our dissatisfaction we pronounce that effect meretricious, harsh, or affected. These discords appear when elaborate things are attempted without enough art and refinement; they are essentially in bad taste. Rudimentary effects, on the contrary, are pure, and though we may think them trivial when we are expecting something richer, their defect is never intrinsic; they do not plunge us, as impure excitements do, into a corrupt artificial conflict. So wildflowers, plain chant, or a scarlet uniform are beautiful enough; their simplicity is a positive merit, while their crudity is only relative. There is a touch of sophistication and disease in not being able to fall back on such things and enjoy them thoroughly, as if a man could no longer relish a glass of water. Your true epicure will study not to lose so genuine a pleasure. Better forego some artificial stimulus, though that, too, has its charm, than become insensible to natural joys. Indeed, ability to revert to elementary beauties is a test that judgment remains sound.

Vulgarity is quite another matter. An old woman in a blonde wig, a dirty hand covered with jewels, ostentation without dignity, rhetoric without cogency, all offend by an inner contradiction. To like such things we should have to surrender out better intuitions and suffer a kind of dishonour. Yet the elements offensively combined may be excellent in isolation, so that an untrained or torpid mind will be at a loss to understand the critic's displeasure. Oftentimes barbaric art almost succeeds, by dint of splendour, in banishing the sense of confusion and absurdity; for everything, even reason, must bow to force. Yet the impression remains chaotic, and we must be either partly inattentive or partly distressed. Nothing could show better than this alternative how mechanical barbaric art is. Driven by blind impulse or tradition, the artist has worked in the dark. He has dismissed his work without having quite understood it or really justified it to his own mind. It is rather his excretion than his product. Astonished, very likely, at his own fertility, he has thought himself divinely inspired, little knowing that clear reason is the highest and truest of inspirations. Other men, observing his obscure work, have then honoured him for profundity; and so mere bulk or stress or complexity have produced a mystical wonder by which generation after generation may be enthralled. Barbaric art is half necromantic; its ascendancy rests in a certain measure on bewilderment and fraud.

To purge away these impurities nothing is needed but quickened intelligence, a keener spiritual flame. Where perception is adequate, expression is so too, and if a man will only grow sensitive to the various solicitations which anything monstrous combines, he will thereby perceive its monstrosity. Let him but enact his sensations, let him pause to make explicit the confused hints that threaten to stupefy him; he will find that he can follow out each of them only by rejecting and forgetting the others. To free his imagination in any direction he must disengage it from the contrary intent, and so he must either purify his object or leave it a mass of confused promptings. Promptings essentially demand to be carried out, and when once an idea has become articulate it is not enriched but destroyed if it is still identified with its contrary. Any complete expression of a barbarous theme will, therefore, disengage its incompatible elements and turn it into a number of rational beauties.

When good taste has in this way purified and digested some turgid medley, it still has a progress to make. Ideas, like men, live in society. Not only has each a will of its own and an inherent ideal, but each finds itself conditioned for its expression by a host of other beings, on whose cooperation it depends. Good taste, besides being inwardly clear, has to be outwardly fit. A monstrous ideal devours and dissolves itself, but even a rational one does not find an immortal embodiment simply for being inwardly possible and free from contradiction. It needs a material basis, a soil and situation propitious to its growth. This basis, as it varies, makes the ideal vary which is simply its expression; and therefore no ideal can be ultimately fixed in ignorance of the conditions that may modify it. It subsists, to be sure, as an eternal possibility, independently of all further earthly revolutions. Once expressed, it has revealed the inalienable values that attach to a certain form of being, whenever that form is actualised. But its expression may have been only momentary, and that eternal ideal may have no further relevance to the living world. A criterion of taste, however, looks to a social career; it hopes to educate and to judge. In order to be an applicable and a just law, it must represent the interests over which it would preside. . . .

This scope, this representative faculty or wide appeal, is necessary to good taste. All authority is representative; force and inner consistency are gifts on which I may well congratulate another, but they give him no right to speak for me. Either aesthetic experience would have remained a chaos—which it is not altogether—or it must have tended to conciliate certain general human demands and ultimately all those interests which its operation in any way affects. The more conspicuous and permanent a work of art is, the more is such an adjustment needed. A poet or philosopher may be erratic and assure us that he is inspired; if we cannot well gainsay it, we are at least not obliged to read his works. An architect or a sculptor, however, or a public performer of any sort, that thrusts before us a spectacle justified only in his inner consciousness, makes himself a nuisance. A social standard of taste must assert itself here, or else no efficacious and cumulative art can exist at all. Good taste in such matters cannot abstract from tradition, utility, and the temper of the world. It must make itself an interpreter of humanity and think esoteric dreams less beautiful than what the public eye might conceivably admire.

There are various affinities by which art may acquire a representative or classic quality. It may do so by giving form to objects which everybody knows, by rendering experiences that are universal and primary. The human figure, elementary passions, common types and crises of fate—these are facts which pass too constantly through apperception not to have a normal aesthetic value. The artist who can catch that effect in its fulness and simplicity accordingly does immortal work. This sort of art immediately becomes popular; it passes into language and convention so that its aesthetic charm is apparently worn down. The old images after a while hardly stimulate unless they be presented in some paradoxical way; but in that case attention will be diverted to the accidental extravagance, and the chief classic effect will be missed. It is the honourable fate or euthanasia of artistic successes that they pass from the field of professional art altogether and become a portion of human faculty. Every man learns to be to that extent an artist; approved figures and maxims pass current like the words and idioms of a mother-tongue, themselves once brilliant inventions. The lustre of such successes is not really dimmed, however, when it becomes a part of man's daily light; a retrogression from that habitual style or habitual insight would at once prove, by the shock it caused, how precious those ingrained apperceptions continued to be.

Universality may also be achieved, in a more heroic fashion, by art that expresses ultimate truths, cosmic laws, great human ideals. Virgil and Dante are classic poets in this sense, and a similar quality belongs to Greek sculpture and architecture. They may not cause enthusiasm in everybody; but in the end experience and reflection renew their charm; and their greatness, like that of high mountains, grows more obvious with distance. Such eminence is the reward of having accepted discipline and made the mind a clear anagram of much experience. There is a great difference between the depth of expression so gained and richness or realism in details. A supreme work presupposes minute study, sympathy with varied passions, many experiments in expression; but these preliminary things are submerged in it and are not displayed side by side with it, like the foot-notes to a learned work, so that the ignorant may know they have existed. . . .

Human nature, for all its margin of variability, has a substantial core which is invariable, as the human body has a structure which it cannot lose without perishing altogether; for as creatures grow more complex a greater number of their organs become vital and indispensable. Advanced forms will rather die than surrender a tittle of their character; a fact which is the physical basis for loyalty and martyrdom. Any deep interpretation of oneself, or indeed of anything, has for that reason a largely representative truth. Other men, if they look closely, will make the same discovery for themselves. Hence distinction and profundity, in spite of their rarity, are wont to be largely recognised. The best men in all ages keep classic traditions alive. These men have on their side the weight of superior intelligence, and, though they are few, they might even claim the weight of numbers, since the few of all ages, added together, may be more than the many who in any one age follow a temporary fashion. Classic work is nevertheless always national, or at least characteristic of its period, as the classic poetry of each people is that in which its language appears most pure and free. To translate it is impossible; but it is easy to find that the human nature so inimitably expressed in each masterpiece is the same that, under different circumstance, dictates a different performance. The deviations between races and men are not yet so great as is the ignorance of self, the blindness to the native ideal, which prevails in most of them. Hence a great man of a remote epoch is more intelligible than a common man of our own time.

Both elementary and ultimate judgments, then, contribute to a standard of taste; yet human life lies between these limits, and an art which is to be truly adjusted to life should speak also for the intermediate experience. Good taste is indeed nothing but a name for those appreciations which the swelling incidents of life recall and reinforce. Good taste is that taste which is a good possession, a friend to the whole man. It must not alienate him from anything except to ally him to something greater and more fertile in satisfactions. It will not suffer him to dote on things, however seductive, which rob him of some nobler companionship. To have a foretaste of such a loss, and to reject instinctively whatever will cause it, is the very essence of refinement. Good taste comes, therefore, from experience, in the best sense of that word; it comes from having united in one's memory and character the fruit of many diverse undertakings. Mere taste is apt to be bad taste, since it regards nothing but a chance feeling. Every man who pursues an art may be presumed to have some sensibility; the question is whether he has breeding, too, and whether what he stops at is not, in the end, vulgar and offensive. Chance feeling needs to fortify itself with reasons and to find its level in the great world. When it has added fitness to its sincerity, beneficence to its passion, it will have acquired a right to live. Violence and self-justification will not pass muster in a moral society, for vipers possess both, and must nevertheless be stamped out. Citizenship is conferred only on creatures with human and co-operative instincts. A civilised imagination has to understand and to serve the world. . . .

49 CAN WE DISPUTE ABOUT TASTES?

MONROE C. BEARDSLEY
(1915-   )

We are assured by an old and often-quoted maxim,* whose authority is not diminished by its being cast in Latin, that there can be no disputing about tastes. The chief use of this maxim is in putting an end to disputes that last a long time and don't appear to be getting anywhere. And for this purpose it is very efficacious, for it has an air of profound finality, and it also seems to provide a democratic compromise of a deadlocked issue. If you can't convince someone that he is wrong, or bring yourself to admit that he is right, you can always say that neither of you is more wrong than the other, because nobody can be right.

Remarks that serve to close some people's debates, however, are quite often just the remarks to start a new one among philosophers. And this maxim is no exception. It has been given a great deal of thought, some of it very illuminating; yet there is still something to be learned from further reflection upon it. Nor is it of small importance to know, if we can, whether the maxim is true or false, for if it is true we won't waste time in futile discussion, and if it is false we won't waste opportunities for fruitful discussion.

The question whether tastes are disputable is one to be approached with wariness. The first thing is to be clear about what it really means. There are two key words in it that we should pay particular attention to.

The first is the word "taste." The maxim is perhaps most readily and least

SOURCE: Reprinted from the *Swarthmore College Bulletin,* Alumni Issue, October 1958, with the kind permission of the author and the editor. Compare with selections 45 and 50.
De gustibus non est disputandum.

doubtfully applied to taste in its primary sensory meaning: some people like ripe olives, some green; some people like turnips, others cannot abide them; some people will go long distances for pizza pies, other can hardly choke them down. And there are no disputes about olives: we don't find two schools of thought, the Ripe Olive School and the Green Olive School, publishing quarterly journals or demanding equal time on television—probably because there simply isn't much you can say about the relative merits of these comestibles.

But we apply the word "taste," of course, more broadly. We speak of a person's taste in hats and neckties; we speak of his taste in poetry and painting and music. And it is here that the *non disputandum* maxim is most significantly applied. Some people like Auden and others Swinburne, some enjoy the paintings of Jackson Pollock and others avoid them when they can, some people are panting to hear Shostakovitch's latest symphony and others find no music since Haydn really satisfying. In these cases, unlike the olive case, people are generally not at a loss for words: there is plenty you can say about Shostakovitch, pro or con. They talk, all right; they may praise, deplore, threaten, cajole, wheedle, and scream—but, according to the maxim, they do not really dispute.

This brings us, then, to the second key word. What does it mean to say that we cannot *dispute* about tastes in literature, fine arts, and music, even though we can clearly make known our tastes? It certainly doesn't mean that we cannot disagree, or differ in taste: for obviously we do, and not only we but also the acknowledged or supposed experts in these fields. Consider James Gould Cozzens' novel, *By Love Possessed,* which appeared in August, 1957; consult the critics and reviewers to discover whether it is a good novel. Being a serious and ambitious work by a writer of standing, and also a best seller, it provoked unusually forthright judgments from a number of reviewers and critics . . . "Masterpiece . . . brilliant . . . distinguished . . . high order . . . mediocre . . . bad:" that just about covers the spectrum of evaluation.

The International Council of the Museum of Modern Art recently took a large collection of American abstract expressionist paintings on tour in Europe. Its reception was reported in *Time.* In Spain some said, "If this is art, what was it that Goya painted?" and others cheered its "furious vitality" and "renovating spirit." In Italy one newspaper remarked, "It is not painting," but "droppings of paint, sprayings, burstings, lumps, squirts, whirls, rubs and marks, erasures, scrawls, doodles and kaleidoscope backgrounds." In Switzerland it was an "artistic event" that spoke for the genius of American art. And of course all these judgments could be found in this country too.

Not a dispute? Well, what is a dispute? Let us take first the plainest case of a disagreement (no matter what it is about): two people who say, "'Tis so!"

and "'Taint so!" Let them repeat these words as often as they like, and shout them from the housetops; they still haven't got a dispute going, but merely a contradiction, or perhaps an altercation. But let one person say, "'Tis so!" and give a *reason* why 'tis so—let him say, "Jones is the best candidate for Senator because he is tactful, honest, and has had much experience in government." And let the other person say, "'Taint so!" and give a reason why 'taint so—"Jones is not the best candidate, because he is too subservient to certain interests, indecisive and wishy-washy in his own views, and has no conception of the United States' international responsibilities." Then we have a dispute—that is, a disagreement in which the parties give reasons for their contentions. Of course this is not all there is to it; the dispute has just begun. But we see how it might continue, each side giving further reasons for its own view, and questioning whether the reasons given by the other are true, relevant, and compelling.

It is this kind of thing that counts as a dispute about the possibility of getting to the moon, about American intervention in the Middle East, about a Supreme Court decision, or anything else. And if we can dispute about these things, why not about art?

But here is where the *non disputandum* maxim would draw the line. We do not speak (or not without irony) about people's tastes in Senatorial candidates or missile policies (if the President replied to critics by saying, "Well, your taste is for speeding up the missile program and spending money, but that's not to my taste," we would feel he ought to back up his opinion more than that). Nor do we speak of tastes in international affairs, or laws, or constitutions. And that seems to be because we believe that judgments on these matters can be, and ought to be, based on good reasons—not that they always are, of course. To prefer a democratic to a totalitarian form of government is *not* just a matter of taste, though to like green olives better than ripe olives is a matter of taste, and we don't require the green olive man to rise and give his reasons, or even to *have* reasons. What kind of reasons could he have? "Green olives are better because they are green" would not look like much of a reason to the ripe olive devotee.

The question, then, is whether a preference for Picasso or Monteverdi is more like a preference for green olives or like a preference for a Senatorial candidate: is it *arguable?* can it be *reasoned?*

When we read what critic and reviewers have to say about the things they talk about, we cannot doubt that they do not merely praise or blame, but defend their judgments by giving reasons, or what they claim to be reasons. The judgments of *By Love Possessed* . . . are supplied with arguments, some of them with long arguments dealing in detail with the plot, style, characterization, structure, underlying philosophy, attitudes towards Catholics, Jews, and Negroes, and other aspects of the novel. Collect a number of these reviews together and it certainly *reads* like a dispute. Or here is one person who says, "Mozart's Quintet in E Flat Major for Piano and Winds (K. 452) is a greater piece of music than Beethoven's Quintet in E Flat Major for Piano and Winds (Op. 16) because it has greater melodic invention, subtlety of texture, a more characteristic scoring for the wind instruments, and a more expressive slow movement." And here is his friend, who replies, "The Beethoven quintet is greater because it has richer sonority, greater vigor and vitality, and a more powerful dynamic spirit." There's a dispute, or something that looks very much like one.

But according to the Aesthetic Skeptic—if I may choose this convenient name for the upholder of the "no disputing" doctrine—this is an illusion. The apparent reasons are not genuine reasons, or cannot be compelling reasons, like the ones we find in other fields. For in the last analysis they rest upon sheer liking or disliking, which is not susceptible of rational discussion. The defender of the Mozart Quintet, for example, seems to be trying to prove his point, but what he is actually doing (says the Skeptic) is better put this way: "*If* you like subtle texture and expressiveness in slow movements, *then* you (like me) will prefer the Mozart quintet." But what if his friend cares more for vigor and vitality? Then the so-called "argument" is bound to leave him cold. He can only reply, "*If* you like vigor and vitality, as I do, *then* you would prefer the Beethoven quintet." But this is no longer a dispute; they are talking completely at cross purposes, not even contradicting each other.

The Aesthetic Skeptic would analyze all apparent disputes among critics in these terms: the critic can point out features of the novel, the abstract expressionist painting, the quintet for winds, but when he does this he is taking for granted, what may not be true, that you happen to like these features. You can't, says the Skeptic, argue anybody into liking something he doesn't like, and that's why there's no disputing about tastes; all disputes are in the end useless.

Now this view, which I have here stated in a fairly rough way, can be worked out into a sophisticated and impressive position, and if it is mistaken, as I believe it is, its mistakes are not childish or simple-minded. Consequently, I cannot pretend to give here an adequate treatment of it. But I should like to consider briefly some of the difficulties in Aesthetic Skepticism, as I see it, and point out the possibility of an alternative theory.

The Skeptical theory takes people's likes and dislikes as ultimate and unappealable facts about them; when two people finally get down to saying "I like X" and "I don't like X" (be it the flavor of turnip or subtlety of texture in music), there the discussion has to end, there the dispute vanishes. But though it is true that you can't change a disliking into a liking by arguments, that doesn't imply that you can't change it at all, or that we cannot argue whether or not it *ought* to be changed. . . . Appreciation isn't something you do if you just decide to. But the fact remains that one person can give reasons to another why he would be better off if he *could* enjoy music or painting that he now abhors, and sometimes the other person can set about indirectly, by study and enlarged experience, to change his own tastes, or, as we say, to improve them. There is not just your taste and mine, but better and worse taste; and this doesn't mean just that I have a taste for my taste, but not yours —I might in fact have a distaste for the limitations of my own taste (though that is a queer way to put it). It is something like a person with deep-rooted prejudices, to which he has been conditioned from an early age; perhaps he cannot quite get rid of them, no matter how he tries, and yet he may acknowledge in them a weakness, a crippling feature of his personality, and he may resolve that he will help his children grow up free from them.

The Skeptic does not allow for the possibility that we might give reasons why a person would be better off if he liked or disliked *By Love Possessed* in the way, and to the degree, that it deserves to be liked or disliked. Sometimes, I think, he really holds that it would not be worth the trouble. After all, what does it matter whether people like green olives or ripe olives? We can obtain both in sufficient supply, and nothing much depends upon it as far as the fate of the world is concerned. That's another reason why we ordinarily don't speak of Senatorial candidates as a matter of taste—unless we want to be disparaging, as when people speak of the President's choice in Secretaries of State, to imply that he has no good reason for his choice. It does matter who is Senator, or Secretary of State—it matters a great deal. But what about music, painting, and literature? . . .

Now of course, if we are thinking of our two musical disputants about the relative merits of the two quintets, this is a dispute we may safely leave alone. Both quintets are of such a high order that it perhaps doesn't matter enormously which we decide to rank higher than the other, though there's no harm in trying to do this, if we wish. But the question about *By Love Possessed* is whether it is a "masterpiece" or "bad"; and the question about the paintings is whether they ought to be shown abroad at all. It may not matter so very much whether a person on the whole admires Mozart or Beethoven more, but what if he cannot make up his mind between Mozart and Strauss, or between Beethoven and Shostakovitch?

The fact is that the prevailing level of taste in the general public matters a great deal to me, for it has a great deal to do with determining what I shall have the chance to read, what movies will be filmed, shown, or censored, what music will be played most availably on the radio, what plays will be performed on television. And it has a great deal to do with what composers and painters and poets will do, or whether some of them will do anything at all. But more than that, even: if I am convinced that the kind of experiences that can only be obtained by access to the greatest works is an important ingredient of the richest and most fully-developed human life, then do I not owe it to others to try to put that experience within their reach, or them within its reach? It might be as important to them as good housing, good medical and dental care, or good government.

But here is another point at which the Skeptic feels uneasy. Isn't it undemocratic to go around telling other people that they have crude tastes—wouldn't it be more in keeping with our laissez-faire spirit of tolerance, and less reminiscent of totalitarian absolutism and compulsion, to let others like and enjoy what they like and enjoy? Isn't this their natural right?

There are too many confusions in this point of view to clear them all up briefly. But some of them are worth sorting out. Of course it is a person's right to hear the music he enjoys, provided it doesn't bother other people too much. But it is no invasion of his right, if he is willing to consider the problem, to try to convince him that he should try to like other things that appear to deserve it. . . .

The distinction that many Skeptics find it hard to keep in mind is this: I may hold that there *is* a better and a worse in music and novels without at all claiming that *I know for certain* which are which. Those critics and reviewers who pronounced their judgments on *By Love Possessed* are not necessarily dogmatic because they deny that it's all a matter of taste (even though some of them were more positive than they had a right to be). They believe that some true and reasonable judgment of the novel is in principle possible, and that objective critics, given time and discussion, could in principle agree, or come close to agreeing, on it. But they do not have to claim infallibility—people can be mistaken about novels, as they can about anything else. Works of art are complicated. There need be nothing totalitarian about literary criticism, and there is nothing especially democratic in the view that nobody is wrong because there is no good or bad to be wrong about.

It would help us all, I think, to look at the problem of judging works of art in a more direct way. These judgments, as can easily be seen in any random collection of reviews, go off in so many directions that it sometimes seems that the reviewers are talking about different things. We must keep our eye on the object—the painting, the novel, the quintet. Because the composer's love affairs were in a sorry state at the time he was composing, people think that the value of the music must somehow be connected with this circumstance. Because the painter was regarding his model while he painted, people think that the value of the painting must depend on some relation to the way she really looked, or felt. Because the novelist is known to be an anarchist or a conservative, people think that the value of the novel must consist partly in its fidelity to these attitudes. Now, of course, when we approach a work of art, there are many kinds of interest that we can take in it, as well as in its creator. But when we are trying to judge it *as* a work of art, rather than as biography or social criticism or something else, there is a central interest that ought to be kept in view.

A work of art, whatever its species, is an object of some kind—something somebody made. And the question is whether it was worth making, what it is good for, what can be done with it. In this respect it is like a tool. Tools of course are production goods, instrumental to other instruments, whereas paintings and musical compositions and novels are consumption goods, directly instrumental to some sort of experience. And their own peculiar excellence consists, I believe, in their capacity to afford certain valuable kinds and degrees of aesthetic experience. Of course they do not yield this experience to those who cannot understand them, just as a tool is of no use to one who has not the skill to wield it. But we do not talk in the Skeptical way about tools: we do not say that the value of a hammer is all a matter of taste, some people having a taste for hammering nails, some not. No, the value resides in its capability to drive the nail, given a hand and arm with the right skill, and if the need should arise. And this value it would have, though unrealized, even if the skill were temporarily lost.

So with works of art, it seems to me. Their value is what they can do to and for us, if we are capable of having it done. And for those who do not, or not yet, have this capacity, it is not a simple fact that they do not, but a misfortune, and the only question is whether, or to what extent, it can be remedied. It is because this question sometimes has a hopeful answer that we dispute, and must dispute, about tastes. When the political disputant gives his reasons for supporting one Senatorial candidate over another, he cites facts about that candidate that he knows, from past experience, justify the hope of a good performance—the hope that the candidate, once elected, will do what a Senator is supposed to do, well. When the critic gives his reasons for saying that a work of art is good or bad, he is not, as the Skeptic claims, trying to guess whom it will please or displease; he is pointing out those features of the work—its qualities, structure, style, and so on—that are evidence of the work's ability or inability to provide qualified readers, listeners, or viewers, with a deep aesthetic experience.

50 HOW DO YOU KNOW IT'S GOOD?

MARYA MANNES (1904-   )

Suppose there were no critics to tell us how to react to a picture, a play, or a new composition of music. Suppose we wandered innocent as the dawn into an art exhibition of unsigned paintings. By what standards, by what values would we decide whether they were good or bad, talented or untalented, successes or failures? How can we ever know that what we think is right?

For the last fifteen or twenty years the fashion in criticism or appreciation of the arts has been to deny the existence of any valid criteria and to make the words "good" or "bad" irrelevant, immaterial, and inapplicable. There is no such thing, we are told, as a set of standards, first acquired through experience and knowledge and later imposed on the subject under discussion. This has been a popular approach, for it relieves the critic of the responsibility of judgment and the public of the necessity of knowledge. It pleases those resentful of disciplines, it flatters the empty-minded by calling them open-minded, it comforts the confused. Under the banner of democracy and the kind of equality which our forefathers did *not* mean, it says, in effect, "Who are you to tell us what is good or bad?" This is the same cry used so long and so effectively by the producers of mass media who insist that it is the public, not they, who decides what it wants to hear and see, and that for a critic to say that *this* program is bad and *this* program is good is purely a reflection of personal taste. Nobody recently has expressed this philosophy more succinctly than Dr. Frank Stanton, the highly intelligent president of CBS television. At a hearing before the Federal Communications Commission, this phrase escaped him under questioning: "One man's mediocrity is another man's good program."

There is no better way of saying "No values are absolute." There is another important aspect to this philosophy of *laissez faire:* It is the fear, in all observers of all forms of art, of guessing wrong. This fear is well come by,

SOURCE: From the book *But Will It Sell?* by Marya Mannes, pp. 179–86. © 1964 by Marya Mannes. Reprinted by permission of J. B. Lippincott Company. Compare with selections 48 and 49.

HOW DO YOU KNOW IT'S GOOD? 351

for who has not heard of the contemporary outcries against artists who later were called great? Every age has its arbiters who do not grow with their times, who cannot tell evolution from revolution or the difference between frivolous faddism, amateurish experimentation, and profound and necessary change. Who wants to be caught *flagrante delicto* with an error of judgment as serious as this? It is far safer, and certainly easier, to look at a picture or a play or a poem and to say "This is hard to understand, but it may be good," or simply to welcome it as a new form. The word "new"—in our country especially—has magical connotations. What is new must be good; what is old is probably bad. And if a critic can describe the new in language that nobody can understand, he's safer still. If he has mastered the art of saying nothing with exquisite complexity, nobody can quote him later as saying anything.

But all these, I maintain, are forms of abdication from the responsibility of judgment. In creating, the artist commits himself; in appreciating, you have a commitment of your own. For after all, it is the audience which makes the arts. A climate of appreciation is essential to its flowering, and the higher the expectations of the public, the better the performance of the artist. Conversely, only a public ill-served by its critics could have accepted as art and as literature so much in these last years that has been neither. If anything goes, everything goes; and at the bottom of the junkpile lie the discarded standards too.

But what are these standards? How do you get them? How do you know they're the right ones? How can you make a clear pattern out of so many intangibles, including that greatest one, the very private I?

Well for one thing, it's fairly obvious that the more you read and see and hear, the more equipped you'll be to practice that art of association which is at the basis of all understanding and judgment. The more you live and the more you look, the more aware you are of a consistent pattern—as universal as the stars, as the tides, as breathing, as night and day—underlying everything. I would call this pattern and this rhythm an order. Not order—*an* order. Within it exists an incredible diversity of forms. Without it lies chaos. I would further call this order—this incredible diversity held within one pattern—health. And I would call chaos—the wild cells of destruction—sickness. It is in the end up to you to distinguish between the diversity that is health and the chaos that is sickness, and you can't do this without a process of association that can link a bar of Mozart with the corner of a Vermeer painting, or a Stravinsky score with a Picasso abstraction; or that can relate an aggressive act with a Franz Kline painting and a fit of coughing with a John Cage composition.

There is no accident in the fact that certain expressions of art live for all time and that others die with the moment, and although you may not always define the reasons, you can ask the questions. What does an artist say that is timeless; how does he say it? How much is fashion, how much is merely reflection? Why is Sir Walter Scott so hard to read now, and Jane Austen not? Why is baroque right for one age and too effulgent for another?

Can a standard of craftsmanship apply to art of all ages, or does each have its own, and different, definitions? You may have been aware, inadvertently, that craftsmanship has become a dirty word these years because, again, it implies standards—something done well or done badly. The result of this convenient avoidance is a plenitude of actors who can't project their voices, singers who can't phrase their songs, poets who can't communicate emotion, and writers who have no vocabulary—not to speak of painters who can't draw. The dogma now is that craftsmanship gets in the way of expression. You can do better if you don't know *how* you do it, let alone *what* you're doing.

I think it is time you helped reverse this trend by trying to rediscover craft: the command of the chosen instrument, whether it is a brush, a word, or a voice. When you begin to detect the difference between freedom and sloppiness, between serious experimentation and egotherapy, between skill and slickness, between strength and violence, you are on your way to separating the sheep from the goats, a form of segregation denied us for quite a while. All you need to restore it is a small bundle of standards and a Geiger counter that detects fraud, and we might begin our tour of the arts in an area where both are urgently needed: contemporary painting.

I don't know what's worse: to have to look at acres of bad art to find the little good, or to read what the critics say about it all. In no other field of expression has so much double-talk flourished, so much confusion prevailed, and so much nonsense been circulated: further evidence of the close interdependence between the arts and the critical climate they inhabit. It will be my pleasure to share with you some of this double-talk so typical of our times.

Item one: preface for a catalogue of an abstract painter:

"Time-bound meditation experiencing a life; sincere with plastic piety at the threshold of hallowed arcana; a striving for pure ideation giving shape to inner drive; formalized patterns where neural balances reach a fiction." End of quote. Know what this artist paints like now?

Item two: a review in the *Art News:*

". . . a weird and disparate assortment of material, but the monstrosity which bloomed into his most recent cancer of aggregations is present in some form everywhere. . . ." Then, later, "A gluttony of things and processes terminated by a glorious constipation."

Item three, same magazine, review of an artist who welds automobile fragments into abstract shapes:

"Each fragment . . . is made an extreme of human exasperation, torn at and fought all the way, and has it rightness of form as if by accident. *Any technique that requires order or discipline would just be the human ego.* No, these must be egoless, uncontrolled, undesigned and different enough to give you a bang—fifty miles an hour around a telephone pole. . . ."

"Any technique that requires order of discipline would just be the human ego." What does he mean—"just be"? What are they really talking about? Is this journalism? Is it criticism? Or is it that other convenient abdication from standards of performance and judgment practiced by so many artists and critics that they, like certain writers who deal only in sickness and depravity, "reflect the chaos about them"? Again, whose chaos? Whose depravity?

I had always thought that the prime function of art was to create order *out* of chaos—again, not the order of neatness or rigidity or convention or artifice, but the order of clarity by which one will and one vision could draw the essential truth out of apparent confusion. I still do. It is not enough to use parts of a car to convey the brutality of the machine. This is as slavishly representative, and just as easy, as arranging dried flowers under glass to convey nature.

Speaking of which, i.e., the use of real materials (burlap, old gloves, bottletops) in lieu of pigment, this is what one critic had to say about an exhibition of Assemblage at the Museum of Modern Art last year:

"Spotted throughout the show are indisputable works of art, accounting for a quarter or even a half of the total display. But the remainder are works of non-art, anti-art, and art substitutes that are the aesthetic counterparts of the social deficiencies that land people in the clink on charges of vagrancy. These aesthetic bankrupts . . . have no legitimate ideological roof over their heads and not the price of a square intellectual meal, much less a spiritual sandwich, in their pockets."

I quote these words of John Canaday of *The New York Times* as an example of the kind of criticism which puts responsibility to an intelligent public above popularity with an intellectual coterie. Canaday has the courage to say what he thinks and the capacity to say it clearly: two qualities notably absent from his profession.

Next to art, I would say that appreciation and evaluation in the field of music is the most difficult. For it is rarely possible to judge a new composition at one hearing only. What seems confusing or fragmented at first might well become clear and organic a third time. Or it might not. The only salvation here for the listener is, again, an instinct born of experience and association which allows him to separate intent from accident, design from experimentation, and pretense from conviction. Much of contemporary music is, like its sister art, merely a reflection of the composer's own fragmentation: an absorption in self and symbols at the expense of communication with others.

The artist, in short, says to the public: If you don't understand this, it's because you're dumb. I maintain that you are not. You may have to go part way or even halfway to meet the artist, but if you must go the whole way, it's his fault, not yours. Hold fast to that. And remember it too when you read new poetry, that estranged sister of music.

"A multitude of causes, unknown to former times, are now acting with a combined force to blunt the discriminating powers of the mind, and, unfitting it for all voluntary exertion, to reduce it to a state of almost savage torpor. The most effective of these causes are the great national events which are daily taking place and the increasing accumulation of men in cities, where the uniformity of their occupations produces a craving for extraordinary incident, which the rapid communication of intelligence hourly gratifies. To this tendency of life and manners, the literature and theatrical exhibitions of the country have conformed themselves."

This startlingly applicable comment was written in the year 1800 by William Wordsworth in the preface to his "Lyrical Ballads"; and it has been cited by Edwin Muir in his recently published book "The Estate of Poetry." Muir states that poetry's effective range and influence have diminished alarmingly in the modern world. He believes in the inherent and indestructible qualities of the human mind and the great and permanent objects that act upon it, and suggests that the audience will increase when "poetry loses what obscurity is left in it by attempting greater themes, for great themes have to be stated clearly." If you keep that firmly in mind and resist, in Muir's words, "the vast dissemination of secondary objects that isolate us from the natural world," you have gone a long way toward equipping yourself for the examination of any work of art.

When you come to theatre, in this extremely hasty tour of the arts, you can approach it on two different levels. You can bring to it anticipation and innocence, giving yourself up, as it were, to the life on the stage and reacting to it emotionally, if the play is good, or listlessly, if the play is boring; a part of the audience organism that expresses its favor by silence or laughter and its disfavor by coughing and rustling. Or you can bring to it certain critical faculties that may heighten, rather than diminish, your enjoyment.

You can ask yourselves whether the actors are truly in their parts or merely projecting themselves; whether the scenery helps or hurts the mood; whether the playwright is honest with himself, his characters, and you. Somewhere along the line you can learn to distinguish between the true creative act and the false arbitrary gesture; between fresh observation and stale cliché; between the avant-garde play that is pretentious drivel and the avant-garde play that finds new ways to say old truths.

Purpose and craftsmanship—end and means—these are the keys to your judgment in all the arts. What is this painter trying to say when he slashes a broad band of black across a white canvas and lets the edges dribble down? It is a statement of violence? Is it a self-portrait? If it is *one* of these, has he made you believe it? Or is this a gesture of the ego or a form of therapy? If it shocks you, what does it shock you into?

And what of this tight little painting of bright flowers in a vase? Is the painter saying anything new about flowers? Is it different from a million other canvases of flowers? Has it any life, any meaning, beyond its statement? Is there any pleasure in its forms or texture? The question is not whether a thing is abstract or representational, whether it is "modern" or conventional. The question, inexorably, is whether it is good. And this is a decision which only you, on the basis of instinct, experience, and association, can make for yourself. It takes independence and courage. It involves, moreover, the risk of wrong decision and the humility, after the passage of time, of recognizing it as such. As we grow and change and learn, our attitudes can change too, and what we once thought obscure or "difficult" can later emerge as coherent and illuminating. Entrenched prejudices, obdurate opinions are as sterile as no opinions at all.

Yet standards there are, timeless as the universe itself. And when you have committed yourself to them, you have acquired a passport to that elusive but immutable realm of truth. Keep it with you in the forests of bewilderment. And never be afraid to speak up.

PART VII
SOCIAL AND POLITICAL PHILOSOPHY

51 THE STATE OF NATURE
THOMAS HOBBES (1588-1679)

Nature hath made men so equall, in the faculties of body, and mind; as that though there bee found one man sometimes manifestly stronger in body, or of quicker mind then another; yet when all is reckoned together, the difference between man, and man, is not so considerable as that one man can thereupon claim to himselfe any benefit, to which another may not pretend, as well as he. For as to the strength of body, the weakest has strength enough to kill the strongest, either by secret machination, or by confederacy with others, that are in the same danger with himselfe.

And as to the faculties of the mind, (setting aside the arts grounded upon words, and especially that skill of proceeding upon generall, and infallible rules, called Science; which very few have, and but in few things; as being not a native faculty, born with us; nor attained, (as Prudence,) while we look after somewhat els,) I find yet a greater equality amongst men, than that of strength. For Prudence, is but Experience; which equall time, equally bestowes on all men, in those things they equally apply themselves unto. That which may perhaps make such equality incredible, is but a vain conceipt of ones owne wisdome, which almost all men think they have in a greater degree, than the Vulgar; that is, than all men but themselves, and a few others, whom by Fame, or for concurring with themselves, they approve. For such is the nature of men, that howsoever they may acknowledge many others to be more witty, or more eloquent, or more learned; Yet they will hardly believe there by many so wise as themselves: For they see their own wit at hand, and other mens at a distance. But this proveth rather that men are in that point equall, than unequall. For there is not ordinarily a greater signe of the equall distribution of any thing, than that every man is contented with his share.

From this equality of ability, ariseth equality of hope in the attaining of our Ends. And therefore if any two men desire the same thing, which neverthelesse they cannot both enjoy, they become enemies; and in the way to their End, (which is principally their owne conservation, and sometimes their

SOURCE: Part I, ch. 13 of *Leviathan* (1651). The title of this selection has been supplied by the editors. Compare with selections 52, 54, and 56.

delectation only,) endeavour to destroy, or subdue one an other. And from hence it comes to passe, that where an Invader hath no more to feare, than an other mans single power; if one plant, sow, build, or possesse a convenient Seat, others may probably be expected to come prepared with forces united, to dispossesse, and deprive him, not only of the fruit of his labour, but also of his life, or liberty. And the Invader again is in the like danger of another.

And from this diffidence of one another, there is no way for any man to secure himselfe, so reasonable, as Anticipation; that is, by force, or wiles, to master the persons of all men he can, so long, till he see no other power great enough to endanger him: And this is no more than his own conservation requireth, and is generally allowed. Also because there be some, that taking pleasure in contemplating their own power in the acts of conquest, which they pursue farther than their security requires; if others, that otherwise would be glad to be at ease within modest bounds, should not by invasion increase their power, they would not be able, long time, by standing only on their defence, to subsist. And by consequence, such augmentation of dominion over men, being necessary to a mans conservation, it ought to be allowed him.

Againe, men have no pleasure, (but on the contrary a great deale of griefe) in keeping company, where there is no power able to over-awe them all. For every man looketh that his companion should value him, at the same rate he sets upon himselfe: And upon all signes of contempt, or undervaluing, naturally endeavours, as far as he dares (which amongst them that have no common power to keep them in quiet, is far enough to make them destroy each other,) to extort a greater value from his contemners, by dommage; and from others, by the example.

So that in the nature of man, we find three principall causes of quarrell. First, Competition; Secondly, Diffidence; Thirdly, Glory.

The first, maketh men invade for Gain; the second, for Safety; and the third, for Reputation. The first use Violence, to make themselves Masters of other mens persons, wives, children, and cattell; the second, to defend them; the third, for trifles, as a word, a smile, a different opinion, and any other signe of undervalue, either direct in their Persons, or by reflexion in their Kindred, their Friends, their Nation, their Profession, or their Name.

Hereby it is manifest, that during the time men live without a common Power to keep them all in awe, they are in that condition which is called Warre; and such a warre, as is of every man, against every man. For WARRE, consisteth not in Battell onely, or the act of fighting; but in a tract of time, wherein the Will to contend by Battell is sufficiently known: and therefore the notion of *Time,* is to be considered in the nature of Warre; as it is in the nature of Weather. For as the nature of Foule weather, lyeth not in a showre or two of rain; but in an inclination thereto of many dayes together; So the nature of War, consisteth not in actual fighting; but in the known disposition thereto, during all the time there is no assurance to the contrary. All other time is PEACE.

Whatsoever therefore is consequent to a time of Warre, where every man is Enemy to every man; the same is consequent to the time, wherein men live without other security, than what their own strength, and their own invention shall furnish them withall. In such condition, there is no place for Industry; because the fruit thereof is uncertain: and consequently no Culture of the Earth, no Navigation, nor use of the commodities that may be imported by Sea; no commodious Building; no Instruments of moving, and removing such things as require much force; no Knowledge of the face of the Earth; no account of Time; no Arts; no Letters; no Society; and which is worst of all, continuall feare, and danger of violent death; And the life of man, solitary, poore, nasty, brutish, and short.

It may seem strange to some man, that has not well weighed these things; that Nature should thus dissociate, and render men apt to invade, and destroy one another: and he may therefore, not trusting to this Inference, made from the Passions, desire perhaps to have the same confirmed by Experience. Let him therefore consider with himselfe, when taking a journey, he armes himselfe, and seeks to go well accompanied; when going to sleep, he locks his dores; when even in his house he locks his chests; and this when he knowes there bee Lawes, and publike Officers, armed, to revenge all injuries shall bee done him; what opinion he has of his fellow subjects, when he rides armed; of his fellow Citizens, when he locks his dores; and of his children, and servants, when he locks his chests. Does he not there as much accuse mankind by his actions, as I do by my words? But neither of us accuse mans nature in it. The Desires, and other Passions of man, are in themselves no Sin. No more are the Actions, that proceed from those Passions, till they know a Law that forbids them: which till Lawes be made they cannot know: nor can any Law be made, till they have agreed upon the Person that shall make it.

It may peradventure be thought, there was never such a time, nor condition of warre as this; and I believe it was never generally so, over all the world: but there are many places, where they live so now. For the savage people in many places of *America,* except the government of small Families, that concord whereof dependeth on naturall lust, have no government at all; and live at this day in that brutish manner, as I said before. Howsoever, it may be perceived what manner of life there would be, where there were no common Power to feare; by the manner of life, which men that have formerly lived under a peacefull government, use to degenerate into, in a civill Warre.

But though there had never been any time, wherein particular men were in a condition of warre one against another; yet in all times, Kings, and Persons of Soveraigne authority, because of their Independency, are in continuall jealousies, and in the state and posture of Gladiators; having their weapons pointing, and their eyes fixed on one another; that is, their Forts, Garrisons, and Guns, upon the Frontiers of their Kingdomes; and continuall Spyes upon their neighbours; which is a posture of War. But because they uphold thereby, the Industry of their Subjects; there does not follow from it, that misery, which accompanies the Liberty of particular men.

To this warre of every man against every man, this also is consequent; that nothing can be Unjust. The notions of Right and Wrong, Justice and Injustice have there no place. Where there is no common Power, there is no Law: where no Law, no Injustice. Force, and Fraud, are in warre, the two Cardinall vertues. Justice, and Injustice are none of the Faculties neither of the Body, nor Mind. If they were, they might be in a man that were alone in the world, as well as his Senses, and Passions. They are Qualities, that relate to men in Society, not in Solitude. It is consequent also to the same condition, that there be no Propriety, no Dominion, no *Mine* and *Thine* distinct; but onely that to be every mans, that he can get; and for so long, as he can keep it. And thus much for the ill condition, which man by meer Nature is actually placed in; though with a possibility to come out of it, consisting partly in the Passions, partly in his Reason.

The Passions that encline men to Peace, are Feare of Death; Desire of such things as are necessary to commodious living; and a Hope by their Industry to obtain them. And Reason suggesteth convenient Articles of Peace, upon which men may be drawn to agreement. These Articles, are they, which otherwise are called the Lawes of Nature: whereof I shall speak more particularly, in the two following Chapters.

52 LIBERTY, EQUALITY, AND THE STATE OF NATURE
JOHN C. CALHOUN (1782-1850)

... To perfect society, it is necessary to develop the faculties, intellectual and moral, with which man is endowed. But the mainspring to their development, and, through this, to progress, improvement, and civilization, with all their blessings, is the desire of individuals to better their condition. For this purpose liberty and security are indispensable. Liberty leaves each free to pursue the course he may deem best to promote his interest and happiness, as far as it may be compatible with the primary end for which government is ordained, while security gives assurance to each that he shall not be deprived of the fruits of his exertions to better his condition. These combined give to this desire the strongest impulse of which it is susceptible. For to extend liberty beyond the limits assigned would be to weaken the government and to render it incompetent to fulfill its primary end—the protection of society against dangers, internal and external. The effect of this would be insecurity; and of insecurity, to weaken the impulse of individuals to better their condition and thereby retard progress and improvement. On the other hand, to extend the powers of the government so as to contract the sphere assigned to liberty would have the same effect, by disabling individuals in their efforts to better their condition.

Herein is to be found the principle which assigns to power and liberty their proper spheres and reconciles each to the other under all circumstances. For if power be necessary to secure to liberty the fruits of its exertions, liberty, in turn, repays power with interest—by increased population, wealth, and other advantages which progress and improvement bestow on the community. By thus assigning to each its appropriate sphere, all conflicts between them cease, and each is made to cooperate with and assist the other in fulfilling the great ends for which government is ordained. . . .

But some communities require a far greater amount of power than others to protect them against anarchy and external dangers; and, of course, the

SOURCE: Excerpted from *A Disquisition on Government,* published posthumously in 1853. The title of this selection has been supplied by the editors. Compare with selections 51, 54, 55, and 56.

sphere of liberty in such must be proportionally contracted. The causes calculated to enlarge the one and contract the other are numerous and various. Some are physical, such as open and exposed frontiers surrounded by powerful and hostile neighbors. Others are moral, such as the different degrees of intelligence, patriotism, and virtue among the mass of the community, and their experience and proficiency in the art of self-government. Of these, the moral are by far the most influential. A community may possess all the necessary moral qualifications in so high a degree as to be capable of self-government under the most adverse circumstances, while, on the other hand, another may be so sunk in ignorance and vice as to be incapable of forming a conception of liberty or of living, even when most favored by circumstances, under any other than an absolute and despotic government.

The principle in all communities, according to these numerous and various causes, assigns to power and liberty their proper spheres. To allow liberty, in any case, a sphere of action more extended than this assigns would lead to anarchy, and this, probably, in the end to a contraction instead of an enlargement of its sphere. Liberty, then, when forced on a people unfit for it, would, instead of a blessing, be a curse, as it would in its reaction lead directly to anarchy—the greatest of all curses. No people, indeed, can long enjoy more liberty than that to which their situation and advanced intelligence and morals fairly entitle them. If more than this be allowed, they must soon fall into confusion and disorder—to be followed, if not by anarchy and despotism, by a change to a form of government more simple and absolute, and therefore better suited to their condition. And hence, although it may be true that a people may not have as much liberty as they are fairly entitled to and are capable of enjoying, yet the reverse is unquestionably true—that no people can long possess more than they are fairly entitled to.

Liberty, indeed, though among the greatest of blessings, is not so great as that of protection, inasmuch as the end of the former is the progress and improvement of the race, while that of the latter is its preservation and perpetuation. And hence, when the two come into conflict, liberty must, and ever ought, to yield to protection, as the existence of the race is of greater moment than its improvement.

It follows, from what has been stated, that it is a great and dangerous error to suppose that all people are equally entitled to liberty. It is a reward to be earned, not a blessing to be gratuitously lavished on all alike—a reward reserved for the intelligent, the patriotic, the virtuous and deserving, and not a boon to be bestowed on a people too ignorant, degraded, and vicious to be capable either of appreciating or of enjoying it. Nor is it any disparagement to liberty that such is and ought to be the case. On the contrary, its greatest praise, its proudest distinction, is that all-wise Providence has reserved it as the noblest and highest reward for the development of our faculties, moral and intellectual. A reward more appropriate than liberty could not be conferred on the deserving, nor a punishment inflicted on the undeserving more just than to be subject to lawless and despotic rule. This dispensation seems to be the result of some fixed law; and every effort to disturb or defeat it, by attempting to elevate a people in the scale of liberty above the point to which they are entitled to rise, must ever prove abortive and end in disappointment. The progress of a people rising from a lower to a higher point in the scale of liberty is necessarily slow; and by attempting to precipitate, we either retard or permanently defeat it. . . .

There is another error, not less great and dangerous, usually associated with the one which has just been considered. I refer to the opinion that liberty and equality are so intimately united that liberty cannot be perfect without perfect equality.

That they are united to a certain extent, and that equality of citizens, in the eyes of the law, is essential to liberty in a popular government, is conceded. But to go further and make equality of *condition* essential to liberty would be to destroy both liberty and progress. The reason is that inequality of condition, while it is a necessary consequence of liberty, is at the same time indispensable to progress. In order to understand why this is so, it is necessary to bear in mind that the mainspring to progress is the desire of individuals to better their condition, and that the strongest impulse which can be given to it is to leave individuals free to exert themselves in the manner they may deem best for that purpose, as far at least as it can be done consistently with the ends for which government is ordained, and to secure to all the fruits of their exertions. Now, as individuals differ greatly from each other in intelligence, sagacity, energy, perseverance, skill, habits of industry and economy, physical power, position and opportunity—the necessary effect of leaving all free to exert themselves to better their condition must be a corresponding inequality between those who may possess these qualities and advantages in a high degree and those who may be deficient in them. The only means by which this result can be prevented are either to impose such restrictions on the exertions of those who may possess them in a high degree as will place them on a level with those who do not, or to deprive them of the fruits of their exertions. But to impose such restrictions on them would be destructive of liberty, while to deprive them of the fruits of their exertions would be to destroy the desire of bettering their condition. It is, indeed, this inequality of condition between the front and rear ranks, in the march of progress, which gives so strong an impulse to the former to maintain their position, and to the latter to press forward into their files. This gives to progress its greatest impulse. To force the front rank back to the rear or attempt to push forward the rear into line with the front, by the interposition of the government, would put an end to the impulse and effectually arrest the march of progress.

These great and dangerous errors have their origin in the prevalent opinion that all men are born free and equal—than which nothing can be more unfounded and false. It rests upon the assumption of a fact which is contrary to universal observation, in whatever light it may be regarded. It is, indeed, difficult to explain how an opinion so destitute of all sound reason ever could have been so extensively entertained unless we regard it as being confounded with another which has some semblance of truth, but which, when properly understood, is not less false and dangerous. I refer to the assertion that all men are equal in the state of nature, meaning by a state of nature a state of individuality supposed to have existed prior to the social and political state, and in which men lived apart and independent of each other. If such a state ever did exist, all men would have been, indeed, free and equal in it; that is, free to do as they pleased and exempt from the authority or control of others —as, by supposition, it existed anterior to society and government. But such a state is purely hypothetical. It never did nor can exist, as it is inconsistent with the preservation and perpetuation of the race. It is, therefore, a great misnomer to call it "the state of nature." Instead of being the natural state of man, it is, of all conceivable states, the most opposed to his nature—most repugnant to his feelings and most incompatible with his wants. His natural state is the social and political, the one for which his Creator made him, and the only one in which he can preserve and perfect his race. As, then, there never was such a state as the so-called state of nature, and never can be, it follows that men, instead of being born in it, are born in the social and political state; and of course, instead of being born free and equal, are born subject, not only to parental authority, but to the laws and institutions of the country where born and under whose protection they draw their first breath. . . .

53 AUTHORITY AND SOCIETY
ALEXIS DE TOCQUEVILLE
(1805-1859)

At different periods dogmatical belief is more or less common. It arises in different ways, and it may change its object and its form; but under no circumstances will dogmatical belief cease to exist, or, in other words, men will never cease to entertain some opinions on trust, and without discussion. If every one undertook to form all his own opinions, and to seek for truth by isolated paths struck out by himself alone, it would follow that no considerable number of men would ever unite in any common belief.

But obviously without such common belief no society can prosper—say, rather, no society can exist; for without ideas held in common, there is no common action, and without common action there may still be men, but there is no social body. In order that society should exist, and, *a fortiori*, that a society should prosper, it is required that all the minds of the citizens should be rallied and held together by certain predominant ideas; and this cannot be the case unless each of them sometimes draws his opinions from the common source, and consents to accept certain matters of belief already formed.

If I now consider man in his isolated capacity, I find that dogmatical belief is not less indispensable to him in order to live alone, than it is to enable him to co-operate with his fellows. If man were forced to demonstrate for himself all the truths of which he makes daily use, his task would never end. He would exhaust his strength in preparatory demonstrations, without ever advancing beyond them. As, from the shortness of his life, he has not the time, nor, from the limits of his intelligence, the capacity, to accomplish this, he is reduced to take upon trust a number of facts and opinions which he has not had either the time or the power to verify for himself, but which men of greater ability have sought out, or which the world adopts. On this groundwork he raises for himself the structure of his own thoughts; he is not led to proceed in this manner by choice, but is constrained by the inflexible law of his condition.

SOURCE: From Book I, chapter 2, of the second volume of *Democracy in America* (1840); in the translation by Henry Reeve, as edited by Francis Bowen (1862). The title of this selection has been supplied by the editors. Compare with selections 5, 14, and 56.

There is no philosopher of so great parts in the world, but that he believes a million of things on the faith of other people, and supposes a great many more truths than he demonstrates.

This is not only necessary, but desirable. A man who should undertake to inquire into everything for himself, could devote to each thing but little time and attention. His task would keep his mind in perpetual unrest, which would prevent him from penetrating to the depth of any truth, or of grappling his mind firmly to any conviction. His intellect would be at once independent and powerless. He must therefore make his choice from amongst the various objects of human belief, and adopt many opinions without discussion, in order to search the better into that smaller number which he sets apart for investigation. It is true, that whoever receives an opinion on the word of another, does so far enslave his mind, but it is a salutary servitude which allows him to make a good use of freedom.

A principle of authority must then always occur, under all circumstances, in some part or other of the moral and intellectual world. Its place is variable, but a place it necessarily has. The independence of individual minds may be greater, or it may be less: unbounded it cannot be. Thus the question is, not to know whether any intellectual authority exists in the ages of democracy, but simply where it resides and by what standard it is to be measured. . . .

When the ranks of society are unequal, and men unlike one another in condition, there are some individuals wielding the power of superior intelligence, learning, and enlightenment, whilst the multitude are sunk in ignorance and prejudice. Men living at these aristocratic periods are therefore naturally induced to shape their opinions by the standard of a superior person, or superior class of persons, whilst they are averse to recognize the infallibility of the mass of the people.

The contrary takes place in ages of equality. The nearer the people are drawn to the common level of an equal and similar condition, the less prone does each man become to place implicit faith in a certain man or a certain class of men. But his readiness to believe the multitude increases, and opinion is more than ever mistress of the world. Not only is common opinion the only guide which private judgment retains amongst a democratic people, but amongst such a people it possesses a power infinitely beyond what it has elsewhere. At periods of equality, men have no faith in one another, by reason of their common resemblance; but this very resemblance gives them almost unbounded confidence in the judgment of the public; for it would not seem probable, as they are all endowed with equal means of judging, but that the greater truth should go with the greater number.

When the inhabitant of a democratic country compares himself individually with all those about him, he feels with pride that he is the equal of any one of them; but when he comes to survey the totality of his fellows, and to place himself in contrast with so huge a body, he is instantly overwhelmed by the sense of his own insignificance and weakness. The same equality which renders him independent of each of his fellow-citizens, taken severally, exposes him alone and unprotected to the influence of the greater number. The public has therefore, among a democratic people, a singular power, which aristocratic nations cannot conceive of; for it does not persuade to certain opinions, but it enforces them, and infuses them into the intellect by a sort of enormous pressure of the minds of all upon the reason of each.

In the United States, the majority undertakes to supply a multitude of ready-made opinions for the use of individuals, who are thus relieved from the necessity of forming opinions of their own. Everybody there adopts great numbers of theories, on philosophy, morals, and politics, without inquiry, upon public trust; and if we look to it very narrowly, it will be perceived that religion herself holds sway there much less as a doctrine of revelation than as a commonly received opinion.

The fact that the political laws of the Americans are such that the majority rules the community with sovereign sway, materially increases the power which that majority naturally exercises over the mind. For nothing is more customary in man than to recognize superior wisdom in the person of his oppressor. This political omnipotence of the majority in the United States doubtless augments the influence which public opinion would obtain without it over the minds of each member of the community; but the foundations of that influence do not rest upon it. They must be sought for in the principle of equality itself, not in the more or less popular institutions which men living under that condition may give themselves. The intellectual dominion of the greater number would probably be less absolute amongst a democratic people governed by a king, than in the sphere of a pure democracy, but it will always be extremely absolute; and by whatever political laws men are governed in the ages of equality, it may be foreseen that faith in public opinion will become a species of religion there, and the majority its ministering prophet.

Thus intellectual authority will be different, but it will not be diminished; and far from thinking that it will disappear, I augur that it may readily acquire too much preponderance, and confine the action of private judgment within narrower limits than are suited either to the greatness or the happiness of the human race. In the principle of equality I very clearly discern two tendencies; the one leading the mind of every man to untried thoughts, the other which would prohibit him from thinking at all. And I perceive how, under the dominion of certain laws, democracy would extinguish that liberty of the mind to which a democratic social condition is favorable; so that, after having broken all the bondage once imposed on it by ranks or by men, the human mind would be closely fettered to the general will of the greatest number.

If the absolute power of a majority were to be substituted, by democratic nations, for all the different powers which checked or retarded overmuch the energy of individual minds, the evil would only have changed character. Men would not have found the means of independent life; they would simply have discovered (no easy task) a new physiognomy of servitude. There is,—and I cannot repeat it too often,—there is here matter for profound reflection to those who look on freedom of thought as a holy thing, and who hate not only the despot, but despotism. For myself, when I feel the hand of power lie heavy on my brow, I care but little to know who oppresses me; and I am not the more disposed to pass beneath the yoke because it is held out to me by the arms of a million of men.

54 LIBERTY AND EQUALITY
R. H. TAWNEY (1880-1962)

Liberty and equality have usually in England been considered antithetic; and, since fraternity has rarely been considered at all, the famous trilogy has been easily dismissed as a hybrid abortion. Equality implies the deliberate acceptance of social restraints upon individual expansion. It involves the prevention of sensational extremes of wealth and power by public action for the public good. If liberty means, therefore, that every individual shall be free, according to his opportunities, to indulge without limit his appetite for either, it is clearly incompatible, not only with economic and social, but with civil and political, equality, which also prevent the strong exploiting to the full the advantages of their strength, and, indeed, with any habit of life save that of the Cyclops. But freedom for the pike is death for the minnows. It is possible that equality is to be contrasted, not with liberty, but only with a particular interpretation of it.

The test of a principle is that it can be generalized, so that the advantages of applying it are not particular, but universal. Since it is impossible for every individual, as for every nation, simultaneously to be stronger than his neighbours, it is a truism that liberty, as distinct from the liberties of special persons

SOURCE: Chapter V, section 2 of *Equality* (4th ed., 1952). Footnotes have been deleted. Reprinted by permission of the publishers, George Allen & Unwin, Ltd., London. Published in the United States by The Macmillan Company, New York. Compare with selections 52 and 56.

and classes, can exist only in so far as it is limited by rules, which secure that freedom for some is not slavery for others. The spiritual energy of human beings, in all the wealth of their infinite diversities, is the end to which external arrangements, whether political or economic, are merely means. Hence institutions which guarantee to men the opportunity of becoming the best of which they are capable are the supreme political good, and liberty is rightly preferred to equality, when the two are in conflict. The question is whether, in the conditions of modern society, they conflict or not. It is whether the defined and limited freedom, which alone can be generally enjoyed, is most likely to be attained by a community which encourages violent inequalities, or by one which represses them.

Inequality of power is not necessarily inimical to liberty. On the contrary, it is the condition of it. Liberty implies the ability to act, not merely to resist. Neither society as a whole, nor any group within it, can carry out its will except through organs; and, in order that such organs may function with effect, they must be sufficiently differentiated to perform their varying tasks, of which direction is one and execution another. But, while inequality of power is the condition of liberty, since it is the condition of any effective action, it is also a menace to it, for power which is sufficient to use is sufficient to abuse. Hence, in the political sphere, where the danger is familiar, all civilized communities have established safeguards, by which the advantages of differentiation of function, with the varying degrees of power which it involves, may be preserved, and the risk that power may be tyrannical, or perverted to private ends, averted or diminished. They have endeavoured, for example, as in England, to protect civil liberty by requiring that, with certain exceptions, the officers of the State shall be subject to the ordinary tribunals, and political liberty by insisting that those who take decisions on matters affecting the public shall be responsible to an assembly chosen by it. The precautions may be criticized as inadequate, but the need for precautions is not to-day disputed. It is recognized that political power must rest ultimately on consent, and that its exercise must be limited by rules of law.

The dangers arising from inequalities of economic power have been less commonly recognized. They exist, however, whether recognized or not. For the excess or abuse of power, and its divorce from responsibility, which results in oppression, are not confined to the relations which arise between men as members of a state. They are not a malady which is peculiar to political systems, as was typhus to slums, and from which other departments of life can be regarded as immune. They are a disease, not of political organization, but of organization. They occur, in the absence of preventive measures, in political associations, because they occur in all forms of association in which large numbers of individuals are massed for collective action.

The isolated worker may purchase security against exploitation at the cost of poverty, as the hermit may avoid the corruptions of civilization by foregoing its advantages. But, as soon as he is associated with his fellows in a common undertaking, his duties must be specified and his rights defined; and, in so far as they are not, the undertaking is impeded. The problem of securing a livelihood ceases to be merely economic, and becomes social and political. The struggle with nature continues, but on a different plane. Its efficiency is heightened by co-operation. Its character is complicated by the emergence of the question of the terms on which co-operation shall take place.

In an industrial civilization, when its first phase is over, most economic activity is corporate activity. It is carried on, not by individuals, but by groups, which are endowed by the State with a legal status, and the larger of which, in size, complexity, specialization of functions and unity of control, resemble less the private enterprise of the past than a public department. As far as certain great industries are concerned, employment must be found in the service of these corporations, or not at all. Hence the mass of mankind pass their working lives under the direction of a hierarchy, whose heads define, as they think most profitable, the lines on which the common enterprise is to proceed, and determine, subject to the intervention of the State and voluntary organizations, the economic, and to a considerable, though diminishing, extent, the social environment of their employees. Possessing the reality of power, without the decorative trappings—unless, as in England is often the case, it thinks it worth while to buy them—this business oligarchy is the effective aristocracy of industrial nations, and the aristocracy of tradition and prestige, when such still exists, carries out its wishes and courts its favours. In such conditions, authority over human beings is exercised, not only through political, but through economic, organs. The problem of liberty, therefore, is necessarily concerned, not only with political, but also with economic, relations.

It is true, of course, that the problems are different. But to suppose that the abuses of economic power are trivial, or that they are automatically prevented by political democracy, is to be deceived by words. Freedom is always, no doubt, a matter of degree; no man enjoys all the requirements of full personal development, and all men possess some of them. It is not only compatible with conditions in which all men are fellow-servants, but would find in such conditions its most perfect expression. What it excludes is a society where only some are servants, while others are masters.

For, whatever else the idea involves, it implies at least, that no man shall be amenable to an authority which is arbitrary in its proceedings, exorbitant in its demands, or incapable of being called to account when it abuses its office for personal advantage. In so far as his livelihood is at the mercy of an irresponsible superior, whether political or economic, who can compel his reluctant obedience by *force majeure,* * whose actions he is unable to modify or resist, save at the cost of grave personal injury to himself and his dependents, and whose favour he must court, even when he despises it, he may possess a profusion of more tangible blessings, from beer to motor-bicycles, but he cannot be said to be in possession of freedom. In so far as an economic system grades mankind into groups, of which some can wield, if unconsciously, the force of economic duress for their own profit or convenience, whilst others must submit to it, its effect is that freedom itself is similarly graded. Society is divided, in its economic and social relations, into classes which are ends, and classes which are instruments. Like property, with which in the past it has been closely connected, liberty becomes the privilege of a class, not the possession of a nation.

Political principles resemble military tactics; they are usually designed for a war which is over. Freedom is commonly interpreted in England in political terms, because it was in the political arena that the most resounding of its recent victories were won. It is regarded as belonging to human beings as citizens, rather than to citizens as human beings; so that it is possible for a nation, the majority of whose members have as little influence on the decisions that determine their economic destinies as on the motions of the planets, to applaud the idea with self-congratulatory gestures of decorous enthusiasm, as though history were of the past, but not of the present. If the attitude of the ages from which it inherits a belief in liberty had been equally ladylike, there would have been, it is probable, little liberty to applaud.

For freedom is always relative to power, and the kind of freedom which at any moment it is most urgent to affirm depends on the nature of the power which is prevalent and established. Since political arrangements may be such as to check excesses of power, while economic arrangements permit or encourage them, a society, or a large part of it, may be both politically free and economically the opposite. It may be protected against arbitrary action by the agents of government, and be without the security against economic oppression which corresponds to civil liberty. It may possess the political institutions of an advanced democracy, and lack the will and ability to control the conduct of those powerful in its economic affairs, which is the economic analogy of political freedom.

The extension of liberty from the political to the economic sphere is evidently among the most urgent tasks of industrial societies. It is evident also, however, that, in so far as this extension takes place, the traditional antithesis between liberty and equality will no longer be valid. As long as liberty is

*greater force

interpreted as consisting exclusively in security against oppression by the agents of the State, or as a share in its government, it is plausible, perhaps, to dissociate it from equality; for, though experience suggests that, even in this meagre and restricted sense, it is not easily maintained in the presence of extreme disparities of wealth and influence, it is possible for it to be enjoyed, in form at least, by pauper and millionaire. Such disparities, however, though they do not enable one group to become the political master of another, necessarily cause it to exercise a preponderant influence on the economic life of the rest of society.

Hence, when liberty is construed, realistically, as implying, not merely a minimum of civil and political rights, but securities that the economically weak will not be at the mercy of the economically strong, and that the control of those aspects of economic life by which all are affected will be amenable, in the last resort, to the will of all, a large measure of equality, so far from being inimical to liberty, is essential to it. In conditions which impose co-operative, rather than merely individual, effort, liberty is, in fact, equality in action, in the sense, not that all men perform identical functions or wield the same degree of power, but that all men are equally protected against the abuse of power, and equally entitled to insist that power shall be used, not for personal ends, but for the general advantage. Civil and political liberty obviously imply, not that all men shall be members of parliament, cabinet ministers, or civil servants, but the absence of such civil and political inequalities as enable one class to impose its will on another by legal coercion. It should be not less obvious that economic liberty implies, not that all men shall initiate, plan, direct, manage, or administer, but the absence of such economic inequalities as can be used as a means of economic constraint.

The danger to liberty which is caused by inequality varies with differences of economic organization and public policy. When the mass of the population are independent producers, or when, if they are dependent on great undertakings, the latter are subject to strict public control, it may be absent or remote. It is seen at its height when important departments of economic activity are the province of large organizations, which, if they do not themselves, as sometimes occurs, control the State, are sufficiently powerful to resist control by it. Among the numerous interesting phenomena which impress the foreign observer of American economic life, not the least interesting is the occasional emergence of industrial enterprises which appear to him, and, indeed, to some Americans, to have developed the characteristics, not merely of an economic undertaking, but of a kind of polity. Their rule may be a mild and benevolent paternalism, lavishing rest-rooms, schools, gymnasia, and guarantees for constitutional behaviour on care-free employees; or it may be a harsh and suspicious tyranny. But, whether as amiable as Solon, or as ferocious as Lycurgus, their features are cast in a heroic mould. Their gestures are those of the sovereigns of little commonwealths rather than of mere mundane employers.

American official documents have, on occasion, called attention to the tendency of the bare stem of business to burgeon, in a favourable environment, with almost tropical exuberance, so that it clothes itself with functions that elsewhere are regarded as belonging to political authorities. The corporations controlled by six financial groups, stated the Report of the United States Commission on Industrial Relations some twenty years ago, employ 2,651,684 wage-earners, or 440,000 per group. Some of these companies own, not merely the plant and equipment of industry, but the homes of the workers, the streets through which they pass to work, and the halls in which, if they are allowed to meet, their meetings must be held. They employ private spies and detectives, private police and, sometimes, it appears, private troops, and engage, when they deem it expedient, in private war. While organized themselves, they forbid organization among their employees, and enforce their will by evicting malcontents from their homes, and even, on occasion, by the use of armed force. In such conditions business may continue in its modesty, since its object is money, to describe itself as business; but, in fact, it is a tyranny. "The main objection to the large corporation," remarks Mr. Justice Brandeis, who, as a judge of the Supreme Court, should know the facts, "is that it makes possible—and in many cases makes inevitable—the exercise of industrial absolutism." Property in capital, thus inflated and emancipated, acquires attributes analogous to those of property in land in a feudal society. It carries with it the disposal, in fact, if not in law, of an authority which is quasi-governmental. Its owners possess what would have been called in the ages of darkness a private jurisdiction, and their relations to their dependents, though contractual in form, resemble rather those of ruler and subject than of equal parties to a commercial venture. The liberty which they defend against the encroachments of trade unionism and the State is most properly to be regarded, not as freedom, but as a franchise.

The conventional assertion that inequality is inseparable from liberty is obviously, in such circumstances, unreal and unconvincing; for the existence of the former is a menace to the latter, and the latter is most likely to be secured by curtailing the former. It is true that in England, where three generations of trade unionism and state intervention have done something to tame it, the exercise of economic power is, at ordinary times, less tyrannical than it once was. It still remains, nevertheless, a formidable menace to the freedom of common men. The pressure of such power is felt by the consumer, when he purchases necessaries which, directly or indirectly, are controlled by a monopoly. It is felt in the workshop, where, within the limits set by industrial legislation and collective agreements, the comfort and amenity of the wage-earners' surroundings, the discipline and tone of factory life, the security of employment and methods of promotion, the recruitment and dismissal of workers, the degree to which successive relays of cheap juvenile labour are employed, the opportunity to secure consideration for grievances, depend ultimately upon the policy pursued by a board of directors, who may have little love, indeed, for their shareholders, but who represent, in the last resort, their financial interests, and who, in so far as they are shareholders themselves, are necessarily judges in their own cause.

The effects of such autocracy are even graver in the sphere of economic strategy, which settles the ground upon which these tactical issues are fought out, and, in practice, not infrequently determines their decision before they arise. In such matters as the changes in organization most likely to restore prosperity to an embarrassed industry, and, therefore, to secure a tolerable livelihood to the workers engaged in it; methods of averting or meeting a depression; rationalization, the closing of plants and the concentration of production; the sale of a business on which a whole community depends or its amalgamation with a rival—not to mention the critical field of financial policy, with its possibilities, not merely of watered capital and of the squandering in dividends of resources which should be held as reserves, but of a sensational redistribution of wealth and widespread unemployment as a result of decisions taken by bankers—the diplomacy of business, like that of governments before 1914, is still commonly conducted over the heads of those most affected by it. The interests of the public, as workers and consumers, may receive consideration when these matters are determined; but the normal organization of economic life does not offer reliable guarantee that they will be considered. Nor can it plausibly be asserted that, if they are not, those aggrieved can be certain of any redress.

Power over the public is public power. It does not cease to be public merely because private persons are permitted to buy and sell, own and bequeath it, as they deem most profitable. To retort that its masters are themselves little more than half-conscious instruments, whose decisions register and transmit the impact of forces that they can neither anticipate nor control, though not wholly unveracious, is, nevertheless, superficial. The question is not whether there are economic movements which elude human control, for obviously there are. It is whether the public possesses adequate guarantees that those which are controllable are controlled in the general interest, not in that of a minority. Like the gods of Homer, who were subject themselves to a fate behind the fates, but were not thereby precluded from interfering at their pleasure in the affairs of men, the potentates of the economic world exercise discretion, not, indeed, as to the situation which they will meet, but as to the manner in which they will meet it. They hold the initiative, have such freedom to manoeuvre as circumstances allow, can force an issue or postpone it, and, if open conflict seems inevitable or expedient, can choose, as best suits themselves, the ground where it shall take place.

"Even if socialism were practicable without the destruction of freedom," writes Lord Lothian, "would there be any advantage in converting the whole population into wage or salary earners, directed by the relatively few, also salaried, officials, who by ability, or promotion, or 'pull,' could work their way to the top of the political machine or the permanent bureaucracy? ... Is not that community the best, and, in the widest sense of the word, the most healthy, which has the largest proportion of citizens who have the enterprise, and energy, and initiative, to create new things and new methods for themselves, and not merely to wait to carry out the orders of somebody 'higher up'?" In view of the practice, of some parts, at least, of the business world, the less said about "pull," perhaps, the better. But how true in substance! And how different the liner looks from the saloon-deck and the stoke-hold! And how striking that the conditions which Lord Lothian deplores as a hypothetical danger should be precisely those which ordinary men experience daily as an ever-present fact!

For, in England at any rate, as a glance at the Registrar-General's reports would have sufficed to show him, not only the majority of the population, but the great majority, are to-day "wage or salary earners," who, for quite a long time, have been "directed by the relatively few," and who, if they did not "wait to carry out the orders of somebody higher up," would be sent about their business with surprising promptitude. Unless Lord Lothian proposes to abolish, not only a particular political doctrine, but banks, railways, coal-mines and cotton-mills, the question is not whether orders shall be given, but who shall give them; whether there shall be guarantees that they are given in the general interest; and whether those to whom they are given shall have a reasonable security that, when their welfare is at stake, their views will receive an unbiased consideration.

Freedom may be, as he insists, more important than comfort. But is a miner, who is not subject to a bureaucracy, or at least, to a bureaucracy of the kind which alarms Lord Lothian, conspicuously more free than a teacher, who is? If a man eats bread made of flour produced to the extent of forty per cent by two milling combines and meat supplied by an international meat trust, and lives in a house built of materials of which twenty-five per cent are controlled by a ring, and buys his tobacco from one amalgamation, and his matches from another, while his wife's sewing-thread is provided by a third, which has added eight millionaires to the national roll of honour in the last twenty years, is he free as a consumer? Is he free as a worker, if he is liable to have his piece-rates cut at the discretion of his employer, and, on expressing his annoyance, to be dismissed as an agitator, and to be thrown on the scrap-heap without warning because his employer has decided to shut down a plant, or bankers to restrict credit, and to be told, when he points out that the industry on which his livelihood depends is being injured by mismanagement, that his job is to work, and that the management in question will do his thinking for him? And if, in such circumstances, he is but partially free as a consumer and a worker, is not his freedom as a citizen itself also partial, rather than, as Lord Lothian would desire, unqualified and complete?

Lord Lothian is misled as to liberty, because he has omitted to consider the bearing upon it of another phenomenon, the phenomenon of inequality. The truth is that, when the economic sales are so unevenly weighted, to interpret liberty as a political principle, which belongs to one world, the world of politics and government, while equality belongs—if, indeed, it belongs anywhere—to another world, the world of economic affairs, is to do violence to realities. Governments, it is true, exercise powers of a great and special kind, and freedom requires that they should be held strictly to account. But the administration of things is not easily distinguished, under modern conditions of mass organization, from the control of persons, and both are in the hands, to some not inconsiderable degree, of the minority who move the levers of the economic mechanism. The truth of the matter is put by Professor Pollard in his admirable study, *The Evolution of Parliament*. "There is only one solution," he writes, "of the problem of liberty, and it lies in equality. . . . Men vary in physical strength; but so far as their social relations go that inequality has been abolished. . . . Yet there must have been a period in social evolution when this refusal to permit the strong man to do what he liked with his own physical strength seemed, at least to the strong, an outrageous interference with personal liberty. . . . There is, in fact, no more reason why a man should be allowed to use his wealth or his brain than his physical strength as he likes. . . . The liberty of the weak depends upon the restraint of the strong, that of the poor upon the restraint of the rich, and that of the simpler-minded upon the restraint of the sharper. Every man should have this liberty and no more, to do unto others as he would that they should do unto him; upon that common foundation rest liberty, equality, and morality."

55 LIBERTY AND LEGISLATION
BERNARD BOSANQUET
(1848-1923)

Among the antagonistic ideas of human progress which confront one another at the present time, there is no more remarkable pair of seeming opposites than the demand for completer liberty and the desire for more thorough-going legislation.

Both of these aspirations appear characteristic of our era; while by one party to the controversy at least, the two tendencies are regarded as absolutely incompatible with each other. It is curious that those who represent the opposition in its most ultimate form, the Anarchist and the Socialist respectively, have some inkling that there may be a meeting of the extremes; but Stuart Mill and Fitzjames Stephen, or Mr. Auberon Herbert and Sir John Lubbock must be regarded as absolute irreconcilables.

I want to consider with you to-day this very astonishing divergence of opinion, in order to ascertain, if we can, the real direction of the movement which can give rise to such very different estimates. For no one is so wholly a pessimist as to entertain an aspiration which he admits to be fundamentally in contradiction with the whole set and tide of human endeavour. What a man believes to be right, that he believes, in one way or another, at bottom or in the long run, to be tending to come to pass.

And to clear the issue, I would say that I am, as far as at all possible, using the word liberty in its every-day acceptation, that of freedom from felt coercion, and power to do what you please. I do not desire to cut the knot by referring to the more philosophical idea of freedom as submission to a noble law. I want to begin by using those notions of liberty and coercion which unquestionably do hold a place in our daily judgments respecting politics and society. And for that purpose I will take them as I find them; as they meet us from day to day in the great practical and theoretical controversy between those who with Mr. Spencer think all politics an evil, and those who, like most of ourselves, assent with more or less conviction to the overwhelming neces-

SOURCE: Originally a public address delivered at South Place Chapel, Finsbury. Reprinted here from the author's book *The Civilization of Christendom* (London, 1893), pp. 358–83. Compare with selections 16 and 58.

sity which produces year by year a larger and larger statute book. If, however, I should be driven by the sheer force of logical continuity to appeal before I close to a somewhat loftier standard of liberty, it will be only because we shall have found, that the higher liberty is rooted in the lower, and that the lower must necessarily grow upwards into the higher.

Now philosophers are often accused of not taking a side. It is their business to reconcile and explain; and they often cause perplexity by seeming to pronounce that if A is right from one point of view, B is right from another and C from a third, and so on through the whole alphabet. To-day, however, though I cannot but try to reconcile and explain, yet I hope very distinctly to take a side. For I hold that the view of the anti-governmental theorist is not merely an imperfect view, but is a misapprehension of an imperfect view. I do not consider that it is the true balance or counterpart to the convictions of those who believe in social authority. I do not acknowledge that it represents the great and valuable principles of effective individual development, of spontaneity, of robustness, of originality. It would be an imperfect conception to suppose that the largest possible liberty of individual action was the only desirable object and standard of life. Nobility and order would be elements neglected by such an ideal. But the view that social compulsion is bad in principle is not even this demand for liberty, but is a misapprehension of this demand. It is not one remove, but two removes from truth. It not merely aims at an imperfect ideal of freedom, but points the wrong road to this imperfect ideal. Every illusion is founded on a fact, but the illusion may consist in ascribing the fact to conditions precisely the reverse of those which really produce it. This I believe to be the case with the facts on which the anti-governmental theorists base their opinions.

What, in the first place, are these facts? I suppose they are such as the following:—

We expect in modern life, and in some measure we obtain, a progressively greater range and choice of action, and a decrease of certain kinds of restriction to which our forefathers submitted. We should not stand having the fashion of our dress, or our power of travelling about, or our religion, or the hour by which we must be indoors in the evening, prescribed for us by law. And in as far as it is true that most of our fellow-citizens can practically get no choice or variety in their lives, we say that this is a burning shame, and that our system is so far a failure. We will not submit to any difference being made by the general law between one man and another, and we are rapidly coming to object to a difference being made between the rights of men and women.

It is on such facts and feelings as these that I suppose the case against governmental interference must be rested, in so far as it is not merely an inference from the non-moral nature of acts done under direct coercion, to which I have to refer again.

Is it a right interpretation of such facts and feelings as I have mentioned to say that the modern movement is, at bottom, against compulsion and towards *merely* voluntary association?

I answer No; it is not a right interpretation; it is a wrong one. People who hold these views are sometimes called Individualists; and no doubt they mean to be Individualists; but they *are* nothing of the kind. They are pretty well such friends to the individual as the British Admiral was to the British engineer who was alleged to be serving under coercion in a Peruvian man-of-war. The Admiral, so the story goes, let fly a Whitehead torpedo at the Peruvian ship, and if he had hit it the oppressed individual would have been liberated from his oppressors by going to the bottom along with them.

Theorists of this type do not know what the individual is, and in trying to free him from tyranny they are dismembering him. But if they are wrong in maintaining that the true progress of modern society is to cut the cords of social authority, what are we to say about the phenomena on which they must rely, and which I have admitted to be real and to be welcome? Do not these phenomena show an increase of liberty, and do they not therefore show a decrease of restriction?

I reply that they do show an increase of liberty, but they do not show a decrease of restriction. An increase of one quantity involves a decrease of another only when the total of the two quantities taken together is limited. And this wholly false assumption is at the root of the entirely erroneous view, which in my judgment Mr. Auberon Herbert—I mention his name in particular, because his trumpet gives no uncertain sound—which Mr. Auberon Herbert takes with regard to life. If life could be compared to a limited space, like a box, and liberty and compulsion could be compared to sets of white and black balls to be put into it, then no doubt the more liberty, the less compulsion, and *vice versâ*. But so much depends upon your metaphor! Just put the case that life could better be compared to a tree, that liberty might then be expressed as the access of the leaves to light and air, and restriction or compulsion might be typified by the strong fixtures of the stem and branches. Then it is pretty plain that the more compulsion, the more liberty, and *vice versâ*. Try again: let life be like a great city, let its liberty correspond to the variety, number, and area of the rooms, and its element of compulsion to the walls of the buildings. Here again it would seem that liberty and compulsion must increase together.

It is not the fact, then, that increased liberty means decreased restriction. But it does mean some peculiarity in the character of restriction which distinguishes modern life from the life of our forefathers, and of barbarous or savage peoples. It is now a commonplace that the life of savages, instead of being as free as the bird in the air, is hedged in on every side with idle belief and groundless prohibition. What is it that in contrast with this cramped and fettered condition constitutes the freedom of modern life?

The quality of freedom does not depend on the great or small amount of social compulsion and fixed enactment, but on two characteristics which belong to life as a whole; and these are:—

First, its comprehensiveness, and secondly, its rationality.

1. In the first place, then, the range of possible actions presented to the individual for his choice becomes, as society develops, more and more comprehensive. His liberty, therefore, in the common straight-forward sense of doing what he pleases, becomes greater and greater. And the yearly Acts of Parliament, forming a thick volume, to which for the purpose of our argument, we ought in strictness to add all by-laws passed and orders made under Parliamentary powers, do not militate against this liberty, but are the conditions of its existence.

Consider, for example, the great province of legal conveyance and contract, which pervades all the relations of civilized life. The form of a contract or a will is an arbitrary matter. It is of no real importance what are the conditions of validity imposed upon such acts, so long as they are easily fulfilled and definitely recognisable. So that by the *fiat* of a general authority, which settles once for all what the conditions of these acts are to be, the facility of transacting business is enormously increased. A compulsory enactment is here the very organ of an enlarged liberty. It is worth while to mention the special example of compulsory registration conferring an absolute title to land, a measure of coercion so drastic that we have hitherto been afraid to enact it, and yet it would at one blow make the transfer of land a comparatively simple matter, and therefore open up far greater possibilities in the way of buying and selling real property. This is an exceedingly striking example of the relation, which I am trying to illustrate, between liberty and compulsion.

And so it is throughout. Everything that you can do involves a number of things that you cannot do, and the restrictions of a larger life are more numerous than the restrictions of a smaller life, just as the branches of a great tree are more numerous than those of a herb or bush.

If we go through all the great departments of legislation, we shall find the same thing. Everywhere the coercive restrictions are simply conditions and results of immense extensions of life, immense enlargements of the range of possible action. Our manufacturing system, our commercial system, our railway system, our educational system, must all of them have a definite shape sanctioned by the community. The practical question, whether we are over-

or under-legislating, touches only a small proportion of the enactments relating to these great departments of life. It is quite impossible that completely new outgrowths of civilisation or complete transformations of our mode of doing business should fail to be registered under a social sanction. How could railways be made without Acts of Parliament or worked without by-laws? And how could parties of working men, or indeed of professional men or women, go to Venice or to Florence in the Easter holidays without railways? Is it not plain that authority and liberty are here again inseparably interwoven?

But, secondly, there is something further; modern life is becoming not only more comprehensive, but more rational. There is a change in the kind of restrictions which we expect and are willing to put up with. It used to be said, for example, that the tendency of modern law was from status to contract, that is from a classification of persons determined beforehand by the legal system, according to birth, to arrangements or contracts made by themselves at pleasure, and only ratified by the community. Granting that this were so, as to a great extent it certainly has been, it is only a change, though a most important one, in the *kind* of compulsion, for all contracts rest, as all status rests, on legal compulsion—and then it is perhaps doubtful whether change is so exclusively in this direction as has been thought.

I do not myself believe that it is possible to lay down any single definite direction which must be taken by the course of legislative enactment as time goes on. And by giving my reason for not believing it possible, I shall explain, so far as I can see how to explain, the actual positive process by which the nature of compulsion comes to be modified.

Human life—this seems to me to be the central truth upon this question—is a thing which at any given moment has a certain shape and certain properties. The shape and properties vary in the most subtle way, and grow more and more complex; but they are always there, and can be gradually learnt by reason and experience. Now the shape of life is the outward expression of its reasonableness or equilibrium—the arrangement of its parts and of their functions, so that they work. And when I say that compulsion changes on the whole by gaining in rationality, I mean that it becomes more and more identified with the support and maintenance of this shape or balance of life. The beauty of a tree depends very largely on the remarkable ingenuity with which its branches keep out of one another's way. Social compulsion gains the same sort of merit as this, in as far as it supports the figure and balance of the social organism, without causing its parts to thwart or impede one another.

Compare it for a moment to a prop supporting a tree, or to the timbers of a house—as it is something done on purpose, and not unconscious like the tree's own growth. Now a prop, or a bit of scaffolding, or a timber in a house, is reasonably arranged when it is in the right place according to the shape and function of the thing it has to support. You may put a stout pole under the branch of a tree as a prop, and it will be of use and do no harm. But if you tie even a slender stick across the leading shoot you will ruin your tree for ever; and in the same way in building a house you do not put your beams across the windows or through the chimneys, but you put them out of the way.

This illustrates what I mean by compulsion becoming reasonable. I mean that it becomes adapted in detail to the particular definite shape and balance of civilized life, so as to support it, and not interfere with it. And then it is not felt as compulsion. For example, we say, quite truly, that nowadays Government ought not to interfere with private opinion or with free discussion about politics and religion. This is quite agreed upon by every one worth mentioning, but the reason is apt to be misunderstood. It is not that Government does not care about our opinions, nor that Government has no right to touch our opinions; it is that reasonable opinion is a thing of a particular kind, and cannot be beneficially affected by direct coercion or by interfering with discussion. It is like a flower; you cannot make it grow right by pulling it about. We have found this out by very sad experience, and now we can see it by common sense; and so it has become a practical rule that Government is not to interfere directly with free discussion and with individual opinion. But if you coupled this practical rule with a general principle, and said that Government has nothing to do with the reasonableness and morality of its citizens, then that is simple nonsense. The truth of the matter is that the public authority, like any individual, must learn to go to work in the right way; and the right way is only learnt by experience of the needs and functions of society.

And in fact, if you say that the public authority is to do nothing in any way interfering with opinion and religious discussion, that is simply not true. Government ought to do a great deal, and does a great deal, for the formation of rational opinion and a moral temper on the part of individuals. It interferes by public education and the means of education, by putting its special information at the disposal of public opinion—the English blue books are an unequalled repository of social and economical knowledge only obtained through compulsory powers—and again by the definite line which the public authority is forced to take on questions of social and moral importance, and by forcibly removing temptation where this can be done. We think, once more, that you ought not to establish any Church. No not *now,* because there is no Church that represents the nation—but it was not always wrong to establish a Church; if the nation wanted one it had a right to have one, and if it does not want one it has a right not to have one, that is all, as it seems to me, that can be said in general about it. All these, and I might add the question of interference with trade, are matters in which we have gradually and painfully learnt how, in what particular way, to interfere without doing harm. We interfere now with trade rather by Factory Acts than by Protection, as the needs of the community take a shape which demands this kind of interference. But there is no general moral principle which condemns protection; there is not even any general moral principle which condemns taxing the community for the benefit of a class; on the contrary, we are at present very largely doing so, and whether wisely or not depends I think entirely on how the administration is performed. The future of the Poor Law is quite obscure. All must depend on the effect with which it is found to work. General principles cannot decide such a question beforehand, because you cannot tell beforehand under *what* general principle the concrete result may practically come. You have to watch and observe and mould your law so as while preventing the last results of destitution, not to break the springs of character. We are not indeed likely, I suppose, ever again to tax the whole community for the benefit of a *richer* class; that is because our concrete idea of the purpose and working of the community has changed in detail, and we do not now believe in any heaven-born governors, whom it is a privilege to the community to support.

Thus, then, I repeat, liberty, in the plainest and simplest sense of the word, does not depend on the absence of legislation, but on the comprehensiveness and reasonableness of life. The coercive power of England or of the United States of America, which, with all their faults, are the two freest countries that the world has ever seen, is such as would have broken the most tyrannical despotisms of the ancient world as a Nasmyth hammer crushes a walnut shell. But the amount of this coercive power no more interferes with our liberty than the strength of your floor interferes with the serviceableness of your house. It is not weakness of the public power, but its adaptation on which freedom depends. What we have therefore to do, is not to trouble ourselves about the more or less of legislative interference; but, living out our lives in some particular honest endeavour, and making those general arrangements which spring out of obvious felt necessities, to call in the social power whenever and wherever good cannot be done without it, and can be done with its help. And we must remmber that by the infinite subtlety of modern organization the social power is becoming in practice what it always has been in theory, simply the expression of ourselves. Where does the social power reside? Who are its agents? Where does its responsibility rest? On the House of Commons and the County Council only? Oh no! not at all. Show me a man or woman in the full enjoyment of physical and intellectual capacities, who is in no sense an agent of the social power, and I will show you a man or woman who is not doing his or her duty. There is no longer a class of governors and a class of governed. I am not referring merely to the parliamentary and municipal franchise, important as are the duties which these lay upon us. I am referring partly to that detailed subdivision of authority and function by which the power and right of the community are in every district in the hands of a great army of officials, both paid and unpaid, and to a great extent of ourselves, and partly, and more especially, to the great force of public opinion, which is all that gives value or reasonableness to law. Every one who forms a clear and honest judgment on matters that concern him and his neighbours is putting into operation the social power.

Thus mere actual liberty, variety of possible action, is in no way opposed to extensive social coercion. Still less are strength and originality of character endangered by legislation. There is a commonplace set of fallacies, by which the great qualities of human nature are confused with their caricatures: character with perversity, originality with eccentricity, knowledge of the world with experience of its seamy side. It is not true that a laissez-faire society makes original characters, or that a weak social pressure permits strength of mind to develop. Not only is Anarchic Individualism incompatible with liberty, but it is hopelessly opposed to that Individualism which alone is an ethical good—intellectual independence and moral robustness.

The fact is, that such terms as Individualism or Socialism are not in any way fitted to designate moral ideals, unless they are taken in a sense wholly independent of reference to liberty and legislation. There is no necessary connection between the moral strength of the Individual and the so-called Individualism of legal and economical machinery; nor is there any justification for confusing legislative collectivism, under the name of Socialism, with that recognition of the social end which is the basis of *all* possible moral views of Society. I have no doubt that the moral fervour, both of Individualists and of Socialists, arises in great measure from this elementary confusion, by which a doctrinaire theory about legal or economical machinery takes the place of devotion to individual character or to the social purpose. What that purpose is, and how to be fulfilled, *can be learnt only in the concrete;* and it is our task, without prejudices for abstract titles, to labour at giving a reasonable shape to the innumerable details of the great building of life.

56 DEMOCRACY, POLITICS, AND EDUCATION
JOHN DEWEY (1859-1952)

... Democracy is much broader than a special political form, a method of conducting government, of making laws and carrying on governmental administration by means of popular suffrage and elected officers. It is that, of course. But it is something broader and deeper than that. The political and governmental phase of democracy is a means, the best means so far found, for realizing ends that lie in the wide domain of human relationships and the development of human personality. It is, as we often say, though perhaps without appreciating all that is involved in the saying, a way of life, social and individual. The key-note of democracy as a way of life may be expressed, it seems to me, as the necessity for the participation of every mature human being in formation of the values that regulate the living of men together: which is necessary from the standpoint of both the general social welfare and the full development of human beings as individuals.

Universal suffrage, recurring elections, responsibility of those who are in political power to the voters, and the other factors of democratic government are means that have been found expedient for realizing democracy as the truly human way of living. They are not a final end and a final value. They are to be judged on the basis of their contribution to the end. It is a form of idolatry to erect means into the end which they serve. Democratic political forms are simply the best means that human wit has devised up to a special time in history. But they rest back upon the idea that no man or limited set of men is wise enough or good enough to rule others without their consent; the positive meaning of this statement is that all those who are affected by social institutions must have a share in producing and managing them. The two facts that each one is influenced in what he does and enjoys and in what he becomes by the institutions under which he lives, and that therefore he shall have, in a democracy, a voice in shaping them, are the passive and active sides of the same fact.

SOURCE: Reprinted (in part) from *School and Society,* April 3, 1937, by permission of The Society for the Advancement of Education, Inc. The title of this selection has been supplied by the editors. Compare with selections 41, 52, 53, and 58.

The development of political democracy came about through substitution of the method of mutual consultation and voluntary agreement for the method of subordination of the many to the few enforced from above. Social arrangements which involve fixed subordination are maintained by coercion. The coercion need not be physical. There have existed, for short periods, benevolent despotisms. But coercion of some sort there has been; perhaps economic, certainly psychological and moral. The very fact of exclusion from participation is a subtle form of suppression. It gives individuals no opportunity to reflect and decide upon what is good for them. Others who are supposed to be wiser and who in any case have more power decide the question for them and also decide the methods and means by which subjects may arrive at the enjoyment of what is good for them. This form of coercion and suppression is more subtle and more effective than is overt intimidation and restraint. When it is habitual and embodied in social institutions, it seems the normal and natural state of affairs. The mass usually become unaware that they have a claim to a development of their own powers. Their experience is so restricted that they are not conscious of restriction. It is part of the democratic conception that they as individuals are not the only sufferers, but that the whole social body is deprived of the potential resources that should be at its service. The individuals of the submerged mass may not be very wise. But there is one thing they are wiser about than anybody else can be, and that is where the shoe pinches, the troubles they suffer from.

The foundation of democracy is faith in the capacities of human nature; faith in human intelligence and in the power of pooled and cooperative experience. It is not belief that these things are complete but that if given a show they will grow and be able to generate progressively the knowledge and wisdom needed to guide collective action. Every autocratic and authoritarian scheme of social action rests on a belief that the needed intelligence is confined to a superior few, who because of inherent natural gifts are endowed with the ability and the right to control the conduct of others; laying down principles and rules and directing the ways in which they are carried out. It would be foolish to deny that much can be said for this point of view. It is that which controlled human relations in social groups for much the greater part of human history. The democratic faith has emerged very, very recently in the history of mankind. Even where democracies now exist, men's minds and feelings are still permeated with ideas about leadership imposed from above, ideas that developed in the long early history of mankind. After democratic political institutions were nominally established, beliefs and ways of looking at life and of acting that originated when men and women were externally controlled and subjected to arbitrary power, persisted in the family, the church, business and the school, and experience shows that as long as they persist there, political democracy is not secure.

Belief in equality is an element of the democratic credo. It is not, however, belief in equality of natural endowments. Those who proclaimed the idea of equality did not suppose they were enunciating a psychological doctrine, but a legal and political one. All individuals are entitled to equality of treatment by law and in its administration. Each one is affected equally in quality if not in quantity by the institutions under which he lives and has an equal right to express his judgment, although the weight of his judgment may not be equal in amount when it enters into the pooled result to that of others. In short, each one is equally an individual and entitled to equal opportunity of development of his own capacities, be they large or small in range. Moreover, each has needs of his own, as significant to him as those of others are to them. The very fact of natural and psychological inequality is all the more reason for establishment by law of equality of opportunity, since otherwise the former becomes a means of oppression of the less gifted.

While what we call intelligence be distributed in unequal amounts, it is the democratic faith that it is sufficiently general so that each individual has something to contribute, whose value can be assessed only as enters into the final pooled intelligence constituted by the contributions of all. Every authoritarian scheme, on the contrary, assumes that its value may be assessed by some *prior* principle, if not of family and birth or race and color or possession of material wealth, then by the position and rank a person occupies in the existing social scheme. The democratic faith in equality is the faith that each individual shall have the chance and opportunity to contribute whatever he is capable of contributing and that the value of his contribution be decided by its place and function in the organized total of similar contributions, not on the basis of prior status of any kind whatever.

I have emphasized in what precedes the importance of the effective release of intelligence in connection with personal experience in the democratic way of living. I have done so purposely because democracy is so often and so naturally associated in our minds with freedom of *action,* forgetting the importance of freed intelligence which is necessary to direct and to warrant freedom of action. Unless freedom of individual action has intelligence and informed conviction back of it, its manifestation is almost sure to result in confusion and disorder. The democratic idea of freedom is not the right of each individual to *do* as he pleases, even if it be qualified by adding "provided he does not interfere with the same freedom on the part of others." While the idea is not always, not often enough, expressed in words, the basic freedom is that of freedom of *mind* and of whatever degree of freedom of action and experience is necessary to produce freedom of intelligence. The modes of freedom guaranteed in the Bill of Rights are all of this nature: Freedom of belief and conscience, of expression of opinion, of assembly for discussion and conference, of the press as an organ of communication. They are guaranteed because without them individuals are not free to develop and society is deprived of what they might contribute.

... There is some kind of government, of control, wherever affairs that concern a number of persons who act together are engaged in. It is a superficial view that holds government is located in Washington and Albany. There is government in the family, in business, in the church, in every social group. There are regulations, due to custom if not to enactment, that settle how individuals in a group act in connection with one another.

It is a disputed question of theory and practice just how far a democratic political government should go in control of the conditions of action within special groups. At the present time, for example, there are those who think the federal and state governments leave too much freedom of independent action to industrial and financial groups, and there are others who think the government is going altogether too far at the present time. I do not need to discuss this phase of the problem, much less to try to settle it. But it must be pointed out that if the methods of regulation and administration in vogue in the conduct of secondary social groups are non-democratic, whether directly or indirectly or both, there is bound to be an unfavorable reaction back into the habits of feeling, thought and action of citizenship in the broadest sense of that word. The way in which any organized social interest is controlled necessarily plays an important part in forming the dispositions and tastes, the attitudes, interests, purposes and desires, of those engaged in carrying on the activities of the group. For illustration, I do not need to do more than point to the moral, emotional and intellectual effect upon both employers and laborers of the existing industrial system. Just what the effects specifically are is a matter about which we know very little. But I suppose that every one who reflects upon the subject admits that it is impossible that the ways in which activities are carried on for the greater part of the waking hours of the day; and the way in which the share of individuals are involved in the management of affairs in such a matter as gaining a livelihood and attaining material and social security, can not be a highly important factor in shaping personal dispositions; in short, forming character and intelligence.

In the broad and final sense all institutions are educational in the sense that they operate to form the attitudes, dispositions, abilities and disabilities that constitute a concrete personality. The principle applies with special force to the school. For it is the main business of the family and the school to influence directly the formation and growth of attitudes and dispositions, emotional, intellectual and moral. Whether this educative process is carried on in a predominantly democratic or non-democratic way becomes, therefore, a question of transcendent importance not only for education itself but for its final effect upon all the interests and activities of a society that is committed to the democratic way of life. Hence, if the general tenor of what I have said about the democratic ideal and method is anywhere near the truth, it must be said that the democratic principle requires that every teacher should have some regular and organic way in which he can, directly or through representatives democratically chosen, participate in the formation of the controlling aims, methods and materials of the school of which he is a part. . . .

. . . Absence of participation tends to produce lack of interest and concern on the part of those shut out. The result is a corresponding lack of effective responsibility. Automatically and unconsciously, if not consciously, the feeling develops, "This is none of our affair; it is the business of those at the top; let that particular set of Georges do what needs to do done." The countries in which autocratic government prevails are just those in which there is least public spirit and the greatest indifference to matters of general as distinct from personal concern. Can we expect a different kind of psychology to actuate teachers? Where there is little power, there is correspondingly little sense of positive responsibility. It is enough to do what one is told to do sufficiently well to escape flagrant unfavorable notice. About larger matters, a spirit of passivity is engendered. In some cases, indifference passes into evasion of duties when not directly under the eye of a supervisor; in other cases, a carping, rebellious spirit is engendered. A sort of game is instituted between teacher and supervisor like that which went on in the old-fashioned schools between teacher and pupil. Other teachers pass on, perhaps unconsciously, what they feel to be arbitrary treatment received by them to their pupils.

The argument that teachers are not prepared to assume the responsibility of participation deserves attention, with its accompanying belief that natural selection has operated to put those best prepared to carry the load in the positions of authority. Whatever the truth in this contention, it still is also true that incapacity to assume the responsibilities involved in having a voice in shaping policies is bred and increased by conditions in which that responsibility is denied. I suppose there has never been an autocrat, big or little, who did not justify his conduct on the ground of the unfitness of his subjects to take part in government. I would not compare administrators to political autocrats. Upon the whole, what exists in the schools is more a matter of habit and custom than it is of any deliberate autocracy. But, as was said earlier, habitual exclusion has the effect of reducing a sense of responsibility for what is done and its consequences. What the argument for democracy implies is that the best way to produce initiative and constructive power is to exercise it. Power, as well as interest, comes by use and practice. Moreover, the argument from incapacity proves too much. If it is so great as to be a permanent bar, then teachers can not be expected to have the intelligence and skill that are necessary to execute the directions given them. The delicate and difficult task of developing character and good judgment in the young needs every stimulus and inspiration possible. It is impossible that the work should not be better done when teachers have that understanding of what they are doing that comes from having shared in forming its guiding ideas. . . .

The fundamental beliefs and practices of democracy are now challenged as they never have been before. In some nations they are more than challenged. They are ruthlessly and systematically destroyed. Everywhere there are waves of criticism and doubt as to whether democracy can meet pressing problems of order and security. The causes for the destruction of political democracy in countries where it was nominally established are complex. But of one thing I think we may be sure. Wherever it has fallen it was too exclusively political in nature. It had not become part of the bone and blood of the people in daily conduct of its life. Democratic forms were limited to Parliament, elections and combats between parties. What is happening proves conclusively, I think, that unless democratic habits of thought and action are part of the fiber of a people, political democracy is insecure. It can not stand in isolation. It must be buttressed by the presence of democratic methods in all social relationships. The relations that exist in educational institutions are second only in importance in this respect to those which exist in industry and business, perhaps not even to them.

I recur then to the idea that the particular question discussed is one phase of a wide and deep problem. I can think of nothing so important in this country at present as a rethinking of the whole problem of democracy and its implications. Neither the rethinking nor the action it should produce can be brought into being in a day or year. The democratic idea itself demands that the thinking and activity proceed cooperatively. . . .

57 REMARKS AT THE PEACE BANQUET
WILLIAM JAMES (1842-1910)

I am only a philosopher, and there is only one thing that a philosopher can be relied on to do, and that is, to contradict other philosophers. In ancient times philosophers defined man as the rational animal; and philosophers since then have always found much more to say about the rational than about the animal part of the definition. But looked at candidly, reason bears about the same proportion to the rest of human nature that we in this hall bear to the rest of America, Europe, Asia, Africa and Polynesia. Reason is one of the very feeblest of nature's forces, if you take it at only one spot and moment. It is only in the very long run that its effects become perceptible. Reason assumes to settle things by weighing them against each other without prejudice, partiality or excitement; but what affairs in the concrete are settled by is, and always will be, just prejudices, partialities, cupidities and excitements. Appealing to reason as we do, we are in a sort of forlorn-hope situation, like a small sand-bank in the midst of a hungry sea ready to wash it out of existence. But sand-banks grow when the conditions favor; and weak as reason is, it has this unique advantage over its antagonists that its activity never lets up and that it presses always in one direction, while men's prejudices vary, their passions ebb and flow, and their excitements are intermittent. Our sand-bank, I absolutely believe, is bound to grow. Bit by bit it will get dyked and breakwatered. But sitting as we do in this warm room, with music and lights and smiling faces, it is easy to get too sanguine about our task; and since I am called to speak, I feel as if it might not be out of place to say a word about the strength of our enemy.

Our permanent enemy is the rooted bellicosity of human nature. Man, biologically considered, and whatever else he may be into the bargain, is the most formidable of all beasts of prey, and, indeed, the only one that preys systematically on his own species. We are once for all adapted to the military

SOURCE: Published in the Official Report of the Universal Peace Congress, held in Boston in 1904, and in the *Atlantic Monthly,* December, 1904. Reprinted here from James's *Memories and Studies* (New York: Longmans, Green, and Co., 1911), prepared for the press by the author's son, Henry James, Jr. Compare with selections 1 and 3.

status. A millennium of peace would not breed the fighting disposition out of our bone and marrow, and a function so ingrained and vital will never consent to die without resistance, and will always find impassioned apologists and idealizers.

Not only men born to be soldiers, but noncombatants by trade and nature, historians in their studies, and clergymen in their pulpits, have been war's idealizers. They have talked of war as of God's court of justice. And, indeed, if we think how many things beside the frontiers of states the wars of history have decided, we must feel some respectful awe, in spite of all the horrors. Our actual civilization, good and bad alike, has had past wars for its determining condition. Great mindedness among the tribes of men has always meant the will to prevail, and all the more so if prevailing included slaughtering and being slaughtered. Rome, Paris, England, Brandenburg, Piedmont,—possibly soon Japan,—along with their arms have their traits of character and habits of thought prevail among their conquered neighbors. The blessings we actually enjoy, such as they are, have grown up in the shadow of the wars of antiquity. The various ideals were backed by fighting wills, and when neither would give way, the God of battles had to be the arbiter. A shallow view this, truly; for who can say what might have prevailed if man had ever been a reasoning and not a fighting animal? Like dead men, dead causes tell no tales, and the ideals that went under in the past, along with all the tribes that represented them, find to-day no recorder, no explainer, no defender.

But apart from theoretic defenders, and apart from every soldierly individual straining at the leash and clamoring for opportunity, war has an omnipotent support in the form of our imagination. Man lives *by* habits indeed, but what he lives *for* is thrills and excitements. The only relief from habit's tediousness is periodical excitement. From time immemorial wars have been, especially for non-combatants, the supremely thrilling excitement. Heavy and dragging at its end, at its outset every war means an explosion of imaginative energy. The dams of routine burst, and boundless prospects open. The remotest spectators share the fascination of that awful struggle now in process on the confines of the world. There is not a man in this room, I suppose, who doesn't buy both an evening and a morning paper, and first of all pounce on the war column.

A deadly listlessness would come over most men's imagination of the future if they could seriously be brought to believe that never again *in sæcula sæculorum* would a war trouble human history. In such a stagnant summer afternoon of a world, where would be the zest or interest?

This is the constitution of human nature which we have to work against. The plain truth is that people *want* war. They want it anyhow; for itself, and apart from each and every possible consequence. It is the final bouquet of life's fireworks. The born soldiers want it hot and actual. The non-combatants want it in the background, and always as an open possibility, to feed imagination on and keep excitement going. Its clerical and historical defenders fool themselves when they talk as they do about it. What moves them is not the blessings it has won for us, but a vague religious exaltation. War is human nature at its uttermost. We are here to do our uttermost. It is a sacrament. Society would rot without the mystical blood-payment.

We do ill, I think, therefore, to talk much of universal peace or of a general disarmament. We must go in for preventive medicine, not for radical cure. We must cheat our foe, circumvent him in detail, not try to change his nature. In one respect war is like love, though in no other. Both leave us intervals of rest; and in the intervals life goes on perfectly well without them, though the imagination still dallies with their possibility. Equally insane when once aroused and under headway, whether they shall be aroused or not depends on accidental circumstances. How are old maids and old bachelors made? Not by deliberate vows of celibacy, but by sliding on from year to year with no sufficient matrimonial provocation. So of the nations with their wars. Let the general possibility of war be left open, in Heaven's name, for the imagination to dally with. Let the soldiers dream of killing, as the old maids dream of marrying.

But organize in every conceivable way the practical machinery for making each successive chance of war abortive. Put peace men in power; educate the editors and statesmen to responsibility. How beautifully did their trained responsibility in England make the Venezuela incident abortive! Seize every pretext, however small, for arbitration methods, and multiply the precedents; foster rival excitements, and invent new outlets for heroic energy; and from one generation to another the chances are that irritation will grow less acute and states of strain less dangerous among the nations. Armies and navies will continue, of course, and fire the minds of populations with their potentialities of greatness. But their officers will find that somehow or other, with no deliberate intention on any one's part, each successive "incident" has managed to evaporate and to lead nowhere, and that the thought of what might have been remains their only consolation.

The last weak runnings of the war spirit will be "punitive expeditions." A country that turns its arms only against uncivilized foes is, I think, wrongly taunted as degenerate. Of course it has ceased to be heroic in the old grand style. But I verily believe that this is because it now sees something better. It has a conscience. It will still perpetrate peccadillos. But it is afraid, afraid in the good sense, to engage in absolute crimes against civilization.

58 FALLACIES IN POLITICAL THINKING

C. D. BROAD (1887-1971)

I want to discuss and illustrate . . . certain fallacies which we are all very liable to commit in our thinking about political and social questions. Perhaps "thinking" is rather too high-sounding a name to attach to the mental processes which lie behind most political talk. It is at any rate thinking of a very low grade, for a considerable proportion of such discussion in Press and Parliament and private conversation hardly rises above the intellectual level of disputes between boys at a preparatory school.

The first fallacy which I will consider is this. There is a very natural tendency for a person to base his judgments about present trends and future prospects on the quite recent history of a quite small part of the world, in particular on what has happened in his own country during his own and perhaps his parents' lifetime. Now the features which he notices in this restricted segment of space-time, and which he makes the basis of his political and social judgments, may depend on a concatenation of circumstances which have seldom occurred before, are unlikely to happen again, and perhaps never existed outside a small area. This may well lead to an unjustified optimism or an equally unjustified pessimism, and in any case to ill-founded judgments.

. . . Consider an example of this fallacy which is common both to Americans and Englishmen. This is the very usual belief that what we know as "democracy" is a suitable article for export and a form of government which all and sundry could and should adopt. For my part I prefer to avoid the word "democracy" altogether, for it has become little more than an emotive noise with the minimum of cognitive meaning. What in practice it means for us is roughly this. It means that legislation and administration are subject to the control of a representative assembly, chosen at fairly frequent intervals by almost universal suffrage exercised by an electorate organized into two nearly

SOURCE: From "Some Common Fallacies in Political Thinking," an essay that originally appeared in *Philosophy,* vol. XXV (April 1950), and was reprinted in Professor Broad's *Religion, Philosophy and Psychical Research* (1953). Reprinted by permission of the author, the Royal Institute of Philosophy, and Routledge & Kegan Paul Ltd., London.

equal political parties. It is assumed that the electors record their votes and that the representatives conduct their discussions without serious interference from the executive or from powerful individuals or groups. It is further assumed that the magistrates hold their offices independently of the executive, the representative assembly, and the electorate; and that they habitually make their judicial decisions, even in matters which directly concern the government, in accordance with existing law and without being subject to pressure either from the executive or the populace.

Now I am not concerned to discuss the merits and defects of this form of government. What I do wish to emphasize is that it presupposes a certain very special kind of historical background and contemporary conditions; that these are absent in the greater part of the world; and that there is not the faintest reason to believe that it is a practicable form of government for most peoples at most times. Even if it be, as I think it probably is, in the abstract a less undesirable form of government than most of the known alternatives, it does not follow that it is the best form for those peoples in whom the necessary conditions for its success are lacking. It may be better to have a worse kind of government, suited to one's traditions and situation and national character, than a better kind imported from abroad which is a grotesque misfit. . . .

So far as I am aware, this kind of government has never worked even moderately well except in Great Britain, Scandinavia, Holland, Belgium, and Switzerland, and in those non-European lands which were first peopled by emigrants from certain of these parts of Europe and are now occupied by their descendants. It is difficult to say with confidence that it has worked decently in France, and one can say with certainty that it has been a fiasco in central, eastern, and south-eastern Europe. One hardly knows whether to laugh or to weep at the naïvety of the common American belief that it is a suitable system of government to impose upon Japan; and our own talk of "educating Germany for democracy" seems to me little less ludicrous. . . .

. . . An instance of this fallacy which is probably common not only to Englishmen and Americans, but also to most Western Europeans . . . consists in taking as normal the peculiarly favourable economic conditions which prevailed in Europe from about 1850 to 1930, and assuming that, apart from occasional set-backs, they will continue and even grow more favourable. If I am not mistaken, that relatively fortunate economic situation, and the marked rise in the standard of refinement, decency and humanity which it made possible, depended on very special conditions which seem unlikely to recur in the foreseeable future. For a short period the resources of food and raw materials available to Europeans increased at a much greater rate than the population which could exert an effective demand upon them. This happened through the rapid exploitation of the virgin lands of America,

Australia and Africa, and the simultaneous development on a vast scale of methods of cheap and quick transport and of cold storage. As a part of this unusually favourable situation huge numbers of men and women were able to relieve the pressure of population in Europe by emigrating and settling in these empty fertile lands, where their labours not only supported themselves but also produced a surplus for those whom they had left at home. I do not see how anything closely parallel to this can happen again to Western Europeans. On the other hand, the population of these new lands has grown and will continue to grow. Their demands for food and raw materials will increase, and so too will their power of producing cheaply and efficiently all the manufactured goods that they need. They will thus have less and less to export to Europe and less and less inducement to take European manufactured goods in exchange. So far from the economic conditions which prevailed in the world during the lives of our grandfathers and fathers being normal, they may be compared to a tidal wave which has left Western Europe in general and England in particular stranded high and dry on a shelf on the face of a cliff, from which it is impossible to climb up and hard to climb down without disaster.

I could easily give other examples of this fallacy of taking temporary and local conditions as permanent and world-wide and basing one's political judgments and actions on that assumption. But it is time to mention and illustrate other common fallacies. I shall take next a bunch of them which it will be convenient to group together under the name of "causal fallacies," because they all involve a reference to causation though some of them involve other notions beside.

Quite apart from all metaphysical questions, the notion of cause is a complex one which needs a fairly elaborate and subtle logical analysis. It would be inappropriate to enter in detail into this here and now; it will suffice for our present purpose to say that the statement that C causes E sometimes means that C is a *necessary* though perhaps not sufficient condition of E, sometimes that C is a *sufficient* though not perhaps necessary condition of E, and sometimes that C is a set of conditions which are *severally necessary and jointly sufficient* to produce E. Now popular talk about this causing that does not clearly distinguish these alternatives. It is very common, e.g., to start from the fact, which may be quite trivial and even tautologous, that C causes E in the sense that it is a necessary condition of E; then to take for granted that C causes E in the important and doubtful sense that it is necessary and sufficient to produce E; and then to infer various far-reaching practical conclusions from this.

An example is the assertion, often made with a great flourish of trumpets by pacifists, that armaments cause war. Since war involves, by definition, a conflict between the armed forces of nations, it is a tautological proposition that armaments are a necessary condition of wars. From this nothing follows except the platitude that, if all nations simultaneously disarmed and remained disarmed, there would be no more wars. This does not give the slightest guidance as to what a particular nation should do, if it is practically certain that at least one fairly strong nation will retain its armaments. It is obvious that there are situations in which a diminution of armaments by a certain nation or group of nations increases the chances of war, whilst an increase in their armaments diminishes it. . . .

Another common causal fallacy may be called for shortness the "extrapolation fallacy." . . . It is known or reasonably conjectured that a change in a certain direction has produced predominantly good results. It is then uncritically assumed that further doses of change in that direction will produce still further predominantly good results, and that it is desirable to administer these additional doses as soon as possible. It is forgotten that almost any change involves at least some loss in some respects as well as gain in others, and that it often produces certain positive evils which would otherwise not have existed. The gains may well overbalance the losses, and the main positive goods may well be greater than the collateral positive evils, until the process has gone a certain length; but the losses and the collateral evils may begin to predominate if it is carried further. Again, even if it be desirable on the whole to continue a certain process further in the same direction, it is often most undesirable to do so with the maximum possible speed. People who would benefit from a slow development, to each phase of which they had time to adapt themselves or to adapt their children, may be merely bewildered and demoralized if the pace becomes too hot for them.

All this is admirably illustrated by the transition from handicraft to large-scale mechanized production and the continued application of new scientific discoveries and techniques to the conditions of daily life. Up to a point there is clearly an enormous gain in handing over to machines much of the heavy drudgery of human work, in making possible the rapid transport of goods and persons over long distances, and producing and distributing food, clothing and other necessities and even luxuries on a scale which would otherwise have been impossible. But it is plain that there are great and increasing disadvantages to be set against this. The most obvious, and the one which lies not far at the back of the minds of all of us nowadays, is the almost unlimited power of destruction which the later developments of this process have put into the hands of individuals and communities much below the level of intellectual, moral and political development at which they can be trusted not to misuse it. I have little doubt that any benefits which mankind may have derived from the invention of the internal combustion engine are heavily outweighed by the fact that it has made the bombing aeroplane and the submarine warship possible and actual. It would be platitudinous to enlarge on the disasters with which mankind is threatened by the most untimely discovery of a means of releasing atomic energy.

I suspect that the only recent advances of applied science on which we can still on balance congratulate ourselves are in the regions of biology and medicine. But we must not forget that each branch of science and technology is so intimately linked with all the others that the advances which we welcome would be impossible without the conditions which have led to those which we deplore. It is the same great tree which bears the poisonous berries, the refreshing fruits, and the healing balsams, and it may even happen that some of its poisons are an essential ingredient in some of its wholesome products. (Cf., e.g. the use of the products of atomic disintegration as tracer elements in medical research.)

In this connection it may be worth while to note the following fact. Sometimes the development of a certain social trend leads to results which almost all decent and sensible people deplore. Yet the development of that trend in any one society may make that community so powerful in relation to others that they are compelled to follow suit and to impose it on themselves if they will not be rendered impotent and perhaps have it and even worse things imposed on them by others. Large-scale industrialization and the great increase of urban population which accompanies it are a case in point. This is a development from which a nation with a reasonably small well-distributed population and a comfortable balance between agriculture, fishery, manufacture, etc., might well pray to be delivered. But those nations in which such a development takes place become so powerful from a military and economic standpoint that they can and do dictate the conditions of life to all the others. . . .

Industrialization has already destroyed and continues to destroy natural beauty on a vast scale. But there seems good reason to think that it has begun to undermine itself by destroying the natural fertility of the soil and the natural balance of plant and animal life over huge areas of the earth. Nor is this the only way in which its inordinate development cuts away the branch on which it sits. I would venture to suggest that it engenders a psychological condition which in the long run may well be fatal to it. What I have in mind is this. As the organization of industry becomes more complex the connection of individual diligence and efficiency with economic or social reward becomes more and more remote. So, too, does the connection of individual slackness and incompetence with economic or social disadvantage. The remoteness of this connection tends to be increased still further by the methods of taxation and the social welfare legislation which are characteristic of communities in which the balance of political power is in the hands of the wage-drawers. Now there is no evidence for, and much evidence against, the view that the average person under normal conditions will work hard and strive to be efficient in intrinsically uninteresting tasks when not under the stimulus of direct economic or social advantage to himself or his family. A rapidly decreasing number of wage-drawers still have the habit of working hard and efficiently as a kind of hangover from an earlier and simpler social system and the customs and standards of values which accompanied it. A few persons will always do so because they are made that way. A considerable number will do so for short periods under the stress of some crisis which appeals strongly to certain social feelings, e.g. when their country is visibly in danger of immediate defeat in war, or when a revolution is taking place or a new system which appeals to their emotions has lately been set up. But I see no reason whatever to believe that any but very direct and visible motives of economic gain or loss to themselves or their families can be trusted to call forth continued efficient work at dull tasks in most men at most times. Yet the system will not provide a high standard of living and leisure unless it can call forth steady continuous effort in the employees while they are at work, and enterprise and inventiveness and readiness to take risks on the part of the directors, whether they be private individuals or State officials.

I find it hard to believe that the communists have discovered any permanently effective alternative to the direct economic incentives which are now ceasing to operate in Western Europe and will probably in time cease to do so in America. At the moment they enjoy all the advantages of a religious revival combined with such a crisis-mentality as evoked prodigious efforts in England in 1940. Even so, this has to be supplemented by the daily terror of the concentration camp and the political witch trials, and has to be stimulated by increasingly strident propaganda, in which self-adulation and anti-foreign war scares are mingled in a welter of nonsense and mendacity which can rarely have been equalled in the long history of human folly and wickedness. If these things have to be done in the green leaf, what will be done in the dry when the Church Militant shall have become the Church Triumphant? I cannot but suppose that even Slavs eventually become inured to this stuff, and that it will become less and less effective as a stimulant in the dull, daily, irritating round of work in factory and field and mine. Then nothing will remain but naked terror, and I doubt whether this is an efficient method of stimulating production in the long run and on a large scale. I wonder what proportion of the populations behind the iron curtain even now are occupied as policemen, prison warders, *agents provocateurs,* and in the hundred-and-one other non-productive tasks involved in building the New Jerusalem.

For these reasons, quite apart from the high probability of a catastrophic upset in the near future through atomic and bacteriological warfare, I suspect that industrialism, like fermentation, generates by-products which gradually check its development and might even bring it to a not very stable state of equilibrium. I cannot pretend to shed many tears over this. I do not view with any enthusiasm a millennium in which there would be no square inch of the earth's surface that did not stink of petrol and humanity and re-echo with the blare of the wireless loud-speaker discoursing mechanical music, enunciating platitude or nonsense, and ingeminating hatred.

It is high time to turn now to another common causal fallacy, viz. that which has been called *post hoc ergo propter hoc*. From the nature of the case it is extremely difficult to say with any high degree of reasonable confidence whether a certain factor did or did not contribute to an important extent to cause a certain other factor in social or political phenomena. This is because it is practically impossible to isolate the facts to be investigated, to find really parallel cases, to devise and perform experiments intended to answer definite questions, and so on. But fools cannot be restrained from rushing in where logicians fear to tread; and, if some fairly outstanding social phenomenon *A* immediately preceded some other fairly outstanding phenomenon *B* in some part of the world at some period in history, they will promptly generalize and conclude that *A* is necessary and sufficient to produce *B*. It will be entertaining to consider some examples of this.

I have heard it cited as an instance of the truth of Karl Marx's economic theories that they enabled him to prophecy that great wars would happen with frequency in the Western world, that they would be increasingly destructive, and so on, and that we have seen this prophecy abundantly fulfilled. As if wars had not been a regular occurrence in the history of Europe and the rest of the world throughout recorded time; as if they had not always been waged with the maximun resources available at the time to the belligerents; and as if those resources had not enormously increased through industrialization and applied science. How can any particular theory be verified by foretelling what could have been foretold with confidence on almost any theory or on no theory at all?

Another example concerns "democracy" in the Western sense of that word. It is often said by political speakers and writers in England and America that the superior efficiency of our system of government is shown by the fact that we defeated the non-democratic Germans in two great wars. The fact is that Germany came within an ace of defeating us, and that in both wars we had as an important ally Russia, a country which was in 1914 and is now at the opposite pole to all that we understand by democracy. The really relevant factors were that Germany, by stupid diplomacy, blundered into war with too many strong nations at once; that England was an island and the

United States far too remote to be attacked; and that the combined industrial resources of these two countries, if once they were given time and opportunity to deploy them, were enormously greater than those of Germany. It should be added that nothing but the imbecility of the governments of England, France and the United States, due to their dependence on the votes of ignorant and ostrich-like electors, who wanted nothing but a quiet life and would not read the signs of the times nor listen to those who could, made it possible for Germany to re-arm and indulge in a second world-war after its defeat in the first. I think it might fairly be said that the main achievement of Western democracy between the two wars was to prevent those who knew what ought to be done from doing it in the economic and the military spheres and in that of international relations.

A consequence of fallacies of this kind is that what may roughly be called "parliamentary government" has acquired a prestige among peoples who have never experienced it and are most unlikely to be able to practise it successfully, which makes them eager to adopt something that looks like it whenever they emerge from tutelage. We have seen plenty of examples of this in central, southern and south-eastern Europe, and we are now witnessing more and bigger ones in the near and the far East. A little later on I fully expect to see a similar result arising from similar causes in connection with the communist system as practised by Russia and its satellites. It seems to me that the fact is that under almost any imaginable system of government which was not completely imbecile North America would have become one of the wealthiest and most powerful communities in the world. Under almost any imaginable system of government, not completely imbecile, the Russian empire, with its vast and as yet hardly scratched natural resources, will become at least equally wealthy and powerful. In the one case the credit has gone to the system which happened to prevail in North America, in the other it will no doubt go to the system which happens to prevail in Russia. We shall be told, and many of us will believe, that this immense wealth and power is "due to" communism, just as we have been told and many of us believe that it was "due to" democracy in the Western sense. In each case there is very little rational ground for believing that the system of government is much more than a fly on the wheel. Any government which kept internal order over these vast empty rich territories and avoided defeat and invasion, and which either allowed individuals or companies to exploit the natural resources or undertook that exploitation itself on a large scale, would secure much the same spectacular results in these exceptionally favourable conditions.

I will consider one other causal fallacy, which often leads to governments or individuals being unfairly blamed or extravagantly praised. Suppose that there is a critical situation in which a government or a leading statesman has a choice of one or other of a comparatively few practically possible alternative courses of action, *A, B* and *C,* including among these the possible alternative of doing nothing and letting events take their course. Alternative *A* is chosen, and we will suppose that the state of affairs which ensues is admittedly much worse than that which immediately preceded the decision. Then it is very common to hold that a wrong decision was made, and to blame severely the individual or the government which made it. Now of course such a judgment may be justified in some cases. But in most cases a whole nest of fallacies is involved. In the first place, even if a different decision would have had a more fortunate sequel, it does not follow that the maker of the actual decision was blameworthy. Before we can decide this we must know whether, in the situation in which he was placed and with the information which was available to him at the time, he might reasonably have been expected to see that the consequences would be much worse than those of some other alternative which he might reasonably have been expected to contemplate as possible. The mere fact, if it be a fact, that *we* can see all this *after* the event may have very little bearing on this question.

Secondly, the mere fact that the state of affairs which followed the choice of alternative *A* was much worse than that which preceded it is not sufficient evidence that the decision was mistaken. It may be that the ensuing state of affairs would have been much worse than the preceding *whichever* of the alternatives had been adopted, and that the results of adopting any other would have been still worse than those of adopting *A*. Men find it very hard to admit that there are situations in which *all* possible alternative developments will be changes for the worse, and where the wisest decision that can be made will do no more than minimize the inevitably ensuing evil. Suppose that we tacitly and unjustifiably assume that there are no such situations. Then we shall automatically conclude that there *must* have been some alternative open to the maker of the decision which would have averted the evils which in fact ensued and would not have been followed by still greater evils. And so we shall judge that the actual decision was mistaken. But there is no reason whatever to accept this premise, and therefore there is no reason to accept any such judgment as a conclusion from it.

It is on such grounds as these, e.g., that the decision of the British Cabinet to go to war with Germany in 1914, or the agreement made by Mr. Chamberlain with Hitler at Munich, has been confidently asserted by many persons to have been unwise and to have redounded to the discredit of those concerned. Naturally I express no opinion here on the *truth* or *falsity* of these judgments. What I do contend is this. Most of those who make them with so much confidence have not begun to realize how many questions would have to be raised and settled before they had a shadow of justification for their assertions. Moreover, some of these questions can never be answered even approximately, for they involve conjectures about the consequences which would have followed if other alternatives had been chosen.

The last fallacy that I shall consider is of a very different kind. It is more trivial than those which I have noticed above; but it is so common and has such an inhibiting effect on many worthy persons that it seems desirable to mention and expose it. It is this. A citizen of country A condemns some contemporary public action or institution in another country B. Thereupon a fellow-citizen gets up and says 'We did the same,' and produces in support of his assertion some public action which was taken or some institution which existed at some time in the history of their common fatherland. This is supposed by many to provide some kind of answer to the criticism on this action or institution in the foreign country. At any rate it is often felt to be relevant and embarrassing by the critic himself, and the fear that such remarks might justifiably be made often prevents scrupulous persons from condemning publicly incidents in foreign countries which they cannot but deeply disapprove in private.

It is obvious that there must be a number of suppressed premises at the back of such an argument, and when one tries to make them explicit one sees that it is so hopelessly confused that nothing coherent can be made of it. I think we should all admit that a person ought to feel, and very often will feel, uncomfortable if it can be shown that at the same time he strongly condemns x and approves or tolerates y when the only relevant difference between x and y is that the former occurs in a foreign country and the latter in his own. Even this, however, would not show that he is mistaken in condemning x. The fact that a man is inconsistent in his judgments or his emotions does not show that a particular one judgment is false or a particular one emotion is misdirected. Sin is not less sinful when it is Satan who condemns it; and he has the advantage of expert knowledge. But suppose, as is very often the case, that a man not only condemns x in the foreign country but also quite consistently condemns similar actions and institutions in the history of his own country. Why on earth should the fact that something similar to what he condemns in another country exists or has existed in his own be thought to show that it is not worthy of condemnation? And, if he equally condemns similar acts or institutions in the history of his own country, why on earth should he feel embarrassed or diffident in publicly condemning them when they exist in a foreign country? Is bestial cruelty in contemporary Russian labour-camps any less evil because there was bestial cruelty in English slave-ships in the eighteenth century? And must an Englishman, who deplores that incident in English history and whose ancestors abolished that evil after a long and arduous Parliamentary struggle, hang his head in embarrassed silence and refrain from calling slavery and cruelty by their name when practised on a vast scale by foreign countries which claim to be the moral leaders of mankind?

I have assumed so far, for the sake of argument, that there really is something in one's own country which is closely or exactly parallel to that which one condemns in another country, and I have shown that even on that assumption this method of rebutting or silencing criticism is logically worthless. But in nine cases out of ten the alleged parallel will not survive a moment's critical inspection. Often it is merely verbal, as it would be, e.g., if one said that England made use of concentration camps in the latter stages of the Boer war and therefore Englishmen have no right to criticize the use of concentration camps by Germany or Russia. Often the only parallel which can be found to a present-day practice in a foreign country is something which formerly existed in one's own and has long since been abolished there by the efforts of reformers and is now condemned by everyone. Any attempt, e.g., to regard the harsh treatment of factory workers and of paupers in England in the early nineteenth century as a relevant parallel to present-day slave-labour in Russia and its satellites would be open to this criticism. The upshot of the matter is that I should advise anyone to whom this kind of argument is addressed either to pay no attention whatever to it or to answer the fool who uses it according to his own folly.

It is time for me to bring my paper to an end. It is not a cheerful paper, for I do not find mankind in their social and political relationships a cheerful subject to contemplate. Gibbon, who knew something of history, described it as mainly a record of the crimes, the follies, and the misfortunes of mankind. I see no reason to think that it will be fundamentally different in this respect in future from what it has been in the past. I suspect that there will always be, as there have always been, relatively infrequent and not very persistent oases of prosperity and culture in a desert of penury, ignorance and unthinking brutality. And at every stage any experienced and intelligent statesman will have occasion to repeat Axel Oxenstierna's words to his son: "Behold, my son, with how little wisdom the world is governed!"

BIOGRAPHICAL NOTES

These notes are intended to be no more than brief identifications of the authors represented in this book. In most cases, the writings that are cited here are in addition to those from which selections have been taken for this volume.

SAINT ANSELM (selection 31) was an Italian churchman, and served as archbishop of Canterbury from 1093 to 1109. He is most famous for his defense of the Church against King Henry I of England. Philosophically his fame rests on his devising the Ontological Argument for the existence of God, which is included in this volume. His most important works are the *Monologium* and the *Proslogium*.

SAINT THOMAS AQUINAS (selection 32) is generally regarded as the greatest of Medieval philosophers. He was born in Italy but spent most of his life in Paris, where he enjoyed great fame and influence. He attempted to reconcile the doctrines of Plato and Aristotle with the doctrines of the Catholic Church. His most important works are the *Summa Contra Gentiles* and the *Summa Theologica*. Detailed accounts of his life and philosophy can be found in *St. Thomas Aquinas* by G. K. Chesterton, and *The Philosophy of St. Thomas Aquinas* by Etienne Gilson.

ARISTOTLE (selection 40), along with Socrates and Plato, is one of the three major figures of ancient philosophy. He was a student of Plato's, but later founded his own school, the Lyceum. At one time he served as tutor to Alexander the Great. His influence on later philosophy, literature, and science is equalled only by Plato's. Medieval philosophers held him in such esteem that for centuries he was known as The Philosopher. He is known as the founder of logic, and his classification of the sciences has endured, in its main outlines, down to the present day. Author of many works, including the *Organon, Physics, Metaphysics, Nicomachean Ethics, Politics, Poetics, Rhetoric,* and *On the Heavens*. See *Aristotle,* by W. D. Ross, for an account of his life and philosophy.

ALFRED JULES AYER (selections 29 and 34) is one of the best known philosophers of the present day. He was educated at Eton and Oxford. His academic career at Oxford was interrupted by the Second World War, during which he served in the Welsh Guards and in Military Intelligence. In 1945 he became fellow and dean of Wadham College, Oxford. In 1946 he became Grote Professor at University College, London, and he returned to Oxford as Wykeham Professor of Logic in 1959. He is the editor of *Logical Positivism,* a standard source book, and *The Humanist Outlook,* and has been editor for some years of the Pelican Philosophy Series, and also of the International Library of Philosophy and Scientific Method. Author, among other works, of *The Foundations of Empirical Knowledge, Philosophical Essays, The Problem of Knowledge, The Concept of a Person, The Origins of Pragmatism,* and *Russell and Moore: The Analytical Heritage.*

MONROE CURTIS BEARDSLEY (selection 49) was born in Connecticut and educated at Yale University. He has taught philosophy at Mt. Holyoke College, Yale University, and at Swarthmore College from 1947 to 1969, when he became, along with his wife, Elizabeth, Professor of Philosophy at Temple University. He is co-editor (with Elizabeth Beardsley) of Prentice-Hall's Foundations of Philosophy Series. Co-author of *Theme and Form,* and author of *Practical Logic, Aesthetics,* and (with Elizabeth Beardsley) *Philosophical Thinking.*

JEREMY BENTHAM (selection 42) was one of the outstanding English philosophers and political theorists of the 19th century. Educated at Oxford, he studied for the law, but devoted his life to the analysis and attempts at reform of political and legal institutions. He was the outstanding advocate of Utilitarianism, which attracted to it many British liberals, including John Stuart Mill, and was the leader of the reform movement based on this philosophy. He wrote much, but published little. Among his works are *A Fragment on Government, Comment on the Commentaries, The Theory of Legislation, The Theory of Fictions, Deontology,* and *The Limits of Jurisprudence Defined* (some of which were published posthumously).

GEORGE BERKELEY (selection 21) is frequently regarded as the founder of Modern Idealism. Irish by birth, he was educated at Trinity College, Dublin. Along with John Locke and David Hume, he was one of the three most famous representatives of British empiricism. Before he was 30 he had written his most famous and controversial works, which have exerted an extensive influence. He became an Anglican clergyman, and was appointed Bishop of Cloyne. Spent three years in Rhode Island, 1729 to 1732, in an abortive attempt to found a university to educate the Colonial and Indian youth of America. Author of many works, including *An Essay Towards a New Theory of Vision, Three Dialogues between Hylas and Philonous, Alciphron, De Motu,* and *Siris.*

BERNARD BOSANQUET (selection 55) was an outstanding member of the

British idealist school, and a prolific author who contributed to all branches of philosophy. He was educated at Harrow and at Balliol College, Oxford. He taught at Oxford for some ten years, and for a brief period (1903–08) was Professor of Moral Philosophy at the University of St. Andrews, Scotland. Apparently of independent means, his independence of a university connection was a result neither of incapacity, indolence, nor lack of reputation. Among other works, he was the author of *Knowledge and Reality, Hegel's Philosophy of Fine Art, Logic or the Morphology of Knowledge, A History of Aesthetic, A Companion to Plato's Republic, Essentials of Logic, The Philosophical Theory of the State, The Principle of Individuality and Value, The Value and Destiny of the Individual, Social and International Ideals, Some Suggestions in Ethics, Implication and Linear Inference,* and *The Meeting of Extremes in Contemporary Philosophy.*

CHARLIE DUNBAR BROAD (selection 58) was one of the most prominent British philosophers of this century. He taught in a number of British universities (St. Andrews, Dundee, Bristol), was a Fellow of Trinity College, Cambridge, for a great many years, and from 1933 to 1953, the year of his retirement, was Knightbridge Professor of Moral Philosophy at the University of Cambridge. In addition to writing extensively in many areas of philosophy, he was for many years actively interested in problems of psychical research. He was the author, among other works, of *Perception, Physics, and Reality; The Mind and its Place in Nature; Examination of McTaggart's Philosophy; Scientific Thought; Five Types of Ethical Theory; Ethics and the History of Philosophy; Induction, Probability, and Causation;* and *Lectures on Psychical Research.* See *The Philosophy of C. D. Broad,* ed. by P. A. Schilpp.

JOHN CALDWELL CALHOUN (selection 52) was born in South Carolina and educated at Yale University. He served as Congressman from South Carolina (1811–1817), Secretary of War (1817–25) under Monroe, and Vice President of the United States under John Quincy Adams (1825–29) and Andrew Jackson (1829–1832). Served as a Senator from South Carolina for many years, and became known as the outstanding spokesman for the South, States' Rights, and Nullification. Author of the posthumous *Discourse on the Constitution and Government of the United States.* His papers have been collected in six volumes by R. K. Cralle.

C. ARTHUR CAMPBELL (selection 25) was born in Scotland, and educated at the Universities of Oxford and Glasgow. He has taught philosophy at University College, Bangor, Wales, and was Professor of Logic and Rhetoric in the University of Glasgow from 1938 until he became Professor Emeritus in 1961. In addition to numerous contributions to philosophical journals, he is the author of *Scepticism and Construction, On Selfhood and Godhood* (Gifford Lectures, 1957), and *Defense of Free Will* (collected essays, 1967).

LEWIS CARROLL (selection 8) was the pen name of Charles Lutwidge Dodgson, author of the world famous *Alice in Wonderland* and *Through the Looking Glass*. Educated at Rugby and Oxford, he taught mathematics at Oxford from 1854 until his death. Aside from the whimsical, witty, and wise works just mentioned, he wrote, in a somewhat similar style, *The Hunting of the Snark* and *Sylvie and Bruno*, which are not so famous. Was also the author of *Euclid and his Modern Rivals, A Tangled Tale, Pillow Problems, The Game of Logic,* and *Symbolic Logic*. In addition, he was an inveterate writer of verse, and an expert and enthusiastic photographer.

WILLIAM KINGDON CLIFFORD (selection 15) was born and raised in England and educated at the Universities of Cambridge and London. In 1868 he was elected a Fellow of Trinity College, Cambridge, and in 1871 he was appointed Professor of Applied Mathematics and Mechanics at University College, London. His brilliant career was ended by death at the early age of 34. Author of *Elements of Dynamic,* and the posthumously published *Mathematical Papers,* and *The Common Sense of the Exact Sciences* (completed by Karl Pearson, 1885).

MORRIS RAPHAEL COHEN (selections 5 and 37) was born in Russia, came to the United States at the age of 12, and was educated at the College of the City of New York, Columbia University, and Harvard University. He taught mathematics and then philosophy at City College for 36 years, and then for a few years at the University of Chicago, and was known as one of the great teachers of his time. His books include *Reason and Nature, Law and the Social Order, A Preface to Logic, The Meaning of Human History, Reason and Law, American Thought,* and the autobiographical *A Dreamer's Journey*.

IRVING MARMER COPI (selections 9 and 10) was born in Minnesota and was educated at the University of Michigan, from which he received a Ph. D. in 1948. He was taught philosophy at the University of Illinois, was for many years Professor of Philosophy at the University of Michigan, and is presently at the University of Hawaii. He has been a Guggenheim Fellow, a Fellow of the Fund for the the Advancement of Education, and a Research Associate at the University of California. In addition to *Introduction to Logic* (4th ed., 1972), he is the author of *Symbolic Logic* (4th ed., 1973), and *The Theory of Logical Types*.

CLARENCE SEWARD DARROW (selection 23) was born in Ohio, and lived in Chicago a good many years. He practiced law for over fifty years, and became known as an outstanding criminal and trial lawyer. He was an outspoken agnostic and opponent of capital punishment. Author of a novel, *Farmington,* and of *A Persian Pearl and Other Essays, An Eye for an Eye, The Prohibition Mania,* and many other writings on social and economic questions.

BIOGRAPHICAL NOTES

RENÉ DESCARTES (selection 12) was a French philosopher who is often regarded as "the father of modern philosophy." In addition to his philosophical works, he contributed to mathematics (where he founded analytic geometry) and various sciences. In philosophy, his writings have been of major importance in epistemology and metaphysics. These include *A Discourse on Method, The Principles of Philosophy, Treatise on the Passions of the Soul,* and *Rules for the Direction of the Mind.*

JOHN DEWEY (selections 46 and 56) was born and raised in Vermont, and taught philosophy at the Universities of Michigan, Minnesota, and Chicago, and from 1904 to 1929 at Columbia University. He traveled widely, took part in several experiments in educational reform, and wrote a large number of books, including *Democracy and Education, Essays in Experimental Logic, Reconstruction in Philosophy, Human Nature and Conduct, Experience and Nature, The Public and its Problems, The Quest for Certainty, Philosophy and Civilization, Art as Experience, Logic: The Theory of Inquiry,* and *Freedom and Culture.* An account of his life, and a discussion of his philosophy, may be found in *The Philosophy of John Dewey,* ed. by P. A. Schilpp.

FRIEDRICH ENGELS (selection 27), together with Karl Marx, was the founder of Dialectical Materialism, the theoretical basis of modern Communism. After meeting Marx in 1844, he devoted his life to organizing revolutionary movements and writing on the theory of Socialism. In 1848 he and Marx collaborated in writing the influential *Communist Manifesto.* His major writings include *The Condition of the Working Class in England in 1844; Landmarks of Scientific Socialism; The Origin of the Family, Private Property, and the State;* and *Anti-Dühring.* He also edited the second and third volumes of Marx's *Das Kapital.*

THOMAS HOBBES (selection 51) was a forerunner of British empiricism, an early defender of philosophical materialism, determinism, and egoism, and a founder of modern philosophy, whose contributions, especially to political philosophy, have an importance far greater than their bulk. He was educated at Oxford, and traveled extensively on the continent, mainly in the service of various Earls of Devonshire as tutor to young prospective Earls. Despite his ardent desire for peace and safety he took part in many controversies and polemics, on topics ranging from politics to political philosophy and geometry, and was an early translator of the classics (Thucydides and Homer). He was subject to much abuse and some danger during his lifetime because of his writings. For nearly three hundred years a considerable portion of Anglo-American political and moral philosophy has consisted in an attempt to answer Hobbes's arguments, and nearly all of it was influenced by him. Author, among other works, of *The Elements of Law* (in two parts, *Human Nature,* and *De Corpore Politico*), *De Cive, De Homine, De Corpore, A Minute or First Draught of the Optiques,* and *Behemoth.*

BIOGRAPHICAL NOTES

JOHN HOSPERS, JR. (selection 11) is currently Professor of Philosophy and Director of the School of Philosophy at the University of Southern California. He was educated at Central College, Iowa State University, and Columbia University, from which he received a Ph.D. in 1944. He has taught philosophy at the University of North Carolina, the University of Illinois, Columbia University, the University of Minnesota, Brooklyn College, and the University of California at Los Angeles. Was a Fulbright Scholar at the University of London in 1955. Author, among other works, of *Meaning and Truth in the Arts, Introduction to Philosophical Analysis,* and *Human Conduct,* and co-editor (with Wilfrid Sellars) of *Readings in Ethical Theory* (2nd ed., 1970).

DAVID HUME (selections 13, 22, 33, and 41), one of the greatest philosophical intellects of all time, was born in Scotland and educated at Edinburgh. One of the three outstanding British empiricists, along with Locke and Berkeley. Much of modern philosophy may be regarded as an attempt to answer his defense of philosophical skepticism, and his philosophical influence, aided by the beauty of his style, remains strong to this day. He never held an academic post, though he was for a time librarian at the University of Edinburgh, when he wrote his famous *History of England.* Author, among other works, of *An Enquiry Concerning the Principles of Morals; Essays, Literary, Moral and Political; An Abstract of a Treatise on Human Nature;* and *Political Discourses.* Many insights into his thought and character can be obtained from his *Letters* (published 1932).

WILLIAM JAMES (selections 35, 36, and 57), son of the theologian Henry James and brother of the novelist Henry James, became one of the most widely-read and influential thinkers of his day. He was born in New York City and received his education at Harvard University, where he started teaching in 1872 as a lecturer on anatomy and physiology, and then in 1880 as a psychologist and philosopher. Author, among other works, of *Principles of Psychology, The Varieties of Religious Experience, A Pluralistic Universe, The Meaning of Truth,* and of the posthumous *Some Problems in Philosophy* and *Essays in Radical Empiricism.* For an account of his life and thought, see R. B. Perry, *The Thought and Character of William James.*

CYRIL EDWIN MITCHINSON JOAD (selection 18) was one of the best known of contemporary British philosophers, having written forty-six books on philosophy and related subjects during his career. He was educated at the University of Oxford and served in the British Civil Service and Ministry of Labour from 1914 to 1930. In 1930 he became head of the Philosophy Department at Birkbeck College, University of London, a post he held until his retirement in 1946. His many writings include *Philosophies of the World, Guide to Philosophy, Guide to Modern Wickedness, God and Evil, The Recovery of Belief, A Restatement of Christian Philosophy, Common Sense Ethics,* and *A Critique of Logical Positivism.*

BIOGRAPHICAL NOTES

IMMANUEL KANT (selection 43), one of the greatest thinkers of all time, was born and lived in Königsberg, Germany, where he was educated. Lectured at the University of Königsberg in philosophy and various sciences starting in 1755, and in 1770 became Professor of Logic and Metaphysics. Author of numerous works, including *Critique of Pure Reason, Critique of Practical Reason, Critique of Judgment, Natural History and Theory of the Heavens, Religion within the Limits of Reason Alone, Prolegomena to any Future Metaphysics,* and *Metaphysics of Morals.* See A. D. Lindsay, *Kant.*

MARYA MANNES (selection 50) is a well-known journalist and critic. She was born and privately educated in New York City. She was for many years a regular contributor to *The Reporter,* and feature editor with *Vogue* and *Glamour.* The essay reprinted in this collection was originally published in *Glamour.* She has also been associated with public television in New York, and since 1963 she has been a free lance writer. She is the author of several books in addition to *But Will It Sell?,* including *Message From A Stranger, More In Anger,* and, more recently, *Them.*

JOHN STUART MILL (selections 6, 24, and 26), son of James Mill, spent much of his life in the employ of the East India Company, and was for a term a member of Parliament. He has become known as the outstanding liberal thinker of the 19th century, and his work has acquired classic significance in a number of fields. He was the author, among other works, of *Principles of Political Economy, On Liberty, Representative Governemnt, The Subjection of Women, Utilitarianism, Examination of Sir William Hamilton's Philosophy, August Comte and Positivism,* and *Dissertations and Discussions.* His unique and amazing education, administered by his father, is described in his *Autobiography* (1873).

WILLIAM PEPPERELL MONTAGUE (selection 17) was born in Massachusetts and educated at Harvard. He taught philosophy at Columbia University from 1903 until his retirement in 1947. He was one of the leaders of the Neo-Realist school of American philosophy. His works include *Belief Unbound; The Ways of Things; Knowledge, Nature, and Value;* and *Great Visions of Philosophy.*

ARTHUR EDWARD MURPHY (selections 3, 19, and 47) was born in Ithaca, New York, and received his education at the University of California. He taught philosophy at the Universities of California, Chicago, Illinois, and Washington, and at Brown and Cornell Universities, and at the time of his death was Professor of Philosophy at the University of Texas; he also served as department chairman at Illinois, Cornell, Washington, and Texas. He was co-editor of *Essays in Political Theory,* co-author of *Philosophy in American Education,* and a contributor to *American Scholarship in the Twentieth Century,* and was for a number of years editor of *The Philosophical Review.* In addition to *The Uses of Reason* (reissued 1972) and *Reason and the*

Common Good (which contains a Bibliography of his writings as well as a brief account of his life and personality) he was the author of *The Theory of Practical Reason* (1965, ed. by A. I. Melden).

ERNEST NAGEL (selection 5) was born in Czechoslovakia but raised in the United States, and was educated at the College of the City of New York and Columbia University. He has taught philosophy at Columbia University since 1931, and is currently University Professor there. He has twice been a Guggenheim Fellow, and has been an editor of the *Journal of Philosophy* and of the *Journal of Symbolic Logic*. He is co-author (with James R. Newman) of *Gödel's Proof,* and author of *Principles of the Theory of Probability, Logic of Measurement, Sovereign Reason, Logic Without Metaphysics,* and *The Structure of Science.*

CHARLES SANDERS PEIRCE (selection 14) was born in Massachusetts and educated at Harvard University, where he was lecturer in Philosophy 1864–65 and 1869–70. His only other formal teaching was at Johns Hopkins University from 1879 to 1884. Worked with the United States Coast and Geodetic Survey for 30 years. Died in dire poverty at Milford, Pennsylvania. Peirce is known as the founder of pragmatism. He wrote voluminously, though he published little, and the only book he published in his lifetime was *Photometric Research* (1878). His major philosophical writings are gathered in *Collected Papers,* in 8 volumes, edited by Hartshorne, Weiss, and Burks, and a selection from them in *Chance, Love, and Logic,* ed. by M. R. Cohen.

PLATO (selection 39) was one of the three outstanding philosophers of ancient Greece, and one of the most famous and influential philosophers of all time. He was a student of Socrates, and the founder of the Academy, which is reputed to be the first university, and is the most famous school of ancient times. His philosophical writings are in the form of dialogues, which are known not only for their philosophical merit, but for their literary style and, in some cases, their dramatic interest. Socrates is the major character in many of these dialogues and, since Socrates himself left no writings, these dialogues provide us with our main source of information about his philosophy. Some of these dialogues are the *Gorgias, Protagoras, Parmenides, Theaetetus, Sophist, Symposium, Philebus, Phaedrus, Timaeus, Euthyphro, Apology, Crito,* and *Laws.* See A. E. Taylor, *Plato: The Man and His Work.*

JOHN ARTHUR THOMAS ROBINSON (selection 38) was formerly Bishop of Woolwich and is presently Assistant Bishop of Southward in the Church of England. He was educated at Trinity College, Cambridge, and since 1969 has been a Fellow and Dean of the Chapel at Trinity. He has gained an international reputation for his advocacy of a radical reinterpretation of Christian doctrine. Among his published works are: *Christian Morals Today, The New Reformation, But That I Can't Believe, Exploration in God,* and *Christian Freedom in a Permissive Society.*

BIOGRAPHICAL NOTES

ARTHUR KENYON ROGERS (selection 2) taught philosophy from 1900 to 1920 at Butler University, the University of Missouri, and Yale University. He retired from teaching at the age of 52 in order to devote himself to writing, and was the author of *A Student's History of Philosophy, English and American Philosophy since 1800, Morals in Review, A Theory of Ethics, What is Truth?, The Socratic Problem,* and *Ethics and Moral Tolerance,* and contributed to *Essays in Critical Realism.*

BERTON ROUECHÉ (selection 4) was born in Kansas City, Missouri, and graduated from the University of Missouri. For many years he was a reporter with several midwestern newspapers. Since 1944 he has been a staff writer for *The New Yorker* and the author of its "Annals of Medicine". He was awarded the Albert Lasker Medical Journalism Award Book in 1950 and in 1960. Some of his other books in medical journalism, in addition to *Eleven Blue Men,* are *Curiosities of Medicine, The Incurable Wound, A Man Named Hoffman,* and *The Orange Man.*

GEORGE SANTAYANA (selections 30 and 48) was born in Spain and came to the United States at the age of 9. He was educated at Harvard University, and taught philosophy there from 1889 to 1912, when he retired to live in Europe, living for a while in England, and spending the last years of his life in retirement in a convent in Italy. Author, among other works, of *The Sense of Beauty, Interpretations of Poetry and Religion, Winds of Doctrine, Egotism in German Philosophy, Character and Opinion in the United States, Soliloquies in England and Later Soliloquies, Dialogues in Limbo, Platonism and the Spiritual Life, Realms of Being* (4 vols.), *Dominations and Powers,* several books of *Poems,* the novel *The Last Puritan,* and the autobiographical *Persons and Places* (3 volumes).

JEAN-PAUL SARTRE (selection 28) is the most well-known of contemporary French thinkers. Born in Paris in 1905, he studied in Berlin and at the University of Freiburg, where he was influenced by the German existentialist Heidegger. He was captured by the Germans during the fall of France in 1940 and later fought in the resistance movement against the Nazis. In addition to philosophical works, he has written plays and novels, for which he is also world famous. Some of his most important works are *Nausea, No Exit, The Wall,* and *Being and Nothingness,* his *magnum opus.* In his later writings, such as *Critique of Dialectical Reason* and *In Search of a Method,* Sartre has been attempting to demonstrate the basic harmony between his existentialism and marxism.

JOHN SOMERVILLE (selection 7) was born in New York City and educated at Columbia University. He has taught philosophy at the College of the City of New York, Columbia University, Stanford University, and the College of the Pacific, and was on the philosophy faculty of Hunter College of the City of New York from 1939 until his recent retirement. In addition to numerous articles in philosophical and other periodicals, he is the author of *Soviet Philosophy, The Way of Science, The Philosophy of Peace,* and *The Philosophy of Marxism* (1966).

HERBERT SPENCER (selection 16) was one of the most well-known and influential thinkers of the nineteenth century. An ardent evolutionist, even before the work of Darwin, his writings were perhaps even more influential in the United States than in England, his own country. He was informally educated, held no academic posts, and supported himself through editing work and through his writings. He was a prolific author, and the beneficiary of a rare and ingenious plan, whereby his works came out in sections, which were sent to subscribers who had agreed in advance to underwrite his work. He was also, as might be expected, unusually prolific, and contributed extensively to nearly all branches of philosophy. Author of *Social Statics* (1850) and *The Principles of Psychology* (1855). After the publication, in 1859, of Darwin's *Origin of Species,* Spencer attempted to apply the concept of evolution to all areas of knowledge, and did so in a series of works: *First Principles, Principles of Biology, Principles of Psychology, Principles of Sociology, Principles of Ethics,* and *Man Versus the State,* and a vast number of essays and reviews. His influence has now declined, and though he is well known, he is also little read.

WALTER TERENCE STACE (selection 44) was at the time of his death Emeritus Professor of Philosophy at Princeton University. Born in England, he was educated there, and in Scotland and Ireland. He served for twenty-two years with the British Civil Service in Ceylon, and began teaching at Princeton in 1932. In addition to *The Concept of Morals* (reprinted 1962) he was the author, among other works, of *The Theory of Knowledge and Existence, Religion and the Modern Mind, Time and Eternity, The Philosophy of Hegel, Critical History of Greek Philosophy, The Gate of Silence,* and *The Destiny of Western Man.*

CHARLES LESLIE STEVENSON (selection 45) received his undergraduate training at Yale, took a B. A. at Cambridge University, and received his Ph.D. from Harvard in 1935. Taught philosophy at Harvard for five years, at Yale for seven years, and has been on the faculty of the University of Michigan since 1946. Was a Guggenheim Fellow in 1945–6. Author of the extremely influential *Ethics and Language,* he has made important contributions to ethics, aesthetics, and the philosophy of language. A number of his most important papers in ethics have been collected in *Facts and Values* (1963).

RICHARD HENRY TAWNEY (selection 54) was born in Calcutta, India, and educated at Rugby and at Balliol College, Oxford. He was prominent for a number of years in the Workers Educational Association, was a Fellow of Balliol College, Oxford, and for many years Professor of Economic History at the University of London. Author of *The Acquisitive Society, Religion and the Rise of Capitalism, Land and Labour in China,* and *The Attack and Other Papers.*

ALFRED EDWARD TAYLOR (selection 20) was a British philosopher who made significant contributions to such areas of philosophy as metaphysics and ethics, and was also one of the outstanding authorities of his time on the life and work of Plato. He was educated at Oxford, and taught philosophy at Manchester, McGill University in Montreal, and then for a considerable period in Scotland, first as Professor at the University of St. Andrews, and then as Professor at the University of Edinburgh. Author of *The Problem of Conduct; Plato: The Man and his Work; A Commentary on Plato's Timaeus; The Faith of a Moralist; The Laws of Plato; Philosophical Studies; Aristotle;* and *Does God Exist?*

ALEXIS DE TOCQUEVILLE (selection 53) was a French statesman and writer. He was prominent for a time in French politics, and was for a short time (in 1849) minister of foreign affairs. His *Democracy in America,* written after an official mission to the United States to study the American penal system, was the first systematic account of American government and institutions, and has become a classic of its kind. Author of *L'Ancien Régime et la Révolution* and of the posthumous *Recollections.* His writings have been edited in 9 volumes by H. G. de Beaumont.

ALFRED NORTH WHITEHEAD (selection 1) was born in England and educated at the University of Cambridge, and taught, first mathematics and then philosophy, at Cambridge and the University of London. In 1924 he came to the United States to become Professor of Philosophy at Harvard University, a post he held until his retirement in 1937. He has written extensively, in an elegant style, in mathematics, philosophy, and education, and had one of the greatest mathematical and speculative minds of the 20th century. Co-author (with Bertrand Russell) of *Principia Mathematica,* and author, among other works, of *A Treatise on Universal Algebra, The Concept of Nature, The Principles of Natural Knowledge, The Principle of Relativity, Science and the Modern World, Religion in the Making, Process and Reality, Adventures of Ideas,* and *Modes of Thought.*

SELECTED BIBLIOGRAPHY

The following list of books is supplied for the convenience of the student who is interested in doing further reading on the topics covered in this volume. For the most part, works from which selections in this volume have been taken are not listed here. A number of those of a more advanced nature, or which are especially technical, are marked with an asterisk. Those with especially rich or useful bibliographies are indicated by "(Bib.)." The heading "Later Works" is used to cover works published in this century; hence a "later work" can be a classic, and is not necessarily characterized by the trait of absolute-up-to-dateness. But these classifications are not rigid categorizations.

THE HISTORY OF PHILOSOPHY

BURNET, JOHN: *Early Greek Philosophy** (4th ed., 1930)
COPLESTON, F.C.: *History of Philosophy** (6 volumes, 1946–60)
DURANT, WILL: *The Story of Philosophy* (1926)
JONES, W.T.: *A History of Western Philosophy* (2 volumes, 1962)
NAHM, MILTON C., ED.: *Selections from Early Greek Philosophy* (4th ed., 1964)
RANDALL, JOHN HERMAN: *The Making of the Modern Mind* (1926; rev. ed., 1940)
ROGERS, A. K.: *A Student's History of Philosophy* (1932)
SORLEY, W. R.: *A History of English Philosophy* (1937) *(Bib.)*
WEINBERG, JULIUS: *A Short History of Medieval Philosophy** (1964)
WINDELBAND, WILHELM: *A History of Philosophy** (2nd ed., 1900; trans. 1901)

PHILOSOPHY TEXTS AND COLLECTIONS

AMMERMAN, R., ED.: *Classics of Analytic Philosophy** (1965) *(Bib.)*
AYER, A. J., ED.: *Logical Positivism** (1959) *(Bib.)*
BARRETT, W. AND AIKEN, H. D., EDS.: *Philosophy in the Twentieth Century** (2 vols., 1962)
BEARDSLEY, M. AND BEARDSLEY, E.: *Philosophical Thinking* (1965; abridged ed., 1972) *(Bib.)*
EDWARDS, P. AND PAP, A., EDS.: *A Modern Introduction to Philosophy** (3rd ed., 1973) *(Bib.)*

SELECTED BIBLIOGRAPHY

FEIGL, H. AND SELLARS, W., EDS.: *Readings in Philosophical Analysis** (1949)
HOSPERS, JOHN: *An Introduction to Philosophical Analysis* (1953) *(Bib.)*
KAUFMANN, W., ED.: *Existentialism from Dostoevsky to Sartre* (1956)
NIELSEN, KAI: *Reason and Practice* (1971) *(Bib.)*
RANDALL, J.H. AND BUCHLER, J.: *Philosophy: An Introduction* (1942; 2nd ed., 1972) *(Bib.)*
SCRIVEN, MICHAEL: *Primary Philosophy* (1966)
SPRAGUE, E. AND TAYLOR, P., EDS.: *Knowledge and Value* (2nd ed., 1967) *(Bib.)*

PHILOSOPHICAL DICTIONARIES AND ENCYCLOPEDIAS

BALDWIN, JAMES M., ED.: *Dictionary of Philosophy and Psychology** (4 vols., 1905) *(Bib.)*
EDWARDS, PAUL, ED. IN CHIEF: *The Encyclopedia of Philosophy* (8 vols., 1967) *(Bib.)*
HASTINGS, JAMES, ED. IN CHIEF: *Encyclopedia of Religion and Ethics* (13 vols., 1908-26)
RUNES, D. D.: *The Dictionary of Philosophy* (1942)
URMSON, J. O., ED.: *Concise Encyclopedia of Western Philosophy and Philosophers* (rev. ed., 1968)

PART I THE NATURE AND USES OF PHILOSOPHY

COLLINGWOOD, R. G.: *An Essay on Philosophical Method* (1933)
DEWEY, JOHN: *Reconstruction in Philosophy* (1920)
EWING, A. C.: *The Fundamental Questions of Philosophy* (1951)
JAMES, WILLIAM: *Some Problems of Philosophy* (1911)
JOHNSTONE, HENRY W., JR.: *Philosophy and Argument* (1960)
MARITAIN, JACQUES: *On the Use of Philosophy* (1961)
PASSMORE, JOHN: *Philosophical Reasoning** (1961)
PLATO: *Euthydemus*
SIDGWICK, HENRY: *Philosophy: Its Scope and Relations* (1902)

PART II LOGIC AND PHILOSOPHY OF SCIENCE
Classics

ARISTOTLE: *Prior Analytics; Posterior Analytics*
BACON, FRANCIS: *Novum Organum*
BERNARD, CLAUDE: *An Introduction to the Study of Experimental Medicine*
BRADLEY, F. H.: *The Principles of Logic**
JEVONS, W. S.: *The Principles of Science*
KEYNES, JOHN NEVILLE: *Studies and Exercises in Formal Logic*
MILL, JOHN STUART: *A System of Logic*
WHATELY, RICHARD: *Elements of Logic*

Later Works

BARKER, S. F.: *Elements of Logic* (1965)
BEARDSLEY, MONROE: *Practical Logic* (1950)

BLACK, MAX: *Critical Thinking* (1952); *The Labyrinth of Language* (1968)
BROWN, ROBERT: *Explanation in Social Science* (1963)
CAMPBELL, NORMAN: *What is Science?* (1921)
COHEN, MORRIS: *Reason and Nature* (1931)
CONANT, JAMES: *On Understanding Science* (1947)
DEWEY, JOHN: *How We Think* (1910)
DUHEM, PIERRE: *The Aim and Structure of Physical Theory* (1906; trans. 1954)
HUFF, DARRELL: *How to Lie With Statistics* (1954)
KNEALE, WILLIAM AND KNEALE, MARTHA: *The Development of Logic* (1962)
NAGEL, ERNEST: *The Structure of Science** (1961)
POINCARÉ, HENRI: *The Foundations of Science* (trans. 1913)
QUINE, W. V.: *Methods of Logic** (3rd ed., 1972)
ROBINSON, DANIEL S.: *Illustrations of the Methods of Reasoning* (1927)
RUBY, LIONEL: *The Art of Making Sense* (1954)
RUDNER, RICHARD: *Philosophy of Social Science* (1966)
RUSSELL, BERTRAND: *Introduction to Mathematical Philosophy** (1913)
SCHEFFLER, ISRAEL: *Science and Subjectivity* (1967)
SINGER, CHARLES: *A Short History of Science* (1941)
STEBBING, L. SUSAN: *Thinking to Some Purpose* (1939)
STRAWSON, P. F.: *Introduction to Logical Theory* (1952)
TOULMIN, STEPHEN: *The Philosophy of Science* (1953) *(Bib.)*; *The Uses of Argument** (1958)
WHITEHEAD, ALFRED NORTH: *An Introduction to Mathematics* (1911)

Collections

BRODY, BARUCH, ED.: *Readings in the Philosophy of Science** (1970)
COPI, I. M. AND GOULD, J. A., EDS.: *Readings on Logic* (2nd ed., 1972)
FEIGL, H. AND BRODBECK, M., EDS.: *Readings in the Philosophy of Science** (1953) *(Bib.)*
KAHL, RUSSELL, ED.: *Studies in Explanation* (1963) *(Bib.)*
NATANSON, MAURICE, ED.: *Philosophy of the Social Sciences* (1963) *(Bib.)*

PART III   THEORY OF KNOWLEDGE
Classics

BERKELEY, GEORGE: *Dialogues between Hylas and Philonous*
DESCARTES, RENÉ: *A Discourse on Method*
HUME, DAVID: *A Treatise of Human Nature*
KANT, IMMANUEL: *Critique of Pure Reason**
LOCKE, JOHN: *An Essay Concerning Human Understanding*
PLATO: *Meno; Theaetetus*
REID, THOMAS: *Essays on the Intellectual Powers of Man*

Later Works

AYER, A. J.: *The Problem of Knowledge* (1956)
CHISHOLM, RODERICK M.: *Theory of Knowledge* (1966)

SELECTED BIBLIOGRAPHY

DEWEY, JOHN: *The Influence of Darwin on Philosophy* (1910)
LAIRD, JOHN: *Knowledge, Belief, and Opinion* (1930)
MALCOLM, NORMAN: *Knowledge and Certainty** (1963)
MOORE, G. E.: *Philosophical Studies** (1922); *Philosophical Papers** (1959)
PRICE, H. H.: *Perception* (1932)
PRICHARD, H. A.: *Knowledge and Perception* (1950)
ROGERS, A. K.: *What Is Truth?* (1923)
RUSSELL, BERTRAND: *The Problems of Philosophy* (1912); *Our Knowledge of the External World* (1914)
WOOZLEY, A. D.: *Theory of Knowledge* (1949)

Collections

AMMERMAN, R. AND SINGER, M. G., EDS.: *Belief, Knowledge, and Truth* (1970) *(Bib.)*
CANFIELD, J. AND DONNELL, F. H., EDS.: *Readings in the Theory of Knowledge* (1964) *(Bib.)*
GRIFFITHS, A. PHILLIPS, ED.: *Knowledge and Belief** (1967)
NAGEL, E. AND BRANDT, R., EDS.: *Meaning and Knowledge** (1965) *(Bib.)*
SWARTZ, ROBERT, ED.: *Perceiving, Sensing and Knowing** (1965)

PART IV METAPHYSICS
Classics

ARISTOTLE: *Metaphysics*
HEGEL, G. W. F.: *The Phenomenology of Mind**
KANT, IMMANUEL: *Prolegomena to any Future Metaphysics*
LEIBNIZ, GOTTFRIED WILHELM: *Monadology*
NIETZSCHE, FRIEDRICH: *The Genealogy of Morals*
PLATO: *The Republic; Timaeus**
SPINOZA, BENEDICT: *Ethics**

Later Works

BERGSON, HENRI: *Introduction to Metaphysics* (1903; trans. 1913)
BROAD, C. D.: *The Mind and its Place in Nature** (1925)
COLLINGWOOD, R. G.: *An Essay on Metaphysics* (1940)
DEWEY, JOHN: *Experience and Nature* (1925)
DUCASSE, C. J.: *Nature, Mind, and Death* (1951)
EMMETT, DOROTHY: *The Nature of Metaphysical Thinking* (1945)
GRENE, MARJORIE: *Dreadful Freedom: A Critique of Existentialism* (1948)
LEWIS, C. I.: *Mind and the World Order* (1929)
MOORE, G. E.: *Some Main Problems of Philosophy* (1953)
RUSSELL, BERTRAND: *Mysticism and Logic* (1917)
RYLE, GILBERT: *The Concept of Mind** (1949); *Dilemmas* (1954)
TAYLOR, RICHARD: *Metaphysics* (1963)
WHITELEY, C. H.: *An Introduction to Metaphysics* (1950)
WITTGENSTEIN, LUDWIG: *The Blue and Brown Books** (1958)

Collections

BEROFSKY, BERNARD, ED.: *Free Will and Determinism* (1967)
CHAPPELL, V. C., ED.: *The Philosophy of Mind* (1962)
DE GEORGE, RICHARD T., ED.: *Classical and Contemporary Metaphysics* (1962)
ENTEMEN, WILLARD F., ED.: *The Problem of Free Will* (1967) *(Bib.)*
HAMPSHIRE, STUART, ED.: *Philosophy of Mind* (1967)
KENNICK, W. AND LAZEROWITZ, M., EDS.: *Metaphysics* (1966)

PART V PHILOSOPHY OF RELIGION
Classics

AUGUSTINE, ST.: *City of God*
BUTLER, JOSEPH: *The Analogy of Religion*
HUME, DAVID: *Dialogues Concerning Natural Religion*
KANT, IMMANUEL: *Religion within the Limits of Reason Alone**
KIERKEGAARD, SØREN: *Fear and Trembling*
NIETZSCHE, FRIEDRICH: *Also Sprach Zarathustra*
PALEY, WILLIAM: *A View of the Evidences of Christianity; Natural Theology*

Later Works

BERGSON, HENRI: *The Two Sources of Morality and Religion* (1932, trans. 1935)
BRADLEY, ANDREW C.: *Ideals of Religion* (1940)
BURTT, E. A.: *Types of Religious Philosophy* (1939; rev. ed., 1951)
DEWEY, JOHN: *A Common Faith* (1934)
DUCASSE, C. J.: *A Philosophical Scrutiny of Religion* (1953)
HICK, JOHN: *Philosophy of Religion* (1963)
JAMES, WILLIAM: *Varieties of Religious Experience* (1902)
MACGREGOR, GEDDES: *Introduction to Religious Philosophy* (1959)
OTTO, RUDOLF: *The Idea of the Holy** (1917; trans. 1958)
RUSSELL, BERTRAND: *Religion and Science* (1935)
SMART, NINIAN: *The Religious Experience of Mankind* (1969)
STACE, WALTER T.: *Religion and the Modern Mind* (1952)
VAN BUREN, P.: *The Secular Meaning of the Gospel* (1963)
WHITEHEAD, ALFRED NORTH: *Religion in the Making* (1926)

Collections

ABERNATHY, G. L. AND LANGFORD, T. A., EDS.: *Philosophy of Religion* (2nd ed., 1968) *(Bib.)*
BRONSTEIN, D. J. AND SCHULWEIS, H. M., EDS.: *Approaches to the Philosophy of Religion* (1954) *(Bib.)*
FLEW, A. G. N. AND MACINTYRE, A., EDS.: *New Essays in Philosophical Theology** (1955)
HARTSOCK, DONALD E., ED.: *Contemporary Religious Issues* (1968)
HICK, JOHN, ED.: *The Existence of God* (1964)
KAUFMANN, W., ED.: *Religion from Tolstoy to Camus* (1964)

PART VI ETHICS AND VALUES
A. ETHICS
Classics

ARISTOTLE: *Eudemian Ethics; Nicomachean Ethics*
BUTLER, JOSEPH: *Sermons on Human Nature*
HUME, DAVID: *An Enquiry Concerning the Principles of Morals*
MILL, JOHN STUART: *Utilitarianism*
PLATO: *The Republic*
SELBY-BIGGE, L. A., ED.: *British Moralists** (1897)
SIDGWICK, HENRY: *The Methods of Ethics** (1874, 6th ed., 1901)

Later Works

BAIER, KURT: *The Moral Point of View* (1958; abridged ed., 1965)
BOURKE, V. J.: *History of Ethics* (2 vols., 1968) *(Bib.)*
BROAD, C. D.: *Five Types of Ethical Theory* (1930)
DEWEY, JOHN: *Human Nature and Conduct* (1922)
DEWEY, JOHN AND TUFTS, J. H.: *Ethics* (1910)
GARVIN, LUCIUS: *A Modern Introduction to Ethics* (1953) *(Bib.)*
HARE, R. M.: *Freedom and Reason** (1963)
HOSPERS, JOHN: *Human Conduct* (1961; abridged ed., 1972) *(Bib.)*
MABBOTT, J. D.: *Introduction to Ethics* (1966)
MOORE, G. E.: *Ethics* (1912)
RAWLS, JOHN: *A Theory of Justice** (1971)
ROGERS, A. K.: *Morals in Review* (1927)
SIDGWICK, HENRY: *Outlines of the History of Ethics** (6th ed. revised, 1931)
SINGER, M. G.: *Generalization in Ethics** (1961) *(Bib.)*
TOULMIN, STEPHEN: *The Place of Reason in Ethics* (1950)
WARNOCK, MARY: *Ethics Since 1900* (2nd ed., 1966)

Collections

BRANDT, RICHARD, ED., *Value and Obligation* (1961)
DAVIS, PHILIP E., ED., *Introduction to Moral Philosophy* (1973)
GIRVETZ, H. K., ED.: *Contemporary Moral Issues* (2nd ed., 1968)
PAHEL, K. AND SCHILLER, M., EDS., *Readings in Contemporary Ethical Theory** (1970) *(Bib.)*
SELLARS, W. AND HOSPERS, J., EDS., *Readings in Ethical Theory** (2nd ed., 1970) *(Bib.)*
TAYLOR, PAUL, ED., *Problems of Moral Philosophy* (2nd ed., 1972)

B. AESTHETICS
Classics

ARISTOTLE: *Poetics*
KANT, IMMANUEL: *Critique of Aesthetic Judgment**
PLATO: *Ion; Phaedrus; Symposium*

SANTAYANA, GEORGE: *The Sense of Beauty* (1896)
TOLSTOY, LEO: *What is Art?*

Later Works

ALDRICH, V. C.: *Philosophy of Art* (1963)
BEARDSLEY, MONROE: *Aesthetics* (1958)
BOSANQUET, BERNARD: *A History of Aesthetic** (2nd ed., 1904)
CARRITT, E. F.: *The Theory of Beauty* (1914)
COLLINGWOOD, R. G.: *The Principles of Art* (1938)
DEWEY, JOHN: *Art as Experience* (1934)
DUCASSE, C. J.: *Art, the Critics, and You* (1944)
EDMAN, IRWIN: *Arts and the Man* (1939)
GILBERT, K. AND KUHN, H.: *History of Aesthetics* (2nd ed., 1953)
GOTSHALK, D. W.: *Art and the Social Order* (1947)
HAMMOND, W.: *A Bibliography of Aesthetics* (1933)
LANGER, SUSANNE: *Feeling and Form** (1953)

Collections

ELTON, W., ED.: *Essays in Aesthetics and Language** (1954)
HOSPERS, JOHN, ED.: *Introductory Readings in Aesthetics* (1969) *(Bib.)*
KENNICK, WILLIAM, ED.: *Art and Philosophy* (1964)
LEVICH, MARVIN, ED.: *Aesthetics and the Philosophy of Criticism* (1963) *(Bib.)*
MARGOLIS, JOSEPH, ED.: *Philosophy Looks at the Arts** (1962) *(Bib.)*
RADER, MELVIN, ED.: *A Modern Book of Aesthetics* (1935; 4th ed., 1973) *(Bib.)*

PART VII   SOCIAL AND POLITICAL PHILOSOPHY

Classics

ARISTOTLE: *Politics*
BENTHAM, JEREMY: *A Fragment on Government*
GREEN, T. H.: *Lectures on the Principles of Political Obligation*
HEGEL, G. W. F.: *The Philosophy of Right**
HOBBES, THOMAS: *Leviathan; De Cive*
LOCKE, JOHN: *Second Treatise on Civil Government*
MILL, JOHN STUART: *On Liberty; Representative Government; The Subjection of Women*
PLATO: *The Republic; Statesman; Laws**
ROUSSEAU, JEAN JACQUES: *The Social Contract*
SIDGWICK, HENRY: *The Elements of Politics*
SPINOZA, BENEDICT: *Political Treatise*

Later Works

CAIRNS, HUNTINGTON: *Legal Philosophy from Plato to Hegel* (1949)
COHEN, MORRIS R.: *Law and the Social Order* (1933)

DEWEY, JOHN: *The Public and its Problems* (1927)
FAIN, HASKELL: *Between Philosophy and History* (1970) *(Bib.)*
HART, H. L. A.: *The Concept of Law* (1961)
HOOK, SIDNEY: *Reason, Social Myths and Democracy* (1940)
LEOPOLD, ALDO: *A Sand County Almanac* (1949)
MABBOTT, J. D.: *The State and the Citizen* (2nd ed., 1967)
POPPER, KARL: *The Open Society and its Enemies* (1945)
SABINE, GEORGE H.: *A History of Political Theory* (1937; 3rd ed., 1963) *(Bib.)*
TAWNEY, R. H.: *The Acquisitive Society* (1921)
WILLOUGHBY, W. W.: *Social Justice* (1900)
WOLFF, R. P.: *In Defense of Anarchism* (1970)

Collections

ARCHAMBAULT, R. D., ED.: *Philosophical Analysis and Education* (1965)
DRAY, W. H., ED.: *Philosophical Analysis and History* (1966) *(Bib.)*
KENT, E. A., ED.: *Law and Philosophy* (1970) *(Bib.)*
OLAFSON, F. A., ED.: *Society, Law, and Morality* (1961)
TUCKER, ROBERT, ED.: *The Marx-Engels Reader* (1972)
WASSERSTROM, R., ED.: *War and Morality* (1970) *(Bib.)*
WOLFF, R. P., ED.: *Political Man and Social Man* (1966) *(Bib.)*

CHRONOLOGICAL TABLE OF CONTENTS

PLATO (427-347 B. C.) **39.** The Ring of Gyges
ARISTOTLE (384-322 B. C.) **40.** On The Good
ST. ANSELM (1033-1109) **31.** The Necessary Existence of God
ST. THOMAS AQUINAS (1225-1274) **32.** Reason, Faith, and God's Existence
THOMAS HOBBES (1588-1679) **51.** The State of Nature
RENÉ DESCARTES (1596-1650) **12.** Of Doubt and Certitude
GEORGE BERKELEY (1685-1753) **21.** Mind and Matter
DAVID HUME (1711-1776) **13.** Two Kinds of Knowledge
  22. Is a Cause Always Necessary?
  33. On Evil and the Argument from Design
  41. Reason, Passion, and Morals
IMMANUEL KANT (1724-1804) **43.** The Categorical Imperative
JEREMY BENTHAM (1748-1832) **42.** Hedonistic Utilitarianism
JOHN C. CALHOUN (1782-1850) **52.** Equality and The State of Nature
ALEXIS DE TOCQUEVILLE (1805-1859) **53.** Authority and Society
JOHN STUART MILL (1806-1873) **6.** Science and Human Nature
  24. Free Will
  26. History and Determinism
FRIEDRICH ENGELS (1820-1895) **27.** Economic Determinism and Historical Development
HERBERT SPENCER (1820-1903) **16.** Human Fallibility
LEWIS CARROLL (1832-1898) **8.** What the Tortoise Said to Achilles
CHARLES SANDERS PEIRCE (1839-1914) **14.** The Fixation of Belief
WILLIAM JAMES (1842-1910) **35.** The Will to Believe
  36. Faith, Belief, and Action
  57. Remarks at the Peace Banquet
W. K. CLIFFORD (1845-1879) **15.** The Ethics of Belief
BERNARD BOSANQUET (1848-1923) **55.** Liberty and Legislation
CLARENCE DARROW (1857-1938) **23.** Crime and Free Will
JOHN DEWEY (1859-1952) **46.** The Continuum of Ends-Means
  56. Democracy, Politics, and Education
ALFRED NORTH WHITEHEAD (1861-1947) **1.** Wisdom

CHRONOLOGICAL TABLE OF CONTENTS

GEORGE SANTAYANA (1863-1952) **30.** Religion
                        48. The Criterion of Taste
ARTHUR KENYON ROGERS (1868-1936) **2.** Philosophy
A. E. TAYLOR (1869-1945) **20.** What is Metaphysics?
WILLIAM PEPPERELL MONTAGUE (1873-1953) **17.** Is Truth Relative?
MORRIS R. COHEN (1880-1947) **5.** Logic and Science
                        37. Religion and The Will to Believe
R. H. TAWNEY (1880-1962) **54.** Liberty and Equality
WALTER T. STACE (1886-1967) **44.** Ethical Absolutism and Ethical Relativism
C. D. BROAD (1887-1971) **58.** Fallacies in Political Thinking
C. E. M. JOAD (1891-1953) **18.** Epistemological Skepticism
C. ARTHUR CAMPBELL (1897-   ) **25.** A Defence of Free Will
ARTHUR E. MURPHY (1901-1962) **3.** The Philosophic Mind and the
                                  Contemporary World
                        19. The World We Perceive
                        47. The Context of Moral Judgment
ERNEST NAGEL (1901-   ) **5.** Logic and Science
MARYA MANNES (1904-   ) **50.** How Do You Know It's Good?
JEAN-PAUL SARTRE (1905-   ) **28.** Existentialism
JOHN SOMERVILLE (1905-   ) **7.** Umbrellaology and Problematics
CHARLES LESLIE STEVENSON (1906-   ) **45.** The Emotive Meaning of Ethical Terms
ALFRED JULES AYER (1910-   ) **29.** The Elimination of Metaphysics
                        34. The Possibility of Religious Knowledge
BERTON ROUECHÉ (1911-   ) **4.** Eleven Blue Men
MONROE C. BEARDSLEY (1915-   ) **49.** Can We Dispute about Tastes?
IRVING M. COPI (1917-   ) **9.** Truth and Validity
                        10. Science and Hypothesis
JOHN HOSPERS (1918-   ) **11.** On Explanation
JOHN A. T. ROBINSON (1919-   ) **38.** Honest To God